CW01044022

AUTOMATIC FOR THE MASSES

AUTOMATIC FOR THE MASSES

The Death of the Author
and the Birth of Socialist Realism

PETRE M. PETROV

UNIVERSITY OF TORONTO PRESS
Toronto Buffalo London

© University of Toronto Press 2015
Toronto Buffalo London
www.utppublishing.com
Printed in the U.S.A.

ISBN 978-1-4426-4842-5 (cloth)

Printed on acid-free, 100% post-consumer recycled paper with
vegetable-based inks.

Library and Archives Canada Cataloguing in Publication

Petrov, Petre M., 1974–, author
Automatic for the masses : the death of the author and the birth of Socialist
realism / Petre M. Petrov.

Includes bibliographical references and index.
ISBN 978-1-4426-4842-5 (bound)

1. Socialist realism.   2. Modernism (Aesthetics) – Soviet Union.   3. Socialist
realism in art – Soviet Union.   4. Modernism (Art) – Soviet Union.   I. Title.

NX556.A1P48 2015   700.94709'041   C2015-900238-9

University of Toronto Press acknowledges the financial assistance to its
publishing program of the Canada Council for the Arts and the Ontario Arts
Council, an agency of the Government of Ontario.

  Canada Council   Conseil des Arts
for the Arts   du Canada

University of Toronto Press acknowledges the financial support of the
Government of Canada through the Canada Book Fund for its publishing
activities.

To Paola and Mamo.

Contents

AUTOMATIC FOR THE MASSES

The existence of proletarian dictatorship is not enough to influence culture. For this, a true plastic hegemony is needed, a hegemony that would speak through me without my knowing it, or even against my will. I do not feel this.

Boris Pasternak

Introduction

FARMHAND
Who are you?
Whose are you?
THINGS
What do you mean, "whose"?
FARMHAND
I mean, what is your master's name?
THINGS
We have no master.
We belong to no one.

(Mayakovsky, *Mystery-Bouffe*)

This book is an attempt to write the doctrine of Stalinist socialist realism into a story of modernism and modernity. The provisional title of that story is "The Death of the Author" – provisional, because it merely focuses under a single theme several different yet closely linked questions. That title will become dispensable once the issues to which it alludes and which supply all its substance are properly grasped. In placing socialist realism within the framework of modernism, nothing can be further from my intentions than to accuse the latter of being an incipiently totalitarian enterprise. A meaningful relationship between two phenomena need not imply genesis or (even less) a cause-and-effect dependency. As I will argue, the line from modernist culture to the cultural ideology of Stalinism involved complex mediations and transformations. When these are taken into account, facile talk of one paradigm "begetting," "anticipating," "implicitly containing," or "leading to" the other can only be firmly rejected.

Nowhere in what follows do I assume that modernism is a simple thing that one can theorize about in passing before moving on to construct equations between it and other cultural phenomena. Modernism, in this book, will be the common term for a complex of responses – artistic and intellectual – to the situation of modernity, a situation that appears in multiple local variants throughout the West.[1] For all its complexity, this heterogeneous field is amenable to understanding, and understanding necessarily implies the bringing of discrete particularities under the unity of the general, of the concept. The variegated map of modernism is traversed by tendencies and themes that give it a measure of unity; this is what allows us to speak of it as a singular phenomenon to begin with.[2] One of these themes/tendencies is the oft-proclaimed absence of the author from the scene of creation, that is, from the "text" understood in the broadest sense. From a complex cultural paradigm, I have chosen this one facet both because I believe it productively illuminates other important facets of modernism and because it provides an opening onto the fundamental driving forces of Stalinist culture.

Efforts to place Stalinism and socialist realism within a modernist framework are not new. Three decades ago, Boris Groys proposed such a narrative in *The Total Art of Stalinism* (1992). A radical and controversial departure from Cold War studies of Soviet culture, the slim volume undertook to destroy the myth of an innocent avant-garde falling prey to the crudely concocted artistic orthodoxy of Stalinism. As Groys saw it, Stalinism was the sole legitimate heir to the "aesthetic-political project" of the avant-garde. At its most radical, modernist artistic ideology aims to transform the world, no longer satisfied with proffering mere reflections of it. In attempting this transformation, the artistic transcends itself and enters the broad arena of life. "By its own internal logic, the artistic project becomes aesthetico-political" (Groys 21). By the same logic, however, it approaches an insurmountable limit, for marginalized artistic radicals do not possess the means to bring about the grand transformations of reality their manifestos have projected. Only an organized political power – the Party in control of the state – can accomplish such a task. And this, according to Groys, is what actually took place in the Soviet Union in the early 1930s: Stalinism "took over" the unfinished project that the left avant-garde could never finish. In Groys's telling of the story, avant-garde artists are dictators without real power, while the Stalinists are artists without talent.

It is a tidy and provocative story, no doubt. But it is tidy because it is oversimplified.[3] If avant-garde modernism and Stalinist culture fit together so neatly in Groys's account, it is because the complexities of both have been greatly reduced. The commonalities between the two phenomena are easy to spot because their marks of kinship are as vague as can be. No one is going to dispute modernism's anti-mimetic thrust or the "life-building" ambitions of various avant-garde groups. However, much argumentative labour is required before these features can be equated with a proto-totalitarian passion for domination and then made into the defining characteristic of the Russian avant-garde. Not for Groys this labour: he cites a handful of pronouncements by Kazimir Malevich, briefly references Velimir Khlebnikov's posturing as "Chairman of the World" and "King of Time," and considers this sufficient for capturing "the very essence of the avant-gardist artistic project" (20).

Cultural historian Richard Stites has shown that in the wake of the 1917 revolutions, the desire to remake life was expressed by a multitude of disparate voices on the cultural scene. He quotes Isaak Steinberg, Socialist Revolutionary and one-time Commissar of Justice:

> All aspects of existence – social, economic, political, spiritual, moral, familial – were opened to purposeful fashioning by human hands. Ideas of social betterment and progress that have been gathering for generations in Russia and elsewhere seemed to wait on the threshold of the revolution ready to pour forth and permeate the life of the Russian people ... Everywhere the driving passion was to create something new, to effect a total difference with the "old world" and its civilization. It was one of those uncommon moments of self-perception and self-assertion. The storm passed nobody by: neither those who hailed it as a blessing nor those who spurned it as a curse. (qtd in Stites 39)

Clearly, the demiurgic passion was not the monopoly of leftist experimenters in art. As Groys was well aware, life-building in Russia began not with the avant-garde of the 1910s and 1920s but with the theurgic visions of Nikolai Fedorov and Vladimir Solov'ev, before entering the mainstream of Russian symbolism through the influential cultural philosophy of Viacheslav Ivanov.[4] It was Aleksandr Blok, the symbolist poet, who issued a passionate call "to *remake* everything. To organize things so that everything should be new, so that our false, filthy, boring, hideous life should become a just, pure, merry, and beautiful life" (qtd in Stites 38; emphasis in the original).[5] On the eve of the October Revolution, Nikolai Berdiaev issued a very similar injunction: "Art unavoidably must go beyond its confined existence and move on to the creation of a new life" (20).[6]

All of this is to say that the notion of demiurgic purpose is simply not specific enough to serve as a distinguishing mark either of the avant-garde in general or of its Soviet instantiation in particular. The psychological-behavioural portrait that Groys presents is not just schematic – it is also misleading. Whatever the refreshingly defamiliarizing value of seeing the artists of the avant-garde as aspiring dictators, that portrait remains a distortion and thus illegitimate. It allows no space whatsoever for utopian desire that is not a disguised lusting after political power. One could doubt whether Maykovsky's line "We will remake life anew – right down to the last button of your vest" (qtd in Stites 38) implies a definitive plan for totalitarian rule; but there is no doubt that it voices an ardent hope for deliverance from that "false, filthy, boring, hideous life" Blok also bemoaned. Nor does Groys make allowance for desire that may contradict itself – as desire so often does – desire whose self-professed aim is at odds with its true nature.

Lastly, but all-importantly for the purposes of this study, Groys almost completely ignores a feature that could well undermine his account's main premise: those salient gestures of self-effacement and depersonalization without which no account of modernism – in Russia or anywhere else – can be considered complete. Because his story is that of a creative subjectivity inflated to semi-divine dimensions, Groys has no way of dealing with those expressions of modernism that repudiated or sought to suppress subjectivity. These cannot be brushed aside easily: they were multiple and ubiquitous, perhaps nowhere more so than in post-revolutionary Russia. It was none other than Malevich – Groys's prime example of a demiurgic artistic persona – who wrote in 1920 that "if we want to attain perfection, the self must be annihilated – just as religious fanatics annihilate themselves in the face of the divine, so the modern saint must annihilate himself in the face of the 'collective,' in the face of that 'image' which perfects itself in the name of unity, in the name of coming together" (qtd in T.J. Clark 226). This was in Vitebsk, during the early days of Malevich's chairmanship of UNOVIS. At about the same time, in Moscow, during the early days of INKhUK, artistic individuality was assaulted no less forcefully. In her study of Soviet Constructivism, Maria Gough points out that "to suppress any trace of artistic subjectivity" was the movement's guiding imperative from its earliest days (*Artist* 11).[7] The very principle of "construction" (contrasted with that of "composition") was conceived explicitly as an antidote to the kind of demiurgic licence that Groys considers the essential aspect of avant-garde practices (Gough, *Artist* 11–14).[8] Far from exercising absolute "power over the materials" (Groys 21), the

Constructivists saw their work as ordered in advance – one might say *commanded* – by the inherent properties of the material.[9] It is not immediately apparent how this obedience to the demands of the medium can be reconciled with the charge of "aesthetic dictatorship."

In fact, one of the most serious difficulties in providing a unified and convincing account of artistic modernism has to do with reconciling these two tendencies: the touted centrality of the individual self and its frequent suppression, subjectivity hyperinflated and subjectivity renounced. Astradur Eysteinsson summarizes the dilemma (apropos of literature):

> On the one hand, it seems that modernism is built on highly subjective premises: by directing its attention so predominantly toward individual or subjective experience, it elevates the ego in proportion to a diminishing awareness of objective or coherent outside reality … On the other hand, modernism is often held to draw its legitimacy primarily from writing based on highly antisubjectivist or impersonal poetics. (27)

While it is the latter aspect, the death of the author, that will occupy centre stage in this study, I believe it possible to construct a consistent narrative in which subjectivity's foregrounding and suppression are seen not as contradictory features of modernism but rather as possible reactions to the same historical circumstances. Below I try to suggest how such a narrative might go. But first, an explanation is in order regarding the "death of the author" slogan and its meaning for the present study.

Just like its intellectual kin, the "death of the subject," the death of the author presents us with a metaphor. It is most familiar to us as a theoretical-philosophical trope whose content has been elaborated by a long list of continental – mostly French – thinkers in a variety of academic disciplines. At the head of that list are Claude Lévi-Strauss, Jacques Lacan, Louis Althusser, Roland Barthes, Michel Foucault, and Jacques Derrida. This metaphorical death – whether of the author or, more broadly, the subject – has roughly the following meaning: man is constituted, not constitutive; he is authored, not authorial; the human individual is embedded everywhere in structures and dynamics of which he is not the progenitor and which his consciousness can never fully encompass.[10] Language has been the model *par excellence* for all fields of objectivity that can be said to "dissolve" the subject. To explain one metaphor by means of another: with language as his main field of play, the subject is the player that is being played by the rules of that very field.

This "Copernican revolution" set in motion by the foregrounding of linguistic structures threw down a direct challenge to the central and founding role of consciousness, whether registered in terms of Cartesian certainty, Husserlian phenomenology, or the doctrine of individual freedom outlined in Sartrian existentialism. In what was to become the "slogan of the decade" for the France of the 1960s, Lévi-Strauss could thus declare: "the goal of the human sciences is not to constitute man, but to dissolve him." (Burke 13)

But the death of the author is not just a theoretical trope. At an earlier historical moment, it functioned as a practical metaphor as well. By "practical," I mean that it oriented, or enabled, practices of various kinds, including artistic ones. The content of that other metaphor is not unitary and so is not easily stated (among other things, the present study will attempt to show how this content shifted between the 1920s and the 1930s on the Soviet cultural scene). My principal point is this: at the beginning of the twentieth century, the death of the author did not have merely cognitive significance; it was also a symbolic act performed in the specific historical context of the time. It did not merely allude to a universal state of affairs; it also performed desire, enacted a state of the world and of man that could or should be. To put it rather crudely: authors pretended not to be authors, and this pretence, this metaphor acted out on page or canvas, aimed to effect a change in that which had hitherto been called "art" and that which had hitherto been called "man."

Another way of framing the same point is to say that the dispersal of the subject (and hence, of the author) was not a revelation of the 1960s. It was already in full view in Marx, Nietzsche, and Freud. But that earlier view was of a very different kind, insofar as the dispersal was not the end of the story. Rather, the dispersal was an enabling, energizing, state of affairs that opened onto another, recuperative state (in Freud's famous figure of repossession, "Wo Es war, soll Ich warden"). It allowed, nay, demanded, that man be gathered again, as something wholly different, beyond – that is, as something greater than – his former being. Speaking of the three thinkers just mentioned, Paul Ricoeur captures lucidly this subsequent moment, when, after being undermined, man is reinstated again on a loftier plane:

All three begin with suspicion concerning the illusions of consciousness, and then proceed to employ the stratagem of deciphering; all three, however, far from being detractors of "consciousness," aim at extending it. What Marx wants is to liberate *praxis* by the understanding of necessity; but this liberation is inseparable from a "conscious insight" which victoriously counterattacks the mystification of false consciousness. What Nietzsche wants is the increase of man's power, the restoration of his force ... What Freud desires is that the one who is analyzed, by making his own the meaning that was foreign to him, enlarge his field of consciousness, live better, and finally be a little freer and, if possible, a little happier. (34–5)[11]

I will not be unfolding on these pages an exegesis of the epoch-making hermeneutic endeavours of Marx, Nietzsche, and Freud. I merely wish to mark two separate and historically distinct moments in the death of the author: (1) an earlier one, in which the objective logic that "dispersed" the subject could still be imagined as a kind of proto-will (most literally in Nietzsche's "Will to power" but also in Freud's "desire" and Marx's logic of social labour-cum-value) and, as such, "activated" in practice; and (2) a later moment, when this practical aspect was lost, the objective logic that mocked man's mastery of experience was revealed as a mere faceless combinatory of elements, and the death of the subject and author was reduced to a purely theoretical postulate that registered a fact without proposing an act. The present study amounts to a return, in the Russian context, to the earlier of the two moments, when the metaphor of the author's demise functioned as an invitation to practice (an invitation that Stalinism would later recast as a summons).

From the moment that structuralism proclaimed the death of the author, in Barthes's programmatic essay of 1968, that earlier episode was occluded. It is not that Barthes was unaware of modernist writers who had practised the death of the author as an act definitive of their artistic creations. Quite the opposite: these modernist performances were at the very centre of his essay. It is, rather, that Barthes took them not in their historical significance but in their universal value. The main ambiguity behind the metaphor – Is the death of the author a cognitive fact or a historically determined act? – informs the essay from beginning to end. For Barthes, the Author – capitalized consistently in the text – is a metaphysical figure that is kept in place by the ideology proper to the bourgeois world order: "The author is a modern figure, a product of our society insofar as, emerging from the Middle Ages and English empiricism, French rationalism and the personal faith of the Reformation, it discovered the prestige of the individual, of, as it is more nobly put, the 'human person'" (Barthes, "Death" 142–3). This situation holds until some time in the late nineteenth century, when – no reasons given – the belief in the strange apparition begins to wane. When, "diminishing like a figurine at the far end of the literary stage" (145), the Author cedes his former dominion, it is time for writing (lowercase) to shine in all its glory. But this is also when the problems begin for Barthes, whose story meanders uneasily between historicity and universality. On the one hand, when he tells us that "writing is that neutral, composite, oblique space where our subject slips away, the negative where all identity is lost, starting with the very identity of the body writing" (142), there is little doubt that he is describing the mode of being proper to *écriture*, removed from the currents of time and cleansed of all historicity: "No doubt it has always been that way" (142). Yet in the next moment, he refers us to writers like Mallarmé, Proust, and Valéry, who deliberately set out to make their works the uncontested dominion of language. This leaves us to conclude that modernist literature fulfils consciously the program that is implicitly contained in the very nature of writing. A well-nigh miraculous outcome! For Barthes, the false prominence of the author is historically determined, yet the good riddance that modernism supposedly initiates does not appear to be grounded in any concrete situation. The closest he comes to arbitrating between history and universality is the following brief statement: "the removal of the Author is not merely an historical fact or an act of writing; it utterly transforms the modern text" (145). The death of the author, then, is not *just* an act, not *just* a moment of practice (although, it is that too); more importantly for Barthes, it refers to a exemplary *modus essendi* of the text, a universal condition, a timeless paragon: the Text as such.

The stream of history ends up spilling into normative universality (that of pure writing), but how this happens is not entirely clear. Since the vague reference to the rule of the bourgeoisie is quite insufficient to theorize what makes metaphysical ghosts like the Author appear in the first place, Barthes cannot explain what it is that vanquishes those ghosts. Given that in Mallarmé's lifetime the economic dominance of the bourgeoisie was as strong as ever, it is no small surprise that its metaphysical superstructure should have been undermined with the sudden death of the author. As it stands, Barthes's essay fosters the impression that the (re)discovery of the "writerly" is due to the acumen of a few exceptional individuals. Could it be that, having driven the individual genius out the front door, Barthes has secretly let it back in through the rear in order to explain how some modernist writers were able to attain the essential dimension of textuality?

The main reason for Barthes's difficulties with history is fairly transparent. If the author is, indeed, a historical fiction, the question will sooner or later arise: Is the death of that same personage not a fiction in its own right, a historically conditioned performance? Barthes wishes very much to evade that suspicion. As a consequence, he is forced into the intellectually tenuous position of seeing the death of the author as a historical moment that opens onto an ahistorical dimension. By contrast, the present study will frame the same fatality exclusively as a historical fiction, a practical metaphor, a ritual, one that seeks to resolve symbolically a very real cultural crisis definitive of modernism.

Barthes's group portrait of modernist literature – to the names of Mallarmé, Proust, and Valéry he adds those of Flaubert and Brecht and a blanket reference to Surrealism – is very sketchy indeed, yet sufficient to intimate that modernism has a vital role to play in the death of the author. With this I readily agree, but I would challenge Barthes's understanding of that role and the overall meaning of the scene he evokes. The implied image of literary modernism as an anti-metaphysical crusade, with *langue* on its banner, strikes me as thoroughly misguided. Anachronism is clearly at work here, which projects the intellectual rebellions of Barthes's own time back to the beginning of the century. "In the 1970s it became almost routine to analyze the style of a particular writer and then arrive at the conclusion that, when it came right down to it, the writer's work was really about language. Everything was 'text,' 'discourse,' 'code.' Critics were fond of talking about language, and they came to think that the poets they analysed felt the same way" (Cassedy 9). Barthes may not be the sole or principal instigator of this critical practice, but in him it is in full evidence, especially when he deals with Mallarmé. What the critic of the 1960s feels about language is taken to be what the early modernist poet felt. All of this comes to grief when one remembers that what Mallarmé was after was not language as some general signifying environment, but rather the ideal, essential verbal medium; that he envisioned not a self-enchanted play of inscriptions, but the inscription of one ultimate truth: "The imperfection of languages consists in their plurality, the supreme one is lacking: thinking is writing without accessories or even whispering, the immortal word still remains silent; the diversity of idioms on earth prevents everybody from uttering the words which otherwise, at one single stroke, would materialize as truth" (Mallarmé, qtd in Benjamin 77).

The modernist author does not step down from the pedestal of authority in order to open a "field without origin," as Barthes would have it. On the contrary, he does it so that there *will* be an origin for the work of art, an absolute beginning and firm foundation. There is little to learn about the nature of modernist writing when Barthes goes on to add, "no other origin than language itself" (146). That modernist writers privileged the medium of linguistic expression is a truth from the primer of literary history, yet this privileging is very different from what Barthes's theoretical platform proposes. For him, "language denies all origins." But this statement is thoroughly misleading when applied to those most committed of all modernist experimenters in language, the Russian *budetliane*. In language they sought not the ephemerality of pure signification but the density of primordial, archaic sedimentations, where some original fullness of meaning, of the referent's presence even, might be repossessed. Their "word as such" (*slovo kak takovoe*)[12] is never the Saussurean signifier whose default relationality deprives it of substance, but the magic name,[13] the first, most essential word, which holds within itself the intuition of what it designates. I realize it is somewhat bad manners to force on Barthes's text a dialogue with Russian Futurism that it did not itself initiate, but the reasons for this should be clear: if Barthes's theorization is at odds with the thought and practice of modernists who took most seriously and declared most strongly the primacy of language, then his history of the author's death becomes incoherent.

There are other notable absences in Barthes's abbreviated pantheon of modernism. His essay is short indeed, but this is hardly the only explanation for why he fails to mention, next to Flaubert and Mallarmé, the other, no less famous declaration of modernist impersonality: T.S. Eliot's "Tradition and Individual Talent" (1917). Another possible explanation is that Eliot's meditations would immediately highlight the blind spot in Barthes's account. For although they do position the author in a space that Barthes would be tempted to call "intertextual," they do not thereby "disperse" him. On the contrary: to locate the author at the intersection of traditions is to provide his work with a substantiality that it cannot have as an individual creation. And it is in the name of this substantiality that the author is enjoined to become aware of tradition. "What happens is a continual surrender of himself as he is at the moment *to something which is more valuable*" (Eliot 39; emphasis added). Depersonalization here is coterminous with anchoring, not with the amputation that Barthes describes memorably as a writing hand "cut off from any voice." In Eliot, the hand that writes is made that much stronger in that it is sutured to the mighty sinews of tradition. In other words, the movement in which the self is "released" does not stop there. It carries on in order to secure for the act of writing a super-individual essence and authority. In this double act, it is difficult to say where dispossession ends and repossession begins, and one should be careful not stake one's case on the power of mere words. As the self is "dissolved" in the flows of tradition, is it also not regained, albeit in a different form and different measure? To speak of it as ephemeral or vanishing may be just another way of describing its expansion beyond mere individual subjectivity. What else, if not a self, is speaking on the pages of "Tradition and Individual Talent," a self willing to forgo the ambition of absolute originality in order to find a new "home of meaning" (Ricoeur 55),[14] where there will be sense of belonging (to "tradition"), of rootedness (in "something ... more valuable")?

Eliot's "escape from personality" is still performed by a personality; desubjectifying the text is still a subjective act and should be interrogated as such. That is to say, we must ask what is at stake for the subject in this act of abdication. But this means returning the writing subject to the proper historical situation in which the act is performed and seeing the act as one with this situation, as a reaction to it. Only from a position of overall understanding of the modernist moment can we query the true significance of the author's demise, if this indeed is the proper name for it. The point is crucial and warrants repeated emphasis: it is not as a *fact* that we should take the death of the author, as some sort of given that it is the task of anthropological philosophy or literary theory to render explicit, but as an *act*, a moment of concrete happening, an instance of historically determinate becoming.[15]

In his reminiscences of the Dada movement, in which he was a principal actor, Hans Richter emphasizes precisely this fact: the escape from individual will, from creation as the expression of the subject, is still an act of the subject: "We felt that we were coming into contact with something different, something that surrounded and interpenetrated *us* just as we overflowed into *it*. The remarkable thing was that we did not lose our own individuality" (Richter 51; emphasis in the original). And the sway of the unconscious in the art and poetry of Dada is nothing like the primordial subversion of the sovereign ego; rather, it is a willful surrender by the ego to something that might or might not be the unconscious. Whatever it is, the surrender to it is very much a conscious act: "We had adopted chance, the voice of the unconscious – the soul, if you like – as a protest against the rigidity of straight-line thinking. We were ready to embrace, or be embraced by, the unconscious" (58–9). This hesitation between the active and the passive voice is an eloquent testimony: one lunges consciously in order to be embraced by the unconscious. "We were all fated to live with the paradoxical necessity of entrusting ourselves to chance while at the same time remembering that we were conscious beings working toward conscious goals. This contradiction between rational and irrational opened a bottomless pit over which we had to walk. There was no turning back; gradually this became clear to each of us in his own secret way" (61).

Freud's legacy – together with that of Nietzsche – was of course the most important intellectual catalyst for the twentieth-century deconstruction of the subject as well as the author. The unconscious was undoubtedly the figure that cast the most ominous shadow over the *ego cogito*. Yet in the light of the Dada statements, the unconscious appears in a peculiar double exposure. It is not just something that *is,* an invariant of the human psyche, individual or collective; it is also an object of desire, and of conscious desire at that. When Barthes writes about the Surrealist practice of automatic writing (anticipated in some of the experiments of the Zurich Dada), he leaves out of the story this historically specific desire as well as its object (Barthes, "Death" 144). It is not a matter of losing "all origins" but of finding a new pivot whose metaphysical nature is unmistakable. The fading of the subject, of the modernist author, is a fading *for the sake of* something. And this something is often written in modernist manifestos with a capital letter (in Dada: the Unknown, Chance, Nature). There is simply no getting away from the implications of this graphic emphasis: we are being pointed towards a transcendental.

While I do not plan to unfold in the limited space of this introduction anything like a comprehensive description of the modernist enterprise, I would like to follow Peter Bürger's well-known account in *Theory of the Avant-Garde* to sketch the general situation in which the modernist artist finds himself. In Bürger's oft-repeated phrase, the essential fact of this situation is art's "apartness from the praxis of life," an apartness that in the first decades of the twentieth century becomes an object of explicit and problematic awareness. Art is ready to own up to the fact that it does not respond to any genuine social demand. The demand for aesthetic products is now articulated predominantly through the market and is, to that extent, counterfeit. The modernist rebel reacts to this by disowning his audience, going even so far as to utterly erase reception. In some of the most radical views on art articulated in the early twentieth century, the fate of the art work is not to communicate, to reach across; it is simply to exist, in a thing-like manner, alongside other worldly entities.[16] Jean-Paul Sartre traces the birth of this attitude to the middle of the nineteenth century: "from 1848 on, and until the war of 1914, the radical unification of his public led the author in principle to write against *all his readers* … This fundamental conflict between the writer and his public was an unprecedented phenomenon in literary history" (119; emphasis in the original). In a similar vein is Barthes's declaration in *The Pleasure of the Text:* "Our modernity makes a constant effort to defeat the exchange: it tries to resist the market for works (by excluding itself from mass communication), the sign (by exempting itself from meaning, by madness) ... And even so, modernity can do nothing: the exchange recuperates everything, acclimating what appears to deny it" (23–4). Herbert Marcuse states pithily: "The truly avant-garde works of literature communicate the break with communication" (71). And Theodor Adorno generalizes this attitude to a defining principle for all genuine art in the era of liberal capitalism: "What [art] contributes to society is not some directly communicable content but something more mediate, i.e., resistance" (321).

All of these statements point to a crisis of communication. It is important to understand that this is also a crisis of being and belonging, an ontological predicament. The absence of authentic demand for aesthetic productions is an aspect of a more general problem: the rootlessness of art, its ontological "baselessness."[17] And it goes without saying that the apartness of art from life is also the apartness of the subject. The subject's anguished question, "For whom do I write?", is a prosaic version of another, more fundamental dilemma: "Out of what do I write? When entering the world, what is it that my work objectivates?" T.J. Clark reminds us that "the thought of belonging and serviceability (of Economy as an ideal) haunts modernism, all the more so because belonging and serviceability are sensed to be modernity's true opposites – the dimension to experience it most ruthlessly outlaws or travesties" (8). The paradox these words flesh out is only apparent. Developed capitalism outlaws only genuine serviceability while very much enforcing the utility of humans as partial functions of a process they cannot grasp, let alone control. Modernism repudiates this latter, corrupt form of belonging to the social whole while endeavouring to project viable visions of the former. Yet the anguished question of belonging is not to be resolved by declarations or radicalizations of artistic practice. As I argue below, answers to that question can be imagined or "performed," but they necessarily remain vicarious satisfactions. Only history can provide the resolution the question hopes for. Only a radical transformation in the very constitution of social being would supply art with a sense of deep inherence in the world (although it is not at all clear whether, in such a redeemed human universe, it would still make sense to speak of art as a distinct activity). Of the numerous modernist statements describing a threshold moment between an unwanted old world and a new one worth belonging to, few are more concisely eloquent than the proclamation of the International Constructivists: "We stand today between a society that does not need us and a society that does not exist" (Doesburg, Lissitzky, and Richter 315). And if there is such a thing as *the* cultural act of modernism, then this act is as much a repudiation of the "society that does not need us" as it is the symbolic summoning of its worthy successor.

I wish to suggest that the metaphor "the death of the author" has a determinate meaning within modernist culture and that this meaning has to do with the themes of summoning, grounding, and belonging. The death of the author takes place in representation, be it artistic or programmatic-theoretical. One might indeed say that it takes place "in effigy"; but as soon as this is stated, something important needs to be added: "in effigy" does not take away from the reality of the phenomenon, it does not make it vaporously unreal. Rather, its reality consists precisely in this abstract, detached existence. Because art is constitutively sundered from the totality of social practice, any attempt at redemption or reversal of fate must be abstract by definition. It must be a performance from a distance, a kind of magic ritual that seeks to exert real effects upon an object from which it is objectively separated. A poem by Elena Guro – the only woman among the Russian Futurist poets – presents in concrete imagery both the predicament and the solution of which I have just spoken:

A frightened man was saying:
"I've been left all alone, I'm wretched"
– – – – – – – –
But the snow was melting above the roofs,

Flocks of daws were circling.
– – – – – – – –
I sat alone once in an empty room

The pendulum whispered gloomily.
I was tied up by gloomy thoughts,
Like a drowned man.
The room was made hideous
By someone's imminent parting,
In the disorder of things, and on the sofa:
Books covered with dust and ennui.
The merciless light of the lamp was going bald on the walls,
The closed door was keeping watch
The merciless tomorrow was keeping watch:
"You won't get away this time!."
And I suddenly thought: what if I turned

The chairs and the couches upside down,
And tinkered with the clock? ...
Then a new era would begin,
New lands would open up.
Here, in the room was hidden the thread
That ties all things in one,
Blotted out by yesterday's unkind day
By the calendar of dates.
Here, in the room it was, nearby!
I suddenly believed that it is so.
And that one need not fear anything,
But need search for the secret sign.
And I took it on faith; without fear
I now looked at the room's closed square ...
At the dead door.

– – – – – – – –

The wind was tearing the slushy, grey sky,

The wind was flying 'round the city;
Destroying blind alleys and walls.
All that was left was the snow slush of change,
Mixed with manure.

– – – – – – – –

The man was bouncing on the droshky,

Not afraid of unfaithfulness.   (104–5)

Do we not have here, in this eccentric lyrical script, the acting out of the essential predicament in which the modernist author finds himself? First, the moment of being-apart, of exile from the fullness of social life, the isolation in the sphere of the singularly personal, for which the dreary private room serves as a figuration. The separation (*razluka*) at first appears to be likewise a personal affair, no more than an intimate drama between two lovers: she has betrayed, she has left, his world now lays barren. But if the narrowness of the individual self is precisely the problem, this cannot be remedied simply by "her" coming back. A more radical solution is required, one that cannot be contained within the private sphere, for it is this sphere itself that needs to be abolished. Nothing less than a transformation of the entire world is called for so that that the happiness or ruin of a single "I" will no longer depend on another single "I." And it is this kind of transformation that the second half of the poem imagines. The walled-in space of atomized individuality opens with a crash, and beyond the crumbling enclosures there rises the promise of a new era and unknown new lands (*Prilshlo by nachalo novoi pory / otkrylis' by strany*).

But how can such a broad and radical revolution be accomplished by the meagre powers of the singular, abandoned self? This kind of feat is patently impossible. And herein lies the poetic paradox that Guro pursues and exploits. The feat acknowledges its hopelessness through a spectacular success. It is accomplished, but in a manner that serves only to confirm the powerlessness of the hero. It is a magical act, a manipulation from a distance. One works on the objects in one's room, overturning chairs and sofas, tinkering with the clock, and by a miraculous homeopathy, these eccentric actions, still contained within the realm of isolated individuality, bring about the desired change in the world at large. Unbelievably, the key to an unheard-of metamorphosis of human life happens to be hidden in one's private room.

If the helpless isolation of art from social praxis is the right diagnosis – and I believe it is – such action from a distance is characteristic of the modernist project as a whole. One works with the objects in the delimited realm of artistic craft – words, sounds, surfaces, lines, and colours – in the hope that this manipulation will affect the whole from which the artist and his work have been cut off. Much of modernist literature, beginning with Flaubert and the Symbolists, can be grasped as such a magical ritual in the face of the impossible. The solution is of course "unreal," imaginary. But its unreality is also its ultimate claim to reality, since it is a testimony to something that truly is the case. For the artistic act of modernism truly is destitute, it really is groundless, without foundation, sundered from the rest of social labour: "Modern artistic culture can scarcely be accounted an indispensable element of general culture any longer, for the simple reason that art has ceased to play a part in the general organism" (Meier-Graefe 54). That this lonely act should wish once again to matter, to act meaningfully – this desire is its truth, an authentic testimony to the predicament from which it springs. The delusion begins when the artist starts to believe that the magic trick might succeed or has succeeded, that the manipulation of the medium has in fact initiated a transformation in the world at large, that art has in fact redeemed the irredeemable.

The death of the author should be understood within this essential modernist scenario. It too partakes of the character of magic ritual. In no way should it be taken as a *fact* that modernist theories or manifestos register. Rather, the death of the author is a symbolic *act* whose aim is as much to bury as to summon. It buries the individual self in effigy so that something more real can appear in its stead. Neither the interment nor the miraculous appearance is real in any factual sense. But real is the desire that drives the ritual and that makes it comprehensible to us. The modernist author does not turn over chairs and sofas; rather, he turns his own self inside out and reads on the reverse side the promise of a new art for a new world.

> If the whole of modern art can be understood as the perpetual intervention of the subject, one that is at no point disposed to allow the unreflected governance of the traditional play of forces within the artwork, the permanent interventions of the ego are matched by a tendency of the ego to abdicate out of weakness. True to the age-old mechanical principle of the bourgeois spirit, this abdication takes the form of the reification of subjective achievements, effectively locating them exterior to the subject and mistaking the abdication of the subject for a guarantee of ironclad objectivity. (Adorno 37)

This profound diagnosis appears in Adorno's *Aesthetic Theory*, a landmark text in the theorization of modernism and an extended critical apology for the autonomy of the modernist artwork. In that very "apartness" in which other Marxist critics have seen the problematic status of modernist art, Adorno sees something like a badge of honour. The artist must maintain this distance of alienation, for the alternative is to be complicit in the evil workings of the "heteronomous world." What Adorno fails, or does not wish, to recognize, is that the thing he deplores – the abdication of the ego in favour of "ironclad objectivity" – and the thing he endorses – the resilient autonomy of the text – are inseparable aspects of modernist culture. When one takes only the latter, and treats the former as a peripheral affair – a lapse that might as well not have taken place – one ends up with an account of modernism that is too private to be very useful.

It takes only a cursory glance at the manifestos of the various modernist currents to see that claims of autonomy are very often accompanied by claims of depersonalization. These occur not side by side but rather as complimentary sides of the same declaration. Russian Formalism, which will be discussed in greater detail later, furnishes a substantial and convincing illustration. Art, or the text, is autonomous insofar as it obeys a logic of its own. At any given moment, this logic, this self-sufficient inner life of the text, can be imagined as unauthored, as operating beyond subjective control. But in fact, the logic of the symbolic act is the opposite, as Adorno astutely points out: the abdication of the ego comes first, after which it is possible to imagine that the text has generated itself, that it has emerged from some compelling necessity beyond subjective whim and will.

Nor do I think that the abdication of the ego, whatever its fraught implications or possible consequences, should be taken exclusively in the elegiac meaning that Adorno attributes to it. The fact that it is based on *méconnaissance* should not prevent us from seeing in it an act of protest and an omen of possible deliverance. Fredric Jameson has insisted on just such an understanding of modernism's gestures of depersonalization (*A Singular* 133–6). For him, these are to be read as reactions – often unconscious – to the subterranean tremors of a social revolution to come – tremors that were felt across the Western world at the beginning of the twentieth century.[18] From this perspective, the surrender of the self is not abdication but a foreboding of imminent empowerment: "Yet the forms still, as symbolic acts, testify to immense gestures of liberation and new construction which we can only glimpse retrospectively, by historical reconstruction" (Jameson, *Singular Modernity* 136). The "break with a thousand-year-old tradition" (Ball 225) to which the modernists dedicated so many cries of despair and exhilaration was driven, in part, by a desire to throw off bourgeois individualism as "an annoying burden or too heavy, too confining garment" (Gershenzon and Ivanov 11).

The death of the author is certainly related to what Renato Poggioli has characterized as the "agonistic attitude" of radical modernisms: a performance of sacrifice in which the self-willed or anticipated destruction of the ego is offered as a token of the world's ultimate redemption. "In short, agonism means sacrifice and consecration: an hyperbolic passion, a bow bent toward the impossible, a paradoxical and *positive* form of spiritual defeatism" (Poggioli 66; emphasis added). Modernist declarations about the death of the author were not always imbued with the pathos Poggioli invokes. Yet the meaning of consecration and that "bow bent toward the impossible" – which Guro's poem images so well – are inextricably part of the symbolic act. The problem inherent in Poggioli's account is one that Groys will reproduce later in his treatment of the Russian avant-garde. Each of them reduces the cultural phenomenon to a subjective attitude: agonism in Poggioli, demiurgic ambition in Groys. Yet such character descriptions are bound to remain abstract when they are not grounded in a careful analysis of the circumstances that determine this or that attitude. The death of the author is not just about the subject: it concerns in equal measure the object with which the subject enters a relationship (and that object is, ultimately, the world). It bears repeating: the ego is relinquished *for the sake of something*. We are dealing with a ritual dance unfolding between two partners: the self and that "something" for the sake of which the self stages its own vanishing. To describe the act as simply a matter of a human agent externalizing her dispositions would be to distort it. Although Part I of this study will describe several such dances with objects, it might be useful to provide here an advance summary of the dynamic between self and otherness.

Because it has been segregated from the practice of life, because it does not receive from life what it so sorely lacks, art must produce this missing substance in effigy. In the place of the use-value it no longer carries, art must create a new and unique species of value; it must manufacture its *raison d'être* out of itself.[19] Because an authentic social demand for their creations is not forthcoming, modernist authors construct a surrogate of this demand in the form of what I call a *demanding object*. A demanding object is one that issues an imperative from within itself, an imperative directed back at the subject. The meaning of this back-and-forth dynamic is that the object should "necessitate" or "motivate" the subjective act; more precisely, the subject contrives to necessitate herself via the object.[20] The object is preconceived so that it needs the subject, presupposes her, "calls" for her being and action – that is, for the artistic practice. The subject has projected before herself a pattern of "lawfulness" and treats it as binding. For this game not to descend into solipsistic self-gratification, the laws in question must be posited as if they issue not from the human agent but rather from whatever it is this agent works with in her artistic practice – that is, from the "material" in the variety of its existences. It matters little whether the material is understood in terms of form or content. What is important is that the demand come from outside the subject, from some otherness, so as to have a legitimate claim upon her. In short, the laws must be objective; they must be the immanent dynamics of some external and non-contingent reality. They must bind and constrain so that the artistic practice does not appear gratuitous: "The non-representational or 'abstract,' if it is to have aesthetic validity, cannot be arbitrary and accidental, but must stem from obedience to some worthy constraint or original. This constraint, once the world of common extraverted experience has been renounced, can only be found in the very disciplines by which art and literature have already imitated the former" (Greenberg, "Avant-Garde" 6). The practitioner of art obeys rules that have subjective origins, although those rules are treated in the opposite sense – as objective. This is precisely what Adorno has in mind when he speaks of the "reification of subjective achievements." As the dance plays out, the subject has found a place and anchoring, yet no longer in the role of author. In exchange for relinquishing the claims to origination, the artistic subject has been fastened within an "ironclad objectivity."

To give a brief and easily accessible illustration of the "lawfulness" being discussed here, let us stay with Greenberg a little longer and consider his well-known discussion of the role of surface in modernist painting. Echoing a number of modernist practitioners,[21] Greenberg points out that the flatness of the surface in abstract art serves as the artist's law of conduct.[22] The painterly forms that appear on the surface are treated as objectivations or visualizations of the principle of flatness. They "lay bare the device," reminding us that we are in the two-dimensional space of artistic manipulation (rather than in the three-dimensional world of illusionistic semblances). What the viewer is supposed to see in a painting by Mondrian, for instance, is simply the actualization of painterly-ness as the latter is equated with flatness and the rectangular enclosure of the picture frame. We are also supposed to appreciate that the act responsible for the object before us is not "arbitrary and accidental, but ... stem[s] from obedience to some worthy constraint or original." The constraint in question is, of course, nothing other than the specific character of the medium, which is treated as a binding condition for individual formative activity.[23] Ostensibly, the artist is simply the midwife of the process whereby the essential properties of painting actualize themselves on the canvas, his personality having merged with (surrendered to) the medium's immanent *telos*.

It should be clear from all of this that I do not see the death of the author in modernism as merely a variation on a theme one might discern in earlier cultural paradigms. Whatever the apparent similarities with, say, medieval doctrines of impersonality,[24] these analogies obscure more than they reveal. In modernism, the act of impersonality is one of negation; it is a concerted attempt to erase from the text the marks of individual, "expressive" subjectivity. For the medieval *auctor*, this could not have been the case: the expressive self had not yet been enthroned, so it could not be dethroned, negated. Nor was there in the Middle Ages anything like an institution of art premised on the individual's pursuit of beauty and truth. A similar objection can be raised against perceived affinities between Romantic and modernist impersonality. The former phenomenon accompanied the still-incipient autonomization of art, which had just begun to emerge from its integration within an overall (aristocratic) "art of living," from its dependence on court patronage, and from the strictures of normative aesthetics. In this context, the Romantic doctrines of inspiration served not to problematize the status of art but to place the agency of art on equal footing with that of the divine Demiurge.

The general point of these brief historical excursuses is the same one I made earlier: the modernist ritual of depersonalization is reactive. It is a response to a specific cultural-historical moment, a moment of crisis. This gives it its distinct meaning and identity. Analogies with other historical episodes are bound to be spurious insofar as the context will inevitably prove to be very different. For as long as we hearken only to declarations of artistic impersonality, we could come to believe that the modernist subversion of the author "is ... resplendently anticipated in the Classical and Medieval traditions" (Burke xvii). But once we move beyond such declarations and reflect on the deep contexts that nurture them, it turns out that we are not dealing with the same imagination at all, but rather with discrete metaphors that express in each case an original, situation-bound content.

The October Revolution did not extinguish modernist art in Russia. On the contrary, for at least another decade, it provided modernism with a new and much more concrete impetus, albeit a deceptively objective one. To quote T.J. Clark again, these were times when "modernism could believe, not absurdly, that it was on the side of history" (257). Nor did the Revolution put an end to enactments of the author's demise. These continued, but in a new context: that for the sake of which the demise was being performed, that which was to be the true generator of works, had acquired clear contours and names (the Dictatorship of the Proletariat, the People, the Economy, History, etc.). After the upheavals of the Revolution, foreign intervention, and civil war, and after the chaos, misery, and utopian intoxications of War Communism, the New Economic Policy (NEP; a period inaugurated by Lenin in 1921) placed the radical artistic intelligentsia in a situation at once novel and familiar. The cardinal transformation of life had been initiated but remained woefully incomplete. The present held open a road to Utopia while prosaically bespeaking its remoteness. Art was delivered once more to the vagaries of a market for cultural commodities; but beyond that market, the Bolshevik government was instituting, by fits and starts, incompletely and ambiguously, a space of official patronage, a space that at any moment could contract into nothing or (as it would transpire at the end of the decade) be expanded to encompass everything.[25] That art could once again be a viable part of social being was no longer an abstract proposition; yet the means by which this could be accomplished remained as unclear as ever. Many

radical artists could recognize their situation in the words of Boris
Arvatov: "Since the end of culture is upon us, [artists] have to acknowledge their own purposelessness and uselessness ... The question now is
what artists are to do" (qtd in Gough, *The Artist* 104).

The intelligentsia's gestures of self-erasure were often overtures to a collective subject whose presence had become palpable, but even more to a
new destiny that appeared at once overwhelming, faceless, and unfathom-
able. Against this tantalizing horizon, depersonalization was once again
an act with a double meaning: it could be read as a symptom of weakness
(the abdication of the ego in the whirlwind of historical happenings that
exceeded the bounds of consciousness) or as the tapping of new currents
of power beyond the narrow subjective realm. The literature of the 1920s
has left us numerous portrayals and evocations of the dissolving indi-
vidualist self, from Blok and Mayakovsky to Babel and Platonov. I offer
here two prominent examples of this common theme so as to drive home
the point that the surrender of the (former, limited) "I" was at the same
time a plea for belonging, a summoning and reification of a grand super-
personal power.

The first example comes from Boris Pilniak's *The Naked Year* (1921), in
many ways the defining modernist text of the post-revolutionary period
(despite the derivativeness of its method). Here we find a whole group of
characters exhibiting a threshold psychological state in which a sense of
disaster and destitution is indistinguishable from an experience of radical
freedom and exhilaration. The scions of the noble Ordynin family, Andrei
and the old Prince Andrei (the identical names are a strategic move on the
part of Pilniak, who is very conscious of constructing a composite image
out of discrete fictional figures), are driven from their ancestral home, and
as they set off on foot through the steppe, now owning nothing but the
clothes they are wearing, their inner monologues voice the same experience: material dispossession has given rise to unsuspected and intoxicat-
ing freedom. Later on, young Andrei's thoughts connect this personal
destitution with the fate of Russia: "no possessions, everything renounced ... without even his own linen. What if the trains of Russia
should stop running – was there no beauty in destruction, in starvation,
in disease? One ought to learn to look everything straight in the face –
oneself too from [outside], only look on, belong to no one" (144). The
previous self is released and becomes merely an object in a strangely ec-
static field of vision, which now encompasses the entire harrowing landscape of post-revolutionary Russia. From this "disassociated" point of
view, chaos, tragedy, and destruction become disturbingly aestheticized.

This vision is rearticulated several pages later, now in the words of the archaeologist, Baudek, for whom too the death and the hunger of the "naked" 1919 are the ingredients for a sweeping enchantment (159–60). Finally we are introduced to a mysterious figure, referred to simply as *chelovek* (man), who seems to be a fictional summation of several of the intelligentsia characters in the novel (135). As the "man" lies dying of consumption in a stuffy, overcrowded train car, he feels intensely the dispersion of his former "I" (235). As the private intellectualized self falls away, a delirious urge replaces it in which beastly violence and passionate human communion are fused: "The ... man's heart grew full of most sweet and bestial pain – he had a longing to cry out and let out and fling himself on the first skirts that came along and be as hard and as cruel as possible there and then in front of them all rape her and rape her. Reasoning, decency, shame, stoicism – to hell with them all! The beast it is!" In Pilniak the crumbling of the "I" unleashes something more powerful and no longer individualized: the primordial life of instinct, which floods the trenches of the self and opens the body beyond its apparent limits. The same agonistic release is then shown to be taking place within the larger, social body, as the crust of Western civilization falls away to reveal a primordial, Scythian Russia.

My second exhibit comes from Fedor Gladkov's novel *Cement* (1925), later to be canonized as a paragon of socialist realism *avant la lettre*. Among the working-class characters and party activists who crowd its pages, the reader easily picks out Sergei Ivagin as a special case, a figure deliberately constructed to "make a point" about the intelligentsia and the Revolution. His personal drama culminates near the end of the novel, as Sergei is purged from the local party organization. Paradoxically, his exclusion is what makes him realize he belongs unconditionally to the Party. In Sergei's inner monologue, which comes right after the official notification from the "purge commission," the agonistic scenario plays out in full force:

Only one thing then was necessary: the Party and Party work. No personal life. What was his love, hidden in unseen depths? What were these problems and thoughts which tortured his mind? All were survivals of an accursed past. All came from his father, his youth, the romanticism of intellectuals. All this must be extirpated to the very root. These sick figments of the mind must be destroyed. There was only one thing – the Party; and everything to the last drop of his blood must be given to it. Whether he would be re-admitted or not made no difference; he, Sergei Ivagin, as a personality, did not exist. There was only the Party and he was an insignificant item in this great organism. (296)

This is as much an act of self-consecration to the cause as it is a suicide note. The two deeds are, again, one: letting go of the self is what allows Sergei to dissolve into – and thus fully belong to – the impersonal force through which history is being made.

Automatic for the Masses is not about literary demises of individuality, however, but about gestures of depersonalization performed in literary and artistic theory. My aim is not to document these gestures; for the most part, they are common knowledge among scholars of Russian modernism. I want instead to examine them closely so as to lay bare their inner meaning and common significance. The post-revolutionary decade (1918–28) abounded in artistic doctrines and theories of creativity that challenged, from a variety of perspectives, the authority and autonomy of the author.[26] The decade after that saw the institutionalizing of socialist realism and the thoroughgoing regimentation of cultural production in all spheres within the newly created artistic unions, which were directly controlled by the state. Within these institutional confines, there were people who casually called themselves "authors" (socialist realism proudly proclaimed the unprecedented freedom of individual creativity in the land of the Soviets), but their authorship was only nominal. The connection between the two cultural frames is not causal in any direct or simple way. It is difficult to hold that socialist realism "implemented" the theoretical ideas of the 1920s. Speaking against such an assertion is the violence with which the Stalinist establishment rejected all of the theoretical heritage of the previous period. Yet a connection exists. The symbolic act of the author's death did not end with the end of the 1920s; it continued to be staged within the institutional framework of official Stalinist culture. Endowed with a new meaning, it entered the very definition of socialist realism as a representational system. Thereby, it also became part of the general state project of building socialism. More precisely, the death of the author was now staged as a ritual that confirmed the immanence of socialism in "one separately taken country."[27] In place of the various "demanding objects," which the theorists of the 1920s had posited as regulatory of artistic practice, there was now a single overwhelming positivity: socialism itself. And the enterprise of socialist realism involved, in the first instance, schooling writers and artists to "see" this positivity, which in turn presupposed a new kind of surrender: authors were expected to let go of their individualistic selves so as to be possessed by the materialized grace of history.

My argument that modernism and socialist realism held ground in common will not concern in the least the properties of their respective artistic discourses. It is immediately apparent that modernist and socialist-realist texts have very little in common. The kinship I wish to explore theoretically concerns the *status* of the text, not its formal or semantic features. The death of the author, I will argue, is a symbolic performance wherein the actual text – the cultural artefact that is the finished product of practice – acquires the status of a token. The text-token completes, "materializes," the symbolic act of surrender and, beyond it, the agency that has come to take the vacated place of the author. This token-being of the text characterizes socialist realism no less than artistic modernism.

Of course, there is a sense in which any text, from any time or place, can be taken as a token of something. For instance, we can take Dostoevsky's writings as a token of his Great Russian chauvinism or Nietzsche's as an index of his problematic relationship with women. But such taking-of-something-as-a-token – a taking guided by our own interests and by what we think we perceive behind the author's back – has nothing to do with the situation in which something is produced and given to us as a token. In the latter case, the object being offered does not wait for the recipient to invest it with evidential value; it is not in that recipient's hand that it first becomes a token. The object is a token beforehand, insofar as it circulates in a pre-existing sphere of symbolic exchange in which certain symbolic behaviours have become a matter of convention. Similarly, it is not for us to assign the status of a token to modernist texts such as Vladimir Tatlin's counter-reliefs. They come to us as such, because they were imbedded in a symbolic plot of willed depersonalization and cannot be adequately apprehended outside of it. From within their own immanent context, they address us as tokens of necessary practice, a practice guided by a demanding objectivity that complies with the intrinsic properties of utilitarian materials. When we contemplate Tatlin's constructions, we are contemplating not just the objects before us but the entire "plot" whose materialized outcomes they are. Otherwise, the objects would remain inscrutable for us.

To say that the text is a token is to make a vital distinction between what is conveyed *in* the text and what is conveyed *by means of* the text. In the latter case, the text is apprehended *in toto*, as a single gesture. Its "insides," the signs from which it has been woven and which may refer us to the world we know, have congealed into a unitary externality, one total sign, namely, the token. Let me offer a small, mundane example to illustrate the distinction. I could show a friend of mine a picture of Kazan Cathedral in St Petersburg so that he can become acquainted with an interesting architectural monument he has never seen before. Or I could send him more or less the same view from the Nevsky Prospekt framed as a postcard. In the first instance, I would be showing my friend something *in* the picture;

in the second, I would be showing him something *by means of* the picture. The object being pictured is the same (the photograph might even be identical) but the context of communication is not. Even if I do not write anything on the back of the postcard, it will still function as an easy-to-read token of my having visited St Petersburg and having thought of my friend while there. Of course, nothing rules out the possibility that my friend will carefully examine the depiction of the cathedral, making it the primary object of his interest. But even if he does, this will not in any way change the "objective" status of the sign. For this status is determined not by how one particular recipient treats the picture sent to him but by the already established culture of symbolic gestures (here, the sending of postcards). Since I have mailed the picture as a postcard, I certainly expect that my friend – whatever his idiosyncrasies – will read not only the photographic representation but also the cultural ritual in which this representation has been embedded. When the recipient is aware of the ritual and participates in it adequately, he is able to look past the photographic image, abstracting from its wealth of details and treating it simply as one total sign, a representative "view" of St Petersburg that betokens the sender's sojourn in the city.

In artistic modernism, the text's representational message is reduced or even extinguished altogether in favour of the gestural message, the showing-by-means-of the artefact. Marshall McLuhan's famous dictum, "The medium is the message," can be reinterpreted along these lines: the modernist text is a token of the formative dynamics that have brought it into existence. The text is a materialization of these dynamics, a sample of their impersonal "work." By means of the text, the artist demonstrates what it is to let Language speak, the Surface dictate its painterly appropriations, the Material reveal its structure and utility, and so on. But in socialist realism, too, the text has the status of a token. Stalinist literature and painting are representational through and through, but that representational content – like the postcard photograph of Kazan Cathedral – is embedded in an institutionalized ritual of communication. The ritual is not something external to the text. We cannot abstract from it, for then the objective status of the sign would be lost to view. To adequately apprehend the socialist-realist text, we must inhabit, analytically, the cultural-ideological performance within which it functions and grasp the symbolic act of which it is the material token.

To that end, my focus throughout this book will be not on the artistic texts themselves but rather on the discourses – cultural theories, artistic programs, ideological pronouncements, and the like – through which the status of the text as a token is framed. I hope to extract from these discourses the general logic of the symbolic performances, their common "plot," through which artistic practice assumes the appearance of a work mandated by imperious objectivity. To that end, Part I offers an analytical survey of some of the most prominent artistic and theoretical platforms of the post-revolutionary decade. In order of presentation, these are Formalism; the sociological method of Valerian Pereverzev and his followers; the "science of organization" (tektology) expounded by Aleksandr Bogdanov; the Constructivist movement; and the artistic-ideological platform of the "Onguardists." My analyses do not aim to capture some agreement, or even vague similarity, on the level of stated positions. In those years, allegiances were few and far between antagonisms and collisions.[28] But underlying the sometimes ferocious clashes among artistic organizations and academic and ideological factions, there persisted one secret and stubborn life common to them all. I will be attempting to capture this life, which animated the thought of the Formalists as well as that of their Marxist critics, the aspirations of the neo-Futurists, and the political manoeuvrings of their sworn enemies in RAPP. This was not the life of thought, not the stirring of some essential idea that the opponents, in the heat of their disputes, did not recognize as common. Rather, it was the life of the object in general, the cultural existence of "this," before "this" became concretized as this or that, before it was apprehended as "form," "content," "product," "word," "consciousness," "history," and so on. Under these various names are to be found different versions of what I have referred to as the demanding object. So I will not be writing the history of organizations and movements, but rather an abbreviated biography of this demanding otherness – of the general "this" – that both knowledge and practice take as their field. In this field I hope to delineate something like common plot, a shared order of happening in which heterogeneous phenomena participate.

What united the theoretical and artistic platforms of the 1920s was a distinctly modern desire to save the creative act from contingency, to motivate it, by anchoring it in a determinate "law of conduct." Formalized as this or that artistic method, the law in question was derived directly from the nature of the medium and interpreted as binding upon the subject. In responding to the demand implicit in the object, the human agent is less a creator than a technician, less an originator than an executioner. The insubstantiality or insufficiency of the subjective – this essentially negative fact – then acquires a positive, enabling, and prospective aspect. The displacing of the subject from the centre of creation instantiates a new kind

of truth. This happens in a single motion, a single act: as individual consciousness and will are found incapable of accounting for the essential constitution of "this," there opens, beyond their limits, the territory of the
"objective." Its shapes are different: for the Formalists, objective are the
workings of the "constructive principle" (against the traditional emphasis
on intended meaning and expression); for the Pereverzevians, objective
are the workings of the "socio-psychological complex" (once again, as
opposed to the author's intent and explicit semantics of the text); for the
Constructivists, objective are the dynamics of social movement in its various permutations (in opposition to the movement of individual invention);
for the Onguardists, objective is the "knowing" of class ideology (rather
than the unmediated cognition whereby individual proletarian consciousness apprehends the world).

Two things take place in the plot we shall follow: (1) something true
is brought out of concealment and instantiated as a now-manifest "construction," "organization," "operative principle," "tectonic," and so on;
and (2) in the same movement, the individual expressive self dissolves into
the impersonal mechanism of a cognitive or practical operation ("method"), accessory and transparent to the essential operations of history, society, language, consciousness, and so on. In short, depersonalization
appears as accessory to the act of demonstration. As noted earlier, it is
important to understand that these two aspects are interrelated, that indeed they belong to a single order of happening: the constitution of otherness ("this"), its production in the dimension of the "objective," is
predicated on the self-induced fading of the "I," its relegation to the impersonal. This is one event, one symbolic act.

Stalinism "fulfilled" the desire implicit in the symbolic death of the author that modernist culture enacted: the desire to belong. That fulfilment
was purely formal, of course. The socialist-realist author was *posited* as
someone fully integrated with the life of Soviet society. The cognitive
transparency to which every realism lays claim was, in Stalinist socialist
realism, premised on belonging: only he who truly was part of the struggle
for socialism could represent the world truthfully. In Stalinist ideology, the
Soviet Man was supposed to be a new kind of human being, one who not
only worked harder but also felt more deeply and saw more clearly. As for
the empirical socialist-realist writer, he had to impersonate *that* posited
being and enact *that* optimal seeing. The text he produced was thus by
default a token of whether he was or was not a creature of socialism – an
ontological certification. In the doctrinal framework of socialist realism,
to write is to provide an occasion for the world to explicate its immanent

logic; but that occasion will be opportune only if the writer is "one of us," a true Soviet person.

Chapter 6 expands on the kinship between modernism and socialist-realist artistic practices. Important for appreciating this kinship – without overstating its scope – is a notion of the cultural act as a performance that goes beyond the physical limits of the text. In modernism, art must not only convey meaning but also betoken its own meaningfulness. I maintain that both modernism and socialist realism feature symbolic rituals in which artistic practice is presented as driven by imperative objectivity. But the commonality ends when we consider how the symbolic performance takes place. In modernism, it occurs in the context of genuine disquiet over art's lost moorings and the threat of its commodification, against which there takes place a multidirectional and open-ended pursuit of an "art of determinate necessity" (Spengler 293). Stalinism, by contrast, instituted this kind of art as a *fait accompli*, as the axiomatic outcome of a world history that had reached its fruition and that had begotten, at its grand finale, a grand organic style. Socialist realism is the staging of an aesthetic that springs directly from the soil of collective life, a compelling formative force that uses individuals as transitory vehicles for its realization.

The ideological scenario for how this force takes hold of individuals is the subject of chapter 7. Here I define in a preliminary way the relationship between the representing and represented in the world of "advanced socialist construction" (which in Stalinist Russia was ushered in by the ahead-of-schedule completion of the First Five-Year Plan). These two instances, I argue, do not relate as "subject" to "object." To procure a true image of reality, a very different relationship must be instantiated. The world of Stalinist socialism constitutes a peculiar kind of representational object. Comparing it to the objects considered in Part I, we find that this one is not *about to* perform its own analysis; it has already done so. The culture of the 1920s is essentially futural; Stalinist culture is essentially perfective. Because it *has* understood itself already, in the present the world *shows*. It is exhibitionistic. In this quality – which, translating an expression of Sergei Eisenstein's (*uvidennost'*), I will call "seen-ness" – it proves to really *not* be an object in any accepted sense of the word. Nor, for that matter, is the position of the representing "someone" the position of a subject. In the place where we would expect to find the subject, we find an empty spot. That empty spot is reserved for any potential "one" in whom the self-knowing of the world, its being-foreseen, would be confirmed.

Chapter 9 further develops this dialectic in order to show how the empty spot was filled concretely, how the Soviet writer was recruited to it. Before this step, however, chapter 8 attempts to both clear and map the territory on which the question of recruitment, or subjection, will be asked – the territory of ideology. It goes without saying that socialist realism was an ideological phenomenon. What is usually understood by this is that the cultural establishment retransmitted the dogmas of the political establishment. But in this chapter I explore a different sense in which socialist realism was ideological: it was not that it clothed the party line in the persuasive garb of aesthetics, but that it staged the very functioning of ideology, in that broader and value-neutral sense in which ideology can be taken as synonymous with culture. Because socialist realism was the name not just of an artistic method but of a project for a sweepingly new human culture, it simulated the objective existence of culture, its well-nigh automatic generation by the socio-economic process.

Analogous to the distinction between the representational message of a text and its token-value, we should distinguish between two levels in the operation of Stalinist ideology. On one level, it produced substantive claims about the world (how the world is and how it should be) and supplied facts that seemed to confirm those claims. On another level, it offered statements about ideology itself and administered rituals that demonstrated how people were possessed by (or dispossessed of) ideology. This meta-level, which I refer to as the ideology of ideology, concerns not the factual content of this or that cognition but the very status of knowledge and the genesis of consciousness in general. Ideological assertions about the real world can be verified by facts; but claims about what it means to have (the right) ideology, to be a subject possessed by a given form of consciousness, cannot be: the truth of such claims can only be "exhibited" through symbolic acts and tokens.

I draw on Louis Althusser's classic essay "Ideology and Ideological State Apparatuses" to show the kind of relationship between ideas, social practices, and individual subjectivities that the (meta-)ideology of Stalinism stages. Althusser maintains that individuals are the supports of an objective and impersonal structure of social (re)production; because it needs its supports, the structure produces the individuals as subjects – that is, it supplies them with the requisite beliefs for performing the requisite tasks to which they are assigned. Because the mechanism of social (re)production is the primary given, it could be said that this mechanism endows subjects with ideology and "acts" them in their respective roles. Althusser's is a critical theory of ideology, but it leaves room for a positive interpretation of ideology-cum-culture. On such an interpretation, ideology would still be a necessary outgrowth of the social infrastructure, it would still have a firm hold on the individual-as-subject, but now this recruitment would not be coterminous with misrecognition, alienation, and exploitation. Such, I argue, is the meta-ideological vision native to Stalinist culture.

It is easy to see how this vision turns specific ideological representations into tokens: it is not enough for me to hold such-and-such views and beliefs, or to profess these in my art; I must show, *by means of* my artistic representations, that I belong firmly to the social whole and, insofar as I do, that an objective historical process has engendered me as a subject and endowed me with views, beliefs, and so on. In short, I must believe in such a way as to show that history believes in my stead. In chapter 7, I suggest that the Soviet writer came to be in an empty spot circumscribed by the power of Stalinist socialism to make things apparent, to lay bare. In chapter 9, I illustrate and develop this argument by examining the grand founding event of socialist-realist culture: the First All-Union Congress of Soviet Writers (August–September 1934). I approach it as a public spectacle that afforded writers the opportunity to come face to face with socialism-in-the-flesh and perform the symbolic act expected of them (i.e., show themselves as being "acted" by the self-revelatory movement of "our (Soviet) life"). As previously suggested, the possibility of depicting the world in its essential reality was predicated on belonging, on being-Soviet, which, for its part, was made synonymous with being-acted. Following the logic of these conditions, I arrive at the ideological character of representation in Stalinist culture: representation (in the sense of "depicting," showing, reflecting upon) was an agency that had become detached from the person; he was more its object than its master; as a function of his belonging to "our world," this agency happened *to* him in the manner of grace.

By way of conclusion, chapter 10 expands these reflections beyond the realm of artistic practices. I discuss Mikhail Chiaureli's film *The Vow* (1946), which offers a striking fictional presentation of ideal Stalinist subjecthood. The film presents us with a group of characters, builders of socialism, whose lives we follow from the mid-1920s to the end of the Second World War. The story of each and all of them tells us that their achievements are not their own. Through their efforts, socialism has been built and victory in the war has been won, but the power that propels them in this effort, and that guarantees in advance that it will succeed, comes to them from somewhere else. It springs into their lives from that same empty spot discussed previously as an abstract space, now rendered in *The Vow* with vivid literalness. What in regard to the act of artistic representation has manifested itself as the power of exhibition, of making-see, now manifests itself as the general power of fulfilment, of making-happen. In the film, among other things, that power charts the trajectory of individual human lives. It does so by recruiting and then "acting" these individuals-cum-subjects in the quotidian enactment of a world whose ways have been objectively preinscribed and that, for this very reason, has as its only destiny fulfilment as such.

PART ONE

Chapter 1

The Imperative of Form

In the writings of those who have come to be known as the Russian Formalists,[1] "form" is the conceptual space in which the death of the author occurs, even if it is not announced in quite so dramatic a fashion. It has traditionally been argued that in their pursuit of "scientific" objectivity, the Formalists sought to eliminate the subjective factor both from the history of aesthetic phenomena and from the analysis of specific texts – that they arrived at something like "system" by taking language as their model and jettisoning the stuff of genetic explanation, intellectual speculation, psychological conjecture, and social commentary.[2] The German tradition of *Kunstwissenschaft* (Hildebrand, Worringer, Wöfflin) and the work of Aleksandr Potebnia (1835–91) and Aleksandr Veselovskii (1838–1906), in Russia, are then cited as significant precursors in this endeavour.[3] But should we not be wary of positing the "new pathos of scientific positivism" (Eikhenbaum, *Literatura* 120) as a *prima causa*?[4] Perhaps it was just the opposite – that the Formalist "science of literature" became practicable because some change had already occurred in the life of the object, a change that made it possible for art, folklore, or *belles lettres* to be conceived as fields of verifiably objective cognition. What I have in mind is a kind of object (of study, but also of practice) whose life is fully internal to itself; in the present case, this means internal to the "literary" or, more broadly, the "artistic." No meaningful relationships, no causes of significant permutations in the object, are to be found outside of it.[5] This is what makes it "systematic," and this is what first grounds any claim to scientific rigour. The human agent – the artistic subject, the author – is just one of those extrinsic factors that will prove inessential in the constitution of the object; and this, in turn, will render the very appellation "author" problematic if not vacuous. To anticipate a bit: the only way the figure of the individual writer can remain pertinent is insofar as its doings are synchronized with the logic of the "literary"; the human agent simply executes that which the object's intrinsic dynamic already presupposes. In other words, the literary field is posited in such a way that one can imagine something like a volition on the side of the object, a volition that the individual writer obeys; and only insofar as he obeys it can he be considered a worthy inhabitant of this field.

In art, the Formalists descried a movement that occurred fully outside the subjective sphere and that carried art through time while also carrying the promise of a scientific study of things aesthetic. This movement traversed singularities – of this person, of this "school" or "movement" – yet the force that propelled it belonged to the object itself. Something in the very nature of art provided the impulse towards new harmonies and cadences, new perspectives and compositions. This impulse reverberated in the soul of every true artist, but no soul, no matter how great, was to be for art's principle either an absolute beginning or even a privileged abode. Osip Brik, the "astute Formalist impresario" (Erlich 67), expressed this most emphatically when he vouched that even if Pushkin had never been born, his immortal *Evgenii Onegin* would have been written all the same ("T. n. Formal'nyi metod" 213). It is as if this work, whose author was, ultimately, Pushkin, had been programmed, "scheduled," in some arcane computation of form. Even if we disregard Brik's aphoristic foray, we should take note of the new meaning it gives to the old phrase "work of art" (*proizvedenie iskusstva*). The genitive attribution becomes more intimate, more engaged: "work of art" means not just a thing that belongs to some predefined category, "art"; it means, almost literally, actual work, activity of production (*proizvedenie* approaching *proizvodstvo*), performed by the impersonal agency of art itself. Brik is really saying this: *Evgenii Onegin* is a particular instance of work that needed to be done, that would have been done even without Pushkin. For art is no longer merely a collection of things with ascertained aesthetic properties; nor is it the generic activity performed on an object that turns it into something beautiful. Outside of these definitions, art is primarily something that *works* autonomously, a device that performs tasks that have been programmed into it. As such, it is susceptible to objective description in terms of elements and functions.

It is rather significant that the manifesto of Russian Formalism was an article by Viktor Shklovskii titled "Art as Device," even if *priem* in the Russian title ("Iskusstvo kak priem") does not quite support the point I am making. *Priem* is "device" only in the more archaic meaning of the English word, which allows us to "leave someone to their own devices."

Priem has a more instrumental inflection; it presupposes human agency. It keeps us in the still human sphere of strategy, dexterity, and ploy, of possible unpredictability and cunning winks. Machines do not operate through *priemy* (pl.); the provenance of *priem* is decidedly not the mechanistic or the technological, unless it is that original *techne* with which Aristotle designated the skill of the artisan-artist.[6] Still, the English "device," precisely in its most mechanistic sense, conveys an essential aspect of what Shklovskii and the other Formalists understood to be the true nature of art.[7]

Artistic form is an autonomous mechanism whose functioning can be described synchronically as well as diachronically. In "Art as Device," Shklovskii emphasized the latter aspect as he spoke of art's ability to renew our perception of things. He made very few references to "form," but he made extensive use of the term *ostranenie:* "making strange," "defamiliarization."[8] For too long had form been viewed as something imparted onto the object and thereafter belonging to it as an unalienable property; what Shklovskii wanted to underscore was not a property but a process, a shift (*sdvig*) rather than a shape. The function of "making strange" constituted for him the positive phase in the life of form; the negative phase was that of "habitualization," or what the Czech Formalists will later term "automatization." The former encompassed the realm of the artistic proper, yet the latter was equally integral in the generation of aesthetic shapes. Each phase not only presupposed the other but actively called it forth: every artistic form fades with time, making necessary the emergence of a new one; conversely, as soon as a new form appears, its irrevocable aging begins, bringing ever closer the twilight hour when it will sink below the threshold of vivid perception: "Each art form travels down the inevitable road from birth to death; from seeing and sensory perception, when every detail in the object is savored and relished, to mere recognition, when the object or form becomes a dull epigone which our senses register mechanically, a piece of merchandise not visible even to the buyer" (Shklovskii, *Khod* 88).[9] Above and beyond the particular forms that have superseded one another throughout the history of art, one can think of Form as the general logic of this supersession, as that which perpetuates itself in ever new instances.

It should be emphasized that there is no contradiction in Shklovskii between the imperative of deautomatization and the automaton-like logic of Form. One pertains to the subjective side, the pole of reception; it tells us what art is (or should be) on the level of perceptual experience: an event of defamiliarization. The other concerns the objective side of textual generation, the inner workings of art; all we find here is an impersonal logic of deformation and differentiation. The objective logic makes possible the subjective effect, the experience of renewed perception. Shlkovskii's starting point was to identify art with that experience. Yet equally important for him, and for the new science of literature, was the vision of art as an impersonal will-to-form that objectified itself in identifiable (and analysable) "devices." There is a good reason Shklovskii was so fond of popular fictions and fairy tales: where authorship is immaterial, one is able to observe the form-giving impulse in its primal, unadulterated manifestations.

In the mid-1920s, Iurii Tynianov would describe the objective aspect of art's genesis in a much more satisfactory ("systematic") manner, as the historical unfolding of pure oppositions:

> And so in the analysis of literary evolution, we encounter the following stages: 1) in regard to the automatized principle of construction, there emerges, dialectically, the opposite constructive principle; 2) its application commences – the constructive principle seeks the easiest employment; 3) it spreads over the greatest possible mass of phenomena; 4) it becomes automatized and calls forth the opposite principle of construction. ("Literaturnyi fakt" 108)

And so art traverses time in the dialectical shuttle of oppositions, perpetually rediscovering itself in what the Formalists called "differential quality" (*differnentsial'noe kachestvo*)[10] – an evanescent quality, to be sure, since it exists only in the momentous motion with which the new form distances itself from the old (the latter no longer experienced as "form" but as the habituated existence of the content).

Human intelligence, skill, imagination, and talent are, of course, involved throughout the life of form. At each moment in time, it is general human experience that brings about the habitualization of the object, and it is human creativity that rescues the object from its tarnished existence. But the agency of the individual, of the human subject in the singular, is now subsumed within the impersonal agency of the general mechanism. Even if he was to reach to the most intimate of his being, to the most idiosyncratic of his subjectivity, the individual author could not be the originator of the artistic work. To a very significant degree, the object over which he labours is "conceived" somewhere else: in the impersonal logic of his craft's historically operative logic, in the diachronic automaton of form.[11] Of course, such a "conception" does not prefigure every detail of the artistic object: there is an inner wealth in each text or artefact that cannot be accounted for by the simple interplay of differentials, and this wealth is still the work of the artist. Yet what sets him to this work, what "employs" him in the task of creativity, is the necessity underlying the life of form: "Art is not created by the individual will, by the genius. The creator is simply the geometrical point of intersection of forces operative outside of him" (Shklovskii, *Khod konia* 22).[12] What previous ages referred to as the "artists' calling" still resounds, but now it is the impersonal logic of literary history that calls: "The freedom of the individual writer lies in his capacity to hear the voice of history ... Creation is an act of historical self-awareness, of locating oneself in the stream of history" (Eikhenbaum, *Skvoz' literaturu* 236). For the aesthetic thought of the past, it had seemed obvious that the individual selects the means for his artistic expression. But now it has become possible to conceive of a scenario in which the artistic device "selects" its master: "a set of artistic forms brought forth by the inner laws of their development, seeks out an adequate milieu *or creative personality* for its realization" (Jakobson, "Randbemerkungen" 373; emphasis added). The symbolic achievement of Formalism – the achievement that interests me most here – is to imagine literature as a work driven by necessity, as a kind of practice that satisfies an objective demand. It is not a social demand (at least not in any direct way), but the impersonal need of the craft itself, the imperative issued from its own inner logic.

By what name should we call the producer of the artistic text in such a scenario? Does he deserve the title of "author," if the formative impulse guiding his activity antecedes his creative will? It is best to call him operator of the device, since the device – even if only *in potentia* – is there before him ("brought forth by the inner laws" of form) and needs to be put to work. The demanding object demands its realization. "Hitched" to it by a necessity of which he is not aware, the artist works with it, on it, and for it. So that form can implement its new operative principle,[13] it must employ a human agent. Thus the individual, in realizing his "artistic calling," becomes just that: an employee of form,[14] or, as Foucault will describe him half a century later, an "executant in a pure economy of the Book in which the discourse would compose itself" (*The Order of Things* 306).

But there may be, still, a prouder mission and a higher title for the human subject in the world of art. Does he not exceed the role of a mere technician when, in a sudden leap of consciousness, he comes to recognize his craft for what it really is: a contrivance, in which there is nothing more than the interplay of conventions? When in self-awareness he undertakes to unveil the play of form as play, to show us the artifice of art, does he not become once again a subject of the text in the full sense of the word? For the Formalists, this promise was burdened with the same ambiguity that characterizes the problem of authorship. An individual, it is true, is capable of consciously apprehending the conventionality of this or that form; it happens all the time; innumerable are the moments in history when a particular aesthetic convention becomes the object of parody, stylization, exaggeration, inversion, and so on – all the different modes in which the device can be "laid bare." But the individual consciousness cannot claim too much credit for such revelations. For here, too, consciousness is only registering – sometimes early, sometimes late – an effect that proceeds from the objective movement of form through history. Carried in the abrasive stream of human experience, art itself brings about the exposure of its conventional nature.[15] When a form wears out and its mystical union with the object is no more, it shows itself for what it truly is: merely a manner of presentation. Its routine perpetuation turns into "mannerism," and the time comes for it to be exposed, for the device to be laid bare.

The diachronic life of form is a sequence of deformations in which each new instance does violence to a pre-existing norm. But synchronically as well, artistic form is just that – deformation, an instance of "organized violence" (Jakobson, *O cheshskom stikhe* 15). In the simultaneity of every moment, no less than in a historical perspective, form deforms. It is actively opposed and effectively negates its other – the habitualized existence of the medium. Verbal discourse, for example, is at its most habitual in its quotidian communicative function. And so poetic language can be defined, for each moment in time and generally, in opposition to conversational, practical speech:[16] "poetry, which is nothing other than *utterance oriented toward expression*, is ruled ... by immanent laws; the communicative function, which characterizes both practical and emotional language, is minimized here" (Jakobson, "Noveishaia" 30; emphasis in the original).[17] Such a definition does not mean that poetry or literature can be grasped as substance, even if, a little later in the same article, Jakobson speaks of "literariness" (*literaturnost'*) as the distinguishing quality of literature and the object proper of literary studies. The literariness, perceptibility, or *faktura*, of the text is a relational quality,[18] indeed, an effect: this quality is "in effect" only against a specific background (a linguistic norm, a textual tradition)[19] and only for as long as this background remains pertinent.[20] This is why the value of a literary text can be appreciated only after a careful historical study. The task of the literary historian is to re-create faithfully the background against which the text had "actualized" a certain set of devices.[21]

In every text now, in the place of the old duality of form and content, we have the dynamics of the deforming and the deformed, dynamics that belong wholly to the domain of form. Only by way of a sloppy schematism can one speak of "content" that inertly awaits its other – a shaping force approaching from somewhere else.[22] When analysing narrative, Shklovskii distinguished between *fabula* and *siuzhet* – a series of events given in the proper temporality and sequence of their occurrence versus the manner in which they are presented in narration ("Sterne's *Tristram*" 296–8)[23] – but this does not mean that the "story told straight" is somehow prior to its deformation. On the contrary: the story can only exist as deformed, as *siuzhet;* only in retrospect, after the *siuzhet* has taken its course, can the *fabula* be reconstructed.[24]

The Formalists were particularly fond of those moments in literature when form could be shown to engender "content" from its own inner necessity.[25] Is not the plot of the fairy tale – this purest of narrative forms – at its purest an enchanted meandering whose sole destination is the postponement of the end? For this enchantment to proceed along its winding path, there is a need for material, for some pliant stuff from which twists and turns can be made. The little hen cannot just take water from the sea and bring it to the choking rooster; first, she must give the sea a wild boar's tusk; but the wild boar will part with his tusk only in exchange for an acorn; when asked for an acorn, the oak tree (for some unknown reason) demands cow's milk; the cow, of course, wants hay; the reaper needs bast for his shoes; and so the little hen's journey continues through another dozen places and another dozen helpers (Shklovskii, "Sviaz'" 43). "Of course, these crooked roads are caused by specific conditions – by the requirements of the *siuzhet*" (Shklovskii, "Sviaz'" 48). In seeking its fulfilment, a form calls forth "content" not as an antinomic – if complementary – other but as its own second term.[26] So instead of "content," it is proper to speak of "material," since "the idea of 'material' does not lie beyond the limits of form; the material itself is a formal element" (Tynianov, "Literaturnyi fakt" 261). Unlike content, material does not exist for itself: it exists solely for the functioning of the dominant formal device; it is there to be moulded, deformed.

But let us take note of this apparent theoretical oxymoron: for the Formalists, form is violence and deformation only to the extent to which it is also law and organization. Shklovskii's early definition of the text as the "sum total of all artistic devices employed in it" (*Rozanov* 15) eventually gave way to the vision of a systematic ensemble of functions:

> We should no longer speak of a literary work as a "sum total" of its various aspects: plot, style, etc. These abstractions are far outdated: plot, style, etc., exist in interaction – the same interaction and relation that exist between rhythm and semantics in verse. A work of literature represents a system of

> interrelated factors. The relation of any one factor with the rest constitutes its
> *function* in regard to the whole system. (Tynianov, "Oda" 227; emphasis in
> the original)

Since formal devices are not planted haphazardly in it, but are coordinated
into a totality, the text itself is a device, a higher-order mechanism.[27]

And if we were to ask once more, "Who is the subject of this mechanism? Who is responsible for this organization of elements and functions?,"
the author would be, as before, the wrong answer. The author's subjectivity
is, once again, insufficient to "cover" the formative work performed by the
text. In Romantic aesthetics, the mystical conception of the Genius had
served to account for the organic unity of the work of art.[28] But no depths
of the human being, no matter how mystically conceived, can account for
the same work of art seen as a systematic totality. Such a totality has no
subject, no human "coordinator." What totalizes the sum of elements into
a textual whole is their subordination to a governing constructive
principle:

> It is abundantly clear that every literary system is formed not by the peaceful
> interaction of all factors, but by the domination, prominence, of one (or a
> group) of them that functionally subordinates and "colors" the rest. Such a
> factor bears the name ... *dominanta* (Christiansen, B. Eikhenbaum). This
> does not mean, however, that the subordinated factors are not important and
> that they deserve no attention. On the contrary, the action of the governing
> factor, the *dominanta*, is manifested precisely in this subordination, transfor-
> mation, of all factors. (227)

In Gogol's "Overcoat," for instance, it is the "devices of verbal mimicry
and gesture" that play the dominant constructive role (Eikhenbaum, "Kak
sdelana" 46). As they are "actualized," the element of plot is subordinated,
deformed. The slim story line is there to support ("motivate") the deployment of the *dominanta*.[29]

What the constructive principle "does" can never be entirely intended by
the author. Just as the author cannot control the ways in which the constructive principle of his work was generated – here the evolutionary laws
of formal differentiation have their say – so he is incapable of fully control-
ling the ways in which this constructive principle fulfils itself within the
text. His intention is inevitably overridden by a necessity programmed into
the very functioning of the device:

Let us add: the author's intention can be no more than a ferment. In handling the specifically literary material and obeying it, the author departs from his intention. Thus [Griboedov's] *Woe from Wit* was supposed to be in a "high," even "magnificent," style, but turned out to be a political, "archaistic," pamphlet comedy. Thus *Evgenii Onegin* was supposed to be, at first, a "satirical poem," in which the author "chokes on bile." But while working on Chapter Four Pushkin already writes: "where is my satire? There is no trace of it in *Evgenii Onegin*."

The constructive principle, the relatedness of elements within the work, turns the "author's intention" into a ferment, no more. The "creative freedom" proves to be an optimistic slogan, which does not correspond to reality, and gives way to "creative necessity." (Tynianov, "O literaturnoi evoliutsii" 278)

It is rather easy, from our current place in history, to take issue with the theories of the Formalists, to approve or disprove, to be critical (in the good sense of the word), to interject with a "Well, yes" or an "Oh, no." We are, understandably, tempted to evaluate their writings in the light of subsequent conceptual developments and to apply to them the standard of more current truths. "Well, yes, we know that the author's intention matters little, that it tells us next to nothing about what the text really does. The intentional fallacy is a truism for us." "Oh, no, the text is never such a fully coherent system of elements and functions as to warrant analysis in terms of some absolute laws of artistic construction or aesthetic evolution. Poststructuralism has taught us to be wary of such totalizing conceptions."

I am consciously resisting this temptation to be critical, to arbitrate between the Formalist "contribution" and subsequent theoretical thought. The perspective I have adopted excludes the very idea of "contribution," of the "lasting value" of this or that conceptual legacy. It is not even a question of whether the Formalists were right or wrong, whether their notions did justice to the object of their study. Once again: I take the theories of the Formalists not from the point of view of truth, but from the perspective of pure happening; not as a cognitive claim, but as a symbolic scenario. We must refrain from asking, "Is this knowledge adequate to its field?," in order to ask, "How does this theory script the act of creation? What symbolic role does it give to the practitioner of art, and how is this role justified?" From this kind of perspective, analytical concepts are not claims to truth; they are *figures,* in the present case – figures of thought. They are arranged in a topology, where they "take place," do something. We are allowed to view them as "actants," as heroes of sorts.

A declaration made by Jakobson in 1921 lends support to such a vision: "If the study of literature wants to become a science, it must recognize the artistic device as its only 'hero' [*geroi*]" (*Noveishaia* 32). A few years later, Vladimir Propp faced a terminological dilemma when analysing fairy-tale plots in terms of typical actions ("functions"). Since these were performed not only by humans but also by animals and all kinds of fantastic creatures, the designations "hero" and "character" were bound to be misleading. Propp labelled this larger category of narrative agents "dramatis personae" (*personazhi*). To accommodate the same non-coincidence between human subjects and subjects of the narrative action, A.J. Greimas introduced the term "actant." Are we not in a similar situation when we discover that, in the world of art, a function traditionally centred in the human subject is suddenly being performed by the decidedly non-human figure of the "device," or the *dominanta*? Considered in a purely functional way, the *dominanta* does, approximately, what the "genius" or the "poet's immortal soul" has done before. They all have the same function in artistic creation; they are the same "actant" in different guises. Here is how Friedrich Schlegel spoke of Goethe's *Wilhelm Meister*, more than a century before the first Formalist manifestos:

> But the reader who possesses a true instinct for *system,* who has a sense of totality or that anticipation of the world in its entirety which makes Wilhelm so interesting, will be aware throughout the work of what we might call its personality and living individuality. And the more deeply he probes, the more inner connections and relations and the greater intellectual coherence he will discover in it. If there is any book with an indwelling genius, it is this. And if this genius could characterize itself in detail and as a whole, then there would be no need for anyone else to say what it is all about, or how it should be taken. (65; emphasis added)

I have highlighted the word "system" as a reminder of its central place in Formalist poetics. Like Schlegel, the Formalists spoke of the artistic text as a system; they too saw in it a "totality," a "coherence" of "inner connections and relations."[30] Yet for them, it was not the "indwelling genius" that, by fulfilling itself, makes the text into a totality, but the "governing constructive principle." The "personality and living individuality" of a work was, for them, not the correlative of a subjective presence (the author's), but the result of an objective process, which could be analysed in its discrete moments.

Another crucial difference prevents us from seeing the Formalist notion of system as a variation on a theme already rehearsed in Romanticism. While in both cases we are dealing with a process of totalization, it is important to note how differently this totalization is brought about. The constructive principle is something fully autochthonous to literature. After all, the Formalists' main preoccupation was to distinguish the operative logic of the literary from that of any other "series." The Romantic genius, on the other hand, is found at work in a great many worldly phenomena. This is what allows it to mediate the principal dichotomy of Romantic thought: that between natural creation and human artistic production. And one last, all-important, divergence: the theme of dissimulation is missing in the Romantic corpus of aesthetic writing. Paul Ricoeur's contrast between the hermeneutic of Freud and that of religious phenomenology is applicable for setting apart the Formalist and Romantic visions of the artistic text: one pivots on the problematic of distortion and concealment, the other on the problematic of depth (Ricoeur 7).

As the text thus loses its anchorage in the figure of the author, another persona enters the plot in what seems, at first, to be a merely ancillary role. I have in mind the persona of the analyst. In the Romantic "work of genius," the generative spirit is immanently present, it is always already realized. From then on, it is up to the "reader with a sense for system and totality" to apprehend it. If this reader were never to come along, the text would not be deprived of the genius that inhabits it. Not so in Formalist poetics, where the effectiveness of the artistic device is always relational. For any moment in the past, there is reconstructive work to be done so that the (differential) qualities of novelty, originality, transgression, and so on can re-emerge in their original pertinence, no longer felt today. But in a synchronic perspective too, the text's "in itself" is never given to us directly. What for the reader is the undefined experience of individual style, is the objective work of a dynamic system, one whose elements and functions are susceptible to meticulous and exhaustive analysis. Only when this analysis is complete can the preconscious experience of style become the conscious apprehension of the text's identity.

Thus, in order to show itself as what it truly is, the text must "pass" through this new place – the repository of hermeneutic knowledge. The analyst is, to be sure, hardly more than the "guardian" of hermeneutic cognition. But since the place he occupies is indispensable to the historical existence of the text, the importance of his role cannot be underestimated.

To convince ourselves of this, we need only consider the place of the analyst in Freud's theory of the unconscious, which is roughly contemporaneous with the Formalist movement in European art criticism. In the Freudian analytical situation, the "text" that issues from the subject behaves in the same way as the artistic text in the vision of the Russian Formalists. We find a similar plot operating here, albeit from the perspective of content. With the Freudian dream – the psychoanalytical "text" *par excellence*[31] – we are once again at the site of a deformation: the dream thoughts (the "latent content" of the dream) appear disfigured in the dream representation (the "manifest content"). Their ostensible author – the dreaming subject – cannot be expected to know what the dream truly represents. All she sees is the enigmatic, ludic hieroglyphics presented to her in her sleep (the manifest content), and even these are often blotted out by waking consciousness. The dream images are, of course, related to the original "message" by hard links of determination. But between "message" and "presentation" a deforming instance intervenes, a mechanism, a device. Employed by what Freud calls the "censor," this device has every right to be called poetic, since the principles of its functioning – displacement and condensation – are also the principles of figurative speech:[32]

> A psychic force is expressed in dream activity which on the one hand strips elements of high psychic value of their intensity, and which on the other hand creates new values *by way of over-determination* from elements of small value, these new values subsequently getting into the dream content. If this is the method of procedure, there has taken place in the formation of the dream a transference and displacement of the psychic intensities of the individual elements, of which the textual difference between the dream and the thought content appears as a result. The process which we assume here is nothing less than the essential part of the dream activity; it merits the designation of *dream displacement. Dream displacement* and *dream condensation* are the two craftsmen to whom we may chiefly attribute the molding of the dream.
>
> I think we also have an easy task in recognizing the psychic force which makes itself felt in the circumstances of dream displacement. The result of this displacement is that the dream content no longer resembles the core of the dream thoughts at all, and that the dream reproduces only a disfigured form of the dream wish in the unconscious. But we are already acquainted with dream disfigurement; we have traced it back to the censorship which one psychic instance in the psychic life exercises over the other. Dream displacement is one of the chief means for achieving this disfigurement. *Is fecit, cui profuit.* We may assume that dream displacement is brought about by the

influence of this censor, of the endopsychic repulsion. (Freud 286–7; emphasis in the original)

Several places in this lengthy passage warrant added emphasis. First, there is the personification of objective psychic forces as "craftsmen," which, after the earlier remarks on typical actions and "actants," I take as more than a stylistic embellishment. These are Freud's new "heroes," just like the device was to be the "only hero" for Jakobson and his colleagues. Second, there is Freud's note concerning "textual difference," which should remind us of the textual difference that exists between *fabula* and *siuzhet* in Formalist theory. Is not the latent content of the dream precisely the *fabula* that becomes distorted on the plane of representation (*siuzhet*)? The fact that Freud operates on the side of content becomes significant here: while, for him, the "this is it" of the dream text is its *fabula* (the concealed wish-thoughts, which he seeks to decipher by undoing the "crooked" ways of their signification), it is just the other way around for the Formalists (who seek to make perceptible the "crookedness" itself).[33] For Freud, it is the meaning of the text that is hidden (behind the apparent triviality or sheer nonsense of the dream narrative); for the Formalists, the meaning of the text hides the determining role of formal construction. Still, from a purely formal point of view, the scenario is the same: in both cases, the "this is it" of the text, its "moment of truth," is systematically occluded and must be systematically recovered through an analytic method that is transparent in relation to the original production of the text.

With Freud, but also with the Russian Formalists, we enter through the front gate into a distinctly modern existence of the textual, characterized as it is by an essential split. In this new existence, what presents itself "initially and for the most part" as *the* text, the manifest, is manifestly *not* it. Behind it, in an obscurity neither too heavy (since it can be dispelled almost routinely by a hermeneutic that claims scientific status for itself) nor too light (since it inheres in the very being of representation), lies the latent actuality of the text, its *raison d'être*. Yet this split is not as dramatic as the one we find in Hume, Kant, or Schopenhauer – the rift between "the world as representation," on the one hand, and the world as it actually is, on the other. Starting from some moment in the second half of the nineteenth century (in Marx this moment is already current), dissimulation is lodged in the very heart of representation. By its nature, that which comes forth as *the* text comes forth as something other than it truly is.[34] But – a crucial qualification – this is a *systematically produced dissimulation*, and not the chasm of some post-lapsarian divorce between essences and appearances, the thing-in-itself and its renditions by finite human consciousness. And because it is systematically produced and systematically sustained, this dissimulation can be systematically overcome.

Freudian psychoanalysis is the prototype for what Ricoeur has theorized as the "hermeneutic of suspicion." Marx and Nietzsche are its other two great practitioners.[35] The hermeneutic in question approaches symbols with the conviction that they conceal truth rather than reveal it. "Interpretation is lucidity's answer to ruse" (Ricoeur 159). Meaning lies hidden behind a false appearance and is to be uncovered only through an act of demystification. The reader must cast away the manifest externality in order to possess, beyond it, the latent yet genuine meaning. As such acts of demystification are the main items of interest in Part I of this study, I should state how my perspective differs from Ricoeur's. As a philosopher, Ricoeur treats the hermeneutics of faith and suspicion as universals. He opposes them as two principal modes of interpretation before showing, through (and beyond) a reading of Freud, how their antithesis can be overcome dialectically. By contrast, I adopt a more historicizing approach. I discuss modernist procedures of knowledge in which the dissimulative constitution of the object motivates (i.e., enables and legitimizes) certain practical comportments and "interventions" on the part of the subject. As I see it, the demystifying act is practically oriented from the outset, for the principle of dissimulation it uncovers furnishes the subject with a "project" (to do away with dissimulation) and a binding law of conduct. In chapter 3, I will have more to say on the relation between this hermeneutics and the practice it authorizes. Presently, I note that in the cases I consider, starting with the Formalists, it is not a matter of some subjective attitude – "suspicion" instead of "faith" – setting the parameters of truth. Rather, it is a matter of certain historically and culturally specific "vis-à-vis" with an object-field whose inner logic creates the conditions for its misrecognition. By the same logic, the object invites – nay, demands – a particular kind of interpretive and practical comportment (this is what makes it a demanding object). Yet it is not a mere question of wresting covert truth from overt falsity. It is a question of grasping as truth, as essence, the very principle that generates false appearances.

In Freud, the manifest content of the dream is a dissimulative show insofar as the *Traumwerk* presents itself as a random formative activity that juggles together the trifles of the quotidian and thus conceals the all-important message of desire. For the Formalists, we read in reverse: the text is dissimulation in the sense that it almost always comes forth as "substance" (content of some kind, a message, a story, a personal expression), while its in-itself, its true being as literature, consists in non-substantive deformation – the pure negativity of form. And this is where the hero of hermeneutics comes in. He exposes the dissimulation and overcomes it. His competence bridges the gap between the two hypostases of the text – in Freud's terms, the latent and the manifest – and makes it one again, restores its identity/truth. It is not just a matter of discovering the particular message of desire or the particular formal construction hidden behind the manifest appearance. At a more radical level, the hermeneutic in question demonstrates that Desire and Form are the very engines of dissimulation; they run the show of false appearances.

In the moment the dissimulation is exposed, the text – a dream or a piece of literary writing – acquires a new status. The analyst has taken it as a token of something (a repressed wish; a constructive principle at work). To wit, he has read it not for what the text says or shows overtly, but for what is being conveyed covertly through it. Something is bespoken without being spoken of. Something is being fulfilled, or realized, *by means of* the text without actually being represented *in* it. The Freudian dream is anything but a representation of desire. The crux of the psychoanalytic approach is precisely this: that desire cannot appear directly in dream images and words lest it overwhelm the ego. Desire exists in the dream not as the object of representation but as representation's organizing principle – as the rule of deformation, which is also a rule of deception. As such, it is everywhere and nowhere. It is realized by the totality of the dream signs (the entire dream narrative is the acting-out of the illicit wish), but nowhere in those signs is it pictured or spoken as such. And so it is with the constructive principle in the great majority of texts handed down by the literary tradition. The deformation of the material betrays the workings of a non-human agency, an autonomous mechanism, but the mechanism itself is not represented as such. The status of the text as a token (in the eyes of the analyst) is a direct consequence of the fact that its veritable origin and *raison d'être* are dissimulated. If the text itself spoke of them, one would not have to search for something behind its signs and read those signs, in their totality, as a token of the hidden; there would be no need to read *through* the representation so as to get beyond it, where the principle of its organization lies; there would be no need for the hermeneutic. And vice versa: the text needs the hermeneutic, it calls for the exercise of method, because it is constituted through a systematic and objectively operative dissimulation; this is what makes it a demanding object.

Before bringing this first enactment of the plot to a conclusion, one seeming contradiction remains to be addressed. Why is it that, on the one

hand, artistic form in the writings of the Russian Formalists appears –
both synchronically and diachronically – as the "work of the negative,"
while, on the other hand, there is talk of some latent actuality of the text,
of its "in itself," of the text as it truly is, and so on? Why does Jakobson
speak of the "literariness" of literature in the same way Shklovskii speaks
of the "stoniness" of stones? And are not terms such as "device," "system,"
and "totality" meant to convey a more substantive understanding of the
aesthetic? What we are witnessing here is not a contradiction proper but a
peculiarity of the plot that interests us. True, when taken by itself, in the
Formalist perspective, the textual can only be grasped as unfolded negativity, the evanescent interplay of differentials. Thus the object, the "text,"
is lost – it is, really, nothing.[36] Yet it is *grasped,* and this hermeneutic grasp
is inscribed as something substantive that pertains *to the object*. The per-
formative of knowledge is included within the known as the very "soul" of
the latter.

In its most typical application, the Formalist hermeneutic demonstrates
how the artistic object systematically defies understanding in terms of content. But for this purely negative characteristic to be seen as immanent to
the text, as its positivity, we must suppose that the text is capable of somehow retaining within itself that which its formal movement negates, distances, "makes strange": "for the older technique or content must somehow
subsist within the work as what is cancelled or overwritten, modified, inverted or negated, in order for us to feel the force, in the present, of what is
alleged to have once been an innovation" (Jameson, *A Singular Modernity*
128).[37] Taken on its own – as printed words on a page, as daubs on a canvas, or as audible vibrations in the air – the text does not seem to possess
such a power. Thus for it to subsist in its original and true being (as a specimen of the Literary), it must be understood as containing and carrying
through space and time that which appears external to it – its own expert
reader; but optimally, it must contain and carry him in such a way that
"he" is no longer "he" – some principally detachable instance of human
intelligence – but somehow a part of the textual mechanism itself, a built-
in reader,[38] as it were, a reader-device.

This is difficult to imagine, but it does point us to the horizon of the
most radical modernist experiments in literature and art: to create a sign
that would be its own interpretant, that is, a sign that would not depend on
knowledge of conventions in order to exercise its effect. If every violation
holds its significance only for as long as the violated canon is in place, then
the sole possible way to eschew historical relativity is to perpetrate an act
of absolute violence. To inflict on the material a deformation so radical

that it will be read everywhere and always as deformation. Not to under-mine a *particular* idiom of artistic communication, but to subvert commu-nication as such. Not to speak differently, but to jettison representational discourse altogether so that the text will exist as pure and unequivocal be-speaking. Not to introduce a new formal device, but to make Form *as such* the *dominanta* of the work, its sole generative principle. One could write so as to make it seem as if Literature were writing itself or Language were speaking itself. One could string words so as to make it evident that the words themselves have generated their compelling sequence (in accordance with their phonetic, morphological, or graphic properties). That is, one could perform literary work as a symbolic act of submission to the neces-sities of form, and the product of this work would be read, everywhere and always, as a token of literature's ownmost essence: the Word as Such.

Russian Formalist theory was more than modernist poetics, but it was that too.[39] The personal ties between the members of the school, on one hand, and Futurism and its Soviet avant-garde offshoots, on the other, are well known. So are the parallels between the theoretical formulations of Opoiaz and modernist artistic programs. The seminal concept of defamil-iarization is to be found in "vernacular" form in declarations pre-dating Shklovskii's essays.[40] The generation of content out of (verbal) form was an idea taken directly from Futurist manifestos.[41] The cult of the self-valuable word found its first priests not in the Formalist critics but in Khlebnikov and Kruchenykh. In the writings of the latter one also finds the imperative for deformation and the initial theorization of poetic *faktura* and *sdvig*;[42] the emergence of new perception from the devices of irregularity;[43] and the stipulation that words be combined according to their phonetic valences, not their semantic properties.[44] All of this is to say that the Formalists' philological poetics cannot be easily separated from the Futurists' "poetic philology."[45] The intimate relationship often made it difficult to determine whether an idea had been generated by avant-garde artists and subsequent-ly taken over by the philologists or the other way around. The main reason "formalism" became the term under which, in Stalinist times, every kind of modernist experimentation was censured was that the school of criticism was seen from the outset as an expression of modernist tendencies in art.[46] Thus it is perhaps more productive to see Formalism not as a school of critical thought and discipline-specific theory but rather as part of a broad-er cultural movement in which textual and metatextual practices inter-twined, each drawing from the other.[47] On this view, it cannot be said, as Burke does, that Formalism's treatment of the author is but a matter of methodological convenience, a provisional manoeuvre that clears the way to the object proper of literary science (*The Death* 71). It is also a symbolic act that motivates the practice of art by anchoring it in a (supposedly) objective dynamic. The death of the author is, at the same time, the projected rebirth of Art as a fully autotelic principle. He who no longer is an author acquires a new function, or "calling": to hearken to the laws of form and thereby ensure that the autotelic movement, on page or canvas, is such indeed.

Chapter 2

The Imperative of Content

It is bound to seem a scandal of sorts that in my approach to the culture of socialist realism the first step should be Russian Formalism – a movement that was to be forcefully extinguished at the end of the 1920s, a movement whose name was to become that of a heresy in both aesthetic criticism and artistic practice during Stalin's time.[1] Perhaps it would have been more prudent to head straight to some properly Marxist aesthetic doctrine, which, whatever its shortcomings or unorthodoxies, could not but prove more akin to the spirit and the letter of socialist realism. After all, from very early on the Formalists were recognized as the main ideological enemies of Marxism in the field of aesthetics and art criticism.[2] This objection falls with the reminder that we are not tracing the genesis of socialist realism as a genesis of ideas. The kinships and genealogies, the thematic affinities and resemblances, that emerge dutifully in that venerable mode of inquiry called "history of ideas" have little argumentative weight here. But this means that no criteria are available for anticipatory judgment on whether this or that theory, this or that methodology, "approximates," "foreshadows," or "prepares the ground for" socialist realism.

Soviet cultural history adds a supportive footnote to this methodological position. It is well known that nothing like a Marxist aesthetic doctrine was bequeathed to the 1930s by the 1920s. All attempts to formulate such a doctrine, to elaborate a critical methodology on the basis of historical materialism, failed to survive Stalin's "cultural revolution"; between 1928 and 1932, such attempts were branded as so many deviations from the proper study of things aesthetic, thus virtually sharing the fate of Formalism. Schools of critical thought that only a few years earlier had been the main players in the vigorous debate on Marxism in the arts – the followers of Bogdanov, the leaders of RAPP, the group around Voronskii at Pereval, Pereverzev and his disciples, the theorists of LEF – had been neutralized by the early 1930s (the most tenacious of them, RAPP, survived until the Party resolution of April 1932). By the late 1920s they had already acquired the derogatory suffix "*-shchina*" (*bogdanovshchina, voronshchina, pereverzevshchina*); during Stalinism, these verbalized essences would be used – depending on the context – as either cautionary references or terms of indictment.[3] And it is difficult to say whether being charged, say, with *voronshchina* – a reactionary blend of intuitivism, irrationalism, and voluntarism that was said to distil Trotskyism in the realm of literary scholarship – was any less stigmatizing than being charged with formalism.[4] Still, these instances of knowledge, these schools of (professedly) Marxist thought, which Stalinism would eventually abolish, have legitimacy for us in the present context – a legitimacy perhaps no greater but also no less than that of Formalism. This is not because they anticipate or approximate a later theoretical orthodoxy, but because they rehearse one and the same general scenario: the emergence of the work of art from "behind the back" of its (supposed) author.

The most elaborate, internally consistent, and methodologically rigorous attempt to formulate a textual analytic and to implement a corresponding practice of critical reading was that of the "Sociological" or "Pereverzevian" school – an academic group formed in the second half of the 1920s.[5] The group's programmatic statements are contained in a collection of critical essays, *Literaturovedenie* (Literary Studies), published in 1928.[6] These essays were remarkably consistent with the earlier writings of the group's leader, Valerian Pereverzev (1882–1968),[7] but went beyond them – especially two substantial contributions by Genadii Pospelov – towards elaborating a full-fledged science of the literary.

In Pereverzev and his followers we find something quite contrary to the theories of the Formalists, whom the former attacked on numerous occasions.[8] For the Pereverzevians, as for most Marxist-minded critics of the time, Formalism was a survival of bourgeois consciousness,[9] an offspring of the divorce between reality and its ideal figurations, with the latter perceived as an autonomous realm that sustained itself, in the air as it were, through powers all its own. The falsity of this view accounted for the principal methodological falsity of Russian Formalism: its fundamental disinterestedness in the genesis of the artistic fact and its propensity to treat that fact descriptively rather than etiologically.[10] Against the Formalist science of literature, based on a study of the intrinsic laws of the "literary series," the Pereverzevians never tired of repeating that the literary fact can only be known objectively in its causal relation to the extraliterary. More than a

mere principle of scientific investigation, etiology was for them synonymous with the scientific itself: "All that is required is that the critic see the
work of art as a causally conditioned phenomenon of life, that he consider
his main task to be discovering this causal relationship, i.e., the scientific
explanation for the appearance of the work of art" (Pereverzev, "Theoretical
Premises" 39).

Obviously, we are dealing not with mere differences but with a fundamental rift that is as much methodological as ideological. Formalism, on the
one hand, and the brand of Marxist analysis of literature practised by
Pereverzev's group, on the other, present themselves as irreconcilable experiences of the literary. With the latter, indeed, with all traditional Marxist
literary criticism, an entirely new dimension is adjoined to the manifest
"there-ness" of the artistic text – the dimension of socio-economic being,
which is absent as such from classic Formalist theory. Yet as we register this
heterogeneity of positions, we must also register the dialectical twist whereby it is taken up and sublated within a higher level homology. For did we not
witness, in the discussion of Formalism, that the experience of the textual is
characterized precisely by a displacement such that what is manifestly there
as *the* text is really "not it" or, at least, cannot be relied upon to ground any
definitive truth about the text? And so it is that precisely when they opposed
themselves to Formalist readings of literature, when they denied the self-
sufficient existence of the literary series, the Sociological critics showed
themselves to be fully partaking of this very experience. When they insisted
that the seeming autonomy of the aesthetic realm, its (mis)representation as
something detached from the coarse reality of social existence, should be
unmasked as the ideology of one particular social formation (the bourgeoisie), they too were confronting this realm as a scene of dissimulation. For the
Formalists, it was the "overgrowth" of content and referentiality, of ideas
and subjective expressions, from underneath which the mechanisms of formal construction must be brought out; for the Marxist Sociologists, it was
the independent and ideal existence of the literary that had to be demystified
in order for us to see the mechanisms by which social life reproduces itself.

To identify and dispel the dissimulation of literature's ideal being involves identifying and dispelling also the illusion of its privileged relation
to the personal "inner world." Thus, just as inevitably as Formalist methodology displaced the individual author by "hitching" him to the broader
movement of objective "forces operative outside of him," we find this
displacement in the methodology of the Sociological school. Here, the
movement of external forces is also objective, but the objectivity in question is different:

It is not in subjective process that a literary scholar operating on the basis of Marxist methodology should seek an explanation for poetic phenomena, but in objective reality, not in the movement of ideas but in the movement of material reality ... Nothing in the poetic fact can be explained by the poet's intentions, because from the Marxist standpoint it is not thought that is definitive, but being. It is not the idea on which a work of art is based, but being; and literary scholarship must discover not the idea but being as the basis of the poetic phenomenon ... A literary scholar's task consists in discovering the objective reality in a work of literature which provided the material for it and determined its structure. Marxist research consists in discovering this being and elucidating the organic, necessary connection between the given work of art and the being in question. (Pereverzev, "Essential Premises" 55–6)

Once again, there is no need to arbitrate between the Formalists and Pereverzev in order to decide which dimension should count as the truly or ultimately determining one: the objective dynamics of form or the objective mechanism of social being (just as there is no need to arbitrate between Marxism and psychoanalysis as to whether the ultimate unconscious is not, after all, the socio-economic). At this point, all we need to do is take note of the fundamental fact that emerges at the formal convergence of these two otherwise irreconcilable currents of thought: the author is not the author, the individual subject is not enough. But this fact does not emerge in isolation; it stands as the centrepiece, the main event, of a plot whose constitutive moments were sketched out apropos of Formalism. Now, in the writings of the Sociological school, we can follow this plot as it unfolds in the dimension of "content."

Anterior to every literary text stands the social being of which Pereverzev speaks, as a unity of objectivity and subjecthood, that is, as an objective world, which is also and equally consciousness (Pereverzev, "Theoretical Premises" 41–2; "Essential Premises" 59).[11] The textual is always a manifestation of the latter, but in such a way that the duality-in-unity we find outside the text is also to be found within it. Since consciousness cannot become manifest except through representations ("images," *obrazy*, as Pereverzev calls them), the literary text also gives us a "world" (represented objectivity) that is equally and simultaneously a self (representing subjectivity).

Pereverzev's monism – inspired by the empiriomonism of Bogdanov – allowed him to solve rather easily the question of whether literature is capable of adequately reflecting the objective world beyond the page – a question that had been a stumbling block for the materialist critics of the preceding century (Chernishevskii, Dobroliubov, Pisarev). They had thought literature fully capable of proffering such a reflection; but in those cases – hardly incidental – when the world appeared crooked in the mirror of representation, there was little for them to do but deliberate on the inadequacies of this or that author's world view.[12] Now Pereverzev could dispense with the problem altogether by confidently declaring that representation is always adequate to reality, provided that the two terms are properly understood: "Yes, art reproduces reality exactly, retaining its unity of object and subject; it reproduces the objective basis of consciousness, which is actual reality" ("Theoretical Premises" 43). The key word in this statement is "reproduces." Art does not "reflect" reality; it *reproduces* reality; it participates in the larger process through which a form of collective life, an instance of social being, perpetuates itself. When "reality" is understood to be synonymous with this very social being, its reproduction in literary artefacts can only be more or less successful, never "false."

Of course, it is possible, in a heuristic abstraction, to separate the world depicted from its depicter and to speak of how the former is a distorted copy of the world as it actually is or was; just as it was possible, for the Formalists, to distinguish between the events of the story as they actually took place (the *fabula*) and the arrangement of those events in a story (the *siuzhet*).[13] But such a heuristic abstraction should not lead to the idea of an objective world pre-dating and awaiting a consciousness that may or may not represent this world adequately. Just as the story can only exist as narrated – that is, as (de)formed by the movement of storytelling – *the* world can only be given to us as someone's world – an objectivity already in the shape of subjecthood. As with the Formalists, for whom formal distortion is prior to – what comes, *a posteriori*, to be perceived as – the distorted material, in Pereverzev the "subjective" deformation is ontologically prior to the deformed "reality." He often reaches for the apparent pleonasm "actual reality" in order to dispel the notion of some naive and simple objectivity unadulterated by the presence of the subjective. An "actual reality" is one in which the "subjective," hence also the "distortive," is factored from the very beginning.

Because the distortive work of consciousness – including, of course, artistic consciousness – has no positive "outside" (this consciousness, at least for Pereverzev, can never be fully transparent to its own objective determinations), distortion itself turns into a positive characteristic of the object under investigation, that is, the literary text. Since every representation is at the same time a misrepresentation (of the objective conditions underlying a given form of social life), misrepresentation does not come with a negative sign, as a lie or mystification. For those same objective conditions of social existence that have been "misrepresented" in the text have also determined, in some moment anterior to the text's production, the specific character of this very misrepresentation.[14] Because we can always count on it to be there, and because – even more importantly – we can always count on it for the key to undoing its own masquerade, misrepresentation must be thought as one with the objectivity it camouflages, as in fact belonging to it. But thus conceived, what we have been referring to as "misrepresentation" is, really, dissimulation; and the new objectivity, to which dissimulation belongs not as a negative moment, a deterrent, but as a positive determination, is none other than Pereverzev's "actual reality": objectivity grasped together with the immanent laws of its subjective deformation.

Pereverzev was fully aware that the Formalists had spoken of deformation as an essential fact pertaining to things literary and artistic. Yet he insisted that the Marxists "knew [this fact] long before Shklovskii" and that they knew it differently: "They [the Marxists] know that the *mechanism* of deformation, a *device* through which social reality is formed, is determined by the base and causally dependent on the base, and that it is in the base that an explanation and understanding of deformation must be sought" ("Formalists" 138; emphasis added). When the base – which is to say, the material conditions of social existence – is thought in a dialectical unity with the mechanisms whereby these conditions shape human consciousness, we end up with Pereverzev's monistic "social being." As it "deforms," the base also determines and structures social reality (in its "subjective" manifestations).

The same mechanism of dissimulation-organization is found operative within the artistic text, which is always a concretion of a particular class "character," "attitude," or "will" – that is, of the subjective aspect of social being. On the most general level, the text dissimulates, inasmuch as this concretion of social being comes across as a reified world, as depicted objectivity, thus concealing its subjective dimension and occasioning the "realist" or "referential" illusion. We fall prey to this illusion when we try, for instance, to relate Pushkin's *Captain's Daughter* to the historical reality of Pugachev's rebellion. In doing so, we fail to see the "depicter within the depicted" (Pereverzev, "Essential Premises" 59–60). In this particular case, the "depicter" is a rather different reality: the class reality of the urbanized and well-educated small landed gentry. The reality of Pugachev's rebellion, in being depicted, is also being *subjected*. In other words, it is being reconstructed in accordance with the laws of perspective immanent to another world. But this means that it is also subjected to deformation. The irreducible measure of non-coincidence between the artistic representation and its real-life referent had been viewed by the Formalists as a result of the laws of artistic construction. The critics of the Sociological school saw a similar discrepancy but attributed it to the immanent laws governing the historical process.[15]

It should be amply clear by now that when the latter spoke of the subjective, they did not mean the individual subject, the author, or even the social group to which he belonged. What they had in mind, rather, was the "character" of reality itself, the "subjective aspect of social relations between people" (Pospelov, "K metodike" 67). The text is the place where the immanent principles of the social world's organization become the immanent laws of the unfolding artistic content: "In the artistic works' system of imagery, social reality (a unity of representation and essence, 'form and content') presents itself as detached and consciously apprehended in the image. The whole system of images, in its interconnection and logic of development, is none other than the interconnection, logic, and lawfulness [*zakonomernost'*] of reality itself, given as an artistic consciousness" (Bespalov, "Problema" 26). This consciousness, which belongs to social reality *in toto*, both "contains" and transcends each individual subjectivity. Clearly, the individual subject is incapable of knowing, willing, and intending everything that the trans-individual consciousness "does" by way of artistic representation. Much of the work takes place behind his back, eludes him.[16]

With regard to the bourgeois author, this drama of consciousness is particularly poignant, for he misrecognizes even the basic fact that he belongs to a class collectivity and that he is writing as part of it. His understanding of himself is that of a unique consciousness, free to encounter the world on its own and to make sense of it. In its manifest being, therefore, his text offers us, typically, a personal quest for knowledge and beauty, for self-expression and identity (usually within the narrow limits of individual ethics and psychology). But we discover "the depicter within the depicted," the latent actuality of the text within its manifest being, when we ask, "What social reality immanently tends to present itself as a 'world' to be known and conquered through the individual's own powers and skills (including artistic skills), through independently accumulated experience and hard-won sense of self?" The answer is forthcoming: the reality in question is one in which the relations of production imply the (latent) fact of ever greater interdependence between the individual members of society, while also posing the (manifest) imperative for competition, specialization of skills, disassociation from traditional forms of collectivity, and so on.[17]

As social being is reproduced in the text, so also is the dissimulation peculiar to it. Manifestly, Maksim Gor'kii's early stories depict the conflict between two character types: the "restless" – those who yearn for an escape from the bleak reality of their social existence – and the "fellow-travellers" – those who acquiesce to it. Around these two poles, a series of semantic oppositions is established: "the exceptional and the ordinary, the free and the bounded, the rebellious and the conceited" (Bespalov, "Stil'" 301). In Gor'kii's legendary-allegorical tales, the conflict is usually recast as one between the anarchic and virulent freedom of the "natural man" (Larra, Danko, the Man) and the stifling enclosures of the man-made world (the domain of civilization). Yet, the Sociological critic informs us, these manifestly irreconcilable opposites are in fact two sides of one and the same "socio-psychological tendency" (*sotsio-psikhologicheskoe ustremlenie*)[18]: in the age of industrial capitalism, the urban petty bourgeoisie in Russia is threatened with extinction by the spread of large-scale, machine-driven production; the class's unstable position, above the social bottom but below desired material prosperity, translates into a psychological oscillation between rejection of reality and hopeful reconciliation with it (301).[19] This is a single psychological "complex," whose moments have been separated in artistic representation and embodied as different and indeed conflicting realities (300–1). But the masquerade of representation does not end here; it scrambles also the vectors of desire. The desire for stable prosperity on the part of the lower urban bourgeoisie, frustrated as it is by the actual socio-economic conditions in Russia at the turn of the century, dissimulates as a dreamy striving for freedom opposed by a monotonous and stagnant life. Along the same lines, an idealized "state of nature" emerges as a redeeming alternative to the artificiality of human civilization. The actual fear of an impoverished and declassed existence (*bosiachestvo*) is represented/deformed in Gor'kii's stories as a romanticized vagrancy (*brodiazhnichestvo*) outside the bonds of a social group, family, and property (297), while the actual but impeded desire – to belong permanently to the prosperous bourgeois world and its culture – is represented/deformed as its own wishful denial.

And lest we think that these transmutations are due to some idiosyncrasy or bad faith on Gor'kii's part, Bespalov sets the record straight: "The social tendency expressed in the central image [of the 'restless'] is not the author's commission, his conception or intention, not his political, ideological convictions; this is the objective directionality [*napravlennost'*] and social content expressed in the image, independent of the will and intentions of the author" (280). If, in the writings of the Formalists, an objectively ascertainable dynamic of form traverses/overcomes the author's individual consciousness, in the theories of the Sociological school the same function is performed by the "objective ... social content." And the function in question is that of an impersonal, supra-individual volition. One and the same cognitive scenario is played out in two ostensibly heterogeneous dimensions. Ostensibly, two different sets of phenomena are being encountered, divergent realities are being asserted and known as "real," incompatible positivities are being called upon to ground epistemological certainties. Yet despite their divergent paths, the idealist poetics of the Formalists and the materialist hermeneutics of the Sociological school arrive at the same vision: the formidable weight of a new objectivity has come upon the individual subject; it now envelopes him and "instrumentalizes" his consciousness towards its own ends; it summons him forth in a voice that is misheard and, *as* misheard, it is always obeyed; it acts through him so that he is never equal to what he himself has "done"; an impersonal agency is now accountable for this work, concretized within each particular text as the agency of a particular "device" or, as we are about to see, the agency of a particular "image." Consequently, for the literary analyst the text assumes the value of a token inasmuch as it – regardless of the specific plot, genre, or style – furnishes an example of this agency at work.

To identify an extraliterary determinant, a socio-psychological "character" (Pereverzev), "tendency" (Bespalov, Ulrikh Fokht), or "complex" (Pospelov, Vasilii Sovsun), was insufficient if this determinant could not be shown to be immanently *of* the text, to have a uniquely literary existence.[20] Just because they denied the independence of the literary series, the critics of the Sociological school were not going to deny the specificity of literature among other superstructural phenomena – or, for that matter, the possibility of poetics as a discipline distinct from economics, sociology, social psychology, and socio-economic history.[21] With no less passion than the Formalists, Pereverzev insisted on the particular character of the literary sphere (Poliakov 21–2); he too was a committed "specifier" (*spetsifikator*).[22] Closely following the doyen of Marxist aesthetics in Russia, Georgii Plekhanov, Pereverzev saw "play" (*igra*) and "image" (*obraz*) as determinants of artistic phenomena in general and of literature in particular:

The concept of art is closely associated with that of the image as a specific feature of art. Art is always action; it consists in reproducing behavior characteristic of a particular form of life, behavior otherwise known as psychology or character. When this form of life reproduces the system of behavior characteristic of it, apart from the immediate battle for life, it is playing. The system of behavior reproduced or, what is the same thing, the character or psychology reproduced, is the image. It is impossible to reproduce behavior, to play, without the image. The image constitutes the essence of play. Play without the image, without reproduction of the system of behavior or character, is simply unthinkable, it is simply impossible. Art is play and art is image are essentially equivalent formulae, because play can be realized only in the image, because to play means to present an image. In play, the image is merged with the organism at play and has no existence apart from that organism ... In art, the image becomes separated from the player; it becomes objectivated and takes on an independent existence ... It is in this objectivation that the act of artistic creativity consists. It is through the objectivation of play, through its embodiment in the matter of the external world, that the artist creates images. In art, social character, the subject of play, becomes the object known as the image. (Pereverzev, "Problems" 155)

Partly because of its lingering connotations as the word for "icon," the Russian *obraz* resolves more easily the tension between sensuousness and sense – between the depictive as such and its semantic fulfilment – that characterize its English counterpart. So even when Pereverzev speaks of the "objectness" of the image, its independent existence in the materiality of the artistic medium, the next step is inevitably implied: to show that a representation is always inhabited by the (social) subjective, that it is not only a sensuous concretion ("image" in its most literal meaning) but also "character." This transition is facilitated by the fact that in one standard usage, *obraz* indeed means a depiction of a person, a character, a verbal or iconic figuration-individuation of the human.

The capaciousness of the Russian term allows Pereverzev to think of the artistic image as an agency, almost a living entity;[23] but it also allows for a common misreading of his argument. That misreading collapses the social character (*kharakter*) reproduced *in* the text with a fictional character (*obraz, geroi, personazh*) *from* the text.[24] Although a fictional persona (a literary "type") can exemplify a class psychology,[25] such a relation does not exhaust the reproduction mechanism that Pereverzev has in mind. The first thing to be said of this mechanism is that it is one of *structural* reproduction.[26] A structure of social relations, once it has been subjectivized as a "system of behaviour," is reproduced (objectivated) in the text as a *structure* of images.[27] In other words, the social "character" is identified with the structure as such and not with separate instances of representation within it (fictional characters).[28] An appeal, therefore, must be made to a more general meaning of *obraz,* as well as "image," so as to allow both terms (not without some semantic strain) to stand for the totality of what the text depicts (an "image of the world" or an "image of reality") and thus be virtually synonymous with two broader terms: respectively, *izobrazhenie* and "representation."

This might be an opportune moment to remember that in the Formalists' theorizing of artistic construction, "device" appeared on two distinct levels of analytical description: as a designation of a particular instance within a totality (an individual device within the text), and as a figuration of that very totality (the artistic text, or even art itself, *as* a device). And the same is the case with *obraz* in the poetics of the Sociological school: it appears both as an individuation within the text (a portrayal of something or someone) and as an individuation of the whole (a historically and class-specific representation of reality in its subjective dimension). In that it is a dynamic interaction of formal devices, the text in Formalist poetics is itself a Device, something that functions in a certain way, a working mechanism. Similarly, by virtue of being a peculiar organization of images, the text can be imaged forth by Pereverzev and his followers as an entity that *behaves* in a certain way, as an *Obraz*, a character-image.[29]

In Formalist theory, the identity of these two levels – the particulars of artistic construction and its totality – is secured through the "governing constructive principle" (*dominanta*): because all formal elements in the text are governed in their functioning by this principle, they function as a whole, a Device. A similar situation obtains when the text is considered from the point of view of socio-psychological content. Here the totalizing media-tor is called, variously, a "tendency," "principle," or "complex." Because, as bearers of meaning, all individual image-motifs serve to articulate a ten-dency or principle, they are not an inert cumulation but constitute a sys-tematic whole. In this way a transition is also implemented from object to subject, from the depicted to its depicter: through the manifest "thereness" of a represented world, a trans-individual agency becomes intelligible so that this image of the world is now, equally, a Character. For the analyst, therefore, it is a question of identifying the "tendency" or "principle" that has thus totalized the text: "Marxism approaches literary phenomena with confidence, in full awareness of the fact that it will be able to dissect the whole fabric of the poetic with the sharp scalpel of its method, reaching the core where the object and subject, both the depiction and the expres-sion of being, are organically combined, where the principle of its regular laws and necessity reveals itself" (Pereverzev, "Essential Premises" 63).[30]

The scalpel referred to above is, obviously, a tool of dissection only to the extent to which it is also a tool of reconstitution. For it is through this surgical intervention alone that the text handed down to us by tradition can be reinstated into its truth. Only at the site of the analytical incision does it reconnect with itself, revealing its true nature as a reproduction of social being. That this truth is in no way manifestly given, but is subsequent to the hard labour of the analyst, is emphasized time and time again by Pereverzev and his colleagues:

> [The] first step in a Marxist investigation of the poetic text consists in finding the subject in the object depicted in the literary work, in discovering the depicter in that which is depicted. It is not so very easy to do this. Finding the subject in question in the object depicted requires a close examination of all the elements of the poetic structure, strenuous attention to the smallest details of the scene portrayed, persistent thought, scholarly sensitivity, and even vigilance and perspicacity. (Pereverzev, "Essential Premises" 60)

The moment when the textual *Darstellung* is shown to be a necessary and lawful structuration governed by a single principle/tendency is the moment when the anagogic level is attained, when the "scene portrayed" acquires the features of a living being, a trans-individual personality (*Obraz*).[31] But, from this, it follows once again that the anagogic (Social-) World-cum-Character should be identified with the textual structure as a whole and not with a particular embodiment within it (a fictional character, "hero");[32] it is to be found in the totality of interrelations that constitute this structure.[33] He who brings these interrelations to the light of knowledge and shows their "regular laws and necessity" – the carrier of specialized knowledge, the analyst – is an indispensable agency in the biography of the text.

Once the content-generating principle or tendency has been identified, the textual elements, on all levels of the structure, can be seen as falling into two distinct categories: the "autogenic" and the "heterogenic" (Pospelov, "K metodike" 101). In the former, the organizing principle has been realized more or less directly; the latter, by contrast, contribute indirectly to its realization. In the former, according to Pospelov's terminology, the principle is "subjectified" (*sub"ektivirovan*); in the latter, it is only "objectivated" (*ob"ektivirovan*):

> The organizing [socio-psychological] complex can be subjectified in the literary work, in which case the work would contain an organizing *image* or *images*, those images into which the organizing complex is subjectified. In the

other case, the organizing complex can be only objectified in the literary work, and then the latter *would not* feature an organizing *image*. [Griboedov's] *Woe from Wit* can serve as an example of the first instance: the socio-psychological complex subjectified here in the character of Chatskii organizes the structure of the play. [Gogol's] *Dead Souls* can be cited as an example of the second instance: none of the socio-psychological complexes subjectified into the character-images of the "poem" organizes it fully; the organizing complex here is objectivated in all these images and organizes them from outside. (Pospelov, "K metodike" 83–4; emphasis in the original)

Pospelov's taxonomy of images parallels the Formalist theory of the *dominanta*. The latter assumes all textual elements to be formal but still distinguishes two general classes of these: the foregrounded, or dominant, ones, and those that function – relationally – as supporting material.[34] With the Sociologists, by contrast, all we find in the text are elements of content; but here too it is necessary to introduce an internal hierarchy: some of these elements (images) are direct conveyors of the generative subjectivity, while others participate in its manifestation only indirectly. Through Pospelov's abstruse language we can glimpse the reason for the rather symptomatic misreading discussed earlier. In principle, all character-images in the text are equally important for the realization of the "organizing complex," but in certain circumstances, some of them (i.e., the "autogenic" ones) come forth as "more equal than others."[35] In these circumstances, one character-image – let us say, Griboedov's Chatskii – can seem to have determined from within, through an agency all its own, the textual presentation. It would then seem that, in our example, all other characters in the play, their roles and trajectories, the manner in which they are presented, are subordinated to the character of Chatskii.

But is it even possible to conceive of a character-image as fully autochthonous in relation to the structuring principle of the text-as-totality, and thus as fully embodying the anagogic Character (*Obraz*) that reproduces itself through the text? For the critics of the Sociological school, the answer was firmly negative. A positive answer would have implied that the much-sought-for nexus of the representational structure – the point where a represented world "turns into" a self-reproducing/representing subject – was not hidden at all, but was there, on the surface of representation, in the body of a fictional character. Rather than residing in the space of hermeneutic cognition, this nexus would have been found in the space of the diegesis itself: in the figure of one of its characters, the text would have appeared to have always already "read" itself; its latent actuality would also have been its manifest "face," rendering the intervention of specialized knowledge quite unnecessary.

The principal fault for which the Pereverzevians were always condemned, in Soviet and Western criticism alike, was their "mechanical sociologism." Their method passed far too easily from social world to text. Reality reproduced itself as literature almost automatically. There were not enough "transmissions" from one to the other, and there were never, in the authors and texts analysed by the critics of the Sociological school, instances of incompleteness or ambiguity. The reproduction succeeded every time, and thoroughly. Each writer they discussed turned out to be an optimal medium for this or that socio-psychological tendency. Indeed, the impression was created that the author was, in each and every case, fully permeable in relation to the transpersonal *ustremlenie*.[36] As a critic of today expresses it, "Persons, organized by class, molded by material conditions, and fixed in their destiny by economic laws, had become as predictable as things" (Emerson 79). Because of this predictability, the figure of the author was regarded by the Pereverzevians as methodologically inessential. After all their talk of subjectivity, the Sociological critics had to suffer being reprimanded for underestimating the subjective factor in literary creation. Indeed, the *individual* subjective had no role to play in their study of literature other than to fulfil unconditionally the dictates of being.

All of this is true enough. The simplifications and failings of Pereverzevian criticism are plain to see. Yet as with the Formalists, it is not my intention to evaluate the intellectual solidity of the theoretical enterprise. What interests me is the imagination that sustains the theory and plots out the field of literature, regardless of the cognitive sins that may accrue to this imagination in the process. The most intriguing aspect of the Pereverzevian legacy is precisely its biggest intellectual *zagib*,[37] the point where matters are obviously pushed too far so that the result becomes untenable. I have in mind the picture of "reality itself, and not the artist ... recreat[ing] itself in the work" (Poliakov 30), and the cognate vision of the "poet ... swallowed up by being" (Poliakov 32). Here we are in the realm of metaphor proper, where one thing is substituted for another: being replaces the individual artist as the actual creator of literature. The metaphor's value lies not in what it might teach us about literary matters, but in the covert desire it channels: to imagine art as driven by necessity, to see creative writing as unconditional, well-nigh automatic, activity. For if the individual creator is "swallowed by being," he is thereby also secured, anchored, in it. His productions are rescued from arbitrariness by default, for they are the autobiography of being (in one of its class-determined forms).

Note that the metaphor not only declares but also proposes; it is not just analytic but programmatic; it is a trope not merely for what *is* but also for what *could or should be*. It projects a new kind of artistic practice that would be the conscious appropriation of the theoretical vision. It would be the conscious attempt, on the writer's part, to understand the *napravlennost'* of reality and synchronize himself with it, to submit himself to the objective volition implicit in his world, so that his work would be, indeed, the autobiography of being. But this implies that artistic practice is to be premised on the practice of self. Since it is a transpersonal subjectivity that is always objectivated in literature, the individual must begin by fashioning his self in the image of that subjectivity. Whereas Formalism places the writer face to face with Art-as-Device, Pereverzevian criticism places him in relation to Being-as-Character. The first is otherness in the shape of objecthood, the second, otherness in the shape of subjecthood. But both are forms of "demanding" otherness, whose dissimulating systematicity is no sooner registered as a fact than it becomes the motivation for an act – an imperative addressed to the very individual whose right to authorship has just been revoked. How this imperative became a practical project for refashioning the writer's consciousness is the subject of chapter 5.

Chapter 3

Knowledge Become Practice

Thinking as a modern, which is to say, being part of intellectual modernity, often meant finding oneself as an actor in a scene of dissimulation similar to the ones described in the previous two chapters. It meant regarding particular fields of experience as fields of false appearances whose falsity was, even so, a moment of truth. Grasping truth, then, was a matter of showing how appearances are generated, laying bare the device that has produced them and ordered them. It involved proceeding, by rigorous method, from the manifest to the latent actuality of "this," steering one's way, for the most part, in the blind spot of the average empirical consciousness. This amounted to practising objectivity in the realm of knowledge. The very definition of the "objective" in such a scenario was premised on this game of law-governed hide-and-seek. Lenin, whose was most certainly a modern mind, wrote in 1908:

> The paramount thing is that the *laws* of these changes [in social being] have been discovered, that the *objective* logic of these changes and their historical development have at bottom and in the main been disclosed – objective ... in the sense that social being is *independent* of *the social consciousness* of men. The fact that you live and conduct your business, beget children, produce products and exchange them, gives rise to an objectively necessary chain of events, a chain of development, which is independent of your *social* consciousness, and is never grasped by the latter completely. (*Materialism* 339; emphasis in the original)

For Lenin, then, "objectivity" is that aspect of social being that is constitutively in excess of the operative consciousness with which individuals play their part in that very social being. It is not a simple opposition between the logic of the whole process and the partial perspective of any single actor in it, as if the whole were just too big, too complex, to be grasped by those who occupy but a minuscule point within it. Rather, the very logic of the whole is such that it operates *by means of* its own misrecognition. (Any form of social life would implode if the majority lived in full consciousness of being exploited while the minority beheld, without ideological embellishments and mystifications, the naked truth of their class existence.)

Twentieth-century humanistic knowledge has made three realms of such dissimulating objectivity especially prominent: the socio-economic sphere, human interiority, and language. For us so far, "this" has been "text," and "this" has turned out to be a systematic organization of elements and functions, a dynamic ensemble of interrelations, a totality, whose objective determinations exceed the purview of the individual who is its putative master. From the middle of the nineteenth century to the early twentieth, the same basic fact was registered by political economy, psychoanalysis, and linguistics: "this" exceeds the grasp of he who possesses and uses it. With Marx, the economy was seen as exceeding the market, with its laws of supply and demand; with Freud, the psychic apparatus was seen as exceeding the jurisdiction of the *ego cogito;* and with Saussure, "language" was seen as exceeding the immediacy of its own deployment in speech. The measure of this excess was defined, respectively, by the production of (surplus) value; the operations of the unconscious; and the (differential) mechanism of signification. Instituting a peculiar modern cryptology, these items are more (or less) than mere facts, more (or less) than "real." For they set the terms for a completely new experience of what is true and what is real, and they are, to that extent, immune to ontological or epistemological challenges. In relation to the individual subject, they define the extent to which the fullness of the empirical, of "this," evades her. These are the names of modern hungers, the respective obstacles that prevent an adequate consciousness of social existence, the full absorption of the inner into the self, and the possibility to truly author one's meanings. Because there are those "primary processes" called the production of commodities, the unconscious, and signification, we must understand that sociality, self, and meaning are not fully *present to* the individual subject. Rather, they are *presented away* from her, *re-presented.*

What separates the thing of use from the commodity, the psychic act from its true significance, the intended from the realized meaning of speech, is a movement of re-presentation with no subject. "Re-presentation" here stands for the process of casting away values supposedly present to the individual, where "casting" is equally "throwing" and "giving shape."

Through commodity production, signification, and the "primary process," the elements that constitute the individual's material, linguistic, and psychic life are "cast away" to another place, onto "another scene" (*andere Schauplatz*, as Freud has it). In the sense I attribute to it here, "re-presentation" is tantamount to transvaluation: both a transposition and an assignment of value somewhere else.

Who is the author of re-presentation, understood in these terms? Who imparts the definitive value-form to the materialities of outer and the intangibles of inner life? Thus far we encountered only very particular answers to this question, arising from two particular experiences of "this" as "artistic text." The answers have been "formal construction" and "socio-psychological complex." With respect to the experience of "this" as "social life," "interiority," and "communication," other particular answers could be phrased, respectively, as the "economic system," the "psychic complex," and the "mechanism of signification." Obviously, the nominal terms in these phrasings are readily substitutable for one another (we can just as well say the "complex of economic relations," the "psychic mechanism," the "system of signification"), which points us to the general answer: the generator of representations, their true "author," is the system in its systematicity, the Device as such. Far from being mere cumulations of facts or events, the economic, the psychic, and the linguistic-semiotic were found to be *systematically working* aggregates. Never mind that the "work" in question appeared sometimes with the grinning face of deceit and sometimes under the countenance of play (the play of the signifier, the ruses and jokes of the unconscious, the ludic existence of the commodity form).[1] To be sure, deceitfulness, or dissimulation, is not a characteristic of the Device and the work it performs, but rather of its relation to the average individual consciousness.

This basic situation – which warrants the label "predicament" only insofar as we are assuming the point of view of the "castaway" (i.e., of the supposedly centred individual subject) – becomes "plot" when we figure into it the act that ends the masquerade and exposes the dissimulation. Thus far, we have encountered that act as a hermeneutic exercise, a deployment of a cognitive method, a conquest of specialized analytic knowledge. But this is only half the story. Next I would like to consider how this same hermeneutic serves to ground praxis, how it motivates or legitimates particular practical interventions. Just as the hermeneutic can have various fields of application, so the practices in question can be found in various spheres of modern life, one of which is the artistic. But their common form is this: to act as if my act is the unfolding of a (previously concealed) objective logic, as if it is called for by imperative if latent necessity, as if it is the impersonal work of the Device itself.

The dynamic between theoretical and practical hermeneutics is illustrated most easily with the example of Russian Formalism and Futurism. As noted earlier, the former was much more than the coming to consciousness of an extant poetic practice, although it was that too. The kinship between the two movements is undeniable and was often commented upon during the 1920s.[2] Without pretending to scientific rigour, the Futurists were writing their own rudimentary Formalist theory in the manifestos and proclamations that accompanied their works. Already by 1913, a few years before the first Formalist publications, Kruchenykh had pointed to "this absolutely new way" of making poetry, which "will be the combination of words according to their inner laws, which reveal themselves to the wordwright, and not according to the rules of logic or grammar, as was the case before us" ("New Ways" 72). He also spoke about the deformation of the linguistic material, of "our new devices" (75) and the resultant "new perception of the world" (73) – all of this before Shklovskii formulated his theory of defamiliarization. In large part because the poetic practice of the Russian Futurists aimed to bring about that liminal moment in the existence of art, when the text would be nothing more than the blunt exposure of its own formal (phonetic) determinants, someone like Jakobson could be convinced that "the language of poetry strives to reach, as a final limit, the phonetic, or rather ...the euphonic phrase – in other words, a trans-sense speech" (*Noveishaia* 313).

The critical analysis of literature in terms of formal devices was rendered possible because there already existed a species of literature that performed a practical analysis of textuality and language. Most conspicuously in the poetry of Khlebnikov and Kruchenykh, the act of writing itself became the overcoming of dissimulation, as it demonstrated the essential dimension of poetic speech (hitherto concealed behind representational content and the "rules of logic"). And this concrete demonstration was in turn always ready to become a general statement, to be abstracted into "theory" by those who carried it out. The transition from theory to practice, and vice versa, was more than routine – it was necessary. To draw a rigid distinction between the two is very difficult. It is most sensible to think of a single programmatic activity with two aspects: the production of literary texts, and the production of statements about literature and art. The two aspects complemented each other: the poems were offered as illustrations of how real literature was (to be) made, that is, as tokens of its essential dimension; while the "theory" explained how the poems were to be received, that is, it substantiated their token-value. Because the enigmatic and often nonsensical words on the page did not explicate their own *raison d'être,* another type of discourse was needed that would make clear, not their representational signification, but their gestural significance. Such was the common procedure of Kruchenykh's manifesto pamphlets: this or that principle of the new poetry was proclaimed, after which a poetic text – his or somebody else's – was quoted in order to show the said principle at work. For instance, Kruchenykh offered his own famous verse "Dyr-bul-shchyl" as a token of the liberated Word after he meditated thusly on the new procedures of poetry[3]:

> The structure [*struktura*] of the word or of verse consists of its component parts (sound, letter, syllable, etc.); let's symbolize them as a – b – c – d.
>
> The *texture* [*faktura*] of the word consists in the *arrangement* of these parts (a – d – c – b, or b – c – d – a, or in still other ways); texture is the *making* [*delanie*] of the word, its construction, layering, accretion, the distribution in one way or another of syllables, letters, and words. (*Faktura* 2; emphasis in the original)

In Kruchenykh's usage, *struktura* refers to the systematicity of language and poetic speech as latent, while *faktura* refers to the moment when this systematicity is made manifest through literary practice, through poetic "making." The structure of the word is a fact, the truth of its immanent organization. This fact is treated as binding upon poetic practice, as its motivation. It calls for the act of poetic *delanie*, which is nothing other than the laying bare, the demonstration, of that same immanent organization. The end result of this is *faktura*. *Faktura* is *struktura* made visible. The object – in this case the poetic text – is a "thing made" (*sdelannaia veshch'*). It cannot be judged on the basis of what it itself articulates as verbal meaning (which could be quite minimal indeed or outright nonsensical). Its true significance can only be apprehended if we are aware of the symbolic performance that is its inalienable context. "Dyr-bul-shchyl" does not tell its reader: "I am a concrete example of poetic *faktura*, a token of Language-laid-bare." This message is nowhere in the signs of which the experiemental piece of poetry is composed, just as desire as such is nowhere to be found in the images or words of a dream. The significance of the text, rather, resides in the principle of its construction. And insofar as this principle – the combination of sounds, morphemes, and verbal forms according to supposedly immanent affinities – actualizes the anonymous agency of Language itself, the text functions also as a token of the author's demise.

We now turn to that other side, the side of the "real world," where the making of words and things takes place: from the systematicity of "this" as discovered by knowledge, to the systematicity of "this" as a motivation for practice. This is not just a thematic turn serving the purposes of the present discussion; it is just as much a call that resounded in Soviet culture of the post-revolutionary years:

> Our epoch is characterized by the fact that mankind, because of the increasing collectivization of the productive forces of society, *is moving from systematicity in knowledge* (in this case, theoretical linguistics) *to systematicity in practice, to organization* (the construction of language). Mankind is beginning consciously and intentionally to create and advance those elements of life that, up to now, seemed to be beyond the jurisdiction of society's organizational-practical interference (psychology, the laws of physiology, the labor process and along with these, language). (Arvatov, "Rechetvorchestvo" 91; emphasis in the original)

While his essay's main theme was the possibility of creating a new language for a new society, Arvatov obviously had a much broader frame of reference. He envisioned a transition "from systematicity in knowledge ... to systematicity in practice" across a multitude of spheres of human experience, of which the linguistic was but one. The "elements of life" in all of these spheres, hitherto constellated in the shadow of empirical, individual consciousness, had begun to emerge from that shadow. And there had opened now the prospect of a human creation – of "construction," as Arvatov calls it, of "making" (*delanie*), as Kruchenykh calls it. But this proud, revolutionary activity will not reinstate the individual's alienated rights to authorship, nor will it simply transfer them onto some collective subject. Whoever their subject proper, "making" and "construction" do not quite amount to authorship, for "making" here does not mean original creation, and "construction" is not to be understood as erection *ex nihilo*. The kind of praxis these acts constitute is less originary than regulatory. And thus it is not by chance that where Kruchenykh uses "making" and "construction," he also speaks of "arrangement," and where Arvatov writes "construction," he equates it with "organization."

"Organization" became a buzzword on the Soviet cultural scene of the 1920s, when it was very common to speak of items as different as clothes, films, and human physiques as needing to be "organized." In large part, this grew out of the theoretical work of Aleksandr Bogdanov (pseudonym

of Aleksandr Malinovskii [1873–1928]), Lenin's chief opponent in the
fractional struggles of 1907–9 and the principal target of the Bolshevik
leader's vitriol in *Materialism and Empirio-Criticism* (1908).[4] Long before
founding the Proletkult movement (in 1917, on the eve of the Revolution),
Bogdanov was working on an analytic of universal life in which the project
of a revolutionary culture would be firmly grounded. He believed that
Marx's hermeneutic had to be expanded towards the utmost horizons of
the empirical world (Bogdanov, *Tektologiia* 134). The positive knowledge
derived from studying the historical experience of mankind was to be co-
opted by the positive findings of the natural sciences. At their meeting
point, these two hitherto disconnected pursuits were to coalesce in a new,
truly universal science (50–2, 78–9), a "strict, structured system of universal understanding" (*Filosofiia* 13).[5] In his Marxist-positivist crusade,
Bogdanov drew substantially on the work of Ernst Mach (1838–1916) and
Richard Avenarius (1843–96), dutifully reproducing in his own copious
writings the empirio-monistic amalgamation of the psychical and the
physical, of acts of consciousness and facts of nature.[6] The *Tektology*
(1912–29), his grand theoretical project, was to institute a monistic science
of all experience by generalizing the apparently heterogeneous existence of
physical phenomena, on the one hand, and human ideas and doings, on
the other.

The sprawling treatise, on which Bogdanov worked to the very end of his
life, was conceived as the culmination of an intellectual trajectory compris-
ing the three-volume *Empiriomonism* (1904–6) and *Philosophy of Living
Experience* (*Filosofiia zhivogo opyta*, 1912). *Empiriomonism* was an exposition of Bogdanov's own philosophical method, which the author did not
hesitate to place above all preceding philosophical thought. The goal in
Empiriomonism had been to renew philosophy; in the 1912 book it was to
transcend philosophy. Here Bogdanov undertook, in a popular form, a
critique of philosophy both as a type of knowledge and as a tradition of
specific, historically bound systems of thought. Even as he touted the superiority of his empiriomonism over Mach's empiriocriticism and Marx's
dialectical materialism, he insisted on the limitations of the philosophical
enterprise as such, including his own version of it, and pointed beyond it
to a yet unrealized "science of the future" (*Filosofiia* 259–66). Where philosophy ended, a wholly different type of knowledge was called for that
would be not so much a making sense of experience as a methodology for
its concrete transformation. The *Tektology* was intended to be the systematic exposition of this last, superior – because immediately practical – type
of cognition, an instrumental science of organization that would take the

place of philosophical reflection: "as it develops further, tektology renders philosophy superfluous; it stands, from the very beginning above philosophy, whose universality it supplements with a scientific and practical aspect" (*Tektologiia* 142–3).[7]

Where others saw heterogeneity, Bogdanov saw a common mode of being for all things available to experience. And the name of this common mode of being was "organization":

Drawing on the facts and ideas of contemporary science we reach the only exhaustive, the only monistic understanding of the universe. The universe presents itself as an endlessly unfolding panoply of forms at different degrees and levels of organization: from the unknown to us elements of the ether to the human collectives and the planetary systems. All these forms – in their interweaving and mutual struggle – constitute the universal organizational process: endlessly dividing itself into parts, boundless and seamless in its wholeness. Thus, the realm of organizational experience coincides with the realm of experience as such. Organizational experience is nothing other than *all of our experience considered from an organizational point of view*, i.e., as a world of organizing and disorganizing processes. (*Tektologiia* 73; emphasis in the original)

In this world-picture, embracing as it does the human and natural realms,[8] every fact can be understood as composed of activities and resistances,[9] of "organizing" and "disorganizing" elements (Bogdanov, "Taina" 398–401, *Tektologiia* 118–25).[10] To that extent, every moment of experience, regardless of its provenance, falls under the competence of tektology, the general science of organization ("Taina" 401).

As can be seen, both "experience" (an *Ur*-concept for Mach and his followers) and "organization" are fundamental notions for Bogdanov; their jurisdictions coincide, covering the entirety of being. To speak of the world is to speak of the sphere of experience and also of the sphere of organization: "Never in the world, in experience, has there been something which has not been organized" (Bogdanov, qtd in Jensen 158). Yet the cognitive weight of the two terms, "experience" and "organization," is different, just as the relative value of the subject is different from that of the predicate in the elementary structure of the judgment. "Experience" functions as the subject, the empty position for which content needs to be supplied in the further movement of thought. "Organization" is the predicate that supplies the content; it is the "punch" of Bogdanov's most basic argument. Just as "God" is something completely abstract, indeterminate, until the predication is completed (e.g., "God *is* love"), so is "experience" before Bogdanov supplies the all-important determination: "Experience *is* organization."

A derivative of this basic argument is that the science of all experience is the science of organization, the all-embracing discipline of tektology. As Bogdanov explains (*Tektologiia* 92), the word "tektology" derives from the Greek sememe for making, building, constructing (*teuchô, tekton*). A science of organization it is, but a science that wants to make and do just as much as it wants to know.[11] Like Pereverzev and many other leftist thinkers of the time,[12] Bogdanov was wont to quote Marx's imperative for a cognition that does not just interpret the world but transforms it.[13] That the world is ubiquitously "tektological" means that it is ubiquitously open to "organizational-practical interference."[14] If everywhere we turn we find only a factually existing organization of things, ideas, or activities, then all of these fields of objectivity, in their bewildering multiplicity, offer themselves as fields for organizational praxis (106). The world is one enormous demanding object. It calls for organizational doing. And it is a real shame that language, as we have it and use it, does not bear out this universal demand. For we can say "to organize a party," or "to organize a meeting," but why do we still say "to write" rather than "to organize" a book, to "construct" rather than "to organize" a building (95–6)?[15] Yet the construction of a building and the writing of a book are both organizational activities, for they involve coordinating multiple elements into an effective whole (99). The linguistic impediment proceeds from the impediment of history; it is the stuttering of a defective historical world in which human endeavour has been disjointed, split into specialized "occupations," and is no longer recognized as common and one.[16]

Note that Bogdanov uses "organization" in two different senses, which hold in English usage as they do in Russian: organization as a *fact* and as an *act,* as an objectively existing state of affairs and as activity.[17] The duality is highly analogous to that of *struktura* and *faktura* in Kruchenykh. The first term stands for an implicit demand, a latent imperative; the second is that same imperative taken up in practice, a putting-into-action of what the demanding object calls for. As long as we are in the world of nature, the distinction between organization as a fact and as an act poses no problem. Crystals, planetary systems, and living bodies are all organized entities; the agent is implied and irrelevant: nothing is to be gained by identifying Nature as the "organizer" of these structures. The fact has precedence over the act. As soon as we cross over into the man-made world – that part of Nature's region that has been processed through human labour and thought – ambiguity sets in. "A society of men" is both a fact and an implicit mission; it is both a neutral description and a tacit call to action. The genitive works both ways: to assign to the organizational structure (society) its constitutive elements (men), leaving in abeyance the question of agency; or to charge these same elements (men) with the responsibility for their own creation (society). Alternately, man stands as that which is being "organized" and as that which organizes, as the object and subject of tektological activity.

In thinking and toiling, ordering and executing, man is the organizer of materialities *and* ideas, of materialities *through* ideas, of life. Yet for the entire expanse of human history, this very life, as an objective system of interrelations, has exceeded the purview of its supposed organizer.[18] The *fact* of organization has been in excess of the *act*. In the bourgeois world, this discrepancy manifests itself as a conflict between an individual, "specialized," subjective consciousness and the objective-latent communality of human experience:

> The "absolute" individual "I" expresses the socially fragmented experience of man and his existential opposition to others. It is clear that the unity of the social whole is outside of his field of vision. Not only is this unity invisible to the individual: it is also imperfect, elemental, unorganized, full of existential contradictions. The individual is *overcome* by these contradictions of the unattainable and incomprehensible whole; he is powerless in front of them; the elemental forces of social life reign over him. ("Sobiranie" 37; emphasis in the original)[19]

Closely following Marx,[20] Bogdanov rehearses here the already familiar scenario in which a totality of interrelations outstrips the powers of the individual and thus remains transcendent to his consciousness. When he says "man," Bogdanov, clearly, does not mean this atomized individual. Rather, "man" is an ontological imperative *addressed to* the individual. As he explains earlier in the same essay, "man" is more than either the corporeal or psychic-ideal identity of the individual subject: "Man is the *entire world of experience*" (29; emphasis in the original). Such a definition, of course, in no way means that a single person could possibly possess all experience accumulated by mankind through its history (43). What one *could* possess, however, is the *common element* of all human experience: those organizational forms and methods that underlie and unify the life of nature and human civilization. This optimal condition would permit each person to relate to and assimilate, if necessary, the experience accumulated by any other (43–4).

We are given to understand that the atomized individual of the bourgeois epoch is a historical distortion-dissimulation of man's genuine being.
A historically specific organization of socio-economic relations has "presented" man away from himself and into the "individual." The predicament of this re-presentation can be reversed through what Bogdanov calls
the "conscious-systematic gathering of man" (42).[21] Man is to be gathered
back from his incomplete and dissimulative existence as an individual-
subjective monad, he is to be retrieved from his being-represented. But
what and whose is the agency through which such a lofty project would
become reality? Does this agency rest with "us who know"? Is it a matter
of "us who know" installing consciousness in "them who don't," of edu-
cating the masses, of organizing their communal existence? Bogdanov's
answer is equivocally affirmative: the "conscious-systematic gathering
of man" can be "our" doing only because it is the immanent doing of
the objective historical process itself. For *there*, in the historical reality of
today, the gathering of man is already under way. The same inexorable
mechanism that has fragmented human being is now working towards
manifesting the truth-reality of that being.

Definitive of the productive activity of every individual is the fact that it
takes place within a specific organization of society's productive forces. As
the forces of production develop, they obscure ever further this essential
fact. In advanced bourgeois society the process reaches a crisis, which is at
the same time anastasis. The specialization of production, the furthest
alienation of labour from labour's true character (as humanity's collective
contest with Nature), has made man a "cog in the machine," it has reduced
him to a mere accessory. Yet there, where he is at his most atomized, where
he has become one blind motion, man is inexorably driven back to the fullness of his genuine being. And what brings him back from re-presentation,
what "retrieves" him or "gathers" him, is, once again, a Device:

> The machine was born in the world of competition and social antagonism.
> As we know, the machine sharpened and brought to the limit this competition
> and this antagonism. But, thereby, it also sharpened and increased the *need
> for development*. In each sphere of [capitalist] competition there arises the
> need for ceaseless, planned perfection of technologies. This need is satisfied
> through the elaboration of new technical methods.
>
> The common technical methods bring machines ever closer to their high-
> est type: the automatic mechanism. This process ... decreases, immediately
> and directly, the importance of specialization by increasing the homogeneity
> between various forms of labor. (41–2; emphasis in the original)[22]

And further still, the increased homogeneity of various labours calls forth a future in which the machine will relieve man of all but one task: that of supervision and organization (Bogdanov, *Tektologiia* 108). As it becomes more self-sufficient, the machine progressively eliminates the great divide in man's existence – the one between intellectual and manual labour, between command and execution (Bogdanov, "Sotsialisticheskoe obshchestvo" 93; "Kollektivisticheskii stroi" 300). It calls into existence a new type of human being in whom the "practical" is immediately the "intellectual," and vice versa: his practical involvement *is* the exercise of his organizational intelligence (Bogdanov, *Filosofiia* 320–1).

As it works, the automated mechanism of the machine also *works out* the latent reality of human existence. As it manufactures material goods, it also produces the realization that this existence is communal and shared, that it is, essentially, organization. In other words, the machine produces (tektological) consciousness.[23] And thus, as history draws closer to its great turning point, the machine comes to manifest in a powerful metaphor the nature of the historical process itself. For is history not just such a mechanism that works systematically and works out in the determinate course of its operations the genuine organization of human life?

If the machine can be experienced as a maker of a veritable historical revolution, it is just as true that the Revolution taking place in history can be experienced as a machine-like process, inexorably precise and effective in the execution of its "iron formulas":

> The materialist dialectics of class struggle – here is the genuine algebra of the revolution. What the naked eye sees on the arena [of history] is chaos, turbulence, formlessness, and boundlessness. But this chaos has been calculated and accounted for. Its stages have been foreseen. The lawfulness [*zakonomernost'*] of their succession has been anticipated and clasped into iron formulas … Revolutionary strategy is not formless, like an elemental force, but complete, like a mathematical formula. For the first time in history we see the revolutionary algebra in action. (Trotsky, "Vneokt'iabr'skaia literatura" 2)

For Bogdanov, however, the machine was not so much a diachronic as a synchronic metaphor. It offered, in a single image, the character of an entire historical epoch, a stage in the organization of production that was just being inaugurated at the time he was writing. The machine was a synecdoche for the entire complex of modern industry ruled by advanced technology – and on a higher level of generality, for the dawning age of automation. And since every major period in history was characterized

(synchronically) by a definite tektological configuration, the machine, in its
singular presence, announced a qualitatively new moment in the organizational genesis of mankind. And because of this, it also stood as an omen
for a radically different gradation of consciousness, an epistemological
leap. The self-regulating machine complexes would revolutionize not only
the relations of production, but cognition as well. This is because, in
Bogdanov's meta-history, every major epoch of tektological development
produced its own distinct episteme as the organizing tool of a particular
dominant class. "A different practice gives birth to a different logic"
(Bogdanov, *Filosofiia* 222).

For its part, the episteme, that is, the configuration of knowledge characteristic of this or that period of civilization, was based on a specific way
of understanding causality (21, 221). Thus the eras through which human
cognition had passed were just as many as the types of causality mankind
had known. In *The Philosophy of Living Experience*, Bogdanov distinguished two such paradigms in the previous history of human knowledge,
one based on authoritarian social relations, the other born out of relations
of exchange.[24] In the former model, every cause is modelled on executive
will, whose prototype is the will of the patriarch or sovereign;[25] in the latter,
cause and effect are in a relationship of necessity, whose prototype is the
impersonal necessity with which the market confronts each individual
Homo economicus (*Filosofiia* 21–46).[26] In its highest development, machine
production promised to inaugurate a third, terminal form of causality and
with it one last episteme.[27] So we should add one last item to the list of
what Bogdanov's machine stands for: the automated mechanism is the material image of something immaterial, of the most basic notion, which coordinates all other elements of knowledge into a system, the relationship
of relationships – causality as such.

What, then, is this last form, or scheme, of causality that Bogdanov saw
instantiated in the operations of automated mechanisms? He calls it "labour causality" (*trudovaia prichinnost'*), and he imagines it as a relationship in which there is no subordination of one term to another (as had
been the case in the authoritarian model), nor are there any fetishized principles, primal matters, unknowable things-in-themselves (as had been the
case in the paradigm of abstract causality). There are only transformations
from one quality into another. All entities and concretions are provisional.
At the same time, nothing is ever destroyed; it only passes into a different
form of existence. The direction of change is reversible, which means that
"cause" and "effect" are not absolute coordinates or values; at root, they
are one and the same (*Filosofiia* 223–4). The age-old question about the

true nature of things is foreclosed; since things are only transient moments in a total energetic flow, one should ask about functions, not origins; everything is process, and nothing is essence; relations and interactions erode all substances; being is fully dissolved into becoming.

Engine-driven machine technology emblematizes this type of causality insofar as its operation is premised on the transformation of force and the conversion of energy (222). The machinic complexes offer to view, over and over again, the spectacle of absolute mutability: the chemical combination of oxygen and coal passes into heat; this heat produces steam, which gives rise to pneumatic pressure; the pressure brings pistons into motion; this motion itself mutates from one kind into another as it is communicated to wheels, belts, and finally to machine tools that work directly on the material and give shape to new products (222). And what this spectacle reveals to the consciousness of men is that every force, every type of energy, can become the source for any other; they are substitutable, vanishing moments in the enduring effort of overcoming Nature's resistance (222). Since energy passes into energy, the initial and final terms of the process are identical; the cause is, essentially, the same as the effect – or, differently put, their distinction–opposition is rendered obsolete (227).

The labour of men, too, figures in this cycle of potentially limitless transformation:

And so, the practice of machine production contains within itself a new point of view. This point of view aims to become, and indeed becomes, universal. Human activity finds its place among the series of mutating forms that energy assumes. The laborer's effort is one of the links in the chain of production; it engenders other links, it is capable of replacing those links or be replaced by them ... As regards those elemental forces of nature that have not yet entered the chain of production, exact science ... reveals their homology, or identity, with those forces that have entered [production]. This means that every phenomenon, every natural process, *is for the labor collective a possible source for the generation of any other desired processes.* In this consists the practical connection of phenomena, the practical unity of nature. (223; emphasis in the original)

When Bogdanov says that "machine production contains within itself [*zakliuchaet v sebe*] a new point of view," we are given to understand that, whatever its uses in industry, the machine is also an epistemological catalyst. To all its other powers, this one should be added: the power to make see, to render perceptible. Its operation, then, can be viewed as analogous to how the Futurist text of Kruchenykh operates (at least ideally). As we saw, the latter presents the reader with *struktura* as *faktura*, which is to say that the inner constitution of the linguistic medium, the Word as such, is rendered perceptible. The reader experiences how sense is born from the combination of basic morphological elements and – hopefully – comes to realize the identity of form and content. Content turns out not to be a world subsisting apart from the verbal means, but a (subordinate) moment in the process of *rechetvorchestvo* (language- or word-creation). In Bogdanov, engine-powered machine production presents the worker with a dynamic aggregate in which all substantive moments vanish. Because matter passes into force and force returns again to matter (in the finished industrial product), the opposition of these two terms collapses in plain view. With it collapses also the more general opposition of means and ends. Just as everything, including matter itself, turns out to be a form of energy, so every end proves to be a means.

Both the ideal Futurist text and Bogdanov's idealized machine are contraptions for awakening perception. And because of this homology, it is not difficult to visualize the Futurist text as a machine (since it is a working aggregate of elements) and the machine in Bogdanov as a text (since it is something the labourer's mind reads to discover the truth of his own existence). The analogy can be extended further, towards the concept of the "device laid bare." For the Formalists, all texts are instances of formal organization, but not all of them show themselves as such. And only in the present day, in modernist poetry, do we have a type of literature that consciously sets out to lay bare its true nature as a formal Device. For Bogdanov, we can state the following: everywhere in the universe there are to be found tektological processes, and everywhere in mankind's history we come across forms of social organization of labour. But only in the present day do we begin to see the outlines of a process that is unitary (i.e., social) not just *in* itself but also *for* itself. Automated machine production lays bare the Device of human history as a whole: the collective effort "to gain mastery, step by step, over phenomena and things so as to derive some of them from others in a purposeful [*tselesoobraznyi*] manner, and use some of them for the overcoming of others" (226). Only with an organization of labour in which everything is treated as a technical matter, that is, as a potential that can be rationally exploited, does the world reveal itself for what it is: the arena of mankind's organizational activity.

It may appear that the name with which Bogdanov christens the third, ultimate type of causality – *trudovaia prichinnost'* – is poorly chosen. After all, every causality is labour causality insofar as every method of knowledge is rooted, in the last instance, in social practice, in the labour process.[28] Yet it is also true that in the course of history, this primary given – labour – has been mediated through power–authority and the process of exchange. And when it is mediated, it is also obscured, lost to consciousness (63). In the dissimulated perspective, the primary given becomes the sovereign will of the master-organizer or the anarchic and abstract will of the market-place. Only in the third and final historic frame is the authentic source of all causality recovered and made native to consciousness. So it is proper that only the final form of causality should be called *trudovaia prichinnost'*. Only here is human practice allowed to become aware of itself as that which bonds the "unity of nature," the cause of all causes.

As can be seen from the foregoing discussion, the theme of dissimula-tion and its overcoming is central to Bogdanov's thinking. It should be emphasized, however, that this theme is played in a register more radical than anything we have encountered so far. To wit, the dissimulation in question concerns not this or that blindness of knowledge, the inadequate cognizing of one field of phenomena or another, but the very nature of knowledge itself. If we go back to Lenin's words quoted at the beginning of this chapter,[29] we can see that they register the inability of everyday consciousness to grasp the general logic of social life. The dissimulation Lenin has in mind, then, has to do with the way the socio-economic pro-cess presents itself *to knowledge* (in its unscientific, existential–practical form). With Bogdanov, however, the ultimate problem is not what knowl-edge knows or fails to know, but what knowledge *is*.

It is a peculiarity of the human (as opposed to the natural) world that organizational activity proceeds through the mediation of knowledge. This is the very pinnacle of creation, the highest level of the universal tektologi-cal process (256); but it is also where the unitary principle of organization betrays itself. It appears no longer as a unitary principle, but as a duality. In the human kingdom, unlike anywhere else in the universe, the tektological process unfolds in two guises: as "practice" and as "knowledge." They are one and the same thing, just as, for the Formalists, "form" and "content" are ultimately homologous. Knowledge is simply another type of practical organizational activity. It is an extension of practice, just as "content" is an accessory of "form." In both cases – with Bogdanov *and* with the Formalists – there is really just one principle ("practice," "form"). Yet this principle is such that its very operation produces something other than itself, a seem-ingly heterogeneous nature, an appearance of radical otherness ("knowl-edge" and "content," respectively). This is just how the principle works: dissimulation is programmed into it. But a return to identity is too …

In itself, knowledge is practice. But it must become this also for itself. The latent fact must turn into explicit awareness. Knowledge must know itself for what it truly is, that is, as an aspect of a unitary organizational process through which humankind makes a home for itself in nature. How can this coming-to-consciousness be attained? Bogdanov hashed together a putative prehistory of mankind whose goal was to show that, originally, discourse was nothing other than action in verbal form (19–20). The first words were formed from primal cries with which our most distant forefathers urged action upon one another. Verbs, therefore, hold priority in the inventory of language, both because they were its very first items and because they are the most authentic testimony to the derivation of speaking from doing (228). In the beginning was the deed, indeed (198). Language is originally and essentially actional, and so is knowledge. With time, however, this essence was obscured, mystified. The organization of social practice is responsible for the dissimulation, and only it can bring about the lifting of the veil.

When advanced, machine-driven industry demonstrates that every motion, quantity, and thing is but a form of energy, a moment in a selfsame process, this realization has direct bearing on the nature of knowledge as well. Now practice and cognition, too, can be seen – potentially, by everyone – as moments of a selfsame activity. Their natures will no longer stand opposed, for in the dawning socio-economic world it will be possible to witness them as passing into one another as a matter of course, just as heat passes, through the evaporation of water, into steam, and steam into mechanical movement. The terminal form of knowledge, for which labour causality will be the *dominanta,* will apprehend fully "the practical connection of phenomena, the practical unity of nature." But this means that this knowledge will treat itself as participant in this unity, that is, as an integral moment of practice. And when it does so, it will in fact *be* an active participant. The coming-to-awareness will produce a qualitative change in the nature of knowledge so that it will actually behave as a practical agent in the world.

Bogdanov identified knowledge with practice much more directly than Marx ever related the superstructure to the base. Bogdanov's principle of sociomorphism postulates that the methods for knowing reality are nothing other than the methods of socio-economic practice transposed onto a different realm: "first come the actions of people, in a certain interrelation and interdependence engendered by the very course of their struggle with nature; thoughts come after, as the abbreviated images of these actions: the practical organization of labor efforts precedes the cognitive organization of the elements of experience and produces [the latter]" (242). And a little further in the same text: "*thinking takes its forms, in the last instance, from social practice*; or put differently: *the relation of elements within cognition is based on the relationship between the elements of labor activity in the social process*" (243; emphasis in the original). Hence, it would not be an exaggeration to say that for Bogdanov the individual thinks with the social organization to which he belongs,[30] or, even, that when he thinks, it is the social organization that "thinks" him. This may sound very similar to certain formulations of the structuralist critique of the subject, to be found in the writings of Lévi-Strauss, Althusser, and Foucault.[31] My use of the term "episteme," which Bogdanov himself never put to paper, was a conscious gesture to indicate this affinity. But, presently, I would like to indicate also the significant divergence between the two enterprises. This will allow me to rearticulate on a concrete example a thesis concerning the death of the author that I advanced in the introduction to this book.[32]

In both cases just mentioned, individual consciousness is seen as determined and is denied authorship of its own cognitions by a largely unconscious "logic": the paradigm of socio-economic organization in Bogdanov; the combinatory of *pensée sauvage* in someone like Lévi-Strauss. But the kinship between the two theories goes no further. The structuralist symbolic logic is the ultimate given: it does not articulate some further, "higher" significance; it is not the "story" of anything; it is the field in which meaning is produced, but this field itself is without meaning. Hence, the structuralist dispersal of the subject, too, is a terminal condition; no horizon opens beyond it. We are dealing with a universalizing postulate: the subject is dispersed in a field of signs because this is just what it means to be human, to live through language, to be in a state of culture. Things stand very differently with Bogdanov, for whom universality is something that works itself out in history. For him, as a follower of Marx, the trans-subjective logic issues from a single principle and can therefore be expected to return to it one day, which means, become true to it. The principle in question is "labour," or even better, the effort to make a home for man in nature. Even when the structure of human knowledge is at its most alienated and "meaningless" – when an abstract system of total exchange, mediated through monetary signs, dictates its laws to thought – it does not cease to be rooted in this most essential fact, it does not cease to be a logic of labour. In other words, the symbolic logic with which Bogdanov is dealing may appear "meaningless" in one of its historical manifestations, but in itself it is endowed with meaning, or essence, which some ultimate stage of history and human knowledge can repossess.

Bogdanov, then, is a modernist thinker of the lineage (if not the stature) of Marx, Nietzsche, and Freud, because for him the dispersal of the subject is not a terminal but a provisional moment that enables a subsequent project of repossession – the very project he calls the "gathering of man." His critique of subjectivity, unlike that of the structuralists, lives in history. It speaks from a determinate moment in time and, from there, assaults a particular historical form of subjectivity: bourgeois consciousness.[33] Where this consciousness is found to be "false," the prospect opens for its transcendence in a further historical episode. In other words, the very plotting of Bogdanov's theory is projective: it opens to a qualitatively new future and provides a blueprint for it (no matter how schematic). The scenario of dissimulation that we find in Bogdanov has the value of an omen and a summoning. For if one positions himself within history and is able, from that point of view, to regard the scene of social-practical organization as a spectacle of dissimulation, this by itself is a most telling sign. It means that the conditions are already ripe for the inauthentic state of being to be overcome. The very act of cognition by which the dissimulation is revealed as such implies that a new form of organized human practice is already on the historical scene, for this is the only place from which the new demystifying cognition can spring.

To convince ourselves of the projective, anticipative, future-oriented character of Bogdanov's thought, we need only open to the very last words of his *Philosophy of Living Experience*:

Philosophy is living out its last days. Empiriomonism is no longer fully philosophy, but a transitional form, since it knows where it is going and to what it should cede its place. The foundations of a general organizational science will be laid in the years just ahead, its blossoming is a result of that gigantic, feverish organizational work that will create a new society and will end the painful prologue of mankind's history. This time is not so distant. (272)

The present-day organization of practice is treated here as a demanding objectivity. This objectivity is already shaping the future and demanding a form of knowledge appropriate to it. The fact that such an organization is emerging *there,* in the world of today, is taken by Bogdanov as an imperative; the fact calls for an act. And the act in question is not this or that particular undertaking in industry, politics, or administration, but primarily the project of making knowledge itself *actional*. Bogdanov is inserting himself, his own work, within the plot of dissimulating and demanding objectivity. This work itself is the taking up of the said imperative and the attempted implementation of what is being called for. "Philosophy is living out its last days" because the type of cognition that philosophy epitomizes no longer corresponds to the most advanced forms of practical organization. Bogdanov's empiriomonism is philosophy's final act by which the entire enterprise is laid out, taken in with a parting backward glance, before being abandoned. It is the ultimate philosophical "point of view" (*tochka zreniia*); and what this point of view makes visible is both the inherent limits of philosophy and the necessary emergence of a new system of knowledge, a general organizational science, "with the help of which humanity would manage to organize in a planned manner all its creative powers, its life" (271).

Now we can see why Bogdanov could not have proceeded directly to the project of the *Tektology*, even if the work had shaped itself fully in his mind in the first decade of the twentieth century (which was far from being the case). A prior, facilitating step was necessary, a general "theory" (for lack of a better word). This theory, developed most extensively in *Empiriomonizm* and *Philosophy of Living Experience*, provides the "motivation" for the subsequent work by explaining why it is necessary. It draws up the plot within which the writing of the *Tektology* will count as the culminating symbolic act. And the act itself is nothing other than the implementation of what the theory had found to be necessary in the current historical moment: the realization of the latent-authentic nature of knowledge as a practical-organizational agency. A very peculiar act it is, for its outcome is not this or that empirical state of affairs, but activity as such. In other words, the symbolic act the *Tektology* executes is the act by which knowledge effects, from within itself, a passage into the dimension of practical activity.

Chapter 4

The Organization of Things

"The things are coming!"

Mayakovsky, *Mystery-Bouffe*

Largely left out of the previous chapter was Bogdanov's theory of culture, which constitutes a distinct and important aspect of his oeuvre and is certainly the main focus of interest for students of Soviet culture. Part of the reason for this omission is that Bogdanov's view of culture is simply a variation of his view of knowledge. Literature and the arts are for him elements of the ideological sphere, just as scientific cognition is. All of these participate in the scenario of dissimulation that plays itself out over the entire course of human history. And just as with cognition, the artistic forms of ideology presuppose the moment of laying-bare, of return to their hidden but authentic character as practical-organizational endeavours.[1] These ideas of Bogdanov's became foundational for the program of Proletkult, a movement that – at least in its blueprint – set out to create the culture and science proper to the new dominant class.[2] Carried by such emissaries as Arvatov, Valerian Pletnev, Nikolai Chuzhak, Sergei Tret'iakov, Nikolai Tarabukin, Dziga Vertov, and Sergei Eisenstein, these ideas travelled beyond the studios of Proletkult, significantly shaping what came to be known as the Soviet avant-garde. In this sense, the concerns of the present chapter will not take us too far from Bogdanov's positions.

What I wish to consider in the following pages is not a knowledge that gathers its history in order to change its own nature but rather a cultural practice (formerly called "art") that aims for an analogous transformation. This practice, which shuns the label "aesthetic" and instead calls itself "organization,"[3] "construction," "engineering," "production," or simply "making" (*delanie*), takes its bearings from the material on which it works. In the material, which can appear in a wide variety of forms, the cultural agent – formerly "artist" – imagines an immanent dynamic that prescribes in advance how the material is to be treated, how it is to be fashioned into a thing (*veshch'*). In short, the agent confronts a demanding object. And because the object is able to specify its own making, the agent proceeds as if he exercised no originary agency, as if he were not an author but merely the executor of the will that issues from the demanding object. The duality of fact and act discussed in the previous chapter will return over and over again in the present one: a latent organization discovered as something factual, existing *there*, will furnish the maker with a binding "law of conduct,"[4] supplying an authoritative motivation for the cultural act.

In one of the inaugural statements of the newly formed Left Front of the Arts (LEF), Nikolai Chuzhak expressed eloquently this essential relationship between a nascent practice and the imperative objectivity of its field: "*There* – an entire uprising of things [is taking place] as a result of some process of dialectically developing matter, produced by an unknown collective artist-creator; and *here* – even the very construction of the thing, even the production of values [exists] as some barely reachable, dreamed-of ideal!" ("Pod znakom"13; emphasis added). Ostensibly, "here" is my studio, my writing desk, the place where something called "art" is still being made – the sanctified domain of aesthetic creation. "There" are the streets and the masses, the factories and production, the exertion of labour at its most pragmatic, and the procession of life at its most mundane. But "here" and "there" are also the essential coordinates of representation in the traditional sense, the places, respectively, of the representing subject and the object to be represented. And the project of the Soviet avant-garde should be understood, most broadly, as an attempt to collapse the distance between the two, to make them one. This project, in its various modes and phases – from "objectism," through Constructivism and production art, to the biography of the object and the literature of fact (*faktografiia*) – unfolds in the dramatic divide between "here" and "there," between a point of departure, where the subject and his expressions still subsist, and a point of anticipated fulfilment, where they are to be abolished, swallowed up by the movement of "dialectically developing matter."

A type of cultural agency is thereby constituted whose character consists in the symbolic disavowal of one's being-here. Saying this amounts to much more than restating Bakunin's famous "I don't want to be 'I', I want to be 'We'." Certainly, the space from "here" to "there" can be understood as the separation between the individual and the collective and further thematized within the drama of the Russian intelligentsia, ongoing since the middle of the nineteenth century: its desire and inability to merge with the masses, to be the true voice of the *narod*, and so on; much in the history of the Soviet avant-garde would testify to a similar desire and a similar inability. But if we are to avoid uncritical conflations, we must see how the masses of the 1920s are different from "the people" of the nineteenth-century Russian populist movement – and, for that matter, from any other figuration of the communal in Russian cultural history.

To start, the masses of the 1920s are *working* and *producing* masses, by which I mean some fairly obvious and some not-so-obvious things. Empirically speaking, these are proletarian masses working in factories that produce material goods. In so doing, the empirical masses stand in, "fill in," for something beyond them, something non-quite-empirical: modern-age productivity, the working totality of the economy as such. The masses are not quite *it*. They are not quite "there" yet. These millions of bodies, minds, and muscles are still not one with the Device that works through them, the Device whose most truthful figuration is not the organized working collective but the perfect cohesion and regularity of the machine. In this sense, the Soviet machinism of the late 1910s and early 1920s was driven as much by sober utilitarian concerns as by the anxious realization that the human mass is an imperfect subsidiary to the machine-driven mechanism of production.[5] In those days it was possible to claim, as Aleksei Gastev did, that the people were not yet worthy of the infrastructure created through Lenin's electrification program (*Vosstanie* 21).[6] Gastev's attitude was echoed in the exasperated words of Sergei Tret'iakov, a leading spokesman for LEF: "Every movement, every step of the people, their inability to achieve harmony in work, even their inability to walk in the street in a sensible way, to get on a streetcar, to get out of an auditorium without crushing each other, is a sign of the counterrevolutionary action of tonguetiedness, blindness, and lack of training" ("Otkuda" 202).[7]

Just under the streets, with their hustle and bustle, beyond the exertion of labour at its most pragmatic and the procession of life at its most mundane, lies the essential but latent reality of all these things: the actuality of the masses as an organized communal collectivity, the actuality of labour as a totality of productive activities, and the actuality of life as a process of "dialectically developing matter." To say that the (empirical) masses, the forms of labour, and quotidian life in general, are "not there yet" is to say that these are things to be worked on, organized, interfered with, that these are the demanding objects of a revolutionary practice. For the Soviet avant-garde, this practice begins from an inherited state of affairs characterized by falsehood and distortion, from a "here" as a dissimulative plane of being. Here is the proletarian multitude, still not living, still not acting as the total unity that it is; here is language, whose communicative efficiency lies dormant beneath a multitude of unnecessary conventions passed down from hoary pasts; here are all the things we use in our daily life – food, furniture, clothes – still cast in obsolete shapes and volumes; and, finally, here are all the things called "works of art."

In the realm of artistic production, the predicament of not-being-there-yet arose from the inherited relation between a representing instance and represented objectivity. The very difference and distance between one and the other was seen by the cultural workers grouped around LEF as the source of falsehood and distortion. For them, the page, the canvas, and the stage – those traditional enclosures of artistic representation – framed the disingenuous existence of the object. The "creative personality" was its equally disingenuous subjective counterpart.[8] It seemed obvious that if the object were made *in absentia,* re-presented, it could not possibly be the "real thing" as it existed out there in the real world. The truism of this proposition did little to soften Mayakovsky's passionate rejection of "celestial delights and bookish passions" in favour of "rye bread to chew [...]/living woman to live with" (*Misteriia* 170). Art as the distortive making of the object was to be abolished in favour of a true "creating of things" (*tvorenie veshchei*); the creative personality was to be succeeded by a skilled maker, something between a dexterous artisan and a disciplined technician. From the pages of the Futurist "Art of the Commune" (*Iskusstvo kommuny*), Osip Brik demanded: "Not to distort, but to create [*tvorit'*]. And not an ideal haze, but a material thing ... We love our living, material, carnal life ... If you, artists, are capable of creating, of making, then make for us our human nature, our human things" (qtd in Mazaev 134).

The task was simple: to produce useful material things, things to be chewed on and lived with. For the word "art" to retain any positive meaning, it would have to refer exclusively to this task. In Brik's definition, "art is the direct, material creation of things" (qtd in Mazaev 136). But much more vocal on the cultural left were the likes of Arvatov, Tarabukin, Aleksei Gan, and Igor' Terent'ev, who felt that the word "art" was irredeemably tainted by what it had previously named and who preferred to speak instead of "craft" or simply "qualified labour." As Voronskii, an unsympathetic contemporary, observed:

In our times, writers and critics of the so-called left front ("Lef," "Gorn," the Formalists belong here as well) are leading a rather energetic campaign against the interpretation of art as a *creative act*. "Artistic creation," "intuition," "inspiration" are subjected to vicious derision: some consider these concepts bourgeois or aristocratic, to others they seem unscientific. They attempt to replace them with "work," "skill," "craft," "energetic word-treatment" [*slovoobrabotka*], "device," "technique," "the making of things." (qtd in Dadamian 203; emphasis in the original)

Many years later, Eisenstein recalled the same scene (in which he had been one of the main actors): "Everywhere around – an irrepressible clamor on the ever-same theme of art's destruction: to liquidate its central feature – the image – by means of the material and the document; its meaning – by means of nonobjectivity; its organics – by means of construction; its very existence – through abolition and replacement with the practical, real transformation of life [*zhizneperestroenie*] without the intermediacy of fictions or fables" (qtd in Dadamian 205).

Because they were "aesthetic," the objects of traditional art were not "real" or "material" enough; they belonged to the order of "fictions or fables"; the process of their production was understood as one of dematerialization or derealization. Now all of this was due for reversal: having left the illusionistic space of bourgeois aesthetics, creativity would rediscover itself in the open "there," where social life produced and reproduced itself. Malevich's famous *Black Square* and Rodchenko's less well-known *Pure Red Colour* (1921)[9] had seemed to mark a turning point, or rather, an exit point; having reached the utmost limit of dematerialization here, on the canvas, the object now had only one way to go – it would have to pierce the surface of representation, move outward, and take its place on the other side, among the material things of life.[10] Referring to Malevich's painting, Lisitskii wrote: "If the slab of the square has blocked up the narrow channel of painterly culture (perspective), its reverse serves as the foundation for a new, volumetric growth of the concrete world" (334). Representation "in reverse" was simply the fattening of the world's consumable materiality, the augmentation of "our living, material, carnal life."

The cultural act that overcomes the dissimulation of the object – or, which is the same thing, overcomes re-presentation – deals initially with something called "material." It imparts a form on this material en route to producing useful things. Whatever the object is to be made from – stone, wood, linen – is to be found "out there": a prosaic fact that now acquires an additional significance. The material for what Brik christened as the practice of "objectism" (*veshchizm*) is found in such a state that it does not lend itself to arbitrary, voluntaristic appropriations. It most certainly cannot be dragged "over here," into the sphere of subjective artistic invention, into the studio, that parlour of aesthetic indulgences and idealistic levitations. It needs to be worked "there." In other words, the material is embedded in a determining context of social need and cannot be extracted from it. Furthermore, the formative work performed on the material is of a peculiar kind: in creating, this work does not really create; in transforming, it merely brings out what is already "there" (as the material's immanent usevalue). This kind of work faithfully obeys the implicit demands of the demanding objectivity it confronts and in so doing showcases its own disciplined, non-contingent character. Here we might recall the stone from which Michelangelo made his famous statue, reportedly carving away everything that was not David. Just as mysteriously as David had resided in the formless slab about to be sculpted, social need inhabits the material about to be made into a productivist *veshch'*.

Unlike the Formalists, who were also deliberating on the relationship of form to material, the theorists of objectism – and, later, of Constructivism and production art – saw material as the active agency and form as its subsidiary function.[11] As if soaked beforehand in potential social use, the material was endowed with an immanent preliminary structure, a utilitarian tectonic. The formative activity involved the bringing out (*vyiavlenie*) of this structure, its actualization: "In 'industrial craftsmanship,' the 'content' is the utilitarianism and expediency [*tselesoobraznost'*] of the thing [*veshch'*], its tectonism, which determines its form and construction and justifies its social purpose and function" (Tarabukin 18). The allusion to Bodganov can be gleaned not so much in Tarabukin's use of the word "tectonism"[12] as in the symbiotic encounter between organization as an act (the making or construction of the object) and as a fact (the material's inherent structure).

Arvatov, an associate of Bogdanov's in the early years of the Proletkult movement, believed he had identified the moment in history when the act began to betray the fact, when the construction of material things departed from social utility as preinvested in the material.[13] Throughout the Middle Ages and the Renaissance, art had existed as craft and the aesthetic quality of the object had been a function of its technical perfection. The celebrated "artists" of those days had been simply the most qualified artisans. "Giving form" to the material at hand had meant realizing its social value in a competent manner, in accordance with current technical knowledge. The seventeenth century saw a radical break with this tradition.

Highly qualified artisans began founding workshops for the production of luxury items. No longer part of the communal process of social construction, these craftsmen saw their own work as somehow different from that of "manufacturers." Their craft became "art." "Now artistic production was guided not by *socio-technical tasks*, but by *socio-ideological* ones" (Arvatov, *Iskusstvo i klassy* 12; emphasis in the original). The material was now conceived as a means to an end, and this end (in itself) was "form":

> They started making the legs of chairs in the shape of paws, door handles – in the shape of lilies, book covers – in the shape of grottoes, that is, they completely perverted the essential meaning of every production: instead of turning the elemental forms of nature into socially-utilitarian forms, they started modeling the socio-technical forms after the forms of nature, began copying their external appearance, forgetting that this appearance is the result of an organic structure …that has nothing in common with the construction of the particular objects. (13)

No longer the carrier of a social function, the material became a vehicle for "representation." In that it now served to represent a lily, the metal of the door handle had been violated, its socio-technical *struktura* obscured.

If aesthetics had been the dissimulation of the thing's utilitarian tectonic, the negation of aesthetics was the laying bare of that same tectonic. In their early days, the Formalists saw the purpose of artistic construction as "making stones 'stony'" (Shklovskii, "Art" 12). For Arvatov, "construction" worked towards a similar end: it was the act that demonstrated the useful properties of materials. *Veshch'*, the thing, was simply the product of this demonstration. Yet it is not enough to say that a Constructivist table, for example, is the result of making wood "woody" (instead of "pawy"). Constructivism demonstrates not the natural properties of the material, not its "organic structure" (see above), but rather its socio-utilitarian tectonic. Marx's table, which "stands on its head, and evolves out of its wooden brain grotesque ideas,"[14] is stood on its feet and firmly supported by objective social demand. Yet in the hands of the Soviet Constructivists, it continues to be a curious thing. While still a piece of wood, it already possesses a brain of sorts, for it knows in advance that it will become a table with a very determinate shape.

To show how another material, textile, can "know" its socio-utilitarian structure, let us take an article on clothing design by Varvara Stepanova (writing under the acronymic name "Varst"), published in the second issue of the journal *LEF*. The article begins with a fairly typical declaration: in the revolutionary present, design that hearkens to the whims of aesthetic taste and market-dictated vogues must give way to "clothes [purposefully] *organized* for specific social action" (65; emphasis added). Of course, taken by itself, the textile from which these clothes are to be made does not "know" anything, it does not dictate any specific cuts or stitches. But this is exactly the point: the material does not come by itself; it comes with its own particular "there" – the place where this or that costume is to be deployed – and it must be worked "there." The work required is not just the tailoring of the costume. Just as important is its *demonstration* in "action," at the workplace: "The most important component [of workers' clothing] becomes its *faktura*, i.e., *execution*. It is not enough to offer a design for a comfortable, ingeniously conceived costume – the costume must also be *made* and demonstrated at work; only then we can see it and have a conception of it" (65; emphasis in the original). If in the experimental poetic practice of the Futurists the linguistic *faktura* is the making visible of language's function (predicated on demystifying poetic language's aesthetic properties),[15] the *faktura* of the material in Constructivist practice is the making visible of the material's utility (similarly predicated on demystifying its aesthetic appropriations). Because the act of laying bare is definitive in the making of Constructivist things, Christina Kiaer speaks of them as "transparent": "The transparent thing demonstrates its expediency or *tselesoobraznost'* – the connection between its material form and its purpose – by showing us how it was made" (90).

The Constructivists never work with plain raw matter (*syr'e*). Woven into the textile for workers' clothing is an objective social commission (*zadanie*; Varst 65). This commission should not be thought of as something separate, detachable from the material at hand – an ideal moment that must be "consulted" and "applied" in the process of making clothes. As Kiaer emphasizes (apropos of Tatlin's utilitarian objects), "the materiality of everyday life determines form in a way that is not external to the material ... but intrinsic to it" (52).[16] As with Michelangelo's David, the social commission has somehow entered the Constructivist material beforehand. Now it needs only to be made manifest, that is, rendered as *faktura*: "The organization of the contemporary costume must proceed from the commission to its material modeling; from the specifics of the work for which the costume is intended – to the system of the cut" (Varst 65). Once again, the act of organization – the modelling of the costume, the "system of the cut" – has met the fact – the specific organization of labour within which the costume is to realize its function. Thus the act is no more than the demonstration of the fact, a laying bare, a letting be. Nothing is added to "this," nothing is subtracted. In "making it," "giving it form," the executor is simply letting the essential being of "this," its being there (as an object within a systematic organization of social forces and needs), emerge from latency.

The Constructivists were not always consistent in their terminology and not always agreed with one another.[17] Still, it seems fair to generalize that by *faktura* most of them understood a certain optimal result of practice, a normative state of "laying bare" fixed in the material,[18] with *konstruktsiia* as the organizational act that brought it about.[19] We owe to Maria Gough the insight that the state in question concerns not just the object but equally the subject of practice. On the level of the act, *faktura* – from which Gan coined a verb, *fakturit'* (*Konstruktivizm* 62) – marks the "transfer of the will to form (or the generative or 'moving' principle) to the material itself" (33–4). Gough shows how the term's evolution through the various phases of the avant-garde movement followed an anti-subjectivist trajectory until, with Tatlin and Rodchenko, it came to designate the maker's submission to the otherness he (ostensibly) was shaping, that is, to an objective, "materiological" volition. Gough also explains, apropos of Tatlin, the ultimate rationale behind this ritualistic surrender of authorship: "Once 'liberated' from the task of representation, Tatlin sought ways in which to justify his artistic practice, to prevent its slippage into the realm of a merely arbitrary manifestation of his individual will or subjective choice. In taking up the principle of materiological determination, Tatlin found a means by which to motivate his practice" ("Faktura" 49). Motivation was, indeed, explicitly part of the Constructivist program. In Gan's manifesto, the bourgeois epoch was marked as much by the reign of art as it was by the reign of accident (*Konstruktivizm* 60). Both were to be erased in the era of conscious Constructivism now dawning. Gan quotes with approval his colleague, Rodchenko, regarding the need "to bind [*sviazat'*] the constructor by the law of the expediency of applied forms, their lawful integration" (65). In the eye of a non-partisan observer, Constructivism's artefacts – whether clothes, furniture, or architectural models – may seem thoroughly subjective, voluntaristic creations. Yet they are offered as tokens of determinism at work, instances of necessary practice.

The principles of Constructivism laid out by Gan can be read as a chain of motivation, one that begins with the character of the revolutionary age, passes through the material, and ends by "binding the constructor."[20] Gan took as absolutely primary the fact of ascendant communism. At the next step, he imagined communism as something immanent to materialities, a kind of dynamic that belonged to them and foreshadowed their optimal deployment.[21] This is what he termed "tectonics" (61). We can think of it as the communist volition of the material itself, a volition that knots the ideological and the formal together in the very flesh of the thing.[22] To look at something "tectonically" is to look at it as harbouring a certain essence, an inner character that is waiting to erupt and give the thing its proper shape: "Tectonics is synonymous with organicity, with the irruption of an inner essence" (61). To look at Soviet objects tectonically, then, is to see them in terms of a communist character that is awaiting realization; it is to read material reality as a demand, or commission. "Construction" is the next step in the progression;[23] for Gan, it is the moment of organizational activity through which the demand is taken up. Here we are on the side of the human doer; but in his role as a "constructor," this doer merely hearkens to the will of the material; only insofar as he synchronizes his doings with the implicit tectonic volition will they count as an instance of "construction." *Faktura* is the third, summative and evidential, moment in the chain. It is not in any sense the "highest" one; rather, it is the aspect in which the other two are brought together in a qualitative expression. From Gan's paratactic explanations, it seems that *faktura* characterizes the state of the material after it has been subjected to constructional activity in accordance with its tectonic. Put differently, *faktura* is the point at which evidence is rendered that the execution of the object has in fact obeyed the material's implicit demand: "The material, taken consciously and used expediently, in a way that does not impede the movement of construction and does not limit tectonics is *faktura*" (62).

Glancing back at Stepanova's discussion of workers' clothing, we can now see that the moments of Gan's program are all in evidence there. The social commission that determines the "material modelling" and the "system of the cut" is nothing other than Gan's communist tectonic. The construction of the *prozodezhda,* insofar as it fulfils this immanent imperative, returns the material in a state both other and same: as *faktura.* Other, because now the utilitarian character, previously latent, has been rendered manifest, or, as Stepanova has it, "demonstrated." Same, because when the material is fashioned into an optimally functional piece of clothing it is made more true to itself than before. It should also be obvious by now that Gan's materiological paradigm of *tektonika–konstruktsiia–faktura* is in every way analogous to Kruchenykh's poetological triad of *struktura–rechetvorchestvo–faktura.* In both, the initial term is organization-as-fact; the second is organization-as-act; and the third is the quality that comes to characterize the utilitarian object or the poetic text if their production has been, indeed, fully determined by the demand implicit in the material.

Earlier, I referred to the experimental poetics of the Russian Futurists as a "practical analysis of language." Constructivist practice can justifiably be called the "practical analysis of things";[24] the end result of this analysis is the same: *faktura*, which is to say, the becoming-manifest of their social character *cum* social construction. These need not necessarily be material things: all material or ideological values count as *veshchi* (Chuzhak, "Pod znakom" 15, 37–8).[25] And so does the entity "man" – itself a complex of material and ideological values. Just as the trans-sense verses of the *budetliane* analysed language in order to lay bare its morphological and phonetic tectonic, Meyerhold's Constructivist theatre was to be the practical analytic of human movement that lays bare its physical tectonic. Here the "material" was the human body itself, a biomechanical ensemble whose economy – the efficient generation, distribution, and application of force and motion – obeyed determinate laws. These laws, hitherto neglected, mystified, repressed, fell within the practical-analytical competence of biomechanics:[26]

[On] the basis of studying the human organism, biomechanics strives to create a human being who knows the mechanism of his own construction, who is able, ideally, to manage and perfect it. The contemporary person, living in the conditions of mechanization, cannot not mechanize the kinetic elements of his organism. Biomechanics establishes the principles for the measured analytical execution of every motion, the differentiation of every motion en route to achieving the greatest clarity, demonstrativeness, specular taylorism [*zritel'nyi teilorizm*], of the motion … The contemporary actor must be shown from the stage as a perfect auto-engine [*avtomotor*]. (Meyerhold, qtd in Rudnitskii 265)

It is difficult to imagine a more literal rendition of the Formalist injunction to "lay bare the device." Freed from randomness and sloth, from all the impediments Tret'iakov bemoaned, the Taylorized body of Meyerhold's actor is an object of demonstration, or, rather, an object *as* demonstration.[27] It does not "represent" anything; it simply enacts its own analysis and in doing so becomes a token of biomechanical efficiency. In the "measured, analytical execution" of movements, the body abolishes representation and manifests what it truly is: a device.

And because this body is not only a motion device but also the physical vessel of consciousness, the act that demonstrates and the fact being demonstrated coalesce, furnishing the already well-familiar duality of organization:[28]

In art, we are always dealing with the organization of material ... The art of the actor consists in his organizing of his own material, that is, in the ability to use correctly the expressive means of his body. Within the actor, the organizer and the organized (that is, the artist and the material) are brought together. The formula of the actor would be an equation like this: $N = A1 + A2$, where A1 is the constructor, conceiving the task and ordering its execution, A2 is the body of the actor, the executor who puts into action the directive given by the constructor (A1). The actor must train his material – his body – in such a way as to make it capable of executing immediately the directives it receives. This is necessary, because every expression of force (including the living organism) obeys the solitary laws of mechanics.[29] (Meyerhold 10)

To all appearances, we are witnessing the traditional encounter between subject and object within the human dyad, between soul and body, between the agency of consciousness and its most immediate malleable otherness. But these appearances are deceptive. The directives given to the body are certainly not the imperatives of subjective interiority seeking expression. They are the specific articulations of that same social commission, now injected into the muscles and sinews of the human physique: "1. absence of superfluous, non-productive movements, 2. rhythmicity, 3. correct positioning of the center of one's body, 4. stability" (Meyerhold 10).

We saw that in Gan the "demanding" character of the material issued, ultimately, from the socio-economic context, which is to say, from the dawning age of communism. The same holds true for Meyerhold: the laws of the human body and, hence, the techniques of acting, are for him not truly universal. They are derived from the general physiognomy of the present-day world as it stares at its imminent future:

In the past the actor has always conformed to the society for which his art was intended. In the future the actor must go even further in relating his technique to the conditions of production. For he will be working in a society where labor is no longer felt as a curse but as a joyful necessity of life ... The work of the actor in a society of labor will be regarded as a [form of] production necessary for the correct organization of all citizens' work.[30] (Meyerhold 10)

The movements of the actor are dictated by the properties of the physiological material, but these properties are, in turn, dictated from "there," from the world of industry and the "conditions of production." So that when it executes the biomechanical movements "here," on the theatrical stage, the body of the actor demonstrates its being-there, that is, its socio-economic conditioning, its belonging to an objective organization of labour, to the imperative rhythms of industrial production, to the machine. Thereby, the Meyerholdian actor also acts out the disappearance of the subject. Far from being a reinstatement of the creative subject under a new name, the figure of the "constructor" – not just in Meyerhold, but in the Soviet avant-garde in general – should be seen as a figure of willing subjection, as "the material's assistant" (Gough, "Faktura" 52), which is to say, as a figuration of the subject's absence.

We should remember, however, that this was not a factual absence, but a moment in a cultural performance, an acted-out disappearance. To emphasize once more: the modernist death of the author is a symbolic act; and Russian Constructivism shows us plainly why this is so. It is not enough for the constructor to work upon and simply make the thing. He must do it in such a way as to create the appearance that the thing has willed its form and worked itself out by realizing its own immanent potentials. This is why the constructor's act is not just practical (the practical significance of the various Constructivist designs tends towards zero), but also and primarily symbolic. And the thing that comes out of it is not immediately a utilitarian object, but, first of all, a *token* of social utility. It does not ask, simply, to be taken and used. Rather, it asks to be appreciated as a model-example of communist utility, a showpiece of how social usefulness has methodically and thoroughly predetermined its final form. In simpler terms, the thing cannot be just useful; it must also make a display of its objective usefulness. With the appropriate modifications, the same can be said of the kind of poetry Kruchenykh envisioned and practised. This was not immediately literature, but a token of how literature is made, a display of literariness. And its production was a symbolic act insofar as it was the conscious fashioning of such a token.

We can now give the enigmatic "here" and "there" their proper significance, which so far I have illustrated rather than articulated. "Here" and "there" do not stand for anything in particular; they are not specific, concrete places in either the actual or the discursive geography of the Soviet 1920s. Rather, they are the placeholders in the general relay between the false (dissimulative) being of "this" and its genuine, demystified existence. For every particular practice, these placeholders are "filled" with different realia, so that a specific opposition is expressed on the level of cultural discourse. In Constructivist theatre, such is the opposition between the artistic conventionality of the "stage" and the grand stage of real life. In the anti-passéistic discourse of the Comfuturists (*komfuty*),[31] such is the opposition between the bourgeois art of representation and the revolutionary art of life building. Finally, throughout the history of the Soviet avant-garde, such is the opposition between the individual creative personality (*tvorcheskaia lichnost'*) and the communal creativity of the factories and the streets. As stated earlier, the project of the avant-garde was to abolish the former and actualize the latter, it was a movement from "here" to "there" that could be thematized differently and on various levels: "the individual and the masses," "conventions and facts," "the studio and the factory" ("representation and production"), "bourgeois past/present and revolutionary present/future," "subjective expression and objective social commission" – all of these were different figurations, articulations, of a basic condition that I described a little earlier as the condition of representation, hyphenating the word so as to suggest its more general application, beyond the specialized meanings of artistic, linguistic, or psychological representation.

The agency of the "constructor," no less than the agency of the Formalist literary critic, consists in a demonstrative analysis of how things essentially are. And since their immediate appearance is a (systematic) betrayal of their true nature, since their "here" is not their authentic "there," the constructor's task is to free the object from dissimulation and demonstrate its being-there. In the vacated place of the author, we now have a vehicle for demonstration/analysis – a vehicle that can still be imagined in a human guise (as a constructor, organizer, or engineer) but whose functioning has nothing particularly human about it. If we have to give it a name, we should call it a "conveyor," retaining both meanings of the word: a vehicle that both "conveys" objects, taking them from here to there, and "conveys" them in the sense of demonstrating what they truly are. With regard to the cultural act I have been analysing, these two meanings are identical, they are one. For to convey what the object truly is means to convey it "there," that is, to demonstrate its belonging to a systemic totality of things in the world. And while it might be flattering to imagine that a person, a human being, could perform this function, it is hard not to see that the "conveyor" is a mechanism, and thus is best represented by a mechanism:

I am a kino-eye. I am a mechanical eye.

I am a machine, I am showing you the world as only I can see it.

I am in ceaseless motion, I approach objects and move away from them, I get underneath them, I get on top of them, I move apace with the horse's muzzle, I spear into the crowd at full speed, I run in front of the running soldiers, I fall on my back, I rise together with the airplanes, I fall and soar together with the falling and soaring bodies ...

I decode in a new way the world unknown to you. (Vertov, "Kinoki" 141;
emphasis in the original)

This is Dziga Vertov speaking on behalf of the movie camera or, rather,
speaking *as* the movie camera. Vertov's most powerful statement on screen
remains his *Man with a Movie Camera* (1929); yet the truest statement
of his conceptual position – indeed, of the conceptual position of
Constructivist cinema – is the metaphoric identification between man and
the mechanized medium of filmmaking: man *as* a movie camera, the human eye *become* a cinematic apparatus (*kino-glaz*, *kino-oko*).[32] In the figurative substitution of one for another, "man" is the vanishing term, whose
properties are displaced by those of the vehicle.[33] And the vehicle is the
movie camera, also a vehicle in the sense suggested above: a conveyor
of things.

The camera is an intriguing piece of machinery. By its very construction
and functioning, it inhabits two places at once. It is *here,* sitting on a tripod
or handheld, attached to the eye of the cameraman. But it is also *there,*
with the things of the world, attached to them, spying on them, studying
them. It is simultaneously with the "seeing" and with the "seen." This double habitation is a source of tension, of conflict, which can be expressed in
terms of a schizophrenic denial: "Where I am is not where I am." This dilemma offers two ways of being for the movie camera, and, hence, two alternative modes of existence for cinema: a here-being and a there-being.
The camera can draw the world to itself, to its own absolute position is
space, it can arrange the world around itself, stage it in front of the lens,
invent a world of its own making.[34] Or it can surrender to the world, adapt
itself to the world's structure and rhythms, become the eye of the world's
objectivities as they stare back at us. These alternatives – one inauthentic,
the other genuine – are not a matter of abstract choice. Now, after the
October Revolution, they could be seen as an actual historical sequence,
two moments in the biography of a still very young medium.

Initially, like many other things, the movie camera led a false life, untrue
to its own nature. At the very dawn of cinema, it had been quite sufficient
to show the public such simple facts as a galloping horse or a train arriving
at a station. Very soon, however, the infantile delight in watching moving
objects on a screen was outgrown (Brik, "Fiksatsiia" 44–5). There appeared the need to show more elaborate attractions. What could be easier?!
All that was needed was to enact some kind of dramatic performance and
record it on film (45). It was the age of theatre-become-cinema. The audi-
ences were happy and were quite willing to ignore the glaring distortion of

theatre's three-dimensional space on the flat surface of the movie screen (45). But tastes do change, and soon the cardboard sham and buffoonery of these early spectacles began to offend the eye. The demand for "photogenic model life" (*natura*) was now to be heard. It became clear that some objects and situations easily lend themselves to the camera's "naked eye," while others need some preparatory work (45). New contrivances had to be invented in order to capture the *natura* inaccessible to the camera:

> The studio appeared. The studio is a place where photogenic *natura* is prepared through artificial means: from the entire system of lighting devices to the complicated constructions with the help of which one could create anything, all the way to earthquakes and naval battles; everything in the studio serves one purpose: to create artificially that which the camera is incapable of creating in living reality. In this way, the camera's imperfections, instead of fostering efforts to improve its mechanism, led filmmakers to begin from the other end: from the artificial transformation of the life to be filmed. (45)

The studio circumscribes the disingenuous, here-being of the cinematic apparatus. It is where objects are being re-presented.

The obverse of the concocted studio act is the arrested fact of real life: "life caught unawares,"[35] in Vertov's sloganized expression. Instead of bringing the world to the camera, the camera must go out into the world, "to flee – the sweet embraces of romance, the poison of the psychological novel, the clutches of the theater of adultery ... to flee – out into the open, into four dimensions (three + time), in search of our own material, our meter and rhythm" (Vertov, "We" 7). Although Vertov says "our material," the warning is still in effect: the material is not free to be appropriated in each and every way "we" choose.

Every object, every event, that captures the camera's attention is not a free-floating monad; rather, it belongs – less obviously – to the world's determinate totality and – more immediately – to the social infrastructure (Vertov, "Kino-Eye" 66). Only there, as part of that totality, do objects and events become "facts." And since it is the kino-eye that shows them as such, being their optimal conveyor, they are properly called "film facts."[36] From within the chaos of visual phenomena, the camera must provide a "scientific illumination of reality" (Vertov, "To the Kinoks" 51), placing each event within its effective context. Vertov calls this practice the "decoding of life as it is" ("The Essence" 49, 50), or in another place, the "communist decoding of what actually exists" ("To the Kinoks" 50), and in still another, the "documentary cinematic decoding of both the visible world and that which is invisible to the naked eye" ("From Kino-Eye" 87). Perhaps more explicitly than any other Constructivist project,[37] Vertov's cinematic method – with its scouts (*razvedchiki*), informants, hidden cameras, and sudden "attacks" – is a procedure of unmasking (Hicks 33–8).[38] It is a practice of analysis,[39] one that rescues the object from its dissimulative existence and demonstrates it in its truth (i.e., as a "fact"): "Kino-eye as the possibility of making the invisible visible, the unclear clear, the hidden manifest, the disguised overt ... making falsehood into truth. Kino-eye as the union of science with newsreel to further the battle for the communist decoding of the world, as an attempt to show the truth on the screen – Film-truth" ("The Birth" 41–2).

Let us briefly observe how the camera does its work as a conveyor of things. In this example, taken from another article by Brik, it is a photographic camera – itself a rather sophisticated device – and the thing at which it is aimed is a house. Of course, the house can be captured on film as just a house. But such a perspective, Brik tells us, underlies the falsity of traditional representation: "It is impermissible to present in isolation one house, one tree; this might be very beautiful, but this would be art, it would be aesthetics, it would be an aesthetic savoring of the particular object at the expense of its relation to the other phenomena of nature or the phenomena of human labor" ("Ot kartiny" 33). According to Brik, the vision that foregrounds an object, extracting it, as it were, from its real-life context, is the artistic vision *par excellence;* it is somehow inherent in the practice of painting (31). Photography offers the technical possibility for overcoming this limited, distorting perspective: "Photography is not forced to isolate a particular person in order to capture him; it has the ability to capture him together with his surroundings, to capture him in a way that would make obvious this person's dependence on his environment; the photographer has the ability to solve a task that an artist is unable to solve" (32). In Brik's estimation, photography is uniquely equipped to show the interconnectedness-in-totality of worldly phenomena. And so our house is no longer just a house: "this house is not interesting all by itself ... It is interesting as part of the overall structure of the street, of the city ... Its value lies not in its visual contours but in the function it fulfills within the social environment" (33). Through the photographic lens, the house is "conveyed": it is taken to where it belongs – there, on that street and in that city, within the determinate structure of urban life – and is thus enabled to show what it truly is – a functional element of social existence. It is now a house-fact, a house-truth.

I noted earlier that in order to manifest its identity, to be what it latently and truly is, "this" (in my earlier context, the literary work) must pass through a special place in the topology of our plot: the analytical apparatus, the repository of hermeneutic cognition.[40] As re-enacted in the project of Constructivist cinema, this same movement passes through the kino-eye. It is by way of the kino-eye that the object – a house or anything else – is conveyed to its being-there, that is, to the totality that holds its truth. The kino-eye is not just the camera lens, nor is it the camera mechanism as a whole. Rather, it is a figuration of the entire apparatus of analysis – before, during, and after the shooting – that utilizes the camera's revolutionary potential. The preliminary research, the scouting of locations, the drafting of the shooting plan; the determination of angles, distances, cadences; the actual recording of visual data; the cataloguing of the recorded fragments; the process of the final editing – all of these moments belong to the physiology of the kino-eye.[41]

In the end result, "if the material is correctly analyzed, i.e., if the work of its passportization [*pasportizatsiia*] (the place and time of shooting, the content of the filmed object) is completed, and the meaning of the separate fragments is made clear – not only in regard to their source, but also in regard to the various juxtapositions necessitated by the thematics – the [montage] gives facts their true voice" (Pertsov 35). Although the auditory metaphor runs against the silent nature of the medium, Viktor Pertsov's point is clear: like the material of other Constructivist practices, the material of cinema possesses authoritative and binding dynamics of its own. And like all others, the practice of *kinochestvo* must submit to this authority and abandon the claim to authorship. The cinematic organization of the visual world is stringently determined by the dynamic organization internal to objectivities: "*Kinochestvo* is the art of organizing the *necessary* movements of objects in space as a rhythmical artistic whole, in harmony with the properties of the material and the *internal* rhythm of each object" (Vertov, "We" 8; emphasis added). It is the immanent logic of visible phenomena, not the will of the film director or cameraman, that governs the analytical operations of the kino-eye. As another eminent representative of the Soviet montage school insisted: "The newsreel must demonstrate events truthfully, and the forms of newsreel montage *are determined not by the author but by the material*" (Kuleshov 32; emphasis added). The world guides its own "decoding." This, undoubtedly, is the main "message" of Vertov's manifesto-film of 1929, replete with visual parallelisms between the motions of the industry-driven urban world and the motions of the movie camera. The operation of the former determines the operation of the latter, as if the mechanism of filmmaking were connected by transmission belts to the enormous Mechanism of industry. We can take this a step further and say that *Man with a Movie Camera* projects not two mechanisms working in synchrony, but only one, with the kino-eye representing that part through which the total mechanism of industrial modernity is able to display visually its true character.

This is a crucial moment in the optics of the kino-eye, for it exemplifies the turning inside out of representation in the visual field. Directed at the world, the kino-eye is at the same time *governed* by the world. The world is its "socket," while being also its target. The subject of visual representation (in the traditional sense) is situated behind the focusing point of impressions received from the external world (anatomically, the retina). Directly opposite this point, behind the socket that is the world itself, we can now begin to imagine a different type of agency, a different kind of "subject." This agency is exercised in an act that is the obverse of "seeing": that other subject does not watch; it *displays*. And the organ responsible for this function is, in turn, the functional inversion of the eye: it is an eye that *shows*, one that *demonstrates* through images, an eye that is, really, a *screen*. Cinema, in its double nature as a recording and projecting medium, is thus situated on a significant borderline. Vertov's method of the kino-eye must be understood as an attempt to traverse the ontological split in the scopic field between seeing and manifesting, to attain the point where "looking" vanishes to emerge on the other side and become a pure "letting it show." But this is none other than the movement we have been following all along, the movement from "here" to "there." It now takes place between seeing and the seen, between the here-being of the visual – my gazing, focusing, observing, and so on – and its there-being: the self-display of things, their exhibitionism, the "showiness" of the world in its true colours.

Vertov's *kinochestvo* is just another example of a practice configured so as to appear obedient to the demands of its object. The object is the modern socio-economic world as a whole. It is a smart device but does not show itself as such. To the unequipped, "all too human" eye, it presents the appearance of myriad uncoordinated happenings. (One is tempted to surmise that in post-revolutionary Russia, this appearance must have been particularly striking.) Insofar as this is a semblance only, a dissimulative show, the world is also an implicit demand. It calls for a new method of seeing. *Kinochestvo* is the practical answer to the demand – a kind of practice that lets the object be what it essentially is. It undertakes to lay bare that essential dimension of objectivity that "is not absolutely unseen but missed by sight, subject to oversight," that "which is not given in appearance but from which things and processes have nonetheless in turn derived" (Vertov, qtd in Michelson xix). But we should note, once again, that we are dealing with a symbolic act. Vertov's kino-eye does not simply show the world. It also shows itself as *adapted* to the world, as necessitated by its essential dynamic, and hence as the world's optimal conveyor. Like any Constructivist project, Vertov's filmmaking is a symbolic act because it must demonstrate, beyond any visual contents, its own non-contingent character.

Chapter 5

The Organization of Minds

So far we have been following a cultural act of "organization" that deals with people and things as things, a kind of praxis aimed at the revolutionary transformation of the world's *objecthood*. To the extent that "man" is thematized at all in the (anti-)artistic doctrines of the avant-garde, he appears as determined by his own "thingness" and by the thingness of the world. As he labours, Gastev's man is composed of muscular forces, expenditures of energy strictly quantified in accordance with the task at hand, movements tailored (Taylorized) to the operations of the machine. As he acts, Meyerhold's man is, similarly, an aggregate of biomechanical variables, vectors of motion and exertions of strength, a device under a human guise.[1] As he records visual phenomena, Vertov's man with a movie camera is an optical device synchronized with the device he operates. Insofar as this generalized "man" can still be conceived as a bearer of consciousness, the consciousness in question has been so fully "instrumentalized" that it is indistinguishable from the objective functioning of the device. And because he thus recedes into the impersonal thingness of whatever it is he is working with, man no longer represents. He is now one with the conveyor of objectivity – the vehicle that allows things to be what they are, to demonstrate their true nature and function.

We now inquire into a different kind of praxis – still a project of organization, but one that takes and deals with human beings in their *subjecthood*. The transition we are making is analogous to an earlier one, when we passed from the Formalist theory of the text to its sociological hermeneutic. What we saw then was, first, the truth of "this" emerging in the mode of objecthood: initially dissimulating as something subjective (the author's "message," an "expression" of one's views or moods), literature turned out to be, on the contrary, an object-like entity, a device, a working mechanism. And just as convincingly, afterwards, "this" traversed the same road, but in the opposite direction: from an initial dissimulative being in the mode of objecthood (depicted world), the literary text showed itself to be, really, a systematic thing possessed of subjecthood (Character, *Obraz*). In the same way, we now pass from a form of praxis where the reality of "what is to be done" is dictated by imperative organization of things as things, to one whose coordinates are set by the authoritative systematicity of consciousness.

If we remember that deluded house from Brik's article – a yellow house to be sure – standing apart from the rest of the world in a narcissistic display of its picturesque singularity, we could follow a line of symmetry to the subjective realm and observe an analogous deviancy. The false being of the object in the world has as its correlate the false being of human consciousness. And the whole movement of praxis that seeks to restore the object to its truth, to return the house to its proper place, will now unfold as an exercise upon consciousness, bringing it back to the native place from which it has been estranged.

It has become customary for us today to speak of "cultural politics" as an inseparable component of culture itself. The production of cultural artefacts, of any discourse or materiality that can be conceived as belonging to the domain of culture, always takes place from a certain position, it serves a certain set of interests, and so on. We can assert confidently that the cultural act is always a political act. Yet this "always" has not always been "always." The realization that culture is unavoidably political is a rather recent one. Even more recent is the praxis that puts this realization into action, the conscious act of "cultural politics" itself. In this sense, it could be argued quite convincingly that nothing like organized cultural politics existed before 7 December 1922.

On that day, a rather mundane event took place: a group of young literati gathered in the headquarters of the journal *Young Guard* (*Molodaia gvardiia*) in Moscow and formed the group October (*Oktiabr'*). This was the core of what eventually became the Onguardist movement.[2] Among the founders were Semen Rodov, Aleksandr Bezymenskii, Iurii Libedinskii, Aleksei Sokolov, and Grigorii Lelevich; the critics Illarion Vardin and Leopol'd Averbakh were to join soon after. Most of the group's members were also members of the Communist Party or the League of Communist Youth; most of them had belonged to VAPP, the All-Russian Association of Proletarian Writers (*Vserossiiskaia assotsiatsiia proletarskikh pisatelei*). In retrospect, the mundane gathering was a pioneering attempt to assert on a grand organizational scale the identity of art and politics. Just a few years later, one Marxist critic had this to say about the Onguardist movement: "History knows of no example of a similar effort to build a literature, and in no other epoch was the demand so loudly sounded that creative inspiration be included in the general plan, and the enthusiasm of the poet subjected to a common task" (Kogan, qtd in Brown 17).[3] What emerged from the Onguardist movement was not just one cultural organization among others, but an organization that proclaimed Organization as its supreme principle, a kind of secular sacrament.[4]

This is enough of a hint that in the present chapter we will be moving again in Bogdanov's shadow. The formation of *Oktiabr'* can be seen as a direct consequence of the blow dealt to Proletkult in 1920–1, when that organization was absorbed by NARKOMPROS and its state funding drastically reduced.[5] Proletkult would languish for the rest of the decade, while the Russian Association of Proletarian Writers (RAPP) (and its many subsidiaries) assumed its place as a mass mobilizer of proletarian cultural forces.[6] The latter movement's leaders were often compelled to fend off accusations of being "neo-Bogdanovites."[7] *Oktiabr'*'s platform contained direct transpositions of Bogdanov's views on culture: "Before the proletariat now arises the foremost task of building its own class culture and, consequently, it own literature, as a mighty means for influencing the sense perceptions of the masses" ("Materialy" 193).[8]

The immediate enemy of the Octobrists, against which the group initially defined its identity and purpose, was *Kuznitsa* (The Smithy) – an association of proletarian poets who had seceded from Proletkult in 1919 and presently supplied the leading cadres of VAPP.[9] The split was between two generations of cultural activists, but also between two very different conceptions of what constituted genuine revolutionary culture. In its first pronouncements, *Oktiabr'* accused VAPP's leaders of failing to expand and unify the movement of proletarian literature ("Iz materialov" 199). For the poets of *Kuznitsa,* literature had become the work of self-proclaimed archpriests of art ("Oktiabr'" 206; Averbakh, "Po etu" 83), who had forged a quasi-religion out of some mystical union of class origin and truth. For them, the poet's belonging to the proletariat seemed a sufficient guarantee of his ability to see and convey the world truthfully. Literature was not so much the product of reflection upon the world as a direct emanation from the quasi-divine essence of industrial labour. The working-class poet was the medium through whom the class character of the proletariat was revealed in texts.

In opposition to this mystical creed, the Octobrists demanded the political indoctrination of both proletarian and non-proletarian writers.[10]

Merely belonging to the working class guaranteed nothing, "and often the proletarian artist is very detrimental to the cause of the working class, just because he is so little familiar with the dialectic-materialist method ... [because he] is unacquainted with his class's system of thought" (Libedinskii, "Temy" 124). The act of artistic creation, Libedinskii continued, was not a seance, "and mere intuition, the hope that the proletarian instinct will show the way, that 'the poet is a medium of his class's ... and truth is, thereby, revealed to him – all this is a simple-minded and dangerous utopia" (124). The poets of *Kuznitsa* had failed to realize that cultural acts are political acts and that "political" had nothing to do with *occupying* a place in the socio-economic structure and everything to do with *assuming* a conscious position. True proletarian literature was not necessarily penned by working-class writers; rather, it was literature that "organizes the psyche and consciousness of the working class and the broad toiling masses in the direction of the ultimate tasks of the proletariat as a transformer of the world and creator of a communist society" ("Materialy" 195). Still, in its main thrust, the platform of the Octobrists did not call on writers from other class backgrounds to adopt the position of the proletariat. The proletarian writer himself still had to take the position proper to him. As Libedinskii made clear, the proletariat was, on the whole, divorced from its own "system of thought."

In those days when proletarian culture in Russia was being institutionalized, this seemingly paradoxical condition (the working class's divorce from its own system of thought) was subjected to a penetrating "psychoanalysis" – where else but in Vienna? – by a thinker who was to play a significant role in Soviet cultural politics during Stalinist times. In one of the earlier essays of what was to become a major text of twentieth-century Marxism, *History and Class Consciousness*, György Lukács wrote:

> Now class consciousness consists in fact of the appropriate and rational reactions "imputed" [*zugerechnet*] to a particular typical position in the process of production. This consciousness is, therefore, neither the sum nor the average of what is thought or felt by the single individuals who make up the class. And yet the historically significant actions of the class as a whole are determined in the last resort by this consciousness and not by the thought of the individual – and these actions can be understood only by reference to this consciousness.[11]
>
> This analysis establishes right from the start the distance that separates class consciousness from the empirically given, and from the psychologically describable and explicable ideas which men form about their situation in life ...

> Thus we must never overlook the distance that separates the consciousness of even the most revolutionary worker from the authentic class consciousness of the proletariat. (51, 80)

Without changing its constituent elements, its "situations," "movements," and "acts," the plot we have been following is now to be played out in the domain of class consciousness. Like every other "this" we have encountered so far, class consciousness is, "initially and for the most part," displaced in relation to its authentic being (witness Lukács's repeated use of the word "distance"). As such, it is "false consciousness." Yet its "falsity" is not some idiosyncratic aberration that could be somehow prevented or avoided. It is a determinately necessary moment in the life of the demanding object, of "this." The displacement and falsity of class consciousness is systematic, and so is its authentic being (the "imputed" cognition appropriate for a given class amounts to a determinate "system of thought").

With the appearance of the proletariat, there appears the unique possibility for one class to overcome this discrepancy and actually be what it truly is. Near the end of history, there is now a social identity that could be imminently equal to the *fact* of its latent-authentic organization. But for this to happen, there must be, first, an *act* of organization, a political praxis that treats class consciousness as its field of operation. In its highest instantiation, this is none other than the revolutionary political praxis of the Party, the vanguard of the working class. But why shouldn't there be also – as a subsidiary, a specialized extension, of the Party's function – a cultural or even just literary "vanguard" of the workers' revolution? It was not a secret that, from its very first day, the Octobrists wanted to play this very role. Their official platform, promulgated at the First Moscow Conference of Proletarian Writers (May 1923) and published in the first issue of the journal *Na postu,* stated:

§4

... with the commencement of planned socialist construction in all areas ... and with the movement of RKP (b) [Russian Communist Party (Bolsheviks)] toward a *systematic* and deep propaganda amongst the widest proletarian masses, there appeared the need to introduce into proletarian literature some kind of *system.*

- -

§5

... the group of proletarian writers "October," as a part of the proletarian vanguard infused with the dialectic-materialist worldview, strives toward the creation of such a *system* and regards the achievement of this possible only on the basis of a unified artistic program, ideological as well as formal, which would serve as a foundation for the further development of proletarian literature. ("Materialy" 194; emphasis added)

The institutional framework through which this strong "system" of proletarian literature was to be implemented was established and expanded between 1923 and 1928.[12] The Octobrists founded the Moscow Association of Proletarian Writers (MAPP, *Moskovskaia assotsiatsiia proletarskikh pisatelei*), which in 1925 was incorporated into a national organization, VAPP. When VAPP in 1928 was itself brought within an even broader institutional framework,[13] it changed its name to RAPP, the Russian Association of Proletarian Writers (*Rossiiskaia assotsiatsiia proletarskikh pisatelei*).[14] The prodigious growth of institutional structures and superstructures within the movement of proletarian literature followed its own "natural" progression. The expansion would continue until every single proletarian writer in the Soviet Union was a member of the organization. There could be no "outside" to it, just as there could be no "outside" to the position that afforded the objective representation of reality.

Around this latter issue irrupted the main cultural polemic of the 1920s: the struggle between RAPP and "Pereval," between *Na postu* and *Krasnaia nov'* (*Red Virgin Soil*), between Vardin, Averbakh, and company on one side and Aleksandr Voronskii (1884–1937) on the other. In the early 1920s, Voronskii was the undisputed kingpin of Soviet literature, the official representative of the Bolshevik government entrusted with finding and nurturing fresh literary talent. When the young Onguardists stepped onto the Soviet cultural scene, he became their primary target.[15] To these young cultural militants, who had recently returned from the Civil War, Voronskii represented the distasteful "grimace of NEP,"[16] the threat of cultural restoration on the cultural front.[17] Although the acronym RAPP would eventually become synonymous with hegemonic ambitions and dictatorial tactics – not just in Western but in Soviet criticism as well – Katerina Clark has argued that the movement was a response to an already established hegemony of non-proletarian literary forces under Voronskii's patronage ("RAPP" 210). It started as a defensive reaction by the proletarian left, which had suffered a major blow with the reorganization of Proletkult, and then evolved into a permanent attack, partly because Voronskii was so well entrenched. The activists of *Oktiabr'*, like so many left radicals during the NEP, were only too eager to continue the class struggle in times of peace.[18] This was a struggle for dominance in the field of literature, for privileged access to publishing houses and printing presses, for material support by the government and political endorsement by the Party.[19] But it was also a struggle over principles.

As director of the Krug publishing house and editor of *Krasnaia nov'*, the first and foremost "thick" journal of the Soviet period,[20] Voronskii surrounded himself with a group of non-proletarian writers, the "fellow travelers," whose acceptance of the Revolution was at best personal and whose allegiance to the Bolshevik regime was at best strategic. Justifying this liberal cultural coalition were Voronskii's views on the nature of artistic representation.[21] In what was to remain his principal conceptual exposition, the 1923 article "Art as the Cognition of Life and the Present Day" ("Iskusstvo kak poznanie zhizni i sovremennost'"), he advanced a rather traditionalist, gnoseological understanding of artistic creativity. As the title suggested, art for Voronskii was a means for knowing the world; this type of cognition could rival and complement the objectivity of science (367, 378, 381). The "objective moment" (*ob"ektivnyi moment*) was attained when the author's subjective position was assimilated to the objective content of the represented reality (368–9). In both science and art, a cardinal act of will made possible this cognitive attunement, which excluded subjective "interferences" and allowed the immanent properties of the object to become manifest (368–9). The practical implications of Voronskii's "objective moment" were favourable for the old artistic intelligentsia: one did not need to carry a Party card to gain admittance to the spectacle of truth.[22]

The Onguardists understood Voronskii's meditations to mean that there was some felicitous state of cognition, a phenomenological encounter between perceiver and perceived, that fell outside the lines of political engagement and class struggle.[23] In the following issue of *Na postu*, Vardin and Libedinskii led the attack: "Well, of course, speaking generally, there exists in nature an 'objective moment.' But comrade Voronskii has lost sight of one trivial detail: he has forgotten to point out precisely which class, which party, which ideology, which social, political, and philosophical movements are the bearers of this 'objective moment' [and] which ... stand as die-hard enemies of objective truth" (Vardin, "Voronshchinu" 11). By this trivial omission, Voronskii had opened the door to an illusory space where truth could be possessed solely through abstract ethics, pure exertion of will, and feats of imaginative synthesis.[24] Even to begin to conceive of such a space was a self-indictment. For only through an atavistic mindset – a disposition characteristic of a previous age – could the artist be seen as hovering above social life and representing it "from the outside" (Libedinskii, "K voprosu" 56). Under capitalism, the artist's (typically, *petit bourgeois*) existence is reflected/distorted in consciousness as a disinterested and unfettered pursuit of eternal truths (56). His intermediate class position in society takes on the form of appearance of a messianic licence beyond the bounds of particular "interests" and "agendas." "[Such] a quality is being ascribed also to the artist in our present time, a time of fundamental destabilizing in capitalist society, when this 'from the outside' is laid bare [*obnazhaetsia*] through particular actions in the clash of class forces" (57).

The relation whereby consciousness disavows its own class nature constitutes the basis of its false existence. Truth is to be found in the obverse. Consciousness must discover itself within the totality of which it is, latently and inalienably, a part: a collection of people, events, and lives, to be sure, but *as reflected in consciousness*. The essence of class – and, it follows, the true home of consciousness – is where this collection of people, events, and lives is raised into a system of thought. It is no longer an inert, "factual" aggregate, but an integral whole held together by cognized relations and necessary prospects. A consciousness engaged in artistic representation, if it is to offer us the world as it really is, must see the world from *there*, from within that totality.

The proletarian writer's road to that new and unique yet native point of view is double: "intrinsically," he is driven there by the momentum of socio-historical change; "extrinsically," he is taken there by a conscious practice of political-cultural organization of which he is the object. Intrinsically, the Revolution has "laid bare" the reality of class struggle and redefined the proletarian writer's relationship to his class (55, 57–9). By the same dynamic, "a new reading public creates its own proletarian writer and establishes a new type of connection with him through the writer's consciousness of the social significance of his work, [of his] responsibility toward the socialist revolution" (58). Extrinsically, "this relationship ... is established by the [working] class through its vanguard in the plane of conscious directorship [*soznatel'noe rukovodstvo*] over proletarian literature" (60). What is the essence of this relationship, furthered by both history and organizational supervision? "This is, first of all, a conscious relationship. The artist must stand equal to his own class' worldview, he must clearly understand every turn in the class struggle and participate in it through each of his actions; he must be a conscious participant in the struggle for communism" (59).

As organizations, MAPP, (the new) VAPP, and RAPP were established nowhere else but "in the plane of conscious directorship over proletarian literature." Their existence as structures ("organization" in the substantive) was grounded in the need for that kind of cultural-political praxis ("orga-nization" in its other, "actional," meaning). And we can see immediately that this praxis, like the ones discussed earlier, purports to do nothing to its object – human consciousness – that is not already *in potentia* contained therein. For the consciousness in question – the proletarian – has this most essential content: that it is not *a* consciousness (in the substantive), an in-dividual self, but consciousness (awareness) of others, of collectivity. So for this content to be laid bare, for light to be shed on the writer's respon-sibility towards his own class, is really nothing more than for him to enter his one and only true existence. In Hegelian terms, his consciousness is to be one whose being-for-self is its being-for-others. In the more specific terms of post-revolutionary cultural jargon, the consciousness of the pro-letarian writer is necessarily consciousness of the "social commission." As Georgii Gorbachev explained: "The social [commission] is the pressure on a personality that the environment makes its own mouthpiece of social or class demands. Everything that meets with any kind of far-reaching social response is made by an individual according to a realized or unrealized social [commission]" (qtd in Dobrenko, *Aesthetics* 94).

Yes, indeed – the very same social commission that we encountered in the writings of LEF. To recall, "their" social commission had found an ingenious way into the material object, before that object was given form as a product, a thing of use; and it had resided there in such a definitive and imperious way that the subsequent process of form giving, or "making the thing," had been simply the laying bare of the thing's dormant func-tionality. Because of this peculiar arrangement, apparently soulless stuff like linen had seemed to "know" its social purpose and the tailoring ap-propriate to it. So it is hardly surprising that consciousness should resem-ble that linen in its capacity to possess the social commission latently before displaying it manifestly.

From the inception of the RAPP movement, its leaders were suspected and accused – with very good reason – of seeking to regiment proletarian literature, to command its course in a quasi-military fashion, through po-litical directives and ideological strictures. While openly and proudly declaring that they were a militant formation, mobilized to fight on the cultural front of class struggle, the Onguardists rejected the charge of ad-ministrative authoritarianism. At the 1927 congress of MAPP, they set out to explain their "conscious directorship over proletarian literature."

Responding to an open letter from one of the fellow-travellers, the writer Marietta Shaginian, in which she had raised in a new context the age-old question of freedom and determination in artistic work, Averbakh expounded the dialectic of the "social commission." The social commission proceeds intrinsically from the individual's class-specific social experience. It seeps through and informs his consciousness *immanently, if latently*. It is not some sort of mandate, conceived at Party plenums and imposed "from above" (Averbakh, "O sovremennykh" 11). Yet many writers (like Shaginian) perceive the social commission as just this kind of extrinsic mandate, a political imposition that limits one's artistic freedom. That perception is normal, even necessary. To a (false) consciousness that does not yet fully reflect its position in the world, the social commission may well appear to be a form of compulsive externality. Not so in the case of the "artist-Marxist, who understands the mechanics of social relations" (11). He is aware that his freedom is determined by the "socio-psychological task" of the current historical moment; hence, this determination "does not appear to him in the form of a compulsively imposed requisition for a literary work" (11).

In this manner, social subjecthood, no less than social objecthood, turns out to be an internally segregated field. Its topology encompasses two moments, a "here" and a "there," that can also be grasped and articulated as a progressive succession – a "before" and an "after." The before-, or here-, being of social consciousness is the inert existence of the social psyche (*obshchestvennaia psikhika*). In its acts and representations, this psyche is objectively determined by its belonging to a class; it objectively fulfils a social commission. "Subjectively," however, it remains opaque to this immanent relation. Only in the after-, or there-, being of consciousness does the social commission immanent to it also become manifest in it. In this second state, the social psyche becomes an assumed ideological position. "Psyche" and "ideology" are not qualitatively different conditions or phenomena. They belong to the same ontological continuum: "Marxism does not find an impassable abyss between [social psyche and social ideology]. On the contrary, [Marxism] views social ideology as a definite form of reflected, organized, systematized social psyche" (6).

The transition from false to genuine subjecthood, from unreflected class existence to the position of true class ideology, occurs as a matter of course in the progressive unfolding of the class struggle in history. Socio-economic development itself makes manifest to consciousness the "mechanics of social relations." But an identical effect can be brought about in another way, through a short cut, as it were: through a hermeneutic capable of explicating those very same relations. Quite apart from any actual knowledge the proletariat may or may not possess, there exists a kind of general knowledge – the dialectical-materialist method – that makes visible what is otherwise concealed. What interests us here is not how the method "works" in representing the world, but rather how, anterior to the act of representation, it allows the representing consciousness to attain the position of radical objectivity. In other words, we are not yet asking about the mind's relation to what is to be represented, but instead about the mind's own disposition.

Anterior to the actual production of specific artistic representations, (the organization of) proletarian literature faces the task of producing the proletarian writer himself. This product, as stressed earlier, cannot be a "natural" one. Just as it was not the natural properties of the material that determined the utilitarian fashioning of the thing in Constructivism,[25] so it is not the natural class origin that defines the writings of the proletarian writer as genuine proletarian literature.[26] A proletarian writer is he "*who sees the world with the 'eyes of the proletariat,' who is infused with the proletarian ideals, world view and world-feeling* [mirooshchushchenie] ... It is clear that here the cornerstone cannot be one's profession or social origin, but the *point of view*, ideology" (Vardin, "Revoliutsiia" 79; emphasis in the original).[27] The cornerstone for the proletarian organization of literature is the imperative movement from "here" to "there," which now occurs on the plane of subjecthood, in the field called "consciousness."

The distance separating the two positions of proletarian consciousness, the immediately given and the immanently possible, is once again the distance between a misguided singularity and a determinate totality. The first position, the disingenuous here-being of the proletarian, is the "subjective" (in a bad sense), particular, contingent, and unmediated absorption of class struggle into the psyche (in Lenin's terms, the position of "spontaneity"). Yet there is nothing whatsoever contingent, arbitrary, or fortuitous about the fact that proletarian consciousness should exist in this way. Its distortion, its being as a false consciousness, is systematically induced; it is a lawful extension of its own true being:

> Regarded abstractly and formally, then, class consciousness implies a class-conditioned *unconsciousness* of one's own socio-historical and economic condition. This condition is given as a definite structural relation, a definite formal nexus which appears to govern the whole of life. The "falseness," the illusion implicit in this situation is in no sense arbitrary; it is simply the intellectual reflex of the objective economic structure. (Lukács 52)

Fortunately, to proletarian consciousness is given – by the same systematic and lawful determination – the possibility of transcending this partial and illusory perspective. By a transposition, it can get *there,* "at the heart of that totality" (52), which is the socio-economic structure; it possesses the "ability to see society from the centre, as a coherent whole" (69). That other place of seeing (very similar to the centre of Vertov's totalizing cine-vision) circumscribes the genuine/predestined being of proletarian consciousness.

When the writer is asked to "see the world with the eyes of the proletariat," that is the vantage point to which he is pointed. En route, his "social psyche" (the here-being of consciousness) must be "organized, systematized." The procedure is non-invasive. It is an act of facilitation, a conveyance, really. The organizational manipulation of the psyche – what Evgenii Dobrenko has called the "fashioning of the Soviet writer" (*formovka sovetskogo pisatelia*) – is conceived similarly to the manipulation of the material in Constructivist practice. Now the "material" is consciousness itself, and its *formovka* is aimed at the bringing-out or letting-be of a latent inner content. Dialectical materialism serves as the conveyor that facilitates this process. In passing through the conveyor, proletarian consciousness does not undergo any transubstantiation. Remaining self-identical, it merely sheds its false being. The method allows consciousness to become transparent to its own "situation," its "position," to see itself as in fact determined by both a synchronic and a diachronic totality of socio-economic facts and phenomena. When it is thus conveyed to itself (in both meanings of the word),[28] proletarian consciousness will possess as subject what it has always possessed objectively: its own function and utility, its "present" and "future" – a social commission in the shape of destiny.

As already noted, the term "social commission" originated with LEF, not with RAPP.[29] The latter adopted it, and its members were quick to declare that only they understood its true significance (just as Pereverzev claimed that it was the Sociological critics, not the Formalists, who truly grasped what "device" means).[30] As the ideologists of RAPP saw it, LEF had cast the creator in the non-committal role of hired hand. As such, he bore no responsibility for the final product, for he merely used his expertise to execute a task in accordance with the customer's bidding (the Big Customer was, of course, the Soviet state). LEF, in other words, furnished the chief example of that inauthentic – purely external, instrumental – understanding of the social commission for which Averbakh upbraided Shaginian. The political diagnosis was easy to make: Constructivists, Productivists, and *tutti quanti* were the surviving class enemy, who under the propitious conditions of the NEP sought employment in cultural production alongside all other "bourgeois specialists" working in industry, finance, agriculture, and administration. Against this ideologically corrupt interpretation of the social commission, RAPP brought to bear its own, organic conception: "the proletarian writer [must] find within himself the social commission of its class, not as something externally given ... but as a living fact of his own inner world. Not for a minute should the artist stray from this genuine social commission" (Gorbov, qtd in Dobrenko, *Formovka* 108). In short, the social commission is immanent to the writer's psyche; it is not some political dictate to which he owes obedience. What the critics of RAPP failed to notice is how much their own effort to imagine the social commission as native to the individual psyche resembled the Constructivist effort to imagine it as residing in the material. This was, structurally, one and the same imagination, one and the same plot, played out in two different dimensions: thinghood in one case, subjecthood in the other. In both cases, however, the imagination served to "motivate" practice by investing its object with a preliminary tectonic, an essential yet dissimulated organization, which a demystifying revolutionary act would make manifest.

In the ranks of RAPP, there was an ongoing debate over whether proletarian literature should have its own method, whether next to the general guidelines provided by Marxism there was a need and a place for a doctrine specifically suited to the purposes of artistic representation. Some considered the distinction immaterial.[31] Others thought it necessary to speak of "proletarian realism," mainly in order to distinguish a new way of artistically apprehending reality from the approach implicit in the bourgeois realisms of the past.[32] Quite often, under the rubric of "style," the problem of artistic methodology was conflated with the question of whether proletarian literature possessed a special character that separated it from all other literary traditions. Nobody could dispute the axiomatic assertion that, by virtue of working-class consciousness's unique perspective on the world, its artistic productions must indeed manifest a unique quality, a distinct style.

Little could be said of this quality, short of restating in qualitative terms the substantive advantages of being "at the heart of that totality," of being able "to see society from the centre, as a coherent whole." The clarity, objectivity, and comprehensiveness afforded by being there meant that the style of proletarian literature was, necessarily, clear, objective, and comprehensive. Borrowing a term once used by Marx, a certain B. Reich proposed that the new literary style be called "sociographics." He went on to explain:

It seems to me that that the term "sociographics" defines the "special style" of the working class, its "special character" expressed in a "special form."

The attributes of sociographics are: *precision* – each of its lines, each of its signs is the exact equivalent expression of precisely quantified magnitudes; *unambiguous, unmediated, demonstrative reproduction* – each of its lines, each of its signs, conveys content in a form which excludes any approximation, any digression into another content, and which demonstrates plainly the inter-relationships within the content. [Sociographics] is *universally comprehensible, concise, concentrated;* each of its lines, each of its signs, is made clear through universally comprehensible means. It brings together homogenous entities and distills their most characteristic features. (21; emphasis added)

In not so many words, the envisioned style of proletarian literature is simply the perfect analytic of every possible social content. In it, writing and reading coalesce. "Each line, each sign" appears on the page only to dissolve into a pure transparency vis-à-vis the object it delineates. To write is to render legible; to apprehend is to demonstrate; to have seen is to have shown.

It is difficult not to see the conceptual symmetry between Reich's vision and Vertov's: both anticipated a universally intelligible sociolect[33] (one on the screen, the other on the page); both emphasized precision and scientific rigour;[34] and both embraced a peculiar dialectic of perception operating in seemingly heterogeneous experiences. Now, in the field of consciousness, which lends itself so easily to analogies with sight and vision, we once again approach that threshold between seeing and the seen, where the first promises to cross over and merge with the second. The eye of consciousness, like the mechanical eye of the movie camera, promises to void the distance separating it from the object of observation and become the pure showing (demonstration) of things as they are.

And just as the camera, once freed from its false existence in the studio, discovers its true position to be literally *in medias res,* in the midst of things, in those interstices of the world where its totality is being knit, so does the proletarian artistic consciousness. It is the same road and the same destination. On the iron rails of objective *pre*destination, "this" accomplishes the trip back from re-presentation, from its alienated, cast-away being. Unlike the theorists of the left avant-garde, the "organizers" of proletarian literature did not aim to abolish artistic representation. On the contrary, they remained strictly within the framework of the traditional vis-à-vis of subject and object, author and portrayed reality. And yet, within this old-fashioned framework, a novel relation between the two terms is established. The author now bears that title through a new kind of endowment. Not he is an author who, keeping reality at the distance of artistic perspective, "depicts" it in writing, but he who apprehends how the reality of which he is part has never ceased to write *through* him and *in spite of* him. Aphoristically, we can call an author the individual who maintains this line of determinism by consciously accepting the "through" so that it is no longer "in spite of." For the theorists of RAPP, genuine authorship amounted to active awareness of lost authorial rights. "One can definitely say that the RAPP's theory of creativity, through all its changes, remained a theory of impersonal creation. In this, the RAPPists remained followers of Proletkultism ... In this respect, they converged with the their enemies from LEF" (Dobrenko, *Formovka* 47).

Having consciously assimilated his work's inevitable dependence on the historical existence of his class (the social commission), the writer enjoys freedom in necessity.[35] Try as he may, he cannot free himself from the social commission. He can only accept it freely and freely employ his abilities in the task of fulfilling it:

> He is free in the choice of his theme. He is even freer in his use of methods for shaping the material at hand. But we know that his freedom is a function of class necessity ... In the free choice of theme, the author is determined by the social-psychological task of the present day. This is how we understand the social commission. This is why we say that the artist-Marxist, who understands the mechanics of social relations ... does not need the illusory freedom of artistic work. (Averbakh, "O sovremennykh" 11)

Averbakh's words do not in the least dispel the ambiguity pertaining to the author's position in the world. Is the proletarian writer seizing upon something, or is something seizing upon him? Is he really "choosing" his theme, or is the theme "choosing" him? As conceived by Libedinskii – himself a proletarian writer of some renown – the subject of a work, its "theme" (*tema*), documents the author's objective relation to the social world ("Problemy" 20). That relation is, certainly, given, not chosen. Developing a theme by means of writing is similar to solving a mathematical problem. The problem as given contains in embryonic form its own solution (20). Hence, the author's activity is the activity of demonstration, of bringing out and making manifest this initially concealed solution. But since he is himself an inextricable part of the problem, since it is *his* objective relation to the social that will emerge at end of the process, he is equally that which demonstrates and that which is being demonstrated, the "subject" and the "object" of representation, the portraying and the portrayed.

Let us turn back for a moment and recall that the theory of Constructivism features two general types of object. One is a thing that does not "know" its social tectonic, does not demonstrate it – that is, it is a thing that abides in a state of dissimulation, or re-presentation. The other is a true *sdelan-naia veshch'*, which is to say, a thing in which the social tectonic is revealed (*vyiavlena*) in the process of making it and that appears as *faktura*. We can think of it as a self-conscious thing, an object whose composition and appearance bespeak the social commission. The second type of object is nothing other than the overcoming of the first. Analogously, the theories of RAPP present us with two contrasting types of subjectivity. One is a consciousness that is oblivious to its class nature and the imperatives issuing from it. The other is a consciousness that has grasped its functionality within the living social whole. The Constructivist dialectic of *tektonika* and *faktura* is restaged in the literary criticism of RAPP as a dialectic of *klassovost'* and *partiinost'*.[36] Every art is, by definition, a bearer of *klassovost'*, for it is objectively in the service of a class. But this may be only a latent moment, just as the social tectonic can be. When *klassovost'* is rendered manifest, we are dealing with *partiinost'*: the conscious taking of a political position in defence of a particular class interest. Put differently, *partiinost'* is the laying-bare of *klassovost'*, its fixation as the determining quality of the text, as the ideological *faktura* of writing. The overcoming of dissimulation is achieved in one case through the method of Constructivism and in the other through RAPP's method of dialectical materialism.

Human interiority, consciousness, appears at first sight to be quite different from, say, linen or stone. But just like linen and stone, consciousness emerges from its dissimulative being to find itself as one "item" in a field of otherness that is knowable and available to praxis. This field consists of things that are coextensive with individual consciousness in such a way that their coexistence forms a systematic and "working" ensemble, a totality. The agency that informs the whole, whatever makes the totality "work" and "behave" in rationally predictable ways, also "disposes" of each particular item in a lawful and necessary manner. Consequently, it gives to consciousness, no less than to stones and linen, a "disposition": a tendency to which it conforms, a function it cannot but fulfil, a shape it will eventually assume. So it is not surprising that object-like and subject-like items alike should be immanently invested with something called social commission and, through it, act as demanding objects. This is the operative principle of the whole of which they are constitutive parts, just as the *dominanta* and the socio-psychological tendency are the operative principles of textual totalities.

As something separate from the totality and its operative principle, there exists the general hermeneutic of "how it all works" and "what it all comes down to." This knowledge is neutral. It does not interfere with the analysed phenomena but simply raises them into clarity. Under its grasp, "this," the cognized field, is conveyed to its own "unconscious": the true if hitherto concealed interrelations among its items. Similarly constituted is the cultural praxis that calls itself now "construction," now "organization," now "systematization." Whatever this praxis approaches proves to be a thing with a disposition and purpose, a thing already headed somewhere. In this way, a cultural "making" becomes possible that is characterized by the unobtrusiveness of pure analysis. To organize items, whether they are possessed or deprived of consciousness, means to convey them to what has always been "there," behind them – to their "unconscious." Human or not, animate or not quite, they prove to be possessing and possessed of a certain "structure," "tectonic," or "organization." Here the ambiguity sets in, for this property of items, whatever its designation, is neither fully within nor fully outside them, it is neither solely *their* property nor entirely bestowed upon them from without. The utilitarian tectonic of material things and the socio-psychological tectonic of human subjects are what relates those things and subjects to the background totality and assigns to them a function therein. It constitutes their identity and, by the same token, refers them to where this identity is no longer theirs to own. For human subjects, the issue of identity is also an issue of agency. It is a matter of that very same "making" and "doing," whether it comes in the form of seeing, building, or writing. In all of these forms, the act apparently issuing from the subject contains two vectors. To be what he truly is, to enjoy identity, the individual must in the same act affirm himself and showcase the operative principle of the systematic totality to which he belongs. He must allow another agency to pass through him uninhibited; another act, an imperious one issuing from the totality as a whole, must come to inform his act.

In Western scholarly literature, it has been customary to see RAPP as a forerunner of socialist realism, a grand rehearsal for the Stalinist cultural orthodoxy. Correspondences are certainly easy to find: the pre-eminence of ideology under the banner of *partiinost'*; the "massification" of literary activity; the bureaucratization of the cultural sphere; RAPP's Five-Year Plan for literature; the insistence on a single correct line in artistic affairs; and so on. Nor should one forget how instrumental were the militants of RAPP during Stalin's cultural revolution of 1928–31, which paved the way for socialist realism. Yet, these facts could serve equally well to measure the radical difference between the culture of the 1920s and the one that came to replace it. Everything in RAPP's theoretical and practical activity was based on the assumption that the class struggle would continue. After all, the distance between false and true artistic consciousness is, at bottom, simply the distance between two positions in that very class struggle.

Socialist realism, by contrast, begins where the staging of a unified Soviet society begins. So it is not surprising that the first act in the institutionalization of socialist realism was the dissolution of RAPP: the organization was deemed incompatible with the era just inaugurated. And so it was ...

This incompatibility had conceptual consequences. *Klassovost'* was central to Onguardist theory, as was the dialectic between it and *partiinost'*. In socialist realism, *klassovost'* quickly lost its significance, with the concept of *narodnost'* (popular character or spirit) gaining prominence at its expense.[37] Insofar as *partiinost'* was no longer interpreted as active partisanship on behalf of a class interest, it came to mean obedience to the directives of the Party, since these expressed perfectly the interests and will of the monolithic *narod*. All of this adds up to one ultimate, summative difference. The project of RAPP, inherited from Proletkult, was to (re)organize the writer's psyche; it followed from the gap postulated between dissimulated and true class consciousness. This was a version of Bogdanov's global imperative for the "gathering of man." RAPP was a zealous implementer of the cultural revolution in part because its leaders assumed, as Bogdanov had, that socialism could not be achieved without such a revolution. By contrast, the orthodoxy of socialist realism, whose founding act was the Party resolution of 1932, was based on the assumption that a cultural revolution was no longer needed. The rhetoric for "raising the cultural level of the masses" remained. But with socialism supposedly "built in its foundations," this was the verbal form of an altogether different narrative: the masses had to be made more "cultured"[38] so as to fit better a stage set that had already been erected. As I hope to show in the second part of this study, a project for reorganizing the individual psyche in accordance with Marxism could have no place in the Stalinist era. This may sound counterintuitive, yet follows straightforwardly from the ontologizing perspective so characteristic of Stalinist ideology. Because the teachings of Marx and Lenin had already become the lived reality of millions, no "organizational-practical interference" was necessary. Instead, the writer was simply enjoined to "know" that reality, which meant to live it fully, to become integrally "one of us," one with the socialist *narod*. (Now conjoined with *narodnost'*, the Stalinist principle of *partiinost* censored not ideological deviations but aberrations in being.) Along with hydroelectric plants and steel mills, the First Five-Year Plan was said to have brought into existence the New Soviet Man (and Woman). Hence, there could be no question of some activist and systematic "gathering of man." This was deemed a *fait accompli*.[39] All that remained was to "show" the fact or, rather, to let the fact show itself.

PART TWO

Chapter 6

The Anonymous Centre of Style

True art can issue only from a purely anonymous center.

Rainer Maria Rilke

Look where one will, can one find the great personalities that would justify the claim that there is still an art of determinate necessity? Look where one will, can one find the self-evidently necessary task that awaits such an artist?

Oswald Spengler, *The Decline of the West*

In the first part of this study, I plotted out several episodes of cultural-theoretical imagination. From the very outset, the assumption was that these imaginations had something in common. And it is this commonality that has justified my referring in the singular to a "plot," a "cultural act," a "symbolic performance," and, of course, *the* death of the author. The story I set out to (re)tell, in a specific national context, was about the anonymous centre that Rilke proclaimed to be the source of all genuine artistic activity. The theories discussed on the previous pages interest me insofar as they seek to define this anonymous centre and place artistic practice in relation (subordination) to it. In defining it, they name it: "dominant," "constructive principle," "psycho-sociological complex," "social commission," "true class ideology." In all cases it is something faceless: a law, a principle of organization, a paradigm for generating form or content. It is something like the unconscious of the text, which a new type of practice would be able to repossess and lay bare. To fix theoretically the anonymous centre is already to anticipate a kind of activity – still within or already beyond art, but revolutionary all the same – that would be its conscious activation, mobilization, demonstration.

The story of the anonymous centre is much broader than the intended scope of the preceding chapters. Although the discussion in them focuses largely on the post-revolutionary decade in the Soviet Union, I have gestured – where appropriate – to the broader context of modernity and modernism. I do not presume that with incantations such as "anonymous centre" and "the death of the author" one can unlock once and for all a phenomenon as complex as modernism. I do believe, however, that if we properly grasp what these incantations stand for, what their genuine content is, we may appreciate better an important aspect of modernist culture.

When we inquire into the death of the author, we come to behold not a fact or a state of affairs but an entire "production," call it ritual, performance, act, or plot. We are not simply registering the existence of an anonymous centre; we are witnessing the positing of such a centre, and we are compelled to ask, "What are the conditions under which someone like Rilke (or Mallarmé, Cézanne, Joyce, Kruchenykh, Tatlin) would posit depersonalization as normative for artistic practice?" Which is to say, we go from a putative fact to an act performed by someone, an act whose significance is to be measured not so much by its effectiveness (practical outcome) but by the larger drama within which – or out of which – it is performed.

As I maintained earlier, what characterizes modernism, perhaps most of all, is the problematic status of art itself, the radical uncertainty as to how and why there should be anything like artistic labour at all.[1] This labour in fact took place, but it did so under a question mark: "What calls for this work? From where does it issue? What necessitates it?"[2] The individual artefacts were the practical responses to this question, yet in them the question was often obliterated as such. In the mere fact of their existence – that is, insofar as they are – they have already left behind the doubt as to whether anything really calls for that existence. But there is more: there is a certain muteness specific to modernist works that prevents them from saying what it is that has brought them to life. When we read a work like Lermontov's *Hero of Our Time*, we do not feel the need to ask: "What occasioned the telling of this story?" The story itself tells us what makes it worth telling: a new psychological and social type can be identified, a character who captures what "our time" is about. To delve into this character's deeds and psychology, to present the motives of his actions or inactions, is to reveal the physiognomy of the present. In other words, the novel draws its significance from its reference to a world of shared significance, in which the intended audience is expected to recognize certain facts as "relevant," "typical," or "essential," but also a world in which an individual human character can be seen as condensing the character of an entire age. Needless to say, this is not the world in which modernist culture took shape.

> When a writer works out a plot, he tacitly assumes that there is a rational structure in human conduct, that this structure can be ascertained, and that doing so he is enabled to provide his work with a sequence of order. But in modernist literature these assumptions come into question. In a work written on the premise that there is no secure meaning in the portrayed action, or that while the action can hold our attention and rouse our feelings, we cannot be certain, indeed must remain uncertain, as to the possibility of meaning. (Howe 144)

Irving Howe's statement raises only one objection: it is not really a matter of a *rational* structure of conduct, but rather of an implied social agreement that a certain order of doings and experiences amounts to a meaningful event.

What the modernist work brings into the world no longer appears with this kind of self-evident significance.[3] Hence the need for motivation, for grounding the act of creation, and, yes, for "theory." What the artefact itself cannot say must often be enunciated somewhere else, somewhere on the side, in a meta-statement, a manifesto, a program, a theoretical essay. No other moment in history had brought together so many artists who also engaged in theoretical meditations on the prerequisites and essential nature of their trade. The names of Apollinaire, Metzinger, Léger, Kandinsky, Eliot, Boccioni, Bely, Zamiatin, Kuleshov, and Eisenstein are but the beginning of a very long list. And this is not by chance. The programmatic pronouncements of modernist artists were not something incidental to their practice, a commentary that might as well not have been offered. They were the integral unsaid of that practice. They were called for by a kind of work that, as it got under way, had to explain what called for it. The problematic status of the text called for the appearance of a meta-text (Cherniakov 88).

From the early days of Russian Futurism – a movement that arguably had nothing but early days – sarcastic observers pointed out the discrepancy between poetic practice and programmatic activity. Vadim Shershenevich quipped, "All that we have of Futurism is the program of the Futurists" (qtd in Ivaniushina 32). And Gustav Shpet chimed in: "Futurism is the theory of art without art itself. A Futurist is he for whom theory is the beginning, cause, and foundation of art" (qtd in Ivaniushina 33).[4]

With even greater force, these diagnoses would apply to the radical currents that made it their goal to dissolve art into life. The work of the
Russian Constructivists never really moved beyond the stage of theorizing
and experimental modelling, and the same can be said of its offshoot, so-
called production art. Yet we could do more with these facts than use them
to indict the said movements for being creatively futile or brand them as
"utopian" (with all the various political accents that word may have under
different scholarly pens). We could take them instead as an invitation to
think of "projecting" and "modelling" as constitutive of the modernist
project rather than as extraneous preliminaries. To do justice to Russian
Constructivism is to recognize that in some essential sense the model *is* the
work. And this is because the work is nothing other than the working out
of the question, "Since the end of culture is upon us ... what are artists to
do?" In this working out, it is a difficult and ultimately unrewarding task .
to fix the border where "theory" ends and "primary text" begins.

I am suggesting that being "faithful to the text" may in fact mean not
losing sight of those conditions that enabled the text to come into being.
Like any other, a modernist text is a sign of a particular kind, with its own
definite inner organization. But this sign, since it is in fact a token, does not
sign on its own, solely from within itself. Its full significance can only be
appreciated within the plot of the symbolic performance to which it belongs. It is one of the great ironies in the history of academic thought that
modernist texts have become the showpieces for formalist analysis, for they
are the least capable of explicating their own import. If it is true that modernism aims at "the wholly manifest, self-sufficient object" (Fox, qtd in
Sayre 9), then it is an error of critical thought to treat its works as if they
were in fact such objects.[5] In so doing, we fail to take into account the aim-
ing itself, that desire for the autonomous existence of the work, which is
itself part of the work. Differently put, the self-sufficient object is not an
accomplishment but a projection; it is a destination, not an arrival.[6] It is
worth insisting, with Barret Watten, that "modernism is not so much what
it *is* as what it *does*" (223; emphasis in the original), that the *fact*uality of
its works cannot be separated from their *act*uality, that is, the projection of
"a deferred or missing horizon of comprehension that it is necessary for
the percipient of culture at large to fill in" (223).

For all of these reasons, it is pointless to ask whether any of the theoretical projections discussed in the previous pages were fulfilled in practice.
Who would venture to say whether some "individual talent" ever made the
wealth of "tradition" fully present in a work of poetry, as Eliot counselled?
And is it not inane to ask whether the Productivist designs were truly

faithful to the "social commission," or whether the *budetliane* did (or did not) attain that moment when "the word as such" spoke in their verse? Eliot's "tradition," LEF's "social commission," and the Futurists' *slovo kak takovoe* mark the enabling/legitimizing horizons of practice. As such, they should be thought as one with that practice; yet they cannot simply be read from its finished product. By the same token, the death of the author cannot be read from the text in which it supposedly occurs. It is a symbolic performance whose effectiveness, or reality, is the same as its intentionality. In simpler terms, we should make sure to count the reaching and not just the getting.

This was the source of Barthes's critical mistake. He took the death of the author and the anonymous being of the "writerly" in terms of simple, unmediated reality, as factual accomplishments of modernist writing.[7] He answered in the affirmative the inquiry I just characterized as pointless: "Yes, indeed, in modernism the text became the domain of pure language, unencumbered by the author, his authority, intentions, etc." Barthes took the modernist manifestoes at their word and thus failed to count the reaching along with the getting. When it seems that "only language speaks," it is really the desire to make language speak that speaks.

The concept of the cultural act presupposes the broader purview that allows us to account for this horizonal nature of the modernist undertaking, for the reaching that may not get its prize, for the projecting that gives full meaning to the now worn-out phrase "modernist project." It also allows theory to be seen as belonging to modernist practice and the work, rather than being a heterogeneous phenomenon located on another (meta-) level. Modernism is inescapably, constitutively theoretical, if by theory one understands the exigency of self-reflection, of justifying the very existence of art, of laying a foundation for that existence. The finished product itself cannot accomplish this. It can merely be, yet it cannot explain why this should be so. To quote the famous opening of Adorno's *Aesthetic Theory:* "It is self-evident that nothing concerning art is self-evident anymore, not its inner life, not its relation to the world, not even its right to exist" (1).

But does this broader scope of hermeneutic vision not open the floodgates for all sorts of circumstantial information to bear upon the analysis of texts – the very licence that the Russian Formalists rejected, thereby inaugurating modern literary theory? Do we not face the danger of regressing to the type of scholarship that Jakobson lampooned as *causerie* ("On Realism" 38), which may well venture to relate "Lermontov's poetry and grain exports in the 1830s" (Eikhenbaum, *Moi* 54)? There is really no need to develop elaborate methodologies in order to meet this objection.

It should be no more than an exercise of common sense to see that Lermontov's poetry does not raise the question of grain exports; neither does "The Overcoat" thematize Gogol's libidinal economy. Of course, one should feel free to use Marxism (vulgar or not) or psychoanalytic theory to shed light on these texts, and the cognitive crops may well be worth the effort. But such deployment of theory has little to do with the hermeneutics that take Vertov's writings on cinema to be relevant for reading *Man with a Movie Camera.* Whether we call the film a theoretical exercise or not, it most patently sets out to answer those general questions about the nature of cinema, of vision, viewpoint, truth, and so on, that Vertov's writings spell out.[8]

Since the example of Vertov's manifesto film may appear too obvious, too "tendentious," let me turn to a work that has nothing like the canonical status and programmatic quality of *Man with a Movie Camera:* Aleksei Gastev's *Pachka orderov* (*Pack of Orders*). It appeared in 1921, at a time when its author had already decided to abandon poetry and devote himself to the scientific management of labour (the previous year he had founded TsIT, the Central Institute of Labor). Gastev's swansong is anything but a song, and to call it poetry in prose says more about one's passion for classification than about the nature of this work.

Before we even get to what should be the "main text," an introductory page written in standard prose serves us Gastev's proclamations on the thunderous march of history, followed by something called "Technical Instruction" (*tekhnicheskaia instruktsiia*):

> "Pack of Orders" is to be read in measured pieces, as if these were fed into an apparatus. In the reading there should be no expressiveness, pathos, pseudo-classical aplomb and strong, pathos-laden accents.
>
> Words and phrases follow each other at the same speed.
>
> A massive action is under way, and the "pack" is offered to the listener as a libretto of thingly events [*veshchevykh sobytii*]. (215)

The need to preface the text with a manual on how it is to be taken and declaimed is itself a rather significant gesture. It suggests – at the very minimum – that what follows is not self-evident, that it does not explicate its own status or significance, the conditions of its production and reception.

What follows are indeed orders, the great majority of them quite extravagant, "packed" in ten numbered clusters. The phrasing throughout is terse, telegraphic. There are no subordinate clauses. As one would expect, the imperative predominates; where it is not expressed grammatically, it is implied; all other forms of the verb have been jettisoned, and so have the tenses. The specialized lexicon of industry, science, and warfare outweighs everything else and frequently morphs into strange nominal compounds and neologisms (*snariadopolet, agitkanonada, inzhenerit', mozgomashiny, elektronervy, arterionasosy*). Action is everywhere urged or imposed, never simply narrated. Verbs are often dropped and replaced by dashes, as if spelling out the action to be performed would take away from its urgency. When declarative sentences do appear, they register rather than describe, reading like entries in some chillingly dispassionate cosmic bookkeeping: "Тридцать лбов слизано, – люди в брак" (216).[9] The orders are issued in the impersonal form of the imperative, the infinitive (e.g., *sdelat'*), and not in the first-person singular (*sdelai*) or plural (*sdelaite*). The implication is clear: the text posits no addressee; the commands directly command being, and not some human agent, individual or collective, whose task it would be to implement changes in being.

As the orders pile on, the scope of their jurisdiction expands hyperbolically in every direction, across spaces and ontological spheres:

> Supply with horses [*oloshadit'*] the inhabitants of Australia.
> Rejuvenate the Canadians by 30 years.
> Take a report in three minutes from half a billion sportsmen.
> Make a summary of the reports in 10 minutes.
> Turn on the sun for half an hour.
> Write on the night sky 20 kilometres of words.
> Dissolve consciousness into 30 parallels.[10]

At times, we are clearly confronted with technical instructions. At others, the tone perceptibly changes and the items of some more familiar, even poetic vocabulary are allowed to make an appearance:

> Requiem in the cemetery of planets.
> Roar in the catacombs of worlds.
> Millions, to the hatchways of the future.
> Billions, stronger than cannon.
> Slavery of the mind.
> Fetters of the heart.[11]

But this allowance is very much calculated. The mixing of registers – from drily technical matters to items like human hearts and emotions – is meant to make a point: all of these things now have been brought together, without much distinction, under some total global management.

What, then, is this text "about"? I would say: it is about every thing but one. It names a great many things indeed: equators and meridians, towns and populations, cubes, colours, the sun, music, literature, lathes, molecules. Ideally, at least, it should name everything. Within its scope falls every item, of whatever kind, that is subject to command. But the point is, precisely, that the whole of being, in all grades, magnitudes, and individuations, is now placed under human control; all is orderable. Yet even if the text extended indefinitely, until it imperatively named every existent, directing it towards this or that practical end, it would still leave one thing unaccounted for: the whatever-it-is that does the directing. The only thing that cannot be commanded is the commanding itself. Here the text reaches its absolute, self-imposed limit. Since only orders are to be given (i.e., naming can come only in the form of ordering, and not as part of a description, narration, or explanation), and since that which does the ordering cannot itself be ordered, it also cannot be named.

At this impassable limit, Gastev's programmatic writings provide the missing perspective, allowing us, in reading, to complete the work. Two years before the publication of *Pack of Orders,* he wrote in an article on working-class culture:

> The mechanization, not only of gestures, not only of production methods, but of everyday thinking, coupled with extreme rationality, normalizes to a striking degree the psychology of the proletariat ... It is this that lends proletarian psychology such surprising anonymity, which permits the qualification of separate proletarian units as A, B, C, or as 325, 075, or as 0 and the like. In this normalization of psychology and its dynamism lies the key to the prodigious elementariness of proletarian thinking ... In this psychology, from one end of the world to the other, flow potent massive streams, making for one world head in place of millions of heads. This tendency will next imperceptibly render individual thinking impossible, and thought will become the objective psychic process of a whole class, with systems of psychological switches and locks. ("Kontury" 330–1)

I do not think we are forcing extraneous matters onto *Pack of Orders* if we assume that it seeks to reproduce something of this depersonalized global consciousness, to make *it* into that anonymous centre from which the text issues. Since this consciousness is proletarian, and thus organizational ("tektonic") in its very essence, for it thinking and discoursing are the same as doing, the practical ordering of the world. Ideas and volitions are indistinguishable from *veshchevye sobytiia.*

"What would it be to verbalize that state of the world in which there is one head in place of millions? How could one render in language that objective psychic process, with systems of switches and locks, that traverses myriads of human minds and is immediately and practically organizational? Not to speak *about* it, but to speak with it, *as* it." These are the questions that open the possibility for something like *Pack of Orders*. The text is the answer. It is, itself, that speaking-as, a token of a voice never heard before. But in the practical answer, the terms of the question disappear from view. Because we get the speaking itself and nothing else, there is nothing to tell us who or what does the speaking. Precisely as speaking, the text remains constitutively mute.

It could, and perhaps should, be muter still. With the 1919 "Contours of Proletarian Culture" before us (and still keeping in mind the theorizations of the principal ideologue of Proletkult, Bogdanov), we realize that to verbalize the organizational interventions of the global proletarian consciousness is already a betrayal of sorts. For Gastev envisions a state of being in which the distance between "planning" or "conception," on the one hand, and "execution," on the other, has been reduced to naught. The utopian horizon of the text is that there shall be no text at all, nothing shall need to be said, for the exigency of using speech already implies an imperfect automatism of transmission. Language is used for communication *between* people, but in the singular and universal proletarian mind projected by Gastev there is no such "between."[12] Here, although millions of people are in fact involved, the pure immediacy of the selfsame reigns; hence we cannot say that "one" speaks to or orders to "another." The demiurgic/organizational process of the future will dispense with words and operate solely by means of "switches and locks," as an all-pervasive current of impulses that pass immediately into executions. The severe terseness of "Pack" can now be read as pointing towards that projected horizon. We are dealing with a completely deindividualized, non-human tongue.[13] This speaking wants to cease speaking and enter into a different, non-verbal dimension. Words no longer want to be human words, but unconditional signals and discharges. Before us is a discourse that delegitimizes itself as such and in discoursing indicts itself for doing so. For what it ultimately wants to be is pure actuation of the transpersonal demiurgic will of the universal class.

Pack of Orders, then, is a *work* to the extent to which it participates in a symbolic performance, a cultural act. It is the working out of a desire, which the text enacts but does not address. The desire is its horizon, not its subject matter; it is not spoken *about*, it is spoken *with*. We do justice to the text by factoring in this horizon as we read. And as we contemplate the scene of the cultural act, we see more than the words on the page, we go beyond the speaking they transcribe. We become aware of a someone (Gastev) who will only write on the condition that what comes from his pen not be taken as "poetry," an expression of one's subjectivity or a crafted verbal condensation of one's experiences. Whether it should be called art or not, this exercise must proceed under a more weighty authority. And so this someone begins to speak as the superhuman, machine-like agency of ordering and execution that proletarian consciousness should be. Or rather, he steps aside, surrendering his authorial position, so that the agency in question can take the stage. This is the symbolic gesture of letting-be, which in the particular case of *Pack of Orders* is enacted as a gesture of letting-It-speak.

If we call "text" that which confronts us directly as speaking in *Pack of Orders,* then the work is the text plus the pretence of an unauthored, deindividualized text. In other words, the work comprises not just the speaking but also the implied yielding, the letting-It-speak. And the perspective of the cultural act is attained when we relate this entire symbolic performance (text-as-produced-in-a-gesture-of-yielding) to a situation, when we understand it as a re-*act*-ion to that situation. This allows us to see the work as a working through of a specific, historically determined problem. We thus move, hermeneutically, from poetics to history, from signs to their ultimate significance.

The yielding is, at the same time, an anchoring. As it gives itself over to an impersonal authority, the act of writing – or painting, or composing – is bound by a law of conduct (Greenberg's "worthy constraint"). It is "methodical," it operates as an autonomous device. This disciplined, "law-abiding" character is immediately obvious in Gastev's text in the strict lexical choices, the curtailing of syntax, and the ascetic regime of expressive means. The "orders" are such not only in name; we are acutely aware that they have been composed "orderingly," as if the writer were trying to transcribe the very essence of commanding volition. Reviewing *Pack* for the first issue of *LEF*, Arvatov applauded what he recognized as the "systematic implementation of a unitary and conscious method" ("Aleksei Gastev" 244). And indeed, the text can be seen as a universe of discourse organized in accordance with a principle of linguistic economy immanent to it. But it would be wrong to stop at this formalist stage of reading (Arvatov certainly did not). If the text can be closed in this way within the limits of an immanent dynamic, the work cannot. Reading should go on until it tells us not just how the method works, but also what it projects. In short, the analysis should lead us to the content of form. In Gastev's case this is not so difficult: behind the law of form there opens a desired and anticipated world of perfected social organization, in which a unity of human practice translates into psychological unanimity and makes every willing authoritative, non-contingent, and immediately effective. The act of depersonalization, that is, the death of the author, amounts to the summoning or evocation of that world, a yielding for the sake of letting *it* speak. The text we have before us is, ultimately, a token of that world.

The fundamental question, "What – if anything – calls for art?", generated diverse theoretical and practical responses within the culture of modernism. This goes some way towards explaining the latter's heterogeneous landscape. Still, in this diversity there are two responses that may serve as boundary markers. One may be termed "activist" or "constructivist": "Nothing calls for art anymore. The entire enterprise, as it has been bequeathed to us from the nineteenth century, should be abandoned. Our practice should flow back into life, into the making of things that are actually called for: 'rye bread to chew ... / living woman to live with.'" At the other end of the spectrum would be the "aestheticist" or "formalist" response: "Art answers for itself only from within itself. It needs no external support, and least of all from the pragmatics of a world debased beyond reprieve. The artistic object stands apart from life's sordid practicalities, subsisting through nothing other than the necessary interrelationship of the elements of which it is composed." One could, then, proceed to distribute the currents and texts of modernism in accordance with this opposition, with the radical avant-gardes at one end, the socially unengaged exponents of pure art at the other, and everything else somewhere in between. A map of this sort would have the additional benefit of orienting us on the scholarly battlefield, where the main point of contest has always been whether the true character of modernism is to be found near the subversive-activist or the reflexive-aestheticist pole.[14]

Yet the very fact that I frame these positions as responses to the same question already suggests that I do not see them as true opposites. It is not, of course, a matter of reconciling politically Kafka's reclusiveness with Marinetti's militarism or Pound's anti-Semitism, but of seeing how activist and aestheticist platforms could be alternative ways of imagining something like a necessary practice. Because in the course of the nineteenth century art lost its moorings – a system of patronage; affiliation with a leisure class; betrothal to a select, privileged audience; a place of moral and political authority in the eyes of that same audience – it had to see itself, eventually, as socially unnecessary labour. And the two ways of dealing with this fact – glorifying the predicament and seeking to eschew it by hearkening to forces and imperatives deemed "essential" – fall within the same symptomatology. And if we need a study case for the compatibility of aestheticist and activist impulses in modernism, we should look no further than the history of the Soviet avant-garde, in whose ranks yesterday's Futurists and today's Constructivists rubbed shoulders with Formalist critics like Shklovskii and Brik. What I wanted to show in the first part of this study was that seeing the text as an autonomous organism and seeing the pragmatic thing as prefigured through general utility are cognate imaginations. The "constructive principle" of Tynianov and the "social commission" of Arvatov, Brik, and Chuzhak play a similar role in the symbolic performance: they provide for the non-contingent character of the practice in question. Bound in one case by the immanent demands of the literary tradition, in the other by the utilitarian demands of a new society, the product is in both cases a non-fortuitous thing, a called-for construction.

In the framework of modernism, envisioning a world of non-contingent practice (whether the practice should be called "artistic" or not depended on the specific ideological vision) was often a matter of imagining what it would be to inhabit a world (re)possessed by *style*. Throughout the previous, nineteenth, century one could hear the recurrent lament that modern civilization had lost a quality that all previous periods in history had enjoyed – a definite unity of artistic form grounded in a social being of a definite and stable shape. Compared to the civilizations of the past,[15] the modern epoch seemed disconcertingly formless. In the words of a twentieth-century thinker:

> Undoubtedly people have always had to be fed, clothed, housed and have had to produce and then re-produce that which has been consumed; but until the nineteenth century, until the advent of competitive capitalism and the expansion of the world of trade the quotidian as such did not exist ... In the heart of poverty and (direct) oppression there was *style* ... Style gave significance to the slightest object, to actions and activities, to gestures; it was a concrete significance, not an abstraction taken piecemeal from a system of symbols. There was a style of cruelty, a style of power, a style of wisdom; cruelty and power (the Aztecs, Rome) produced great styles and great civilizations, but so did the aristocratic wisdom of Egypt and India. With the rise of the masses (who were none the less still exploited) and democracy (the masses still being exploited) great styles, symbols and myths have disappeared together with collective works such as cathedrals, monuments and festivals. Modern man (the man who praises modernity) is the man of transition, standing between the death of style and its rebirth. (Lefebvre 38; emphasis in the original)

"Culture," then, is what you get when there is no more style. The use of the latter term to designate the unique "signature" this or that individual artist places on a body of work[16] became current exactly in the period in which that other "style" – the epochal unity Henri Lefebvre had in mind – was seen as extinct. From that point on, there could only be personal styles as the component parts of something called culture, whose defining trait is its divorce from the realm of work and everyday life. It was the end of *this* culture, no doubt, that Arvatov was announcing when he admonished artists to find something better to do with their lives and skills: the culture of individualism and subjective idealism; of sclerotic academicism, with its impotent rehashing of dead historical styles;[17] of the affirmative mimesis of what is; of beautiful words and assonances oblivious to mute misery; of painstaking dissections of the inner blind to the swelling tumours of the outer; of tight-corseted moralizing, forgetful of lives that had only prostitution as means to survive; of everything that "elevated" the enjoyment of material comforts denied to most; of everything that served to prettify profitability; of humanism that did not mind imperialism; of vacuous spirituality, intimate confessions, and high-minded philosophizing, all made meaningless against the backdrop of mass movements, the global depredations of capital, and the carnages of modern warfare.

Whether or not we countenance nostalgia for civilizations in which even cruelty came with style, the fact remains that in modernism this nostalgia was active and potent (which accounts for the powerful attraction that primitive cultures exercised on modernist imaginations). Georg Simmel identified that nostalgia as a symptom of painfully dilated modern subjectivity, which sought to hide itself, to fold itself, to give itself "an addition of calm breath and typical lawfulness" (70).[18] The perception that style had died some time in the preceding century, and been replaced by fragmented and formatively anemic individualism, was shared by many. Wrote Franz Marc in the *Blaue Reiter Almanac* (1912):

> But the artistic style that was the inalienable possession of an earlier era collapsed catastrophically in the middle of the nineteenth century. There has been no style since. It is perishing all over the world as if seized by an epidemic. Since then, serious art has been the work of individual artists whose art has had nothing to do with "style" because they were not in the least connected with the style or the needs of the masses ...
>
> Nothing occurs accidentally and without organic reason – not even the loss of artistic style in the nineteenth century. This fact leads us to the idea that we are standing today at the turning point of two long epochs. ("Two Pictures" 94–5)

Modernists who saw themselves as standing at such a turning point, a moment "between a society that does not need us and a society that does not exist,"[19] could just as easily describe this condition as one of "standing between the death of style and its rebirth."

"The people itself (and I do not mean the 'masses') has always given art its essential style. The artist merely clarifies and fulfills the will of the people. But when the people does not know what it wants, or worst of all, wants nothing ... then its artists, driven to seeking their own forms, remain isolated, and become martyrs" ("Aphorisms" 275–6). These lines, again by Marc, focus the main premises of my account so far. First, they register the lack that I take as definitive of the modernist moment: the absence of genuine social demand for art ("the people does not know what it wants, or worst of all, wants nothing"). Where such collective calling is silenced, there can be no great style. When it is no longer called for, artistic practice becomes the individualistic pursuit of "expression," of form. And this is nothing other than the elaboration of a "style," but now narrowly understood as the stamp of one person's creative originality. (With the decline of modernism, style will become simply the trademark of a product that no longer resists the exchange, the packaging of a commodity.) As suggested earlier, when artists were "driven to seek their own forms," they were also driven to imagine surrogates for the absent social demand. And the end result was the positing (implicit or theoretically explicit) of demanding objectivities that would supply laws of form and specify terms of constraint – a "disciplined," non-contingent conduct for the human agent in the execution of the work. Along with this went the positing of something akin to Rilke's anonymous centre. The definite unity of form that art could not get from a worthy collective endeavour could only be derived surreptitiously, from a symbolic performance of discipline and depersonalization: "What we demand of art is UNITY, a demand which will never be fulfilled as long as artists use individualistic means. Unity can only result from disciplining the means, for it is this discipline which produces more generalized means. The objectification of the means will lead towards elementary, monumental plastic expression" (Theo van Doesburg; qtd in Baljeu 141; capitalization in the original).

Artists and intellectuals in Russia did not have to wait for the proletarian revolution in order to draw that horizon of compelling creativity grounded in an immanent collective will. From the turn of the century, as elsewhere in Europe, the fatigue, often disgust, with what was then called culture was being expressed in no uncertain terms.[20] Its real, historically effective negation seemed inevitable. In the 1902 *History of Russian Art in the Nineteenth Century*, Aleksandr Benois insisted: "Historical necessity ... requires that an age that would absorb man's individuality in the name of public benefit ... would again come to replace the refined epicureanism of our time, the extreme refinement of man's individuality, his effeminacy, morbidity, and solitude" (qtd in Bowlt 5). In his earliest articles, from 1904, Viacheslav Ivanov also prophesied the end of individualism, which would "reconcile the Poet and the Crowd in one great all-people's art" ("Poet" 714). Needless to say, the revolution of 1917 made the dissolution of individualism and the resurgence of style seem that much closer and more inevitable. The historical necessity of this epochal event now seemed fully confirmed. In Russia of the 1920s, it was a rare artistic current that did not undertake, at one point or another, to announce the imminence of a great style, speculate on its character, and attempt its implementation. Below I quote three from among countless pronouncements on the subject.

Writing at the third anniversary of the Revolution, the Commissar of the Enlightenment, Anatolii Lunacharskii, gave a diagnosis very similar to Marc's:

> The last epoch of the bourgeoisie was unable to advance any style at all – including a life style or a style of architecture – and advanced merely a whimsical and absurd eclecticism. Formal searches degenerated into eccentricities and tricks or into a peculiar, rather elementary pedantry tinged with various, puzzling sophistications, because true perfection of form is determined, obviously, not by pure formal search, but by the presence of an appropriate form common to the whole age, to all the masses, by a characteristic sensation, and by ideas. ("Revolution" 191)

He went on to say, of course, that the Revolution would save both life and art from this formlessness.[21]

In the same year, 1920, the "Realistic Manifesto" by Naum Gabo and Antoine Pevsner, which accompanied their open-air exhibition in Moscow, began with these words:

> The blossoming of a new culture and new civilization, with their unprecedented-in-history surge of the masses toward the possession of the riches of Nature, a surge that binds people into one union, and last, not least, the war and the revolution (those purifying torrents of the coming epoch), have made us face the fact of new forms of life, already born and active.
> What does Art carry into this unfolding epoch of human history?

Does it possess the means necessary for the construction of the new Great
Style?
Or does it suppose that the new epoch may not have a style? (7)

These questions were rhetorical, of course: the answers were beyond doubt.
The Association of Artists of Revolutionary Russia (AKhRR) had an
artistic platform very different from that of Gabo and Pevsner, but the
declaration of 1922 that announced its first exhibition began from the
same assumption:

The day of revolution, the moment of revolution, is the day of heroism, the
moment of heroism – and now we must reveal our artistic experiences in the
monumental forms of the style of heroic realism.
    By acknowledging continuity in art and by basing ourselves on the con-
temporary world view, we create this style of heroic realism and lay the foundation of the universal building of future art, the art of a classless society.
("AKhRR" 267)

From everything said so far, it should be clear that I share the views of
Comrade Lunacharskii (as well as Marc), in that I have treated the modernist pursuit of necessary (self-necessitating) form as a symbolic performance conditioned by the absence of true social demand, which in turn
accounts for the absence of that "form common to the whole age, to all the
masses." In other words, I see the modernist desire for form (which, after
Russian Formalism and the American New Criticism, was to be thoroughly misunderstood) as, ultimately, a desire for the *formative*. And by "the
formative" I mean that organic relation, through belonging, to a greater
social project that would brace the practice of art from the outside, would
give it place and "calling," and, by thus supplying it with essential content,
would impart to it a non-contingent form. In this sense, it could be argued
that what the modernist project ultimately projects, the farthest horizon to
which it points, is the great epochal style.

In Russia after the Revolution, this horizon seemed very near, until one
day it was proclaimed to have been reached. The epoch of socialist realism
began. The death of the author was to have yet another historical enactment. What started, with modernism, as a drama, was to end as a farce.
And it did so not just in Stalin's Russia but also in Mussolini's Italy and
Hitler's Germany. The act of depersonalization, which had been a summoning of the impossible, was now to be performed as an affirmation of

the immanent. Stalinist cultural policy, summed in a phrase, was the staged return of the great historical style.

Because of this, one might be tempted to say, *à la* Groys, that Stalinism was the completion or consummation of the modernist project. But if we wish to maintain credibility in our commerce with words and concepts, we should give proper consideration to the following dialectic. To have a horizon is *not* to have it. In reaching, one does not yet possess what one reaches for.[22] A horizon is what it is by staying always ahead of one, beyond one's reach, even as it orients one's movement. "The phantom that runneth on before thee, my brother, is fairer than thou" (Nietzsche 69). The value of a horizon is in supplying direction, not harbour, impetus, not *domus*. The same dialectic can be expressed in terms of desire. A desire is what it is when it does not have its object or, even, when it does not have *an* object. It is the going-after such an object, the projecting/imagining of what and where it might be.[23] To talk of a satisfied desire is to not talk of desire at all. And so it is that when we speak of the completion of the modernist project, the words we use create the impression that modernism includes its completion. But this is wrong. We must think, instead, of a kind of fulfilment that, insofar as it pretends to have resolved an intrinsically irresolvable drama, no longer belongs to that drama's dynamic.

The fundamental question of modernism, "What – if anything – calls for art?", was not supposed to have a real answer – not at the beginning of the twentieth century, to be sure. There were no historical forces then, just as there are not now, that could overcome in a short time the displacements, fragmentations, and alienations of modernity. The social movements of those days were powerful enough to promise a new world order and a new culture (in a way no movements today can). But this was only a promise, and as such it was ambiguous, as the range of political articulations, from anarchism to fascism, demonstrates. As long as it was a promise with a necessarily indefinite horizon, it was true to the historical moment. When it became a celebration of a redeemed world and attained cultural renaissance,[24] it became false and obscene.

By the same reasoning, it should be said that style as a horizon of possibility and style as a blooming immanence are two very different things that speak of two very different cultures. We should recognize the impulses that socialist realism inherited from modernism and give due attention to that commonality. But at the same time, we must be wary of drawing hasty and schematic lines of descent from one to the other. The notion of unconditional, anonymous creativity was common to modernism and Stalinist culture. But to understand this fact is also to see how differently the act of depersonalization played out in the two cultural frames. To state the most evident: artistic modernism was always the work of isolated individuals, who, even as they huddled together in groupings of dozen or so (trumpeting these cliques as advanced detachments of the future), only gave further evidence of just how cut off from the rest of society they were. And as they allied themselves, here and there, with radical political movements, what they projected on the coarse faces of those movements were still imaginations nurtured in isolation and political irrelevance. The death of the author, as treated so far, was the symbolic act of such individuals. It was *their* doing insofar as it symbolized the true predicament they lived as the performers of a labour no longer called for. Depersonalization was ultimately a subjective ritual that symptomatized this predicament even while mystifying it, even while turning it into the vicarious satisfaction of formal mastery. Under Stalin, as I hope to show further, depersonalization was part of a pre-scripted official plot. Instead of projecting and summoning, it verified. It issued not from subjective reason but from *raison d'État*. It was still individuals who acted in the performance, but the roles were set in advance; it was only a matter of filling those roles and speaking the words the script prescribed.

I will be insisting that we view socialist realism within the framework of style, in the meaning underscored so far. Those who cultivated it referred to it also as a "method." I will not be using the latter term, for it might lead to misunderstanding. A method implies the elaboration and deployment of a determinate set of procedures on a given material – something we do not find in socialist realism. Repeated calls to "learn from the classics" and the technical competence urged upon Soviet artists, composers, and writers are surely insufficient as parameters of a distinct artistic methodology. If, by contrast, we see socialist realism as the staging of an epochal style, we may be able to explain why it never developed the kind of theoretical apparatus that would have qualified it as a method.

Style is an enemy of premeditation. For its existence, it draws from a pre-reflective unity of experience that stamps cultural artefacts with an organic character.[25] It is from life, not from method, that such a character issues. Conversely, the need to follow procedures may be taken as testifying to the drying up of those vital springs that nurture style. As he diagnosed the course of Western civilization, Oswald Spengler described the art of the present as obsessed with method, "meticulous, cold, diseased – an art of over-developed nerves, but scientific to the last degree, energetic in everything that relates to the conquest of technical obstacles, acutely assertive of programme" (I, 289). For Spengler, to create by means of method was the lamentable but also unavoidable consequence of culture's decline. It was the surest evidence that art responded to no deep need and that its shape was no longer imparted by the weight of a common destiny. "The weaker the feeling for the necessity and self-evidence of Being, the more the habit of 'elucidation' grows, the more the fear in the waking-consciousness comes to be stilled by causal methods. Hence the assimilation of knowledge with demonstrability, and the substitution of scientific theory, the causal myth, for the religious" (II, 103). The opposite of the modern methodological consciousness is what Spengler calls simply the "feeling of life" (*Lebensgefühl*; I, 119).[26] Where this feeling is vigorous, where "the necessity and self-evidence of Being" hold sway, there is style:

> It is not the personality or will or brain of the artists that makes the style, but the style that makes the *type* of the artist. The style, like the Culture, is a prime phenomenon in the strictest Goethian sense, be it the style of art or religion or thought, or the style of life itself. It is, as "Nature" is, an ever-new experience of waking man, his alter ego and mirror image in the world around. And therefore in the general historical picture of a Culture there can be but one style, *the style of the Culture*. (I, 206; emphasis in the original)

When we follow Spengler's logic, we have to recognize fascism and Stalinism as two grand ventures to simulate a new historical and cultural cycle, one in which the self-evidence of Being is once again virginally strong, one in which there is a binding destiny for one and all. The unmediated aesthetic imprint of this destiny – Style.

The last quotation replays the leitmotif of all previous chapters. Here again is a vision of some objectivity that transcends the individual, leaving him to will only what "it" wills, "for it is not 'I' who actualize the possible, but 'it' actualizes itself through me" (I, 164). What I then produce – a text, an artefact – is necessarily an instance of such actualization. When I act, "it" acts, and when I speak, "it" speaks. I have argued that modernist artistic practice was often grounded in some such scenario: from an anonymous centre, an "it," the work works itself out through me, and when complete, it stands as the objectivation or demonstration of "it," its extant token.[27] What I read in this common scenario is the desire of modern subjects for whom individual subjectivity has become a form of imprisonment (the same condition Simmel diagnosed more than a century ago). As an imaginary escape from it, they often regarded themselves as subjective "extensions" or attributes of objective happenings that are autonomous and unconditional (but that still somehow need these creative individuals in order to fully manifest themselves). The thesis I will be developing from here onwards is that Stalinism perpetuated this scenario while radically changing its meaning. The desire I have just referred to became institutionalized as its opposite – unconditional fulfilment. Socialist realism, as the staging of style's resurrection, was also the staging of how the subject was overwhelmed by "it," that is, by a truth so powerful that artistic creation meant simply letting go and allowing oneself to be taken by it.

The original German edition of Spengler's wildly popular treatise was one of the volumes that Nikolai Bukharin had at his disposal in the Lubianka prison while he was writing *Socialism and Its Culture*. In the penultimate chapter of that manuscript, "The Style of Socialist Culture," he engaged with Spengler on the issue of "form in relation to society" (*The Prison Manuscripts* 183).[28] He charged that Spengler and other bourgeois ideologists[29] had stolen and disfigured the authentically Marxist understanding of this issue, in which the mode of production stands as the ultimate formative factor and endows the products of intellect and imagination with the commonality of style (184–5). By style, Bukharin understood a unitary "mode of representation" corresponding to a historically specific mode of production (185, 196). He, too, glanced back at the era just past and sketched the same landscape of exhaustion, fragmentation, and formlessness that we have already encountered in Marc and Lunacharskii:

> The bourgeois art of the late nineteenth and early twentieth centuries, reflecting fragmented specialization, the impoverishment of life, the anarchic nature of capitalism, the growing pessimism of its agents, etc. – all this broke art itself into fragments, separated form from content, reduced the latter to the minimum, splintering form itself into its component parts and turning them into separate, distinct "substances" of art ... The wholeness and unity of rich form with diverse content disappeared along with the vitality of fullness and completeness. (192–3)[30]

The bourgeois epoch, with its distinct mode of production, possessed also a distinct culture; but its style was the negation of style, the form of formlessness. Its positive antipode was the style of socialism, a mode of representation arising from the new mode of production installed in the Soviet Union. Bukharin spoke of this style as something already existing.[31] Having begun with a critical jab at Spengler, he ended with a distinctly Spenglerian vision of human beings once again enjoying the sway of destiny. Under the reign of socialism, which is, at the same time, the reign of Style, "the 'individual' knows perfectly well what he has to do and what road he has to follow ... Thus no great role is played by the 'why' questions referred to earlier. This is not a sign of insufficient culture, but a sign that these questions have been ... taken off the agenda by life itself" (199). Bukharin did not elaborate on how this era of manifest destiny affected the role of the artist; yet the answer is implicit in his meditations: once everyone knows what road to follow, once all the accursed "why" questions have been resolved by "life itself," the only possible problem of artistic representation that remains is whether the artist truly belongs to this life or not.

During the 1920s, the campaign for style was still largely a guessing game as to what could or should be the shape of the new Soviet culture. In the 1930s, it became an exercise in axiomatics, of which Bukharin's chapter was but one sample. It was an ideological axiom that socialism had arrived[32] and that a new epoch of human history had thus been inaugurated, with its distinct character already in evidence; now it was only a matter of getting hold of and displaying the evidence. It was no less axiomatic that this epoch had already given birth to a new human specimen, the Soviet Man, and along with it a new style of life. Following this chain of deduction, which Bukharin did, one finally reached the axiom that socialist realism was the artistic dimension of that greater phenomenon, the all-embracing style of life in socialist Russia. To be a socialist-realist author (and a good Stalinist subject), then, implied inserting oneself in the chain of axiomatic reasoning and furnishing evidence that this was not some abstract logic but matter-of-fact reality. One had to demonstrate that one's artistic work was, in fact, the work of the Formative, that is, of life as an overwhelming plastic force. This demonstration took place not *in* the text but *by means* of the text (among other means). That is to say, it was not just a matter of portraying the Soviet style of life (say, in a novel) but of demonstrating *by means of* the novel that he who wrote it had been guided by a deep "feeling of life" while writing it.

I am suggesting, in other words, that with socialist realism we are again compelled to look beyond the text so as to embed it in the symbolic act to which it pertains. The socialist-realist text was produced as a token, just as the modernist one was. As such, it does not wear its value on its sleeve. To appreciate what this value is, to know what the token betokens, it is necessary to consider the situation out of which it is presented. In the first instance, it had to present itself as a token of Style, and as such it had to give evidence of a form common to an entire age. But this is tantamount to saying that the socialist-realist text had to demonstrate its author's belonging to "our reality" (*nasha deistvitel'nost'*), his rootedness in an "unproblematic general foundation for life."[33] Indeed, the products of Stalinist

culture were always read in this light – as certificates of their author's belonging – by well- or ill-meaning official critics and Party overseers of culture. Because the text was assumed to issue straight from life, it became a
standard procedure to use it for diagnosing a wholesome or a sick life, as
the case might be.[34] The categories of *partiinost', narodnost', ideinost'* (ide-
ational/ideological content), and *tipichnost'* (typicality) provided the basic
terms for formulating the diagnosis.[35] It is not enough, though, to point out
that the texts of socialist realism were read in this manner. They were also
produced as to-be tokens of style and to-be ontological certificates. This
was the proper horizon of artistic practice in Stalinist culture: that my
work, once completed, should betoken the existence of socialism as a formative force, which has also formed me, my thoughts and imaginations,
insofar as I truly belong to our great age.

In a sense, then, socialist realism is modernism in reverse. The modernist
text is a token in the symbolic exchange with the possible; the socialist-
realist text is a token in the symbolic exchange with the (ideologically)
given. The former looks ahead, to a state of the world that will render my
practice necessary and endow it with genuine significance. The latter looks
backwards to a pre-existing state of being that not only has made artistic
work meaningful by default but has also supplied it with an essential form,
so that it is now my task to furnish proof, by means of my work, that such
is the case. By proposing a new verbal idiom, a work like *Pack of Orders*
also proposes a new way of speaking, thinking, willing, and thus projects a
new epoch in which these would be the norm. Clearly, they are not the
norm at present; this age is not yet here, it is latent at best; so the work, as
a symbolic act, is to be read as a summoning. In a similar way, the constructions of Le Corbusier, "which ride like so many gigantic steamships
upon the urban scenery of an older fallen earth" (Jameson, *Postmodernism*
36), project out of themselves the conditions that would justify their existence, conditions (infrastructural but ultimately social) presently missing
on the fallen earth upon which the buildings stand. A socialist-realist work
operates in reverse perspective: it has to bear witness to the axiomatic fact
that the earth has been redeemed, that already-present conditions have
precipitated a unitary and binding form of creativity, that is, a Style.

It may first seem strange that I am placing Stalinist art in the same
context as the modernist pursuit of necessary form. Was socialist realism
not wholly about content, the political commitment, the ideological message? Did not Stalinist cultural orthodoxy proscribe formal experimentation? Yes to both questions, of course, but that does not contradict my
argument. After all, form and content are not discontinuous dimensions,

but interact dialectically. At its extreme, each tends towards and passes into the other. The abstractions of Malevich and Rodchenko illustrate well that, at a certain point, pure form is indistinguishable from pure content (in Malevich, the point was supposed to be a breakthrough to the Absolute; for Rodchenko, it was to be the entrance to the factory). By this dialectical logic, absolutely necessary form is to be found not in deliberate attention to form, in its conscious manipulation (Doesburg's "disciplining [of] the means"), but in its opposite: the spontaneous, self-propelled, coming-into-relief of content. Form is truly non-contingent when a certain "material" does not need to be shaped willfully from the outside but is so internally active that its existence amounts to its own shape giving. This is the highest instance of what I referred to as the Formative; Spengler called it the "self-evidence of Being." The ideological fantasy that structured official Stalinist culture – that Being shapes itself and lays itself bare – is the theme of the next chapter.

Chapter 7

The Unbearable Light of Being

"And your painting, comrade Arnol'dov, is remarkable for being a reflection of the life created by our creators."

Panferov, *Bruski*

A certain straightforwardness of life, an uncontainable power of saturation, was staring at him from everywhere ...

Nikolai Zarudin, "The Sleeping Beauty"

The first epigraph, taken from Panferov's epic of collectivization, is meant to give us a first taste of a distinctly new mode of cultural creation. The taste has something of bland pleonasm to it. Comrade Arnol'dov's painting, his creation, reflects what is created by "our creators." This is its value and distinguishing quality. Some of those creators are seated around him: a tractor driver, a *kolkhoz* worker, an aviator, a party activist – a miniature model of the new social world. The person speaking is an old Bolshevik, Bogdanov. He is announcing the arrival of a present in which the ranks of comrade Arnol'dov's profession have expanded enormously. From Lenin and Stalin to common folk like Pavel and Stesha over here – are these not also artists, creators? In all of them, from the first to the last, some new energy pulsates, a "dynamic force," as Bogdanov puts it (980). Let us begin by asking about this force, about its nature, as well as about its pertinence to artistic representation – to the kind of work someone like Arnol'dov performs.

What is so distinct about the situation Panferov describes, other than the pomp of Party rhetoric? After all, people have worked since time immemorial, and inasmuch as they produce something that was not there before, they could be called "creators." And the artist – what has he done, other than depict an episode of socialist construction, a world being made? There does not seem to be any novelty here either. Many of his profession, many times before, have sought to provide a truthful picture of the world, and more often than not that world had borne the traces of an earlier activity, of a making that precedes the artist's. How could any representational art avoid encountering the world as a pre-existing creation, that is, as a cultural, man-made reality? If this is all there is to comrade Arnol'dov's creation, why make such a fuss about it?

The scene we are considering seems rather mundane insofar as we are aware of only one picture in it – the picture Arnol'dov has just completed. But there is one other – the picture the old Bolshevik is drawing for his listeners and for us as he speaks. This outer frame encompasses the "creators," their creations and their creativity, as it wells up from the very foundations of socialist reality. In this second picture, Fenia, Kirillov, Pavel, and Stesha, their labour and their lives, are the immediate outlet and expression of socialism's "dynamic force." If they are artists, they are artists in a sense quite different from what is meant in Arnol'dov's case. Whatever Bogdanov says, our painter occupies an altogether different position from that of the other creators. From all we know about realism – and this is, no doubt, Arnol'dov's method – he has presented on another surface what his eye has captured on the surface that is reality; while those around him are part and parcel of that original surface, their doings blending seamlessly with it. His painting did not emerge in the same way that a tractor station emerges somewhere in the Soviet countryside. In that sense, it is not the immediate blossoming forth of the force generated by socialism, but only a reflection of its manifestations.

The people in whose midst Arnol'dov now stands are representatives of socialist construction; he is no more than their representor. His work is a *Darstellung* of the world now emerging; theirs is a *Vertretung* – not a symbolization, but a direct embodiment, an exemplification.[1] They are not only the creators of the new world under socialism but also its native creatures. Could it be that the artist, with his age-old craft, is excluded from this immediacy? If so, the praise he receives might be read as a concealed reproach, and his success, as success in failure. Or could it be that there is a way to represent that surmounts this dilemma – a kind of representation that is not a reflection *upon* life, but a reflection *out of* it, so that the artistic vision is generated not with the subject but with the object of representation? What if the vital force evoked by the old Bolshevik is so fecund that, besides directly reproducing itself in the labour of people like Fenia,

Kirillov, and Stesha, it is able also to "perceive" and "think" its own workings in the labour of someone like Arnol'dov? What sorts of thoughts and perceptions would those be, and how would they relate to the thoughts and perceptions of those who still call themselves creative authors?

In a speech at a Moscow Party conference on the eve of the Seventeenth Congress of the CPSU,[2] Maksim Gor'kii identified a very similar type of dynamic force: "This energy, which is being embodied in the grandiose construction of a new culture, is at the same time raising new forces, creating conditions and atmosphere that quickly transform the great quantity into a superb quality" ("Moshchnaia energiia" 1). Even before his permanent return to the Soviet Union (in 1932), Gor'kii had become an avid collector of what might be called "tokens of living socialism": facts showing that the new socio-economic order was not an ideological abstraction but rather a potent and life-shaping force. The collection of such tokens was greatly facilitated by Gor'kii's busy program of officially sponsored trips and public meetings. At the Moscow Party Conference, the eminent speaker shared with his audience one remarkable fact he had come across during a recent meeting with the staff of the All-Union Institute for Experimental Medicine. A dozen or so of the institute's employees had been until recently factory workers, farmhands, or disinterested, apolitical intellectuals. "But lo, it turned out that, infused with the energy of the working class, which fertilizes people's feelings and thoughts, [these] dozen workers of the Institute, while researching the organism of animals, *came to the dialectic of development* that constitutes the foundation of revolutionary thought" (1; emphasis added). Gor'kii's telling of the story does not allow us to reconstruct all of its specifics. (What did he mean by "it turned out"? When did it turn out? How? What sort of revelation had come to these people?) Still, its general significance is sufficiently clear: truth had dawned on the institute's employees as a (predictable?) consequence of their work. We are supposed to infer that not just any work will "turn out" this way: only work that is carried out in the atmosphere and conditions created by the victorious class struggle of the proletariat.

Whatever we may want to call the medium in which these people are immersed, we should see that they come to a state of cognition with no agent of enlightenment present on the scene other than the immersion itself. From what we can gather, the "dialectics of development" they finally attained were not precisely the fruit of their efforts or of scientific rigour. Gor'kii's words lead us to suspect that scientists working with equal diligence and passion for objectivity, but working, say, in London, would be presented with a rather different picture of how living organisms evolve.

Unlike "their" scientists, ours – even if they were the dregs of a former world or the bystanders of the Revolution – had been delivered unto knowledge/truth by a power that was, at least initially, outside their awareness. It matters little that prior to possessing this power, they had been blind to or had even blindly resisted the teachings of dialectical materialism. If anything, this fact makes their deliverance that much more wondrous. Wondrously they arrived at the "foundation of revolutionary thought" – a thought that, as something distinct from their own thoughts, had been confidently awaiting them in the depths of their object of study. It is as if, placed in the atmosphere and conditions of socialism, the object had arrived at the thought proper to itself, and the human subject was the site of this happy arrival.[3]

The culture of socialist realism dates from the moment when "miraculous" stories like the one told by Gor'kii became commonplace. The proclamation of a unitary artistic style was a straightforward consequence of the proclaimed immanence of a unitary style of Soviet life. By its very existence, socialist realism served as a token of a formative force reaching far beyond the domain of art. In other words, the affirmation of a single aesthetic was a correlate of the kinds of facts Gor'kii was publicizing, facts that showed socialism to be an immanent force, definitively shaping psychologies, cognitions, and behaviours. As one Stalinist critic explained:

Socialist realism was born when the first "facts of socialist character" emerged, first in the form of mass proletarian revolutionary struggle, then in the form of the first in history proletarian Soviet state. But when the question "Who will win?" [kto kogo?] was finally decided, when "NEP Russia" became "socialist Russia," and when socialism entered the everyday life of Soviet people – a foundation was laid for a new rise of Soviet art, for a new, deeper fusion of realism and revolutionary romantics. And only after this could the concept of socialist realism be promoted as a slogan for all our literature, for all our art. (Bialik 188)[4]

It is not surprising that the official founding act of the new culture, the Resolution of the Party's Central Committee of 23 April 1932, told a story analogous to Gor'kii's. His was about apolitical researches that had miraculously "arrived" at dialectical materialism. The Party's official narrative was about the apolitical artistic intelligentsia, which, under the conditions created by the First Five-Year Plan, had arrived at socialist realism. The resolution decreed a radical reform in all spheres of cultural production, citing as the basis for the decree the "significant successes of socialist construction," which had resulted in a "qualitative as well as quantitative growth of literature and art" ("On the Reformation" 124).

On the same basis, the resolution ordered the liquidation of RAPP and its sister organizations, which by that time had become a hegemonic presence in Soviet culture. According to the Central Committee, RAPP's leaders had fallen out of step with the times. After an initial run (during the NEP period, but especially from 1928 to 1931) during which the organization played a positive role, it had missed a crucial change in the sociopolitical situation. The antagonistic treatment to which RAPP continued to subject the Revolution's cultural fellow-travellers could no longer be tolerated. According to the resolution, in the new conditions created by the progress of socialist construction, the psychology of the fellow-travellers had undergone significant transformation (124). As an editorial in *Literaturnaia gazeta* explained, these new conditions "had not been understood in a timely way and in their depth by RAPP" ("Budem" 1). Its leaders had failed to see how these conditions "had ensured [*obespechili*] the active participation of the main mass of the intelligentsia in solving the tasks of [socialist] construction" (1). As a consequence, the organization's recent activity had been riddled with "grave political errors"; and this, despite the clarity of the said conditions and the Party's repeated instructions (1). According to the Party press, all needed clarifications were contained in Stalin's speech at the Convention of Economic Cadres (23 June 1931), in which the Leader had called for a new approach to the old technical intelligentsia and indicated their changing attitude towards Soviet power. As it turns out, something other than overt political indoctrination – RAPP's approach *par excellence* – had brought the broad masses of previously apolitical writers to the acceptance of socialism.

So, what was this "something" – which, despite its blinding obviousness, had been ignored by RAPP's leaders, and which, almost against the grain of their efforts, had ensured the intelligentsia's participation in the building of socialism? The answer is again somewhat tautological, for this "something" was nothing other than socialism itself. The resolution says, more or less, the following: "The process of building socialism, creates, apart from socialism itself, also the conditions that secure the participation of previously indifferent subjects in the building of socialism." The tautology arises from the fact that socialism is inscribed twice: once as an empirical world in the making, and a second time as pure and practical self-evidence that takes possession of human consciousness and instrumentalizes it towards a predetermined purpose. Without the need for propaganda, socialism's own growth and ontological plentitude had recruited subjects to the cause of socialism.[5]

In the Central Committee's resolution, we find these subjects in two places. First, there are the poor functionaries of RAPP, who were supposed to see but who had failed to do so because of a deeply ingrained "coterie mentality" (*grupovshchina*), which had isolated them from crucial developments in the life of their country. Second, there are the "broad masses" of the previously non-committal intelligentsia, who can indeed see. It seems useless to ask whether this official characterization correctly describes the actual position of writers in either of these groups (how can we ever be sure?). What matters for us here is that both groups set out immediately to show that they were indeed the subjects of socialism. They began acting *as if* they could see. While RAPP's leaders (Averbakh, Libedinskii, Ermilov, Selivanovskii, Kirshon, Chumardin) engaged in cathartic exercises of self-criticism (*samokritika*), former fellow-travellers strove to depict themselves as possessed by the transformative power of the new epoch.

One such newly "possessed" subject was Shaginian – the same Shaginian who, in the mid-1920s, had difficulty reconciling traditional notions of creative freedom with the requirements of the social commission.[6] Speaking in 1932 to a group of young writers, she saw these difficulties as a thing of the past:

> Much has happened since then. Since those days, *socialism has become reality*. It exists on one sixth of the world map, and we exist *in it*. And from all sides, from the depths, as well as from the surface, of our new phenomena, of our new practice, socialism gushes at us, surrounds us, infuses us, and not only changes our attitude toward things and phenomena, but also opens our eyes to the essence and meaning of the transformations taking place within us. (205; emphasis in the original)

Note that the socialism Shaginian inhabits with her passionate discourse is not equal to the sum of its own "things and phenomena." Over and above them, socialism produces cognitive clarity as a kind of para-phenomenon. The things and phenomena that compose the empirical existence of socialism do not lie in quiet repose, as a world that is merely and inertly *there*. They gush, surround, infuse. Through this restless ebullience they are able to possess the subject, opening her eyes and giving her the ability to see clearly not only outside herself but also within. In short, they make sense.

When we say, in casual parlance, that "things make sense," we of course mean that they do so for someone present at the scene, a person who has reached an understanding of a certain state of affairs. And we believe that ultimately it is this person who – despite not being the grammatical subject of the expression – is the one actually "making" the sense. The case I am trying to argue here runs counter to this "pedestrian" logic. In the state of affairs Shaginian describes, it is, literally, the *things* that make the sense. "Oh, well," someone may object, "but what about our speaker and the 'we' to which she belongs and appeals? Obviously, it is to them that socialism makes sense, and, hence, their activity as subjects is implied. Is not Shaginian saying simply, 'We have come to understand the society we live in, its mechanisms, advantages, etc.'?" This would be true only up to the point where we notice that the "we" in which the clarity of understanding and self-awareness is born is itself a product of what it comes to understand. Socialism manifests itself to consciousness in such a way that it transforms this consciousness into something new. The subject who comes to understand was not there prior to the object of understanding (socialist life). The people included in Shaginian's "we" are what they are in the present moment because they were made by socialism. Quite literally, they were *made to understand, made to see* – made in order to be the site where true vision occurs. In Stalinist socialism – considered as a cultural-ideological phenomenon and not as a factual state of affairs – we have a sort of reality that not only unfurls the inner wealth of its content into a manifest externality but also, by means of this luxuriance, secures its own representation. That is, it creates, as one of its phenomena, the subject for whom this wealth is appreciably real. What is more, the transformation of the individual into a subject of socialism may take place outside the individual's conscious grasp: "The socialist tendency, as the general law of development of our reality, *influences consciousness objectively*, radically transforming the character of people's actions, remaking their social nature, *even when they themselves are not fully conscious of this*" (Korabel'nikov 98; emphasis added). As strange as it may sound, one can come into possession of socialist consciousness ... unconsciously.

Let us now consider another fellow-traveller who, in the early 1930s, embraced the cause of socialism. During the previous decade, the name of Il'ia Ehrenburg (1891–1967), a poet, prose writer, and journalist, had been closely associated with modernist tendencies in Soviet culture. His scepticism towards social utopias and his original writing style, which wove satire, playfulness, picaresque adventure, and philosophical gravity into a loose narrative fabric, had made him a favourite target for the zealots of proletarian culture. For vigilant RAPP critics, the fact that he was living abroad (first in Berlin, then in Paris) served only to confirm that he was an "alien" element. But in 1932 Ehrenburg made a long sojourn in his home country, during which he toured some of the major sites of socialist construction. Having gathered impressions and inspiration, he returned to Paris, where he wrote *Den' vtoroi* (*The Second Day*; 1932–3). Despite mild criticism of the author's lingering penchant for fragmentary narration,[7] that novel was welcomed by the Soviet press as Ehrenburg's greatest achievement, his first truly Soviet work.

In 1933, following the publication of *Den' vtoroi* in France, an article appeared in *Literaturnaia gazeta* in which a well-meaning critic set out to explain the recent changes in Ehrenburg's world view. The article is titled "In Search of the Truth" ("V poiskakh pravdy").[8] It begins by presenting to us the Ehrenburg of old, "a disillusioned, cynical skeptic" (4).[9] Under his pen, the Western world (as recently as 1931, in his novella *Spain*) had appeared in scenes of chaos, misery, and moral destitution. A resident of that world, Ehrenburg had failed to see it. In the working people of Western Europe, Ehrenburg had failed to see the harbingers of a brighter future; instead, he had focused on the "monotony, doom, and boredom" of their everyday existence (4). Divorced from the contemporary life of Soviet society, "he did not believe that ... a new world is truly being built, that socialist relations are being created, that new, happy people, the genuine people of the future, are being raised" (4).

After these introductory statements, there is a page break in the article, intended to alert us to a meaningful break in Ehrenburg's career. Below the break, we learn that at the present moment (1933), the capitalist world has entered the fourth year of acute economic crisis. It turns out that the economic depression in the West has had much to do with Ehrenburg's transformation as a writer and person, "for it laid bare [*obnazhil*] so deeply the essence of capitalist society, revealed [*obnaruzhil*] with such clarity the rotting foundation of capitalist economy, so distinctly defined [*opredelil*] the real interrelations between classes, that even for a person not equipped with the method of Marxism-Leninism, there appears the possibility of understanding the deep foundations of events" (4). Faced with a reality that aggressively bares itself, "flashes" the subject, the latter stands defenselessly receptive. How could he help seeing?! "Naturally, in depicting the crisis, Ehrenburg *could not but see* the exposed [*obnazhivshiesia*] lines of class struggle and understand the deep foundations of events" (4; emphasis added). The conviction that Ehrenburg had no choice but to see is restated several paragraphs later and clearly constitutes the conceptual backbone of this short critical biography.

An interesting picture emerges: the artist is confronted with a vision he cannot escape. In the liminal moment at the onset of perception, the moment to which the statement "he could not but see" applies, this vision is not his. It comes from without, already explicated, almost as an assault on him. If we had to describe the activity of our hero in this moment, we could only do it in the passive: the subject is being beamed.

Under the word "beam" in the Collins Cobuild English Dictionary we find, among others, the following definitions:

1. If you say that someone *is beaming*, you mean that they have a big smile on their face because they are happy, pleased, or proud about something.
2. A *beam* is a line of energy, radiation, or particles sent in a particular direction.
3. If something such as radio signals or television pictures *are beamed* somewhere, or *beam* somewhere, they are sent there by means of electronic equipment. (emphasis in the original)

Let us try to think about these three meanings as one, so as to bring together into a single conceptual knot (1) the triumphant faces of those new happy people, the true people of the future, which Ehrenburg had failed to see, but which now, we must assume, have become apparent to him (we shall return to these "shiny, happy people" in chapter 9); (2) the energy evoked by Panferov, Gor'kii, and Shaginian through which socialism "gushes at us, surrounds us, infuses us"; and (3) a concept of representation in which the representing subject, the author, seems not unlike a television set in that the "picture" he presents does not come, strictly speaking, "from inside" (only small children believe that the people and things they see on the television screen live in the boxed space behind it) but rather from someplace else.

Ehrenburg's case tells us that it matters little whether the picture is that of advancing socialism or rotting capitalism, whether the show that cannot but be seen is that of the happy faces of Soviet citizens or that of desperate capitalist enterpreneurs ruined by the Great Depression.[10] These phenomena, seemingly so disparate in character, constitute one kind of reality by virtue of an attribute they share: the ability to "glare" (the contradictions of capitalism, just as the successes of socialist construction, can be "glaring"). How do phenomena acquire such an ability? It is from the fact that the blossoming of life under socialism and its degradation under capitalism were both *meant to be*. They are equally part of a history whose unfolding brings only the confident inscription of its own systematic presuppositions.[11] The events and phenomena that comprise this history are events and phenomena that *could not but* occur.[12] As such, they dictate the position-comportment of the subject confronted with them: he becomes the subject who *cannot but see*.

"Observer," then, would not be a good way to describe this subject, if by "observing" we imply any sort of analytical exertion. When something meant to be takes place, it leaves no room for the analytical attitude. It flies in the face of the observer and disarms him. It says to him, "You see!" (in the sense of, "You see! I told you so!"). This kind of encounter between human subject and objective reality precludes the possibility of original perception. "You see!" does not mean "Begin to observe the situation." It is too late, and there is no need to observe or analyse anything at this point: whatever the situation the subject was supposed to see (but did not), it has now turned into one stark exposure; it *beams,* robbing the subject of the opportunity to *not* see.

In the article chronicling Ehrenburg's transformation, the place of the meant-to-be(-seen) is marked carefully. Right after the statement that the capitalist world has entered the fourth year of crisis, there follows, without a special transition, a quotation from Lenin in which the leader of the Proletarian Revolution explains the inevitable and fatal exacerbation of class struggle in the late stages of industrial capitalism (4). But apart from this explicit indication, the meant-to-be persists tacitly as a backdrop to our author's creative pursuits. Clearly, it is from this backdrop that socialism stares triumphantly at Ehrenburg as the inevitability in which he had not been able to believe.

Before it is actually built, Stalinist socialism is, in a sense, pre-built. Its empirical existence is erected on the ground of unconditional certainty regarding the ways of history and the mechanisms of social life. Thus no collection of empirical facts and observations can give an adequate presentation of this world. For what any conscientiously empirical picture of Soviet life in the 1930s will surely miss is one feature that underlies all "hard facts" and endows them with a surplus quality. This additional feature, which only a cultural investigation can adequately address, is brought out in Shaginian's words quoted earlier. She speaks not simply of socialism but of socialism-become-reality, which is not the same thing. It is a thing whose content is overridden by, folded into, the purely formal feature of fulfilment. Over and above any number of descriptive features that may be proper to it (a particular organization of productive forces, a certain standard of living, a determinate structure of government and political institutions, etc.), Stalinist socialism is that which was meant to be, that which was fore-seen.

It would be quite pedestrian of us to mistake the voice that says "You see!" for the voice of actual people (say, that of loyal adherents to the Party line speaking to previously disheartened non-believers). We should think of it as the voice of the world itself addressing – or rather, beaming – the subject with its manifest truth. The whole point of Ehrenburg's biography is that he needed no people to tell him which way the Western world was headed. What is more, he did not even need the "armament" of Marxism-Leninism. We are, clearly, in a new cultural frame if the "equipped" eye of the observer is rendered obsolete. The otherness confronting the subject has lost the aspect of systematic subterfuge (which can only be overcome by the systematic application of method). It bears no decoding; in its presence, hermeneutical exertions are inappropriate. For it freely emits whatever there is to know and see in the direction of the subject.

While discussing the cinematic theory of Vertov and the *kinoks*, I pointed to a certain place in the objective world that stands in inverse symmetry to the eye of the human subject. Recall that our subject was not happy with his inherited position, he did not want to see the world "subjectively." He therefore strove to attain a position in the world from which the objective interrelations of phenomena would be visible, from which life could be "caught unawares." For the purpose, the subject became the vanishing tenor of a cultural metaphor: $\frac{camera\ (mechanism)}{(human)\ eye}$, $\frac{method}{expression}$, and so on. At the same time, it was abundantly clear that the sought-after fulcrum of the visible world, the space where things make (objective) sense, does not exist as such; it is not an actual place – some sort of "display" or "exhibition" of phenomena that one can attend. Rather, it is the virtual space of the hermeneutic operation itself, the point of the application of method. The same turned out to be the case with the world of the literary text: its fulcrum is not an actual place in the fabric of writing, either a formal property or a semantic element, in which the organization of the whole comes together as a formal or semantic "principle," "tendency," or similar.

Yet in all these instances, I suggested, as a sort of unfulfilled fantasy, a what-if, the possible appearance of a world that, through some device of its own, would "see," "know," "read" itself in our stead. Here, "stead" is to be understood quite literally, in accordance with that word's etymology, as referring to the place where the subject is (supposed to be) standing, that is, in the place where seeing, understanding, and knowing have been known to occur. I submit that Stalinist ideological culture is the fulfilment of this fantasy. Here we encounter a primary cultural substance, which may be called "socialism," "our reality" (*nasha deistvitel'nost'*), or simply "life" (*zhizn'*), which requires no mediation in the ordinary sense of the word. It produces knowledge of itself without the prerequisites of "method," "system of thought," or "position." Rather than being the starting point of consciousness, these are now the end results of a new type of cognition. Let us recall those employees from Gor'kii's speech who "arrived" at dialectical materialism at the conclusion of their empirical research. There we have matter (the living organisms being studied) that, by being subjected to socialist praxis, "knows" itself in the space provided by the individual minds of our researchers. We may say: in the "stead" of their individual views, opinions, prejudices, and so on, dialectical materialism takes place, taking possession of their consciousness.

I am suggesting that socialist realism, as the simulation of Style, begins with the staging of such a quasi-automatic generation of knowledge by social praxis. It is a Marxist insight that the historical forms of consciousness are dependent on conditions of socio-economic existence. But it is Stalinist ideological theatre to demonstrate – as all the examples cited in this chapter endeavour to – that a socialist consciousness and *Lebensgefühl* are generated as a matter of course in the building of socialism. Stalin's postulate that theory lags behind practice (advanced at the very end of 1929 and instrumental in subsequent campaigns to cleanse the cultural field)[13] canonized the following logic: practice configures knowledge in advance; it presupposes definite ways of seeing and understanding the world. Even if these are not yet in evidence (because of the lag), they have been pre-programmed; a space has been reserved for them, an empty "stead" is waiting. In the first instance, it is always the "stead" that "sees" and "knows." The empirical individual partakes of truth only when, and insofar as, he comes to occupy this reserved place.[14] For this to happen, the individual in question must ensure that he resides in the depths of "our life," "our reality."[15]

With the completion of the First Five-Year Plan, the orchestrated euphoria about socialism's miraculous effects reached new heights. A whole rhetoric developed to celebrate the immensely rich material being thrown up from the depths of socialist construction and to attest to this material's blinding power.[16] Ideologists began speaking of the compulsive character of the new order, which left artists and intellectuals no choice but to occupy the "stead" and behold the truth. This was the irresistible, eye-opening, radiance of a "beaming" reality: socialism as an epistemic fate. Some imagined this fate as an almost predatory force: "You cannot hide from the all-embracing socialist life of the Soviet land, this life will overtake you wherever you go, and if you do not respond to its 'summoning call,' 'then you will be deprived of creative life and grow numb'" (Korabel'nikov 95). Taking a glance back from the middle of the year 1935, an editorial in *Literaturnyi kritik* explained why the ideological conversion of writers *could not but* have taken place: "Yet in our very reality [*v samoi nashei deistvitel'nosti*], in the practically developing socialist construction, were contained such mighty 'powers of persuasion,' that it was not to be doubted that the true essence of Bolshevism, of the proletarian revolution, would be fully understood by the writers" ("Sotsialisticheskii" 11).[17]

Mark Rozental', editor of *Literaturnyi kritik* and a major authority on aesthetics during the Stalinist period,[18] elaborated on how these "powers of persuasion" did their work:

> Every writer who deeply studies and observes real objects may come into conflict with his own views on the world; *life itself* [*sama zhizn'*] suggests to him entirely different methods than those dictated to him by his limited worldview. ... *Reality* [*deistvitel'nost'*] bursts into [*vryvaetsia*] the writer's work with tremendous force, and under its pressure the writer's ideological positions weaken and often give in. (qtd in Rozhkov 178; emphasis added)

If we are to believe Rozental', it is not even for the writer to decide whether he will man the "stead" or not. This is because, without waiting for him, life "bursts" into his private room and sweeps him along. This is the same invasion of which Shaginian had spoken ("it gushes at us, surrounds us, infuses us"). Once again, as in Gor'kii's story, the empirical individual begins by studying objects and phenomena through the distortive prism of his parochial mindset. The distortion is nothing to worry about, for whatever in Stalinist culture goes by the name of "reality" can generate a thrust that eliminates the false perspective and installs, in its stead, the proper view of things. What is this aspect or property of objects that makes a (Soviet) person see? Rozental' tells us that these objects are "real," but the triteness of this description obscures more than it reveals. How are we to name the quality of things, the quality bestowed on them by socialist "life itself," through which they assault the eye studying them and pry it open?

For the purpose, we may borrow a felicitous expression used at that time by Sergei Eisenstein (1898–1948), the celebrated avant-garde film director. In an article that appeared exactly a year after the Central Committee's resolution, Eisenstein – who had himself become part of the establishment (albeit not the most reliable part)[19] – called on Soviet writers to provide better texts for the script-starved film industry. He asked them to convey a certain property of contemporary life, which he designated as *sotsial'naia uvidennost'* (2). The first part of the expression is clear: *sotsial'naia* means "social." The noun that follows is a neologism, derived from the verb *uvidet'* ("to see"). *Uvidennost'* operates in opposition to *vidimost'* and *vidimoe*, both of which pertain to what can be seen, the visible, the apparent, and connote phenomenal superficiality. *Uvidennost'*, by contrast, is that which *has been* seen and has, as it were, sedimented inside visible phenomena: the "seen-ness" or (even better, but more awkwardly) the "having-been-seen-ness" of reality. Eisenstein leaves it at that, not caring to further explicate the meaning of the phrase or the implications of his injunction. Still, it is not much of a stretch to include his pronouncement in the line of the present argument.

The social seen-ness of the world must be a property that pre-exists the eye of the individual subject. It must be there before he comes along, or Eisenstein's counsel makes no sense (how could writers capture this property if it were not independent of and prior to their artistic seeing?). That being so, the question then becomes, how does one relate to seen-ness, and what does it mean to "convey" it? Is it a property that one is supposed to see? I suggest that seen-ness pre-exists the subject's eye genetically as well. It is the world's way of being, its demeanour or "disposition," through which it makes the subject see. It refers to the world's ability to beam and be, as the colloquial expression has it, an "eye-opener." This suggestion is in keeping with the two instances of psychological transformation we have just considered: to both Shaginian and Ehrenburg, the capacity to perceive truthfully comes from the laying bare of the world's historical inevitabilities. Seen-ness is the correlate of the empty "stead." It is a way of thinking about the automatic generation of vision, or knowledge, as a quality rather than a place. In the next few pages I will attempt to bring these two themes – the topographic and the qualitative – into a single model.

If we had to discover the primary source from which the sexual excitation of the exhibitionist springs up, our search for a properly corporal point would be – pun intended – pointless. His pleasure does not issue from any part or property of the body itself. Still, an erotogenic zone exists, even if it is not, strictly speaking, somatic. To name this surface, we can redeploy Eisenstein's neologism: the exhibitionist's source of pleasure is his "seen-ness." We can imagine it as an extension of his physical being (since it borders, ultimately, on a climactic sensation that is purely physical), an ineffable flesh woven into his natural flesh. Of what does it consist? Everyone knows that it has nothing to do with the person being simply naked. It consists in appearing naked in front of someone, *for* that someone. If we wish to give a more physiological flavour to our description, we can say that the erotogenic zone of "seen-ness" is made from the same tissue as the enlarged pupils of the other's eye. That eye, with the perplexity and shame that keep it open, is prefigured at the source of excitation. The *dilator pupilae*, those tiny muscles of the other's iris, are somehow also included in the exhibitionist's sexual apparatus. Their stimulation in the other is strictly co-lateral with the exhibitionist's erotic stimulation. It is as if we are dealing with a single sexual organ that begins with what is shown (by itself, quite insubstantial), arches across the way, and incorporates, as its most vital function, the arrest of the other's attention, the capture of her vision, her *could-not-but-see*. Speaking figuratively, we may conclude that the exhibitionist's real organ of pleasure is not his penis, but his eye-opener.

To say that the other's eye is prefigured in the exhibitionist's libido is to say that its place in the coordinate system of the sexual encounter is set much before an actual encounter occurs. When a real person comes along, she is simply slotted into a position that awaits her. What for her is a moment of highly unpleasant surprise, is, from the standpoint of the libidinal plot, a moment of confident fulfilment. In that plot, her eye becomes the concrete instantiation of the pre-scripted glance-from-there. In the assault to which she is subjected – the aggressive laying bare that surprises her – her eye turns into an effective continuation of the exhibitionist's sexual organ. Her individual-particular seeing, as the fulfilment of a general condition that disregards individual characteristics, is subsumed within the function of seen-ness. In her, in the place her eye has come to occupy, his penis sees itself.

These are, then, the constitutive elements in the anatomy of exhibitionistic pleasure: at the beginning, as no more than a "pathological" prerequisite, there is the actual piece of flesh, the carnal member itself; added to it, as the true measure by which it is not merely a penis but an exhibitionistic phallus, is the ineffable flesh of the meant-to-be-seen. To be sure, it is made from the stuff of (sexual) fantasy, but that does not make it any less real. There, in that place, the penis is, so to speak, fore-seen, meaning that the libido knows ahead of time what makes our hero go. It is this part, i.e., the fore-seen (we can imagine it as an intangible foreskin), that the libido casts out into the world as a net in which its fulfilment will eventually be caught. The catch arrives in the form of a pair of "eyes wide open." When they appear on the scene, they do no more than "fill out" the place that was left waiting for them: the place of the meant-to-be- ... In short, they ful-fill the fore-seen.

This reflection in (the stead of) the other is the whole point of the act. In that sense, "exhibitionism" is not a very accurate name for it. The gesture of showing, taken by itself, accomplishes nothing. The dialectic of the act unfolds between these two moments: the fore-seen, which is there as pure potential waiting to be activated; and the moment of "capture," when an unsuspecting subject saunters into the charted libidinal field and arouses what had lain pre-inscribed within it. It is, obviously, difficult to speak of her seeing as an "act," not only because at this particular time, she is helpless and cannot but see, but more importantly because another act has swallowed up and negated hers. This second act, which frames her seeing, is of an entirely different nature. It is not to be understood by analogy with "action." Here we must appeal once again to the other meaning of the word: "act" as a series of scripted actions – more a "scene" or "performance" than a single execution. In this sense, her seeing becomes "part of the act," part of the whole "production" that is the exhibitionistic scene.

For the dialectic of seen-ness to be complete, something in the nature of a raincoat proves necessary. We are mistaken if we think of the raincoat as a mere accoutrement of convenience, something that allows the exhibitionist to remain unnoticed before the "right moment" comes. The drapery is very much part of the right moment itself. It affects the entire meaning of the performance. Without it, we may understand the exhibitionist as saying, "Look at my penis," which is not at all the case. What he really says is, "You see!? I have nothing on!" The distinction is crucial. In the first instance, one is showing *something* (supposedly, an object worth showing, something substantial); in the second, one is showing the *nothing* of obstruction, the very absence of concealment. The actual item on display is not the exhibitionist's body but its non-hiddenness, unconcealment. To the other, he is showing exposure as such.

Only when we pass from "Look at *it*!" to "You see!? *Nothing covers* it!" do we understand the raincoat's true significance. Such is the dialectical logic of the moment that the obstruction, or veiling, must be present in some form for its negation to be effective. The possibility of covering the exposed part must be present on the scene in a sublated form. The Russian verb that translates "to sublate" is *sniat'*, which also means "to take off," "to remove." "In sublated form" would then be "*v sniatom vide*," which tells us with charming literality about the unsuspected meaning of the raincoat: not only is it there in order to be taken off, but also, in being taken off (i.e., when it is there *v sniatom vide*), it represents the possibility of *not seeing* as denied – the veritable fulcrum of the exhibitionistic act. When its flaps fly open, the raincoat stays on as material support for the little *but* that turns the formula of concealment – "(she) cannot see" – into a preserving negation: "(she) cannot *but* see."

My excuse for devoting this much attention to the exhibitionistic performance is that it may help us understand the position assigned to the subject in Stalinist cultural ideology. The parallel should not be taken too far – only so far as to clarify the relationship between consciousness and the general domain of what is called Stalinist "life" or "reality." At first go, we must reverse Vertov's slogan: now it is not life that is "caught unawares" but the subject. Caught by/in what? Caught by and in life's disposition, which is that of seen-ness. I again intend in simultaneity the two meanings of the word "disposition," which makes it possible to both be captivated by it and be captured in it: disposition as "demeanour," a way of being, and as "arrangement," assignment of positions (if someone possesses, say, a melancholic disposition, this fact has a bearing on how we approach the person, what position we take vis-à-vis him or her).

In speaking of Stalinist reality's disposition, I mean to say, in the first place, that we are dealing with something more than an object-like entity, just as the phallus on which the exhibitionistic encounter centres is more than a body part. By the same measure by which the phallus exceeds any physiological definition, this reality exceeds the lifeless abstractions of those diligent historians, economists, and political scientists who seek to establish a factual state of affairs segregated from ideological illusions and mystifications. Against such dissections, I am arguing for an understanding of the object that would include – as with the phallus – the fantasy that permeates it and constitutes flesh of its flesh. Only when we count in one entity Stalinist reality *together with* the ideological fantasy thrust upon it can we begin to ask how reality can captivate the subject so that she becomes *its* subject, the subject of Stalinism. We must reach the point where we grasp the constitution of reality as inseparable from and dependent upon the constitution of identity. When someone like Shaginian, for example, identifies herself as one who has been *made to see,* we witness the birth of a "subject," which in this instance does not mean the centre of sovereign action. As used so far in this chapter, "subject" refers to the "one" who is "part of the act" and who, in this act, is *subjected* to the glaring visibility of "life itself." It is the position, or "comportment," necessary to bring about the erection of the True-Real. Where this "one" appears is also where the order of things called Stalinist socialism celebrates its certainty at its firmest. The victory amounts to this: to have caught this "one" unawares and to have made her see. She is the "one," that is, the one in whom the act attains its satisfaction, not because of *what* she sees but by virtue of the fact *that* she sees. The content, the "what," of her seeing is, as noted apropos of the exhibitionistic scene, the unessential and contingent prerequisite of the act. The thing that really counts is this purely external characteristic: that her eyes are now in fact wide open.

"But wait," someone may interject. "Why is the act of the perceiving consciousness formal? Haven't those employees of the Institute for Experimental Medicine seen the dialectical evolution of living beings? Hasn't Ehrenburg seen how the West declines? How does this not constitute determinate content?" Such an objection would miss an all-important component of what happens in both cases – namely, the presence of the fore-seen, of the empty "stead" in which a certain vision "presupposed" by objective conditions awaits the subject whose vision it will be. When we take this component into account, we are obliged to say: the workers of the institute have seen *that indeed* living beings evolve dialectically, just as Ehrenburg has seen *that indeed* the West declines. The difference between "what" and "that" is the difference between two types of reflection. The first is the kind we are readily familiar with: the active reflection that takes hold of something outside itself, bringing something new out of it, and which, in doing this, feels itself internally,[20] thus constituting itself as an "ego." By contrast with this seeing, whose possession of "object" is correlative with its self-possession, the second kind, with which we have been concerned throughout this chapter, is not self-generative and self-constituting but reactive. We might say that here, it is the object that "feels itself" and firms up into certainty by being reflected in me. "I see" here is tantamount to "I display." I display, externally, the awareness through which the artifice called Stalinist socialism is aware of itself, of its own reality.

To bring this chapter to a conclusion, we can translate the terms of the exhibitionistic scene back into plain ideological matters. For the Stalinist regime, proving the success of socialist construction depended on proving the latter's symbolic efficacy. To wit, showing that "socialism has become reality" meant showing that it had begun producing on a mass scale cognitive, psychological, and ethical "equivalents." But this show could not be realized without the cooperation of the many "ones" in whom those very equivalents were supposed to have been incarnated. What I referred to as the "erection" of Stalinist socialism is nothing other than the moment when the symbolic efficacy of the infrastructure is con-firmed in the words or behaviours of people intent on demonstrating that their "seeing" (i.e., their way of knowing and feeling) has come to them as a gift, quasi-automatically. In sum, the actuality of "actually existing socialism" is best ascertained in its ability to produce its own creatures (subjects). The following chapter will develop these reflections further, towards a fuller conceptual grasp of Stalinist ideology. With the help of Louis Althusser, I will propose to see it as an ideology whose distinguishing character lies not in substantive claims about the world but in the ongoing display ("show") of its unconditional hold on subjects. Socialist realism will remain in the background, yet the discussion will have direct bearing on it. For, as the present chapter has suggested, the road by which subjects arrive at correct ideology is of a kind with the road by which writers and artists arrive at true artistic vision.

Chapter 8

Ideology as Authentication

Disappeared: the term *ideas.*

Louis Althusser

There is a well-known painting by Vitaly Komar and Alexander Melamid, hanging in the Zimmerli Art Museum, titled *The Origin of Socialist Realism.* It belongs to the Nostalgic Socialist Realism series of the early 1980s. Stalin, clad in the white parade uniform of a generalissimo, is seated, expressionless, on a settee. The Muse, a half-undressed figure with long, lustrous hair, holds him gently under the chin. Stalin is the model, the Muse the artist. The palatial neoclassical interior is illuminated by a single oil lamp. The light from it casts an almost perfectly opaque shadow of Stalin's figure onto the plinth at his left. With a stencil in her other hand, the Muse traces the shadow's outline. This, then, is the origin of socialist realism. Like many of Komar and Melamid's paintings, this one offers a pseudomyth. It doubles the official mythology of Stalinism with a whimsical one of its own. Executed in the style of glossy academicism, the painting seeks, as it were, to install itself in the place of its socialist-realist predecessor and subvert the doctrine from within. The realistic manner and classical pomp of the depiction yield a hyper-reproduction of socialist-realist conventions, a sort of a death mask whose verisimilitude to the original turns the latter into a mummy. Behind the tongue-in-cheek glorification of the Leader, we have no trouble reading the true (and trite) message of the painting: socialist realism was hardly more than the cultural tracing and retracing of the overshadowing figure of Totalitarian Power. The original on which Komar and Melamid superimpose their *faux-*mythography is, of course, the widely publicized story of socialist realism as a slogan that came directly from Stalin himself, as yet another manifestation of his inimitable genius.[1]

In the previous chapter, I began sketching a different myth of origin, one that developed immediately after the Party resolution of 1932. This myth is about the subject, not the Master; it is the projection of a blinding light, not the tracing of a shadow. Socialist realism was decreed into existence by a sort of ideological axiom: since socialism was already a fact on the level of the economic base (after the campaigns of industrialization and collectivization), it must also be the case that a corresponding cultural superstructure was likewise already there, at least implicitly.[2] All that remained to be done was to give it a name, remove the survivals of the past that stood in its way, and provide the organizational structure for its manifestation and further flourishing. All of this the Party soon accomplished. The axiom that socialism was an effective force, demonstrably operative everywhere among the masses, presupposed that a distinct style of life had become dominant in the land of the Soviets. This, in turn, presupposed that its cultural manifestation – an art defined and unified by a distinct way of experiencing the world – was also in evidence, definitely if not yet fully or perfectly. In this sense, socialist realism was not a program for something to be attained later and gradually; rather, it was the baptism of something that was already there and that had been for some time. So it was not a paradox that at the time of its formal birth, socialist realism in literature could boast a list of works in which it had already been incarnated.[3]

On this axiomatic logic, being a socialist-realist author meant being told – implicitly or explicitly – that a place had been prepared for you, a place of cannot-but, that needed only be manned.[4] This implied participating in the theatre of perfect visibility (discussed above) in which one was to show oneself as possessed, as overwhelmed by the coming-true of socialism. And definitive of socialist realism, I contend, was the kind of artistic practice that unfolded as the symbolic act of filling out – through writing, painting, composing – this axiomatically predefined spot. The Stalinist version of the immaculate conception was the myth of a social content that dictated its own intellectual and artistic articulations, a life that spontaneously produced its own authentic representations. The conception was immaculate, for it was as if the world conceived itself, thought itself, and this was somehow an objective process to which the subject was urged to surrender. By letting go (of his personal opinions, homegrown world views, studied convictions), he would become one with the process so that the world would know itself in him. This was an ideological myth, to be sure, but of a rather peculiar kind.

When we concern ourselves with ideology, we have as our primary object of interest – what else? – ideas. If we belong to the critical, predominantly Marxist tradition, we interrogate these ideas in order to show how they misrepresent the actual order of things in the world and how this misrepresentation serves to promote the interests of a dominant social group. Alternatively, if we subscribe to the sociological approach to ideology, we want to show how a body of authoritative notions enables social integration by mapping in broad strokes a terrain of infinitely complex (and divisive) experience. In both cases, however, we attend to the *content* of ideas, and it is through this content that we distinguish one ideology from another. For instance, we identify a racist stance with the content of statements like: "People of the race *n* are naturally predisposed toward a life of indolence." On the same logic, many have identified Stalinist ideology with a set of dominant theses: the possibility of building socialism in one country; the necessity for the continued existence, even strengthening, of the state; the inevitable decline of capitalism; the intensification of class struggle in the Soviet Union after the suppression of antagonistic social groups; and so on. Continuing with this line of thinking, one would not fail to describe socialist realism as an ideological art, inasmuch as it unfailingly reproduces these and other official postulates. Stalinist novels, for example, would be called ideological because the stories they tell give an expanded fictional presentation of well-familiar Party slogans such as: "Heroism is becoming an everyday occurrence"; "The capitalist world is handicapped by the very existence of the Soviet Union"; "Collectivism has become a habitual way of life for millions"; "The enthusiasm and initiative of the masses redefine the limits of the possible"; and so on.

This thinking is valid as far as it goes; unfortunately, it does not go very far. The fact that socialist realism was ideological, in this sense, is too obvious to belabour. One is easily convinced of this by picking up just about any novel of the Stalinist era and reading it alongside the *Pravda* headlines from the time it was written. Nor is there a chance that we might confound Soviet writers by pointing out to them that their productions were ideological. The writers were abundantly aware of the fact. On every opportune public occasion they were reminded that their works must reflect the "burning issues of the day" and stay in step with the "leading ideas of the time." This was called *ideinost'*, and it was a fully intentional aspect of creative practice under socialist realism. To remain at this level of understanding would be to forfeit critical work proper, for the latter cannot be satisfied with knowledge already explicit in the object of study. Socialist realism was explicitly and self-consciously ideological. Just because we repeat this with a tone of approbation does not make our pronouncement any less of a platitude.

Stalinist ideology was a phenomenon that went beyond specific ideas, beyond the content of slogans, speeches, and resolutions. And it is this fact that makes it, and socialist realism, worthy of discerning critical inquiry. For anyone familiar with Soviet culture, it should be intuitively obvious that a statement like Shaginian's "Socialism has become reality …" (itself a rehashing of Stalin's triumphalism) holds no epistemological interest whatsoever. Nothing impels us to inquire whether its content is true or false. If it holds our interest at all, it is not as an idea that it does so. We understand that the statement's significance, if any, resides not in its asserted meaning but in the general "setting" from which it comes to us. That is to say, we take it not as a proposition that may or may not stand the test of verity, but as a gesture, a performance that enters into a larger "production." As soon as we adopt this perspective, we should realize that we are no longer dealing with ideology in the sense suggested above. We are not attending to a set of ideas (whose content we could expect to betray illicit agendas or instruct us as to the functioning of a social mechanism), but to the organization and staging of performances. In this chapter, I propose a view of Stalinist ideology that takes this perspective into account. I argue that the peculiar character of this ideology is to be found not in any substantive claims delivered by way of representations but rather in the attempt to stage the functionality of representations. The case I have been making for socialist realism is analogous to the case for ideology: in socialist realism as well, we are dealing with representations (*Darstellungen*) whose significance is not reducible to what they say or show on the level of content, but derives from a general symbolic performance whose aim is to demonstrate how knowledge and vision take hold of the subject.

I will begin with a preliminary illustration in the form of a heuristic scenario. Let us imagine ourselves as the conscientious observers of an activity previously unknown to us. It involves several people and takes place outdoors. We chance upon it and try to make sense of it. After observing it for some time, we notice the following:

1. The activity has no practical significance. The participants derive obvious pleasure from it, yet it does not in any way connect with the lives these people lead when not engaged in it.
2. The activity involves discrete roles for the participants and unfolds according to rules. Both the roles and the rules can be grasped and described by an attentive outside observer.

3. During the activity, the participants seem to forget about the lives they lead when not engaged in it and take on the roles required by the activity. What they do engrosses them completely; they become what they are doing so that it does not seem at all that they have taken on "roles."

4. Even though their motions over time exhibit, to an observing eye, the regularities of rule-governed behaviour, the participants do not appear to be "following rules." Their actions flow with great ease and without any special effort of compliance with prescripts.

As time passes and we come across many occurrences exhibiting the same characteristics, we realize that we are dealing with instances of a general kind. To this general kind of activity we decide to give a name: "play." From that point on, to everyone who asks, we explain what "play" is by summarizing our four principal observations: it is a pleasurable activity that draws you in and away from your real life, so that you partake of it obliviously, and although it does have rules, it is *truly* "play" when the rules fade away to become a spontaneous way of being. For even greater brevity, we decide to capture this characterizing description in a single adjective: "ludic." We agree that from now on, we will call "play" only that which exhibits the traits definitive of the "ludic." Conversely, if an activity does not give evidence of the "ludic," it should not qualify as "play."

One day we chance upon a group of people engaged in something that very much resembles "play." All of the roles and motions are the same. But in addition to all the rules we previously extrapolated, we now become aware of another condition: the participants must act in a way that visibly demonstrates that the activity has drawn them in and has a hold upon them. In their behaviour, they must not only follow the usual course of the game but also show "involvement," even "abandon." Previously, the sole object of play was "to win." Now there is an additional object – play itself, or rather, the "ludic." In playing, the players must create the objective appearance that the activity of play plays them. By showing themselves to be drawn in, involved, spontaneously living the rules and roles of the game, they are, essentially, demonstrating the presence of the "ludic." This strange arrangement does not exclude the possibility that some of them may be genuinely drawn in by the activity and actually possessed by the ludic. Such may very well be the case, since the earlier parameters of the game have been preserved and winning is still an object. Yet as we take a look at the entire set-up, we must ask ourselves: Is this still "play"? We remember our decision to apply the term only to that which exhibits the "ludic." What we now have in front of us certainly does exhibit this general quality. Formally, and by this standard alone, we must concede that we are indeed observing "play." At the same time, it is abundantly clear that the situation now is nothing like before. Now the "ludic" is not something we first produce, on a conceptual level, in order to describe the qualitative distinctiveness of the activity in question. Rather, the activity has changed in such a way that the "ludic" is now produced *by* it, in a premeditated and controlled manner. The *in*-itself, that is, the essence, has become *for*-itself: a conscious performance, or staging, of the essence. What we have before us is "play" as the process of its own authentication.

When we contemplate Stalinist ideology, we are in a situation analogous to the one just described. We are contemplating an activity whose object has shifted in a peculiar, self-referential way. While we are still confronted with statements that could be termed "ideological," that is, with claims about states of affairs in the world (existing, potential, desirable, normative), the activity we have before us goes well beyond the making of such claims. More than the generation and dissemination of meaning, Stalinist ideology encompasses the regulation and self-regulation of behaviours through which the essence of ideology itself is authenticated. Much like "play" in my hypothetical scenario, ideology is at its most authentic when it is experienced not as a convention, a construction, a set of norms, but as a way of life; and when it has a hold upon the subject so that ideological meanings and the social roles they assign are lived not as prescripts, artificial impositions, or ideals, but as the dynamic of reality itself. Stalinism, in my view, should be understood as an attempt to replicate just this kind of positive experience of the ideological.

When we take a Stalinist ideological thesis such as "the triumph of socialism in the Soviet Union leads to the exacerbation of class struggle, while altering its traditional forms,"[5] we notice right away that as political discourse, this thesis functions on two levels. One is the purely semantic or epistemic: the statement accomplishes the assertion of a determinate meaning, it describes a purported state of affairs in the world. On this level, we might be tempted to judge whether the description accurately reflects the reality at which it aims. At the same time, we are aware that the statement had a very concrete life in Soviet society. An entire campaign followed whose goal was to demonstrate that what the thesis asserted was indeed the case. At this second level, we must take into account all the mechanisms by which the ideologeme was transmitted from the political apex to the lowest levels of the Party apparatus and the general population: the meetings convened to discuss the latest pronouncement by the Leader; the directives from the centre urging vigilance and a new optics for viewing what had previously seemed innocuous occurrences; the work of

Party activists in all spheres of social life in unmasking concealed class enemies; and the hundreds of reports published in local and central newspapers that testified to the continued, and now more insidious, resistance of socially alien elements.[6] In other words, after registering what the ideologeme means, we have to also take into account the campaign whose end result was to provide factual backing for the asserted meaning. This second aspect, which we might call validation, is by no means unique to Stalinist ideology. Every ideological system must have at its disposal some means for demonstrating the truth of its propositions. Just as a doctrine of revelation must be able to produce miracles, a political ideology must be able to exhibit facts that validate the claims it advances.

Validation, however, is something different from what I called, just a while ago, authentication. The latter is not about the factual content of this or that particular postulate but about the experience of ideology as such. The procedure of authentication does not aim to convince that such-and-such is in fact the case, but rather to show that knowledge itself – whatever its content, whatever the claims it makes – derives from a genuine source. In the case of "play," authentication referred to the process of staging the essential element of play – the ludic. Analogously, an ideology that functions as its own authentication would be one that stages, or produces, the essential (positive) characteristic of the general kind "ideology": its hold upon the subject, its existence as a second nature.

The distinction between the two modes of operation of ideology may become clearer if we consider the following two pronouncements:

1. "I believe that x is the case" (where x is an ideological proposition).
2. "When I believe, it is socialism that believes in my stead."

At first, it may seem that the second of these could very well be an ideological proposition. If so, we should be able to substitute it for the x in the syntax of the first pronouncement. But when we do this, we end up with an anomaly that is not merely verbal:

3. "I believe that, when I believe, it is socialism that believes in my stead."

The more evident reason for the anomaly is that we are used to having the object of ideological belief be a certain state of affairs in the world, not the status of belief itself. This is why something like "I was falsely led to believe she was pregnant" cannot itself be an object of belief. The less evident reason for the anomaly has to do with the logical conundrum presented by

(3). If all of my beliefs are believed for me, then my belief that this is the case should fall under the same rule. But (3) fails to express this fact. The phrase "I believe" in statement (1) asserts my agency as someone who is free to adopt or reject this or that belief. But statement (2) abrogates this very agency (I am not free in my believing, since this is the work of socialism). Thus, when (1) and (2) are combined to form (3), the result is a contradiction: the two parts of the statement speak at cross-purposes. Because (2) cannot be an object of belief, it also cannot be the object of verification. But it *can* be the object of authentication. That is to say, I can act and speak in a way that makes it apparent that my views are dictated to me by the irresistible immanence of socialism.

To unfold further these reflections on the character of Stalinist ideology, I will presently turn to Louis Althusser's well-known essay "Ideology and Ideological State Apparatuses." Embraced as a revelation by some, harshly criticized by others, this text of 1970, along with other writings by Althusser, remains a major contribution to the conceptualization of ideology in the twentieth century. It does not address Stalinism at all, nor can the argument found in it be applied to Stalinism in a straightforward way. It offers a theorization of ideology in a universal sense, which aims to extract the scientific kernel of Marx's legacy with the tools of psychoanalysis and structuralism. It is not my intention to "apply" Althusser's insights into ideology to the case of Stalinism, as if the latter could prove to be a privileged or at least a very intriguing species of the former. Stalinist ideology is decisively *not* what Althusser claims the universal kind "ideology" to be. But, in a peculiar sense, it *wishes* to be that and stages the kind of symbiosis with the subject Althusser has been the first to theorize.

    The first part of the article, stretched over some thirty pages, is devoted to rethinking the old Marxist duality of base and superstructure. Althusser insists that their relationship is most adequately understood in terms of reproduction (136). Just as the economy encompasses the reproduction of the existing forces of production, so the superstructure is largely responsible for the reproduction of the relations of production (which are also constitutive of the base; 148). In a practical sense, this is accomplished through the legal-political sphere and a number of ideological state apparatuses (ISAs: the church, family, schools, etc.), which Althusser contrasts with repressive apparatuses such as the army and the police (149–56). Although this lengthy discussion has been to a great extent about ideology, it is only midway through the text that Althusser takes a closer look at what ideology is: "When I put forward the concept of an Ideological State

Apparatus, when I said that the ISAs 'function by ideology,' I invoked a reality that needs a little discussion: ideology" (158). This "little discussion" takes up the rest of the article. Here, Althusser advances a universal theory, not of ideologies (which have had documented existence in determinate historical settings) but of ideology as such (161). The latter has no history: it is one and the same always and everywhere (161–2), which is to say, it has an immutable structural role in the social totality. It is this general theory that interests me most, and I will follow the discussion closely, as I find even Althusser's phraseology quite revealing.

Let us pick up the argument from the subsection that has as its heading the assertion, "Ideology Is a 'Representation' of the Imaginary Relationship of Individuals to Their Real Conditions of Existence" (162). The assertion itself we leave aside for the moment. In this section, Althusser asks, without actually spelling it out, a disarmingly simple question: Why does ideology need to lie? He then proceeds to argue against two common answers to this question. The first answer points us to a company of "a few bad men." That is, ideology needs to lie because a few bad men need to lie to the "people" and thus keep them in submission (163).[7] In dismissing the "few bad men" thesis, Althusser does not wish to say that bad men in power do not fabricate deceptive ideas. Even less is he saying that they do not use such ideas to maintain their domination over the people. He simply dismisses the thesis, for even though bad men in power fabricate lies to keep the rest of the people in their power, *this is not what ideology is about.*

From there, Althusser moves on to a second erroneous thesis. This one comes from Feuerbach via the early Marx. The thesis answers the question, Why does ideology need to lie? by pointing not to tyrants and priests but to the people themselves: the people (i.e., not just the "common folk," but men in general) create ideal representations that they superimpose onto the less-than-ideal conditions of their existence (163–4). In other words, ideology needs to lie because men need to escape, even if just in their imagination, the alienating social world they inhabit from day to day. Once again, Althusser denies neither that people construct imaginary worlds for themselves nor that they inhabit these so that they do not have to face straight-on the harsh reality of their daily lives. He simply dismisses the thesis altogether, for even though people may in fact do that, *this is not what ideology is about.*

Having dismissed in this fashion the two wrong answers to the question, Althusser moves on to dismiss the question as well: It cannot be at all a question of anyone "needing" the lies of ideology.[8] Expressed differently, the "need" through which ideology "needs" to lie is not the need of anyone. But a need that is not the need of anyone is not a need at all: it is a necessity. Henceforth, the question of ideology becomes a question of necessity. And here is how Althusser formulates this new question: "Why is the representation given to individuals of their (individual) relation to the social relations which govern their conditions of existence and their collective and individual life *necessarily* an imaginary relation?" (165; emphasis added).

In the last three words we find, I believe, the key to the thesis that opens this section of the article: it is pressingly important for Althusser to distinguish between this formulation and "men represent their real conditions to themselves in an imaginary form" (163). For those who are reading the article for the first time, the distinction may seem little more than a confusing scholastic exercise, and the confusion is only increased by the use of the verb "represent" in the two formulas: in the latter, it has a subject (the people, who "represent ... to themselves," etc.), while in the former it is subjectless ("it is their relation to [the real conditions of existence] that is *represented* to them [in ideology]" [164; emphasis added]).⁹ But the confusion is dispelled once we have the key: ideology rests on a "necessarily ... imaginary relation." This should be read along the lines of the preceding argument: just as it is not a matter of anyone "needing" the lies of ideology, so it cannot be a matter of anyone "representing" what is represented in ideology.

And thus we come by short and quiet steps to what otherwise has the power of a bombshell – the assertion I highlighted in the epigraph to this chapter: ideology is not a matter of ideas. How are we to understand this sudden inversion of the content that "ideology" carries and announces in its very name? Caution is again in order: Althusser does not dispute that people have distorted ideas about the world, ideas of which they are conscious and in which they believe. He simply writes: "Disappeared: the term *ideas*" (169; emphasis in the original). Disappeared from where? – From consideration. Although people have "ideological" representations of which they are conscious and in which they believe, *this is not what ideology is about*.

Ideology is a Representation that nobody has conceived. We should be perfectly clear on this: although people *can* think this representation, they do not *give* it to themselves, in the essential sense of the word. This is why Althusser is very careful to write "representation *given* to individuals" (*la représentation donnée aux individus*). Nor should we be curious to know *by whom* it is given to them: it is simply given, without a "who"; we left the clique of priests and tyrants far behind, and no new "givers" have appeared since. Now we should take the next step, which is strictly consistent with our previous formula: "A need that is not the need of anyone is not a need at all, but a necessity." In a similar way, a representation that nobody can "give" is not a representation at all, but an immanent *relation*. This, then, is what has remained of ideology, after we put aside all the things it is *not* about: an immanent imaginary relation, that is, a relation whose "imaginariness" (*imaginaire*) is not imagined by anyone (supposedly, standing in the real world). If we wish to retain the word "representation," as Althusser does, we need to say: ideology is a kind of representation that cannot be given, only inhabited. We cannot be *with* it, only *in* it. This is the fundamental meaning of the since then sloganized assertion that we all are "in ideology" (166).

Those well acquainted with the article have noticed that my gloss so far has not followed faithfully the order of Althusser's exposition, but instead has jumped ahead and, from there, interpreted what comes earlier. In my defence, I can say that in order to follow the spirit, one must often go against the letter. "By the letter," the exposition is as follows: after Althusser has reformulated the question of ideology ("why is the representation given to individuals … necessarily an imaginary relation"), he suddenly stops and drops the question, promising to return to it later; for the time being, he advances a whole new thesis: "Ideology has a material existence" (165). For those who follow the letter, the transition may appear quite sudden: "Didn't we just say that ideology is not only an imaginary, but *necessarily imaginary* relation? How do we get from there to the thesis that ideology has a *material* existence? Since when are imaginations something material?"

Those who follow the spirit should not be baffled. We should try to understand Althusser's statement by approaching it from a subsequent point – that is, from the thesis advanced only later in the article: ideology is not a matter of ideas (representations, in the sense discussed above). If not, then what *is* it a matter of? The answer: it is a matter of… *matter*, of something *material*. In the article, the order of argument is: "ideology is material, and hence, ideas drop out of consideration." Our way of proceeding here, which is just the reverse of this order, allows us a better grasp of what Althusser means by "material" existence, that is, the real matter of ideology.

The examples he gives of the material life of ideology are curious at best: kneeling, praying, confessing, signing petitions, protesting (167). Supposedly to illustrate the precedence of the material with regard to the ideational, he even quotes Pascal: "Kneel down, move your lips in prayer, and you will believe" (168). Now, these actions can be called "material" only in a very approximate and idiosyncratic sense. Althusser had sought to forestall the problem earlier by asserting that "[of] course, the material existence of ideology … does not have the same modality as the material existence of a paving stone" (166); and then, with a wink to Aristotle, "I shall say that 'matter is discussed in many senses,' or rather that it exists in different modalities, all rooted in the last instance in 'physical matter'" (166). This is coy at best, and self-servingly evasive at worst, but it does make clear the direction in which Althusser wishes to go. He very much wants to show that ideology is hard-wired to the economic infrastructure, so he is doing his best to convince us that it too has a material existence of sorts. And what he means by this is that ideology consists in the performance of concrete actions in concrete institutional settings (those of the ISAs).

In the same way that people do not give themselves ideological ideas, they also do not give themselves (generate) the actions in question. Of course, they are the ones *de facto* performing these actions, just as they were the ones *de facto* thinking those ideas. But like the ideas, the actions are given to them by the institutionalized practices in which the people find themselves embedded:

> I shall talk of actions inserted into *practices. And* I shall point out that these practices are governed by the *rituals* in which these practices are inscribed, within the *material existence of an ideological apparatus*, be it a small part of that apparatus: a small mass in a church, a funeral, a minor match at a sports' club, a school day, a political party meeting, etc. (168; emphasis in the original)

When all is said and done, we have the following enchainment: ideas count only to the extent that they are "performed" in (individual) actions, which are, in each case, the instantiations of practices, which, for their part, take place within institutionalized rituals, the last constituting the concrete life of various ideological apparatuses. Following the logic of the chain, we can say that the individual's ideas are "thought" by his actions, which are "acted" by social practices, and so on. In the ultimate instance, the individual's actions are "acted" by ideology, in the new sense that the concept has acquired by now (i.e., as a Representation *in which* people live their lives).

As always already inserted in an array of such practices, the individual is everywhere and for all practical purposes the *subject*. Being a subject, for Althusser, means just this – to be acted in one's (supposedly free) actions and thought in one's (supposedly personal) thoughts: "It therefore appears that the subject acts insofar as he is acted by the following system (set out in the order of its real determination): ideology existing in a material ideological apparatus, prescribing material practices governed by material ritual, which practices exist in the material actions of a subject acting in all consciousness according to his belief" (170). Should we entertain the hope that we could somehow forestall the moment when, as individuals, we are "interpellated" by ideology, Althusser would inform us that our hope is in vain. Even before we come into this world, a pre-appointment is waiting for us,[10] by which we are slotted into roles we will be playing: "man," "son of ...," "citizen of ..." (176). Hence: "ideology has always-already interpellated individuals as subjects, which amounts to making it clear that individuals are always-already interpellated by ideology as subjects, which leads us to the last proposition: *individuals are always-already subjects*" (175–6; emphasis in the original). If so, "individual" stands for the never truly available (as an actuality) yet necessary presupposition of the existence of the subject.[11] The meaning of "subject" is determined exclusively by its relation to ideology, and vice versa: ideology cannot be thought outside of the necessary imaginary relation in which individuals are constituted as subjects. In fact, ideology is nothing *but* this relation: "The existence of ideology and the hailing or interpellation of individuals as subjects are one and the same thing" (175). Earlier it was said that, in his ultimate instance, the individual is what has been produced by ideology, namely, the subject; the individual is *not*, except as a subject. In reciprocation, we must now say: ideology, in its ultimate instance, is what produces subjects; it does not exist *except* as this production (171). The theory of subjectification conjugates with the earlier thesis of ideology-cum-imaginary-relation as follows: individuals are necessarily subjects insofar as they are *in* a Representation (imaginary relation) that they have not given to themselves; it is given to them by necessity, so that the Representation "acts" them in determinate and necessary ways, while also producing a set of requisite beliefs.

Althusser's principal intervention in Marxist theory is his endeavor to drive a wedge between the early Marx (prior to 1845) and the – supposedly much more scientific – author of *Capital*.[12] The issue of ideology is no exception. Althusser deems unsatisfactory the view advanced in *The German Ideology* (1845–6),[13] where thought unhinged from material life is pilloried as self-glorified vacuity. Such thought is ideological inasmuch as men's practical lives are absent from it; it is a "phantom," a "chimera," as Marx and Engels put it (*The German Ideology* 37), "a pure illusion, a pure dream," as Althusser rewords it ("Ideology" 159). The problem with such a conception is that it lets ideology and reality go their separate ways, leaving us with no means to think one *in terms* of the other. Thankfully, what the early

Marx had put asunder, the mature Marx joined together, or so Althusser believes. His main source of inspiration for a genuine, scientific theory of ideology is the famous section in Volume I of *Capital* (chapter 1) devoted to the fetishism of commodities.[14] In it Marx does not address ideology explicitly, but he does describe a mechanism of illusion very different from the one we find in *The German Ideology*. The commodity form that all products of human labour assume in a capitalist economy can be called a false appearance, insofar as the social character of this labour masquerades as an objective property of the thing (its exchange value expressed in monetary signs). The falsity in question, however, does not come by way of anyone's deluded views. The appearance of people's creations as commodities is not caused by "phantoms of their brains" (*The German Ideology* 37). On the contrary, people come to view products in terms of objective values *because* this is how products actually appear in the myriad quotidian acts of buying and selling. Marx, in other words, is asking us to think of an illusion that exists necessarily and practically,[15] a chimera full of reality, and this is also how Althusser wants us to think of ideology.

Just like the commodity form for Marx, ideology for Althusser is not a representation that people give themselves. Just like exchange value, it exists in acts more than it does in beliefs (we usually do not go to the local supermarket with a creed on political economy). If ideology is an illusion, it is an objective one imparted by the mode of economic life in which people find themselves inserted. It is easy to see now the true source for that inverted order of things in which, for Althusser, actions come before beliefs. If a worker, yesterday's peasant, hires himself for pay in a factory, he does this out of necessity and not out of conviction that labour should be exchanged for money. In the very act of hire, he practically performs the idea that human labour is a commodity like any other. He does not need to believe that this is so (most likely, he never gave a moment of thought to the issue). His actions do the believing for him.[16] It is with similar realities in mind that Althusser is able to write, apropos of ideology, that "ideas drop out of consideration."

If people live "appearances" that are not, strictly speaking, imagined by themselves, yet have a hold upon them, the stage is set for a wedding of Marxism and psychoanalysis. In comes Freud, chaperoned by Claude Lévi-Strauss and Jacques Lacan.[17] In this intellectual company, Althusser is able to cast Marx's scheme of an objective process that assumes a necessary form of appearance in terms of a very familiar intra-psychic dynamic. The ISA essay draws an explicit analogy between ideology, as Althusser wants it, and the dream, as Freud has it. Ideology is not a pure illusion, as young Marx supposed, just as the dream is not a random exercise of an imagination let loose during sleep (Althusser, "Ideology" 160–1). Both are structured and meaningful insofar as a concealed reality is transmitted through them in an organized way. With the dream, we have yet another example of a representation that people do not give to themselves. It is from their own lives that the dream representation issues, but since the true and full content of these lives is not directly accessible to the individuals, it is as if the representation comes to them from somewhere else, from "another scene." Continuing with this analogy, one can think of ideology as a *production* in a sense similar to the production of dreams and symptoms by the unconscious.

The Freudian unconscious, constituted by instincts and their "vicissitudes," became in Lacan a system of pure relations modelled on linguistic signification. In Althusser, a kind of social unconscious is analogously structured by the relations of production. The point Althusser wishes to get across is that the relations of production are effective in a twofold manner: they not only secure the production of goods and the generation of wealth, but also – just like the unconscious – generate a surrogate reality for the human subject whose existence is determined by those same relations.[18] With hardly any mediation at all, we pass from economic conditions of existence, through the forms of social intercourse they impose, to the patterns of thought and behaviour these forms in turn activate. The transmission between the heterogeneous realms is, to all appearances, unconditional, quasi-automatic. It is as if social existence were an enormous dream machine in which the infrastructure does the dreaming, ideology is the dream itself, while human subjects are nothing but the roles that the machine has dreamt up for them.[19] (Remembering the earlier heuristic exercise, I should add: they live them not as "roles" but as life itself.)[20] The domain of ideology, and even of culture as a whole, is viewed as a field of practices programmed in advance and *in toto* by their functionality in reproducing an existing order of things. Lévi-Strauss had already provided the model (indebted to Freud in its own right) by analysing elementary social formations in which an unconscious symbolic logic, a coding automaton of sorts, is at work in configuring the community's mythical plots and corresponding (ritual) practices. Althusser seems to believe that ideology, even in advanced capitalist societies, functions similarly: as an unconscious symbolic combinatory hard-wired to economic reality and configuring most varied and mundane rituals of public life. Because the logic is unconscious, yet practically effective in setting the terms for what people do and believe, a structuralist like Lévi-Strauss, or Althusser, might as well go ahead and declare that the logic "acts" people, "thinks" them, even "lives" them.[21]

This talk was rather fashionable in the 1960s and 1970s, but as E.P. Thompson reminds us, it is far from politically innocuous:

> In the old days, vulgar Political Economy saw men's economic behavior as being *lawed* ... but allowed to the autonomous individual an area of freedom in his intellectual, aesthetic or moral choices. Today, structuralisms engross this area from every side; we are structured by social relations, *spoken* by pre-given linguistic structures, *thought* by ideologies, *dreamed* by myths, gendered by patriarchal sexual norms, *bonded* by effective obligations, cultured by mentalities, and acted by history's script. None of these ideas is, in origin, absurd, and some rest on substantial additions to knowledge. But all slip, at a certain point, from sense to absurdity, and, in their sum, all arrive at a common terminus of unfreedom. (206; emphasis in the original)

It cannot be my goal here to detail the numerous conceptual and political issues with which Althusser's theory is riddled.[22] Instead, I wish to focus the unexpected light this theory throws on a topic it never treats explicitly: official Stalinist culture. After all, that "terminus of unfreedom" to which Thompson draws our attention was not just a theoretical *faux pas* of French academics; it had a very real historical instantiation in Soviet Russia.

The vision of ideology as the "bad dream of the infrastructure" (Eagleton 73, 117),[23] in which people get assigned roles, acted, and thought, is questionable psychoanalysis[24] and even more questionable Marxism, but it does come very close to being a perfectly good Stalinism. All one needs to do is remove the negative marks that ideology bears in Althusser (as inadequate knowledge, alienated form of existence, and dissimulation of the real) so that the bad dream could have the potential to become wholesome and bright.[25] This would leave intact the general sociological thesis that forms the backbone of Althusser's theory:[26] the mechanism by which social-economic being reproduces itself as culture by recruiting subjects and giving them representations to live *in*. This, I would argue, is ideology in its own right, a meta-ideology (since it concerns itself with the generation of ideology) with distinctly Stalinist overtones. It is most certainly a Marxist idea that we can learn much about men's intellectual productions by considering the socio-economic conditions in which they emerge. But it was Stalinist state policy to build socialism by forcing the installation of an economic infrastructure and disregarding, in the process, all the cultural conditions that must be in place beforehand if a socialist community is to be more than a mockery of its name. The ideology implicit in this policy is easy to spell out: the infrastructure is symbolically and psychologically productive; once installed, its cultural extension – the practices, behaviours, and mentalities presupposed by socialism – will follow as a matter of course; it is enough to place people (by force, if need be) in socialist relations of production for the dream of freedom, equality, and brotherhood to become their lived reality. It is also easy to see how very close this is to Althusser's conception. Thompson has pointed out the affinity in terms as blunt as can be:

> If we wished to translate [Stalinism's] practices into a consistent theoretical system, then we would design a Theory ... in which a structuralist reductionism both guaranteed the fundamental health of the Soviet system in its supposedly socialist economic "basis" (thereby displacing all political, legal, and cultural questions into secondary or tertiary status) and disallowed any materialist historical analysis of this system ...; in which men and women were seen as the bearers of ineluctable structural determinations, in which their responsibility and historical agency was denied ... and in which it was, hence, more easy to view them as "rotten elements" or things ... In short, Althusserianism *is* Stalinism reduced to the paradigm of theory. It is Stalinism at last, theorized as ideology.
>
> Thus there is a sense in which we failed fully to identify Stalinism as Theory, because we were waiting upon Althusser for this theory to be invented. (245–6)

This is unmercifully harsh,[27] but the reason I have chosen to dwell for so long on Althusser's concept of ideology is that I believe Thompson's basic intuition to be correct. I am not interested in incriminating Althusser but in understanding, with his unwitting help, the character of Stalinist cultural politics. I do believe that the ISA essay succeeds, indirectly, in theorizing Stalinism in a way that Stalinism could never theorize itself.

I stated earlier that Stalinist ideology is not what Althusser claims ideology to be, just as the organized simulation of the ludic is not really play. Stalinist ideology did not "secrete" from the pores of an established social order, as Althusser believed to be the case for all ideology;[28] it did not function organically and unconsciously; it did not generate a compulsory symbolic logic spontaneously; it did not recruit subjects automatically; it did not hold these subjects fast within some compelling imaginary relation; and no, it did not act their deeds and think their thoughts in their stead. But – and this has been my main point throughout – such is the image it projected of itself; such is the plot of the spectacle it administered. Stalinist ideology was more than the body of dogmas that the ideas of Marx and Lenin had become once their original meaning had been falsified by instrumental *raison d'État* or desiccated through endless ritualistic incantations. It was also the staging of ideology's positive essence, more or less as Althusser envisioned it. It was not merely a matter of propagating and inculcating particular meanings, but of showing how *meaning itself,* any meaning, is a product of a supposedly immanent social process, of "our life," of "practice" (whether it be the reality of class struggle or the victorious work of building socialism), and of demonstrating how it gets hold of people and acts them even before they are able to consciously apprehend it. Beyond any ideational content, it was this "show" that constituted the essential dimension of Stalinist ideology – a state-wide, perpetually renewed production in which people were expected to act not only as if they believed in Marxism-Leninism but also as if their belief was taking place within them by virtue of an objective dynamic operating beyond them.

I will leave this show's sinister enactments for the beginning of the next chapter, and offer here a glimpse of its brighter, affirmative version. My example is a speech by Stalin to a gathering of women shock workers on 10 November 1935.[29] The women, some forty beet farmers from *kolkhozes* in Russia and Ukraine, have gathered in the Kremlin on this "festive day, when the successes and potentials of liberated women's labor are being demonstrated" (Stalin, "Priem kolkhoznits-udarnits" 77). The visit, in other words, is framed from the outset as a moment of demonstration, a show. Stalin begins his short speech by stating what it is that has been shown today to the members of the Politbiuro: "Comrades, what we saw here today is a piece of the new life, the one we call *kolkhoz* life, socialist life" (76). The beet farmers are very much like the characters of Panferov with which I opened the previous chapter – the *Vertretung* of socialism, its creatures. No such women have ever existed before, declares Stalin, only *kolkhoz* life could have begotten their kind. At the gathering, the women have spoken words, and these words have expressed their ideas and beliefs. Now Stalin's speech will frame their words and beliefs as tokens. That is, he will take them not for what they have said – their denotative content – but for what they have manifested – their indexical or evidential significance. "We listened to the simple words of simple working people" (76). It does not matter what those words are about. It matters that they evidence a new state of being, free labour under socialism; and the views these words express count insofar as they can be shown to be "thought" by an objective set of circumstances. The Leader proceeds as follows: these women are the products of the *kolkhoz* system (*kolkhoznyi stroi*); the *kolkhoz* system comprises the practice of remunerating labour on the basis of workday norms (*trudodni*);[30] hence it can be said that women have been liberated by the lived reality of the workday norm.

> The *kolkhoz* gave [*kolkhoz dal*] the workday norm. And what is a workday norm? The workday norm makes everyone equal – women and men ...
>
> By means of the workday norm, the *kolkhoz* liberated the woman and made her independent. Now she no longer works for her father, before marriage, and for her husband, after she is married, but works for herself, first and foremost. This is what the liberation of the peasant woman means, this is what the *kolkhoz* system means, which makes the working woman equal to any working man. Such splendid women could appear only on this base [*na etoi baze*],[31] in these conditions. (76–7)

The first observation I offer concerns Stalin's use of the verb "means" (*oznachaet*). Clearly, he is not treating his listeners to a semantic analysis of the phrases "liberation of the peasant woman" and "*kolkhoz* system." These are items whose semantic content is only too familiar to the people in the hall today and the readers of *Pravda* tomorrow.[32] The Leader's goal is not to herald or clarify an ideological meaning but to authenticate it, and that entails showing us that "*kolkhoz* system" is a meaning operative in life, one that has produced real-life effects, has taken possession of people, beings of flesh and blood, so that when these people come forth, one can point to them and say triumphantly: "This is what a *kolkhoz* system *means*!" It is a meaning that speaks not in propositions but in tokens, not through *Darstellung* but through *Vertretung*. And this brings me to the second point: the women, with their words and views, are those very tokens. In simple terms, they are shown in the Kremlin as examples of what socialism makes of people. In terms more reminiscent of Althusser, the beet farmers are exhibits of what happens when individuals are inserted into practices (*trudoden'*) constitutive of certain relations of production (collectivized agriculture): they become the faithful subjects of socialism, possessed of the views and beliefs appropriate to their position. Lastly, in the terms of Thompson's critique, the women shock workers are presented in Stalin's speech as nothing other than "the bearers of ineluctable structural determinations,"[33] only now in the positive sense of determinations that bestow freedom as a destiny.

Stalin, then, is rehearsing his own version of Pascal's and Althusser's "Kneel down, move your lips in prayer, and you will believe." During the ceremonial meeting, the shock workers have shown that they believe in socialism.[34] Stalin takes the rostrum after them and points out that they believe it because they live it, or rather, because they are "lived" by the practices of socialized agriculture. This is the most striking aspect of the picture presented by the Leader: that freedom, hope, belief, pride, all of these are effects that accrue *to* people by virtue of the place they have been given in the new socio-economic organization (the state gave the *kolkhoz* system; the *kolkhoz* system gave the workday norm; the workday norm gave freedom, hope, belief, etc.). It is as if these are the attainments not of people struggling for a better life, but rather of the place itself, of the "stead" they happen to be manning.[35] Socialism appears not as their work but as an objective set of circumstances (Stalin's "base" and "conditions") that works them en route to its self-realization.

Because socialism was to be built by first constructing the "base" and then installing, in a purely formal way, the corresponding relations of production, it became a question of legitimacy for the regime to demonstrate that the base had been unconditionally effective in producing its necessary supplement – the consciousness, psychological make-up, and patterns of conduct appropriate for a liberated humanity.[36] The Stalinist thesis that (theoretical) consciousness trails behind practice[37] did not contradict this fact. It simply indicated that people had not yet come to awareness of a truth implicit in their own lives and work. This truth thought *them,* even if they did not yet think *it.* Recall that literary critic who avowed that the "socialist tendency" was transforming the lives and minds of people even if they were not fully aware of the fact.[38] On the same assumption, Stalin was able to declare in a speech of 1937: "Our people, unfortunately, do not always realize the height to which history has elevated them under the conditions of the Soviet system" ("Rabotnikov" 236). It was not a great calamity that the "software" of individual consciousness had fallen behind the "hardware" of infrastructural accomplishments, since it was understood that the former was preconfigured by the latter. This did, however, allow the Party to speak on behalf of "practice" and explain to ordinary minds the objective tendencies to which they had to own up. Thus in April 1932, the resolution on literature informed the leaders of RAPP that their consciousness was not in step with the current stage of socialist construction. And thus the institution of socialist realism, from its very first day, was premised on the symbolic act of demonstrating that truth inheres in practice, that it emanates (beams) straight from life and gets a hold of me even before I can consciously get hold of it.

This may be an opportune moment to draw once again the distinction between the ideology found *in* texts of socialist realism and the ideology *of* socialist realism as an institutionalized practice. The former has to do with the reproduction of specific ideologemes in artistic discourse; it is not this aspect that interests me in the present study. The latter is about staging the functioning of ideology itself, in its positive aspect as culture; it is about demonstrating that culture – that is, socialist realism itself – is the necessary form of (artistic) appearance assumed by an objective and symbolically effective social process. Like the words of the women shock workers during the Kremlin reception, the texts of socialist realism are framed by this greater show, or exhibition. They convey meanings discursively, but this is only the trite sense in which they can be said to be ideological. In the first place, they are ideological because they participate in a regime of symbolic behaviour that authenticates the essence of ideology. These are representations that are produced and received – at least in official contexts – as tokens. Tokens of what? – Of the fact that their authors are truly subjects, creatures of socialism, which means that representations are given to them by the immanent symbolic logic of Soviet life. And if they are obedient subjects, the authors will play their part in this performance, they will act and speak not as if it was they who painted socialism, but rather as if socialism painted itself in their work. In short, they will act as if in their artistic practice they were acted by the socio-economic organism to which they belong. This is what I called authentication. It too is a symbolic performance, like the modernist death of the author; and it too transcends the limits of the text; finally, it too aims to show artistic practice as "operated" by some objective agency beyond the individual subject. Unlike its modernist counterpart, however, this performance obeys the script of an ideology in power, an ideology of ideology, which requires that ideas be shown to spring from a necessary "lived relation." Ideological Stalinism shared with intellectual modernism the conviction that individual subjectivity is shaped by forces – heredity, race, environment, unconscious drives, economic conditions – beyond subjectivity's jurisdiction. But only for Stalinism was it a matter of political exigency to stage over and over again rituals affirming that this was the case. To one extended ritual of this kind I will turn my attention in the next chapter.

Chapter 9

The Blind, the Seeing, and the Shiny

We need to fantasize, we need to study reality in such a way that, on the basis of its laws, our fantasy could create actually possible events, which we do not always see.

K. Chornyi, speech at the
First Congress of Soviet Writers

In our country there are no events that occur by accident.

Vladimir Kirshon, speech at the
First Congress of Soviet Writers

The theoretical credo of Althusser and Žižek – the objectivity of ideological belief – was the practical *modus operandi* of the Stalinist ideological regime. As E.P. Thompson remarked, the latter did not develop its own original theory of ideology. In practice, however, this regime consistently sought to demonstrate that personal convictions are merely the coming-to-consciousness of objective circumstances that shape the lives of individuals. Insofar as consciousness did not always keep up with its objective determinants, it was possible for people not to realize just how happy they were, just as those leading cadres Stalin was addressing in 1937 did not realize what a privileged place history had given them. By the same token, it was possible for individuals to be anti-Soviet elements without ever harbouring anti-Soviet sentiments, let alone having a coherent ideological world view. For after all, they were perceived as occupants of determinate positions in the society's class structure; even if they did not believe – say, in the restoration of capitalism – it was assumed that their class position "does the believing for them." Kulaks and wreckers, Trotskyists and right opportunists, imperialists spies and "rootless cosmopolitans" – these were all variations of the "objective enemy," a peculiar breed of human beings, extant only since the early twentieth century and distinguished by the fact that their character and subsequent fate was decided regardless of whether they actually harboured feelings or intentions inimical to the regime.[1] Their classification as so many alien elements proceeded not from what they actually *thought* but from what they supposedly *were*. The alien political character imputed to them did not concern in any essential sense the ideas they might or might not have. If they did in fact have harmful ideas, this was seen as a consequence and as a further – but by no means necessary – demonstration of their being objective enemies, not as a prerequisite for being considered such. By confessing their criminal actions and intentions, they simply inhabited, with their consciousness, the position to which they had been assigned in advance. With the ideas they voiced, they declared to the world the "tendency" whose carriers they were known to be.[2]

Stalin's rise to power in 1928–9 was due in large part to his ability to present his political opponents as people who were objectively undermining the Soviet order, even if, subjectively, they were unaware of that fact. He reasoned by axiom: the petty bourgeoisie continued to exist, and so did the class struggle; this fact *could not but* be manifested within the Party (which had remained the only forum of political representation in the country);[3] deviations from the General Line, both to the left and to the right, were the forms assumed by the class struggle in society at large and the pressures exerted on the Soviet Union from the "capitalist encirclement."[4] In this picture, individuals were no more than supports for objective relations, which is why Stalin could brush them aside: "Those comrades who focus the problem of the right deviation on the persons [*litsa*] representing the right deviation make a mistake. This is an incorrect way to pose the question. Persons, of course, play a certain role. However, it is a question not of persons, but of those *conditions and circumstances* that engender the right danger in the party" ("O pravoi" 223–4; emphasis added). As carriers of a tendency defined by objective "conditions and circumstances," the persons in question might not be fully aware of how the tendency acted them and towards what end: "The right deviation in communism, under the conditions of Soviet development, where capitalism has been abolished, but where its roots have not yet been torn out, is the *tendency* on the part of some communists, *an unformed and not yet conscious proclivity*, but a proclivity nevertheless, to stray from the general line of our party in the direction of bourgeois ideology" ("O pravoi" 225; emphasis added).[5]

When, in the following years, the proclivity was alleged to have became conscious and to have formed itself into a series of monstrous plots against the Soviet Union and its leadership, the general ideological set-up did not change. The enemies of the people pilloried in the Moscow show trials of 1936–8 were still treated as persons whose thoughts and deeds were a function of an impersonal and inexorable logic. With their testimonies, Kamenev, Zinov'ev, Bukharin, and their associates were expected to show themselves before the court and the Soviet public as being precisely that: the *Träger* of necessary determinations. The accused cooperated only to a point. Most of them recited what they were supposed to say.[6] But they, obviously, could not always recite it with authentic passion; not many could show convincingly that they had indeed been compulsively driven to the crimes with which they had been charged. The Prosecutor-General, Andrei Vyshinskii, did his best to remedy the spectacle:

> Is it *by accident* that Trotskyism became the vanguard of capitalist restoration?
>
> No, *not by accident,* because everything was leading to this from the very beginning. *Not by accident,* because even before the October Revolution Trotsky and his friends were fighting against Lenin and the Leninist party, just as they are now fighting against Stalin and the party of Lenin-Stalin.
>
> Comrade Stalin's *predictions have been fully realized.* Trotskyism *indeed* turned into the central meeting point of all powers inimical to socialism, into a gang of mere bandits, spies, and murderers, who put themselves fully at the disposal of foreign intelligence services, into lackeys of capitalism, into restorers of capitalism in our country.
>
> And here, at the trial, with extraordinary fullness and clarity was revealed just this vile essence of Trotskyism. They came to their disgraceful end because for decades they followed this road, glorifying capitalism, refusing to believe in the successes of socialist construction, in the victory of socialism. This is why they finally arrived at a broad program for capitalist restoration, this is why they decided to begin betraying and selling our motherland. (*Protsess* 172; emphasis added)

This passage merely reproduces the logic of Stalin's thinking about the class struggle in the Soviet Union: for as long as that struggle continued, it *could not but* be manifested within the Party. Similarly, for as long as there existed a capitalist encirclement, and for as long as the antagonism between socialism and the bourgeois world escalated, there *could not but* be agents of reaction within the Soviet Union. The history of Trotskyism, reaching back to the years before the Revolution, was given (i.e., concocted) not in order to strengthen the case against the accused, to give their recent crimes a credible background. The goal, rather, was to chart a vector of ineluctable necessity (which I have punctuated by italicizing the emblematic phrases in the quoted passage).[7] Nothing occurred by accident,[8] everything happened just as it was supposed to happen, just as it was predicted by comrade Stalin and inscribed in the logic of history. It *could not but* happen. The show trial was the show of this *could not but*.[9] No ideological conviction, no matter how firm, no matter how resolutely pursued and implemented in action, could travel a road as straightforward and precipitously inevitable as the one Vyshinskii drew for his audience. This could only be the trajectory of a tendency, principle, or function, of a devilish automaton that had nothing subjective about it. We are referred to it when the Prosecutor-General speaks of the "vile essence of Trotskyism." From this essence proceeded the acts that the accused *could not but* commit; from there, they had been irresistibly compelled to ever greater crimes against the Soviet Union.

We should take care when examining the logic of Vyshinskii's harangue, for it follows a course directly opposite of what we might expect. The indictment does not move from a consideration of the deeds, intentions, and beliefs of the Trotskyists to the characterization of these people as anti-Soviet elements ("they did this, intended that, hence they should be condemned as anti-Soviet"). It is just the other way around: these people are Trotskyists – that is, carriers of an objective anti-Soviet tendency – and therefore they could not but do what they did and intend what they intended. In a traditional legal procedure, the criminal's motives are considered in order to substantiate the attribution of the crime. In the Moscow trials, by contrast, crimes were attributed to the members of the anti-Soviet centres and blocs in order to demonstrate to the public the general motive force that had acted these people in their criminal acts. To prove they were criminally culpable was a subordinate task. The primary objective of the macabre spectacle was to show that down to their smallest deeds, the enemies of the people were marionettes controlled by the inevitable workings of history. In a traditional legal procedure, the court begins by collecting evidence and hearing testimonies in the hope that these will coalesce into a clear and consistent picture of the crime. The Moscow trials followed the opposite course: from a picture of historical forces and political subject positions that was known in advance, to making this picture "come alive" in the courtroom.

And here is how the tableau came to life. First, there is the general ideological vision of victorious socialism, implying, inevitably, the reciprocal decline of capitalism, the rising hostility towards the Soviet Union, and so on. But since that vision is merely the scheme of historical necessity at its most schematic, it has to draw material into itself in order to be completed. From the second, darker part of the picture, an "essence" emerges, a concretization of the very inevitability of the tendency. The essence is the anti-Soviet pure and simple – degradation as such. Next, the essence needs a "character" (not unlike Althusser's *Charaktermask*)[10] in order to show itself in human-psychological form. This character is none other than the "Trotskyist," the paramount exemplification of the anti-Soviet person. It contains just what was contained in the essence: subterfuge, undying hostility towards socialism, escalating moral degradation passing into unprincipled bestiality, and so on. For its part, the "character" needs concrete actions, beliefs, and words, through which it will make its appearance on the stage of the world; it needs the components constitutive of a "role." Once all of this is put in place (i.e., fabricated), one last thing remains: the role needs to be manned, an actual human being has to appear in it – a person through whom the actions will be acted, the beliefs believed, and the words spoken – in short, through whom the picture will become complete so that everything that is will be shown to be indeed just what was meant to be.

This is how the spectacle was actually composed. But the effect it sought to produce was something quite different. The accused had to show that their downfall was nothing other than the inevitable downfall of the tendency whose carriers they were.[11] It was not just a matter of delivering self-incriminating evidence. They were also expected to dramatize their own political bankruptcy and ideological insubstantiality. It was not enough to confess to the crimes. It was also necessary to act out and speak out the logic that led to the crimes, as the last resort of creatures crushed by history. Under questioning, Kamenev delivered the following "confession":

> I must admit that we really did not, and *could not have had*, any positive political program with which to oppose the policy of the VKP(b).
>
> In the very beginning of our negotiations with the Trotskyists there were still some faint attempts to discuss the possibility of composing some positive platform.
>
> However, we soon realized that this work is in vain, that *we do not have any ideological-political platform*.
>
> We banked on the insurmountable nature of the difficulties our country was experiencing, on the crisis of the national economy, on the collapse of the economic policies implemented by the Party leadership; by the second half of 1932, this card was clearly beaten.

The country, under the leadership of VKP(b), was overcoming the difficulties and moving successfully on the path of economic growth. We *could not
but see* that.

It might seem that we should have abandoned the struggle. However, the
logic of counter-revolutionary struggle, the base pursuit of power, devoid of
any ideas [*bezideinoe*], led us in a different direction.

The overcoming of difficulties, the victory of the policies implemented
by the Central Committee of VKP(b), infused us with more resentment and
hatred toward the party leadership and, in the first place, toward Stalin.
("Zakrytoe" 305–6; emphasis added)

As paradoxical as it may sound, the oppositionists' *bezideinost'* was only
a further – nay, the ultimate – demonstration of the objectivity of ideological belief. That the Trotskyist–Zinov'evist bloc lacked an ideology does not
contradict the fact that ideology is a lived relation; indeed, it confirms it.
The essence of ideology in general was being authenticated here by a negative example. One can have substantial ideas and a positive political platform only if one occupies a meaningful place in the social (super)structure,
if one represents (*vertret*) some viable forces in society. By 1932 the oppositionists had been left without any "base" and thus without a place in socialist Russia (a fact foreshadowed in concrete terms by the expulsion of
their alleged leader, Trotsky). As such, they could only attract other up-
rooted elements – the pitiful remnants of the vanquished exploiters – and,
of course, the forces of reaction *outside* the Soviet Union. The former poli-
ticians automatically become unprincipled terrorists once socialism has
become the sole effective base of Soviet society;[12] since all ideas and beliefs
are produced by the base, these former people have been reduced to in-
stinctual resentment and brute force. As another of them recapitulated:
"The circle has closed. It is over with the political masquerade, it is over
with the shams of oppositions, discussions and platforms. Opposition was
superseded by conspiracy against the state; discussions and platforms were
superseded by bullets and bombs" ("Last Pleas... Mrachkovsky").

This is what happens when one represents (*vertret*) bankrupt historical
tendencies: one is eventually left without ideological representations
(*Vorstellungen*). By the same logic, but in reverse, we get the following axiom: if one is part of a viable social whole, truly belongs to it, and is thus a
Träger of a progressive historical tendency, then one will live ideology as
second nature, will be possessed by substantial ideas, energizing beliefs,
and so on. This axiom underlay the institution and practice of socialist
realism. The staged revival of Style presupposed the spectacle of creative
individuals in the grip of a transpersonal plastic force. The spectacle was

staged in various forms and on various occasions. One occasion, however, is pre-eminent among all others, for it marked the institutional birth of Stalin's homegrown socialist culture: the First All-Union Congress of Soviet Writers. The House of Trade Unions on Bol'shaia Dmitrovka Street in Moscow, where in March 1938 the last of the show trials took place,[13] was also the venue for the congress – a spectacle in which the members of the literary intelligentsia had to show themselves to be the *Träger* of the opposite, victorious, historical tendency. To this spectacle I now turn.

The congress had been decreed by the Party resolution of April 1932 and was set in motion almost immediately. From the outset, this assembly of writers was seen as a symbolic event of epochal significance. By enthroning the style of socialist realism, the congress was to signal the advent of a socialist renaissance and mark the Soviet Union as the new centre of world culture.[14] Partly because these ambitions were so extravagant, the preparations took longer than expected, and the opening date needed to be moved back on several occasions. The delegates were carefully selected, and selected foreign guests were invited. The order of presentation was set in advance. The key speeches and reports had to be approved beforehand by the Organizational Committee; those texts were made available to all the delegates. Excursions, concerts, and public festivities accompanied the main event. On the street outside the House of Trade Unions, large crowds gathered every day to greet the writers as they entered or left the building.

This festive, effervescent life was not confined to the outside. It made its way inside. At intervals throughout the writers' debates, organized groups of common folk from various walks of life proceeded down the aisle of the magnificent Hall of Columns and ascended the podium. These were the "delegates without membership cards," as Boris Pasternak referred to them: industrial workers, representatives of *kolkhoz* collectives, Young Pioneers, soldiers, scientists – "shiny, happy people." All of them had come to greet the unprecedented assembly, voice their enthusiasm for the epochal event, and testify to the eager attention with which all Soviet people followed the congress's proceedings. Their entrances were more than colourful intermezzos, ceremonial exclamation points in a prosaic text that was otherwise about different matters: artistic literature, the parameters of socialist realism, the organization of the Writers' Union, and so on. They were very much *part* of that text – the frame without which the text could not be properly understood. Their attendance was constitutive of the act whereby socialist realism was being produced, not a sideshow to the deliberations through which, supposedly, the Stalinist cultural program was being formulated. In a sense on which I will elaborate in the following discussion, this was *the show*.

Each such appearance was introduced by the session chair with the words: "Comrades, we have been visited by ..." (*Tovarishchi, k nam prishlil priekhali* ...). Usually, after saluting the delegates and providing a short biography of the collective he or she had been chosen to represent, the speaker presented a *zakaz,* a particular social commission. All of them made, essentially, the same demand: "Show us."[15] In different voices, the people's representatives were demanding that they be represented (*darstellt*). In the voice of comrade Bratanovskii, speaking on behalf of proletarian authors of technical literature: "Our collective order to you, comrade writers, is: get closer to the industry worker, depicting him not only at the machine, but also showing his fight for acquiring high technical qualification, for absorbing all achievements of world culture" (*Pervyi* 554); as expressed by comrade Nemtsova, a representative of a factory-university (*zavodvtuz*) named after Stalin: "Give us a woman-hero, not just a shock-worker, but a woman who raises our next generation ... who combines this exacting, complicated task with the struggle for socialist construction" (366); and as sung by a choir of pioneers from Moscow:

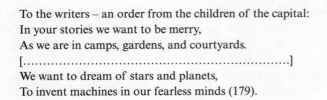

To the writers – an order from the children of the capital:
In your stories we want to be merry,
As we are in camps, gardens, and courtyards.
[..]
We want to dream of stars and planets,
To invent machines in our fearless minds (179).

This was the social commission speaking, commissioning itself. It did not need to be ordered from somewhere else, from "up high." To all appearances, it was life itself, "our reality," that was entering the Hall of Columns and demanding its own artistic rendition.

The assembly was genuinely moved. When a *kolkhoz* farmer carrying a heavy tool on her shoulders took to the podium, Pasternak was so flustered that he lunged at her, seized the tool, and tried to carry it for her. When the Pioneer choir marched through the hall and began singing, Gor'kii could not suppress his tears; many in the audience sobbed along with him. Throughout the proceedings, speakers kept reminding the gathering of this or that memorable appearance: "When, yesterday, those children entered the hall, when all those colors, gestures, applause, the sounds of the orchestra, of the trumpets, the flood of light ..." (206); "Take for example the speech of the *kolkhoz* worker who greeted us. This absolutely fearless, valiant woman ..." (232); "Comrades, Otto Iul'evich Schmidt spoke here.[16] He said something seemingly simple, but quite significant ..." (616); "Comrades, one of the most remarkable moments of this congress was the speech, during the first session, of the Donbas shock-worker Nikita Izotov ..." (654).[17]

The writers understood and agreed that the business for which they had convened, the business of Soviet literature, of artistic representation in general, had to do, in the first place, with showing the builders of socialism. Nikolai Pogodin even equated socialist realism with the task of presenting the biographies of these people (388). The call to depict the new heroes was heard from all sides. The Party emissary, Andrei Zhdanov: "Soviet literature must be able to show our heroes ..." (4); Gor'kii: "The main hero of our books should be labor, that is, the human being organized by the processes of labor ..." (13); comrade Nemtsova: "Give us a hero who lives a full life, give us the kind of hero who is to be found in our socialist construction ..." (367); Aleksandr Fadeev: "Indubitably, our literature lacks the images of monumental, intelligent, integral characters, the likes of which are promoted in ever greater numbers from the ranks of the working class and the peasantry ..." (234).

Yet even as they were urging one another in this way and vowing to fulfil the main social commission, to show in their works the new people of socialism, the writers could not ignore the fact that the social commission itself had "made a showing." Had the people not appeared in front of the congress? Had they not come from the factories and fields, walked down the aisle, and stood before the assembly? Those who had come had done so not just to speak to the writers *about* the building of socialism. They had also come to exemplify it. They had taken to the stage in the Hall of Columns and stood there as living tokens of Soviet reality. This too was a "showing" – one that did not wait to be shown through the agency of the "delegates with membership cards," but was showing itself on its own, from within itself. Once again we come upon the duality hidden behind the word "representation," the duality between *Darstellung* and *Vertretung*, between "depicting" and "standing for," "embodying," "bodying forth." On the one hand, we have a showing that shows something: the depicted object. It is transitive. The second is showing as pure self-exhibition. It is intransitive, for it does not take us somewhere outside of itself, to a thing we should see. It is *itself* the thing we should see, the thing we cannot help but see. The first type of showing is satisfied and extinguished when it gets to the object. The second is satisfied when it "gets" to the viewer. Its "object"

– for it is not as intransitive as it seems – is to possess its audience. Nowhere exceept in this possession does it succeed as a show.

Not nearly everyone in the audience at the First Congress of Soviet Writers understood what was required of them. What were they supposed to do? What was their part in the production that was already under way, the cultural production of socialist realism? And, as a first order of business, how were they to react to the demands being made by the new people? What were they supposed to do in order to show these beings? Because the assembled were writers, members of the intelligentsia, living lives quite different from those of their potential heroes, many thought it was a matter of getting closer to the new people, getting to know them more intimately, and depicting them from that point of intimacy. As in the years prior to the congress, there were reproaches that echoed the old Russian theme of the intelligentsia's separation from the life of the masses.[18] In response, voices – some of them quite authoritative – prescribed a more involved and diligent study of the living subject matter.

In his official report on the Statute of the Union of Soviet Writers, Pavel Iudin mandated:

> The artist must study reality intently, carefully, and persistently, he must know the new man in detail, in all the particulars, his work, everyday life, soul, personal qualities, how he thinks, how he converses with his comrades, what he thinks about himself, what he sees in his dreams, how he loves and hates, how he cries and rejoices. Without this, the writer cannot become an "engineer of human souls." (665)

For a brief initial moment this statement sounds like an invitation to a diligent empirical study. That moment passes once we realize that we are in the Soviet Union of the 1930s, the last place in the world where the writer could be advised to be a mere observer of life (and certainly not by Iudin, a Party philosopher and one of the leading interpreters of Marxism during the Stalinist period).[19] We may also notice that no empirical acquaintance could possibly get to the depths of intimacy Iudin envisions ("what he sees in his dreams").

How, then, is one to attain this intimacy? How deeply into the thick of reality must one reach before reality shows its true face? What is that optimal proximity at which the knowledge of reality becomes authentic and lends itself to truthful artistic synthesis? At what point in the asymptotic approach to the presence of "life itself" does one begin to see that presence truthfully, "in detail, in all the particulars"?

One thing is certain and bears repeating: the desired point is not, as it had been earlier, the point of application of method. Since the first part of this study, since the culture of the 1920s, we have moved beyond this point. The first indication that the attainment of the "real" was no longer the provenance of (professedly) scientific hermeneutic was the controversy, at the beginning of the 1930s, centred on the literary theory of RAPP. Even as their organization was being dismantled, RAPP's leaders had continued to insist that the essential characteristic of Soviet literature was its ideologically superior vantage point upon the world: the so-called dialectical-materialist method. In preliminary meetings between writers and representatives of the Party's Central Committee, this platform was rejected and the slogan of socialist realism took its place. This was more than just a scholastic squabble over words. It suggested a momentous cultural shift. From now on, there was not going to be a mediatory instance ("conveyor") through which truth would emerge from latency and manifest itself. Truth would do so on its own, out of itself.[20] In the Hall of Columns, it did so every time the delegates without membership cards walked down the isle, spoke, or sang.

The shift between the two paradigms of truth was implied in the first published mention of socialist realism, the statement by Ivan Gronskii of May 1932: "The basic demand that we make on the writer is: write the truth, portray truthfully our reality, which is in itself dialectic" (qtd in Robin 39; emphasis added). This gives us to understand that no special apparatus is needed to extract the truth of life, for "our reality" itself makes this truth legible.[21] All that is needed is to "write" what has thus been rendered manifest. The sentence following the one just quoted comes as an inference: "Therefore, the basic method of Soviet literature is the method of socialist realism" (39). In other words, socialist realism is the generalization of this kind of artistic practice for which no method is needed, insofar as it records a truth that has been made explicit already by the movement of life itself. Gronskii's words echo those of Stalin, supposedly spoken two weeks earlier, at a meeting with writers in Gor'kii's residence: "If an artist truthfully depicts our life, he cannot but notice and depict in it that which leads it to socialism. This exactly will be socialist art. This exactly will be socialist realism" (qtd in Ermolaev 145; emphasis added).[22] First comes the world, with its immanent truth; then the writer's contact with it; and only in the last instance, following a line of inevitability ("cannot but"), as a consequence or a point of arrival – the so-called method of socialist realism. This, of course, is none other than the concatenation discussed in chapter 7, on the example of a moving story told by Gor'kii, through which the object arrives at the cognition proper to itself in the "stead" of its researchers. In that earlier instance, we were considering the general mechanism through which the truth of socialism "works." We are now considering the very same mechanism, but with a view to the obligations this truth places on the author.

It indeed appears that the author's "burden is light" (Matt. 11.30), for no special knowledge or intuition is required of him prior to his encounter with the world. As the words of the Leader suggest, all that is needed is sincerity. The person mirroring Stalin's role within the writers' community, Gor'kii, voiced the same imperative in his keynote address to the congress: "Only one thing is required of the person [in our country]: to be honest in his attitude toward the heroic work of creating a classless society" (14; emphasis added). In ordinary circumstances, we would have no cause to pause and ponder the meaning of such common phrases as "being honest" or "being sincere." But we are now in quite extraordinary circumstances that give us reason to doubt whether the sincerity intended by Stalin and Gor'kii is exactly what we have have always understood by this word.

Sincerity, as we know it, presupposes something contained within (feelings, intentions, thoughts, etc.) that is not held in concealment but freely released into the open.[23] It is a motion of letting out. But this is not at all what Stalin and Gor'kii had in mind. The sincerity they were preaching was a letting-in or, even better, a letting-through, more akin to the eighteenth-century notion of sensibility as susceptibility: one's capacity to be affected by life in its various manifestations, to "resonate" with the meaning/emotion intrinsic to life's events, to be moved.[24] With regard to Stalinist culture, we may say, in a preliminary way, that it was a matter of one's capacity to be "moved" (acted) by the *truth* – or, which is the same thing, the *tendency* – of "life itself." Rather than letting out a truth held concealed, it was a matter of being affected by a truth breaking through and manifesting itself. As we now see, the optimal proximity to reality that Iudin and many others urged, the proximity of clear artistic vision, was not to be measured with the yardstick of some expert knowledge or systematic observation but by degrees of "sincerity."

When, in the same speech, Gor'kii complained that "we still poorly see reality" (14), he was blaming the predicament precisely on the dearth of such sincerity. The injunction he directed at his audience pivoted on a verbal usage I find quite revealing:

For the success of our common work, we must understand, feel through [*pro-chuvstvovat'*], the fact that organized socialist labour in our country, the labour of half-literate workers and the primitive peasantry, has created, in a short period of time, a decade, colossal values ... The right evaluation of this fact would show us the cultural-revolutionary force of the teaching that unites the proletariat of the world. (13)[25]

"To feel," whose proper Russian equivalent is *pochuvstvovat'* (perf.), falls a bit short of translating *prochuvstvovat'*. The latter denotes a different kind of relation to the object of sentiment. *Pochuvstvovat'* refers us to the moment a feeling is born, when an emotion emerges out of nothingness or ephemerality. It takes as a direct object this very emotion, whatever its name may be ("love," "resentment," "sadness," etc.). By contrast, *prochuvstvovat'*, used in Russian much less frequently, directs us to an object that has nothing ephemeral about it. On the contrary, it is something that predates the exertion of feeling, a solid, pre-existent reality, an antecedent fact. To feel, in the sense of *prochuvstvovat'*, is not so much to experience the birth of a particular emotion as to inhabit with emotion such a pre-existent reality.

In the passage just quoted, Gor'kii is spelling out clearly for those in attendance the reality that needs to be infused with feeling: it is the "fact" of socialist construction. Given that the fact is already a fact, we may ask: What is to be gained from this additional sentimental operation? Can the fact be made *more* real, *more* present? Indeed it can. When one opens up, "sincerely," to the fact of socialism, a new level is reached. We already know what the qualitatively new moment is, and Gor'kii's words confirm this knowledge: through sincerity, one begins to see "the force of the teaching" on which the entire edifice stands; that is to say, one appreciates the power of this teaching to become reality; one sees that what was meant to be could not but come to be and so is indeed coming to be, amen!

This, of course, is none other than the dialectic of seen-ness discussed in chapter 7. The coming-true of socialism lays bare the logic of history. For those who are on the wrong side of history – oppositionists of various stripes – it spells doom and the absence of (political) vision. For those on the right side of history, the laying-bare is the very source of vision:

> The Soviet dramatist possesses one small advantage, he is relieved of one small worry: he does not need to look for a hero. There is no need for him to light his torch and search in the secret nooks of life for man, the new man – the hero of our epoch.
>
> The epoch came to his rescue. The secret of life *stands revealed, grandiloquently clear*. The hero is everywhere. (*Pervyi* 459; emphasis added)

These are remarkable words. In them, the "epoch" is presented as an agent independent of the writer, a force that comes to his rescue and relieves him of traditional duties. The Soviet author does not need to light his torch and illuminate reality because the reality of the Stalinist socialist epoch is now itself the light of revelation: it is beaming. Projecting this light more powerfully than anything else are the shiny, happy people, the heroes of socialism. Some of the writers speaking from the congress's rostrum testified to having been nearly blinded. Bruno Iasenskii: "To be a Soviet writer means to be in possession of such *blinding* [*oslepitel'nyi*] material, the likes of which was not available to any writer, in any country or historical period" (278; emphasis added). Aleksandr Zharov: "[We] proved to be unprepared for a full-bloodied poetic perception of the grandiose complexity and *blinding* simplicity of the reality that has come to be [*nastupiv-shei deistvitel'nosti*]" (537; emphasis added). Leonid Pervomaiskii: "I want to look in the eyes of Soviet poetry's tomorrow. I want to look into the eyes of truth. This is very difficult. This is how great our time is, this is how *vivid and fierce* [*iarka i iarostna*] this truth is. This is the truth that gave birth to us" (540; emphasis added).

Because the light is already here, upon us, all one needs to do is throw one's torch away and "let the light shine through." The imperative of sincerity, translated into the scopic register, implies that one should open one's being to the point where it becomes translucent, porous, in relation to the light, so that it can transmit it without distortion or attenuation. The verb best suited to describe this unusual relay between world and subject is a near-synonym of *prochuvstvovat'*, only in the reflexive: *proniknut'sia*. It is one of those instances that showcase the wonderful subtleties of expression possible in Russian. The root verb *proniknut'* translates easily and quite accurately as "penetrate." But after it comes the reflexive particle, which changes everything. The semantic result is not "penetrating oneself," or "letting oneself be penetrated," or just "being penetrated"; it is: through one's own activity to render oneself penetrable, to bring about the permeation of one's own being by something initially external (an emotion, the consciousness of something; respectively, *proniknut'sia chuvstvom ... proniknut'sia soznaniem o ...*).

In this single word, I believe, we have a succinct answer to the question posed earlier: How is the Soviet author to achieve the intimate knowledge required for a proper representation of socialist reality and its exemplary inhabitants? The key to such intimacy lies in a particular position that the two partners – the author and raw, unprocessed reality – must assume. The roles are reversed from the relation implied in the very name "author": his

role of actively manipulating the material, shaping it into a creation onto
which he may place the seal of master and originator. In socialist realism,
by ideological default, the artist is confronted with "blinding material"
that already possesses a proto-aesthetic form. The primal beauty of this
self-shaping stuff need only be channelled by the subject. He who by virtue
of a cultural anachronism still calls himself author must assume a position
vis-à-vis the material such that he opens himself to the powerful thrust of
"life-itself" – a surrender in which his being will be possessed to the core.
What we saw, in the previous cultural frame, as an immanent organization,
principle, tectonic, and so on, acquires in Stalinist ideology the prowess of
an invasive force, one that manifests itself precisely where it takes possession of the human subject. In that it produces and "acts" the subject, this
force proves to be real, enjoys presence.

One is able to see clearly insofar as one is truly possessed by this force.
Conversely, the inability to see should be attributed to a certain obdurate-
ness of being and, ultimately, to "foreignness." (When Stalin launched his
offensive against the right opposition, a consistent motif in his speeches
was Bukharin and Tomskii's failure to see the changes in Soviet society;[26]
we saw the same reproach directed at the leadership of RAPP.) At the congress, the distance between these two states of being, between blindness
and clear vision, was addressed in an emotional speech by the young writer
Aleksandr Avdeenko. An abandoned child, he had had a difficult early life
beset with violence, crime, and imprisonment. He was speaking of this past
when he admitted: "My life was such that I looked at people and *did not see
them*" (243; emphasis added). He interrupted the story about his past by
recalling the moment when the Pioneer choir ascended the podium; it was
as if his former, low life had continued all the way to that memorable entrance and had been terminated only by it: "We lived by the day, by the
hour. But in that moment when the pioneers appeared on the congress'
podium, I felt a tremendous desire to live. And my thoughts ran not by
decades, but by centuries .... Then, in front of me, the future *flashed, revealed itself* [*blesnulo, raskrylos'*]" (243; emphasis added). In the lobby,
however, during the intermission, as Avdeenko was looking to share his
enthusiasm with his colleagues, he was taken aback: "But many of the
writers were not shaken by the pioneers' demonstration. That was an offensive indifference. Indifference is the most terrifying thing" (243).

Avdeenko recalled an earlier occasion on which he had been offended by
the indifference of his colleagues. His mentor, Gor'kii, had told him of a
new kind of blade that a Soviet technician had invented: a blade that could
not be blunted, only sharpened. "He [Gor'kii] drew an entire picture of

what lays in store for our economy and our life as a consequence of this invention. He became impassioned. I do not know whether he had ever been as happy or excited as in that moment" (243). When, afterwards, Avdeenko asked other writers about the blade, it turned out that no one had heard of it; not only that, but they were not even interested in learning about it (243). Gor'kii was the antipode of this obtuseness:

> Aleksei Maksimovich harbors a special hatred toward indifference. He has the ability to feel life [*umeet chuvstvovat' zhizn'*]. Once he was telling me that in our country labour is beginning to turn into art. He proved it with facts, examples. I left Gor'kii's house shaken by his passionate attitude towards life. It was uncomfortable for me to walk down the street: I thought that people would stop me and start asking me questions.
>
> I felt that I had become smarter, as if I had read a dozen good books. I wanted to speak, live, dream just as wisely and profoundly, as he, Aleksei Maksimovich. No other writer has shaken me in such a way, from others I have not heard such speeches.
>
> We lack this voracity toward life. We are either unwilling or unable to be voracious toward life's manifestations. (243)

What reads as a sickeningly syrupy profession of feelings, passing into a plea for sensitivity, is, in essence, really about something else. The ability to be moved by life, which Gor'kii exemplifies and which his protégé is happy to evidence as well as eulogize, is a matter of emotion only because it is, first and foremost, a matter of *belonging*. Gor'kii sees better and farther because he feels more deeply; but he feels more deeply because he is organically rooted in Soviet reality (despite his long absence from the country). He does not even need to do what other writers are being urged to do: *proniknut'sia*. His being is already saturated with the tendency characteristic of socialist life. He is moved emotionally by life's "manifestations" because, in a deeper sense, he is driven by the driving force of that very life: driven to *see*.

What is it that Gor'kii sees from his privileged position? According to his disciple, Avdeenko, Aleksei Maksimovich is able to "dream wisely and profoundly." He sees, for example, what will happen as a result of the new invention; he sees a future in which labour will become a creative endeavour. This dream-like futurist vision had a well-known designation in Soviet culture: revolutionary romanticism. It was only fitting that Gor'kii possessed the capacity for it to the extreme, for he was also its foremost exponent. In his keynote address at the First Congress of Soviet Writers – which, along with Zhdanov's speech, remains a *locus classicus* for the doctrine of revolutionary romanticism – he envisioned an epic style that would be supremely realistic precisely because it was also mythical. Myth, Gor'kii reasoned, is something imagined, invented. But if the invention provides a genuine synthesis and expression of what is actually present, then it is realistic (10). Revolutionary romanticism was just this paradoxical coalescence of the mythical and the realistic, which began with available experience and, "following the logic of hypothesis," arrived at the portrayal of the "desired and the possible" (10).

However maligned it has been in Western and post-Soviet Russian scholarship for having sanctioned an illusionist "varnishing of reality," revolutionary romanticism certainly cannot be accused of this one "sin": that it appealed to the power of the writer's imagination. It was, primarily, an appeal to belonging. About it we should say what has already been said about socialist realism: that it was not a certain method of "approaching reality," of manipulating the raw data of experience. After all, as one speaker at the congress assured his colleagues, "the style of artistic work cannot be anything other than the style of life [*stil' zhizni*]" (382). To be a "revolutionary romantic," then, did not mean to fantasize about the bright future after diligently studying Marx and Lenin, but to be organically one with the Soviet style of life – a life that was itself a sort of a oneiric machine, inasmuch as in it the dreams of historical humanity were being fulfilled.[27] Since Gor'kii was one with this device, he was naturally "acted" by it, and hence, just as naturally, the visions of the future appeared before him.

Those writers for whom such natural belonging could not be assumed were in danger of succumbing to "naturalism" – the lifeless registration of what is merely there. Along with the second deadly sin of Stalinist culture, "formalism," the naturalistic copying of reality was viewed as a sure sign of the artist's severed connection to the fullness of Soviet life. Opposed to the lifeless exactitude of the copy was the full-blooded truth of the "invention": "Our work is not a mere imitation, an exact registration, but an invention that emerges from the closest and most intense connection to reality, a reality that gives rise to the possibility of being that could endow dramatic works with the character of a prediction, a foretelling, a prospective plan" (*Pervyi* 460; emphasis added). Decoding playwright Aleksei Faiko's awkwardly phrased pronouncement, we come to realize, first, that for him "invention" does not mean some unencumbered flight of the imagination. The flight is very much restrained in that it aims, optimally, at an objective prognosis – an advance knowledge of what cannot but take place.

Second, we see that the act of prognostication does not begin with the subject, the author; rather, it begins with the "reality" that engenders a unique "possibility of being." The (socio-historical) being in question possesses the unique ability to lay bare and render manifest. Only to the degree to which the writer is part of this being can he believe objectively. More precisely, the being would do the believing in his stead. We find ourselves once again on the territory of what Žižek calls the objectivity of belief.

Criticizing the inability of some writers to provide powerful artistic expressions of the world in which they lived, Faiko's colleague, Vladimir Kirshon, attributed the problem to a disorientation characteristic of the present day. Life was changing swiftly and dramatically; what had been current just yesterday was already obsolete today; new phenomena were springing up incessantly from the fabric of Soviet reality. For many writers, the impression was overwhelming; "they wander through [life's] events like blind people" (405). As a defence against the onrush of this rich and powerful life, which struck them as chaotic, they had taken the path of naturalism: "photographing the present reality, they want to hide behind the photographic depiction their attitude toward this reality" (405). To these people, who covered up their blindness with the exactitude of the copy, Kirshon gave the following assurance:

> What takes place in our country is *not chaos, not an accumulation of random occurrences*, no – this is an expression of the internal laws of historical development, which lie at the foundation of events, the laws of scientific Marxism, which are embodied in tactics and strategy – our Party's general plan.
>
> As it is being implemented, this plan itself becomes a historical factor. On the basis of the Party line in the execution of this extraordinary historical plan, there take place not just foreseen processes of the socialist transformation of life, but also ones that have been elicited and organized by our Party.
>
> In our country *there are no events that occur by accident*. There is diversity in the unity of a single line.
>
> The task of the writer is, first and foremost, to *feel this line organically*. (405; emphasis added)

This is an opportune moment to recall the words of Trotsky quoted earlier in this study, which, similarly, sought to dispel the seeming chaos of historical happening with an assurance that pointed confidently to the "iron formulas" of the "revolutionary algebra."[28] At first glance, the two statements seem to be conveying the same meaning. In fact, they are saying paradigmatically different things, thus marking the distinction between two different cultural moments. Trotsky is saying, essentially, "We are through what we know": the method of historical materialism gives us knowledge of the intractable laws of historical development, turning the apparent chaos into an ordered picture; as convinced revolutionaries, we are guided by this picture; and so on. Official Stalinist culture speaks differently, indeed in reverse: "We know through what we are." Such is the logic underlying the last quoted passage: if you were truly Soviet, you would feel organically the immanent tendency of our life[29] and, hence, be able to behold the picture of ·perfect order and unswerving direction through the apparent chaos of events and phenomena.

But this means that the theatrical stage, the page, and the canvas must somehow become isotopic with the podium in the Hall of Columns, which for its part is isotopic with the stage on which life does its self-showing. Expressed differently, the motion of painting or writing must become absolutely unassertive, ephemeral, so that it can easily be "moved" by the grand movement of self-revelatory life. Is this not the implication we should read into statements like the following, made by Gronskii a couple of months before the Congress: "The direction of historical development, the outcome of the struggle between the proletariat and the bourgeoisie, is now drawing itself out [vyrisovyvaetsia] sufficiently clearly before the artist" (212)? The "drawing" mentioned here is not an artistic activity proper. It is, rather, the drawing of that absolutely straightforward and determinate line to which Kirshon also referred, the line that lets no event fall out of line with necessity and inevitability. It takes place on a surface that we, usually, do not consider contiguous with the surface on which the artist draws. Yet the peculiarity of socialist realism, as a cultural practice, consists precisely in the attempt to splice these two surfaces together, as if they were one. The first kind of drawing, the drawing that depicts, is made a function of the second – the drawing that gives direct embodiment, manifests, and thus manifestly fulfils. Any line of depiction must issue forth from that other line, which the author is enjoined to feel organically.[30]

This is the extent to which, with socialist realism, we find ourselves beyond the traditional understanding of artistic representation. This is also the extent to which we find ourselves outside the notion of authorship proper. We now see that to be a Soviet author – changing only slightly Stalin's previously quoted definition – means to have depicted truthfully; but this means to have seen, which in turn implies – and here the contradiction is already apparent – to have been permeated and possessed by the force of socialism and thus to have been made to see. This force counts as real – or as I previously phrased it, enjoys erection – to the extent to which any given "one" (in our case, a Soviet writer) proves amenable to it. I am choosing both words, "proves" and "amenable," quite deliberately. The former is meant to resonate with the peculiar logic of proof operative at the Moscow show trials. As noted, the court sought not so much to prove the guilt of the accused as to demonstrate the workings of a "tendency" (in fact, the former proof was subsumed by the latter). Ideally, the accused would have been able to show themselves, in their words and behaviour, as being irresistibly driven by this inexorable tendency. Similarly, at the Writer's Congress, the writers had to show that they were indeed those they were supposed to be – beings exhibiting the effects of socialism, irresistibly driven to clarity by a force that possessed them to the core but that was, nevertheless, distinct from them, not truly *theirs*.

In the concrete setting of the Hall of Columns, this force was acting concretely as the force of exhibition. On the podium, right before the writers, it was demonstrating in concrete human form that socialism had indeed become reality, since it was indeed producing a new breed of man, a new attitude towards labour, new forms of ethics, and so on. To wit, in this performance, everything happened just as Gronskii's words had described it: "drawing itself out sufficiently clearly before the artist" was the "direction of historical development." In saying that writers had to prove "amenable" to this force of exhibition, I mean, quite literally, that they had to be able to adopt a disposition of elated resignation analogous to an "Amen!" Since it was the force, and not the artist, that did the essential showing, there was little left for the latter to do but show that his being was not opaque to the show that showed. Verbalized, his attitude had to be something like this: "Yes, now I see! Indeed, it has come to pass before me! And so, I let it be just as it was meant to be; I let it draw itself out and present itself just as it has been drawn up in heaven. Amen!"[31]

This disposition was captured effectively in Pasternak's words that serve as an epigraph to this study: "Proletarian dictatorship is not enough to influence culture. For this, a true plastic hegemony [*plasticheskoe gospodstvo*] is needed: a hegemony that would speak through me without my knowing it and even against my will. I do not feel this" (qtd in *Pervyi* 175). There is no doubt that the hegemony to which Pasternak wished to be subjected was homologous with the force of socialism as a force of concrete and true showing. In the realm of art, this hegemony was tantamount to the manifestation of a great style. The yearning for a "ventriloquized" expression, unconscious and unwilled, was yet another expression of the modernist desire for the Formative discussed in chapter 6. We are reminded here of the psalm refrain, "Into your hands ... I commend my spirit" (Ps. 31.5), in which redemption blends seamlessly with surrender.

The "Amen!" implied in both utterances could be imagined as a certain letting-go whereby one's ontological density decreases: a self-induced ephemeralization of one's being, so it can be "moved" more easily by the force of truth ("For You shall redeem me, Lord of truth").

Pasternak made the pronouncement in 1925, during the NEP period, but he was reminded of it a decade later, during the congress, by one of the speakers, Abram Lezhnev. The main theme of Lezhnev's speech was the theme discussed in chapter 7: the radical conversion of the old intelligentsia in the years of Stalin's cultural revolution. The transformation, he argued, consisted not in the writers' mere acceptance of the new social order, but, much more substantially, in their changed world view (177). The latter he attributed precisely to the realization of Pasternak's "real plastic hegemony" (176). When it came time for him to speak, Pasternak confirmed Lezhnev's conviction. The power for which he had been waiting in vain ten years ago, the one that bypasses the consciousness and will of the author on its way to artistic expression, was finally making itself felt; its effects were palpable even within the official enclosures of the Hall of Columns. Pasternak expounded on one such remarkable effect – the birth of a new poetic language:

> For twelve days we have been united by the dizzying bliss of the fact that this high poetic language was being born on its own in our conversation with our present day, with the present day of people who had cut off the anchor of private property and were freely soaring, floating, whirling, in the space of the biographically conceivable ....
>
> The poetic language of which I reminded you sounded the loudest in the speeches of the people with the most decisive vote: the delegates without membership cards, the members of the delegations that had come to visit us. In all these cases, the poetic language reached such power, that it forced apart the bounds of reality and transported us to that realm of the possible, which in the socialist world is also the realm of the necessary. (549)

This realm is, of course, the provenance of the aforementioned revolutionary romanticism. We need to emphasize here again the way in which it is reached: by a "transport" that begins not with an interior ecstasy that extends into a poetic presentation of an external world (as in Romanticism proper); but rather with the self-presentation of an objectively existing world, which through the pure power of this suddenly manifest presence takes possession of the poet and transports him into an eye-opening vision "of the possible, which is also ... the necessary."

Pasternak went on to sketch, briefly but passionately, a new understanding of poetry and poetic practice:

> What is poetry, comrades, if such is its birth before our eyes? Poetry is prose: prose not in the sense of someone's collected prose works, but prose itself, the voice of prose, prose in action, not in paraphrase. Poetry is the language of the organic fact, i.e., the fact that has living consequences .... Poetry is nothing but this: pure prose in its transferable intensity [*v perevodnoi napriazhennosti*]. (549)

Modifying Pasternak's vision with the insights gained so far, we reach the following ideal picture of how socialist-realist writing should proceed: socialist reality shows or expresses itself in "organic facts"; as long as the writer is "ours," that is, as long as he is made from the same substance as the rest of Soviet reality, he is subjected to and penetrated by the "transferable intensity" of that reality (if he is not quite yet, then he should make himself penetrable, *proniknut'sia*); through him, bypassing his consciousness and his will, the organic fact reaches the page and speaks; only what is spoken in this wise counts as an authentic artistic presentation and, thus, as genuinely "true"; this is socialist realism, which is to say, the return of the grand organic Style.

Inspired by the organic facts being demonstrated before the congress, Viktor Gusev wrote verses that could serve as a poetic illustration of the mechanism just described:[32]

> Interrupting our speeches,
> *Blinding us with the shine* of unimaginable deeds,
> They were offering to us their victories,
> Bread, airplanes, metal –
>   themselves.
> They were *presenting themselves as a theme*,
>
> Their work, love, life ...
> And each of them
>   sounded like a poem,
> Because in each of them
>   Bolshevism thundered. (675; emphasis added)

I can now state explicitly what has been obvious throughout: that the "shine" (*blesk*) of the shiny, happy people is the same kind of radiation I designated earlier as "beaming" – the one through which there is "vision" (in the impersonal). And the mechanism by which, ideally, socialist-realist texts will be produced follows the dialectic of seen-ness, which I rehearsed by analogy with the exhibitionistic scene. The analogy can now be extended so that it comes full circle: the moment in which the penis is reflected in the "eyes wide open," the moment enabling its erection, is analogous to the moment in which the "prose" of reality turns into poetry. It seems that this is a "natural," immanent process, one that does not need the presence of the writer. It seems that the words that "sound like a poem" do so out of themselves and by themselves and that the writers sitting in the audience are merely bystanders. What good could they possibly do when faced with a life that spontaneously turns into poetry?[33]

But even a life that spontaneously turns into poetry still needs an external "turning point." In the exhibitionistic act, this external point of reflection is the passer-by. In the cultural act of socialist realism, this external point of reflection is the artist. Expressed more accurately, in the proper order of realization: he shall be a considered a Soviet artist who comes to the point in front of which the organic fact of life shall bare itself. In other words, first comes the open "stead," where the laying-bare awaits its satisfaction, and only then, the "one" who comes and actually stands there. The subject is the effect of manning the stead. At the congress, this topological arrangement was realized as follows: there was, on one side, the procession of triumphant and radiant life; across from it, corresponding generally to the place from which the audience was watching this show, was the place where the Soviet writer was supposed to appear and stand as just such a "one." This moment would come – speaking here conceptually and figuratively, rather than referentially and literally – when someone stood up and, from that spot, said something along the lines of "Yes, now I see, indeed." As we saw, Avdeenko made this proclamation almost literally. This was also the essence of Pasternak's speech and the overarching thesis of Lezhnev's, as the latter chronicled the short biography of the Soviet writer. This is also what we should read in the following words of Isaac Babel: "The first scaffolding is being removed from the edifice of socialism. *Even the most shortsighted can now see* the outlines of this edifice, its beauty. And we are all witnesses of the fact that our entire country has been enraptured by a powerful feeling of sheer physical happiness" (279; emphasis added). But nowhere was this onset of vision expressed more engagingly than in Iurii Olesha's highly crafted oratory, which, in the general agreement of those present, provided the dramatic climax of the congress's proceedings.

Olesha narrated the story of his personal transformation, which sounded more like a story of religious conversion, cast in terms of blindness and sight. He began by recalling the publication, in 1927, of his novella *Envy* (*Zavist'*), which the vocal proletarian wing had met with harsh criticism, mostly on account of the main protagonist, Nikolai Kavalerov. Unmistakably a descendant of Dostoevsky's underground man, Kavalerov exemplified the bystander of the revolution, resentful of the ethical vigour, robust practicality, and bristling vivacity of the new social world. In him, the proletarian critics saw a reactionary creation, a reflection of Olesha's own personality; Kavalerov looked at the world with the eyes of his creator. Fully conscious of the autobiographical connection, Olesha was that much more hurt to hear his hero being called "a lowlife and a nonentity" (235). In his mind, *Envy* was where his artistic vision had been at its clearest and richest; but lo, what he considered to be clarity and richness had turned out to be blindness and misery. At this point, Olesha's speech takes on the character of a parable, as he retells the plot of a novella he intended to write. The writer imagines himself as a beggar: "There I am, superfluous, vulgar, and insignificant … I am standing on the steps of a drug store, I beg for handouts, and my name is 'writer'" (235). The beggar-writer roams the countryside for years, until one day he finds himself in an open field on a bright, crisp morning. At the edge of the field, near a forest, stands an old, crumbling wall. In it, there is an opening, an arched doorway: "I look through it and see unusual greenery … Maybe goats walk here. I step over the threshold and enter; then I look at myself and see that this is youth: youth has returned" (235).

What is the meaning of this miracle? Whence youth, all of a sudden? And what is this magic threshold that the beggar crosses? The speaker himself provided the clues for deciphering the allegory. Hearkening to the words of his critics, Olesha had "taken it personally"; he had thought that the distorted vision was his, that it was somehow innate in his being. Hence, the self-image of a worthless lowlife, which tormented him for years. The miraculous transformation corresponded to the moment when the writer finally understood that the problem was not in him: "I understood that it is not about me, but about the world around me" (235). Everything changed when he realized that he was not the one who generated the image of the world; he was just the site of seeing. Representations, images, came from the "world around" and entered him. Kavalerov had been one such image, a visitor from the former, "distorted" social world, who had taken possession of his author's self. But a new world was already in the making: "All this time the country was getting younger. There are already youths of seventeen in whose minds there is nothing of the old world" (236). All the writer had to do was *proniknut'sia* – that is, open himself up to these new beings and to the Being that had engendered them:

> I was peeking through the magic arc, but could not understand the most im- portant thing: I could not understand that I believe in the youth of the coun- try, that it is not my youth I want to bring back, but to see the youth of the country, i.e., of the new people. *Now I see them* ... This is how the miracle happened of which I had dreamt while looking through the magic arc. This is how youth came back to me. (236; emphasis added)

The magic arc of Olesha's allegory, then, is not unlike the line separating the audience from the podium in the Hall of Columns. It is the imaginary membrane of the world through which one must pass in order to cease "representing" (in the sense of *Darstellen*) and begin the movement of showing. On this side of the arc, the writer sees from within himself, "sub- jectively." On the other side, he sees, so to speak, "from without"; he sees because he partakes of seen-ness – the general quality of a world whose objective logic has laid itself bare. The symbolic moment of going through the doorway is none other than the moment of this partaking: the writer takes on the part allotted to him in the production of clarity, which, in a broader sense, is the cultural production called "socialist realism."

We can only guess, and never know for sure, how much personal invest- ment went into the kind of verbal performances Olesha, Pasternak, and their colleagues made at the congress, how much authentic belief fuelled these public enactments. The subjective side of the spectacle will always remain beyond our confident grasp. All we have been left with are the words that have been spoken. It is understandable that we should wish to know what was there behind the words: resigned acceptance of an imposed role, pragmatic calculation, sincere engagement? But this we can never know with any degree of certainty, let alone with certainty in each indi- vidual case. The desire to unlock the inner worlds of people no longer alive ends in frustration sooner or later. All that remains for us to do is describe the official spectacle and the roles it prescribed. If, on occasion, these roles were played "in earnest," this does not at all invalidate the fact that they were prefigured by an official script. It is beyond doubt that many Soviet subjects, not just writers, felt that socialism was immanent and imminent in the 1930s, that its already palpable force was transforming not only the landscape of their country but also their own character and consciousness. Still, none of this could change the fact that their sincere personal belief was framed by an ideology in power. Earlier, I called it a meta-ideology, an ideology of ideology, in that it scripted and staged the very production of consciousness; in that it demonstrated, in public rituals, that individuals are possessed by the symbolic power of the socio-economic structure they populate; in that it aimed to prove by live exhibition that people are *in* ideology simply by virtue of being in a particular social formation (and, conversely – outside of ideology if they are the rejects of society). Thus, the symbolic act of surrender to the overwhelming visibility of socialism, to its "plastic" formative power, should be defined not by the subjective investment of this or that individual who performed it, but by the ideological and institutional settings that made such acts a prerequisite for social acceptance, professional success, and, often, physical survival.

Chapter 10

Life Happens

The steps of a good man are ordered by God, and He delighteth in his way.

Psalms 37: 23

In the previous chapter, I presented the First All-Union Congress of Soviet Writers as a complex performance in which the agents of representation – Soviet writers – were not *really* agents but rather pieces in a larger show, during which they were required to show themselves as "moved" by the force of self-revelatory immanence. I hope I have made it clear that the case of the socialist-realist author under Stalinism was, in fact, an instance in the broader problematic of subjecthood, and that the motion of being moved to vision was an instance of a more general movement reaching beyond the sphere of artistic work. In this final chapter, I extend the argument, however tentatively, towards this broader problematic.

I will advance my thesis through a discussion of one of the most remarkable epic narratives of Stalinism: the 1946 film *The Vow* (*Kliatva*), directed by Mikhail Chiaureli (1894–1974), who co-authored the script with writer Petr Pavlenko (1899–1951). I contend that the film shows, on the movie screen, the same thing the Congress showed: that agency does not issue forth *from* the actions of subjects but only registers *in* them. The stage on which *The Vow* makes this apparent is the grand stage of Soviet history; and the cultural act, which has appeared so far in this study from the partial perspective of "seeing" and writing, is featured in Chiaureli and Pavlenko's story in the generalized form of any human "doing." If the Congress staged the "making of the Soviet writer," *The Vow* stages the making of the Soviet subject in a cinematic fantasy whose generic territory encompasses both the modern historical epic and the fairy tale. Stalin's central and functionally unique role in the plot will allow me to address briefly the phenomenon often referred to as the "cult of personality."

The Vow is one of four films by Chiaureli chronicling the life and heroic deeds of the Leader. The other three are *The Great Dawn* (*Velikoe Zarevo;* 1938), *The Fall of Berlin* (*Padenie Berlina;* 1949), and *The Unforgettable 1919* (*Nezabyvaemyi 1919;* 1951). All four belong to the uniquely Soviet genre of the "historico-revolutionary film" (*istoriko-revoliutsionnyi fil'm*), whose Stalinist variation is characterized by the decisive participation of the country's political and military leaders in the epic events unfolding on the screen. The four films also share a principal narrative device: an ordinary hero's life journey joins and follows Stalin's biographical path during a pivotal moment in history.[1] But it is in *The Vow* and to some extent in *The Fall of Berlin*, the two scripts written by Chiaureli and Pavlenko,[2] that this device is radicalized, attaining a new structural quality and introducing a new level of meaning. This new structural and semantic aspect will be the focus of my analysis.

The Vow opens on a stormy winter day in early January 1924, just days before Lenin's death (21 January 1924). As the story begins, we are far from Moscow and from the grand stage of political history, on the banks of the Volga in the little provincial town of Tsaritsyn, among the "little," common people. Stepan, an old Bolshevik, is returning home from a trip to the countryside, where he has been investigating the crimes committed by kulaks sabotaging the organization of *kolkhoz* farmsteads. As he is walking through the snowy fields outside Tsaritsyn with his daughter, Ol'ga, Stepan tells her that it was on this very field that in 1918 he and Comrade Stalin fought against the Whites. His reminiscences are interrupted by an ambush: the kulak "elements" that Stepan has been prosecuting have come to take their revenge. He falls on the very field where in 1918 he and Comrade Stalin... It is a desolate spot, snow and wind swept – a blank spot, seemingly.

Back in town, Stepan's family home is the scene of a heated debate about the country's current political situation. His younger son, Sergei, a student and devout follower of Lenin and Stalin, is arguing with his friend, Anatolii, whose stereotypically Jewish features betray his alien nature even before he begins praising Trotsky and Bukharin; moderating the shouting match that soon ensues is the older son, Aleksandr, an unemployed and politically uncommitted engineer, who devotes his ample free time to drawing blueprints of buildings that will never be built. At this point, having just witnessed Stepan's tragic end, we might expect the younger, more "conscious" son to take over the main role in the film by assuming the symbolic place vacated by his father. In that case, our expectations would be deceived. One of the biggest surprises the film has in store for us concerns precisely the category of "hero" and the qualifications it presupposes. As we will learn in the further course of the narrative, being conscious, having adopted an "ideology," is not among those qualifications.

While Sergei's role in the story will be little more than episodic, the central character will become his mother, Varvara. When she first appears on the screen, she is a cipher: a simple housewife, completely absorbed in the prose of her quotidian life, oblivious to any concern beyond this parochial realm. While the young men are arguing about politics, their mother is – where else? – in the kitchen, fretting about her husband's return and paying not the least attention to the discussion. In the next scene, however, her status suddenly begins to change. Ol'ga rushes in and delivers the tragic news. The family rushes out to find Stepan expiring on the sled that has brought him home for the last time. In a last, dying effort, he hands Varvara a letter and instructs her to deliver it personally to Lenin. Chiaureli does not tell us what is in the letter, not yet. At the moment, it is a white sheet of paper, a blank spot.

We find out what is in the letter only when, having reached Gorki – Lenin's residence during his final illness – Varvara joins up with a group of modern-day pilgrims, representatives of various Soviet nationalities, who, like herself, have come to visit Lenin and tell him their grievances.[3] As she reads to them Stepan's letter, we discover that it is a description of the various kulak crimes that Stepan recorded during his last trip. At the same time, we begin to discover something different, something unexpected and quite miraculous: as Varvara reads, the people who have gathered around her begin to recognize in her words the stories each of them has come to tell. The events described in the letter she carries are identical to the events the pilgrims carry indelibly in their minds. This is the first of several instances in the film when miracles spring from (seemingly) blank spots.

The pilgrims soon learn grim news: Lenin is dead. As they make their way to Moscow, we are introduced to Lenin's potential successors. While Kamenev and Bukharin are scheming, Stalin is taking a pensive stroll through the park in Gorki. In an almost unbearable moment of sublime sentimentality, he comes to a lonely park bench, the mere sight of which brings back to his mind the haloed image of Lenin. This – as every Soviet viewer is supposed to know – is the same bench on which Lenin and Stalin are shown seated in a much-publicized photograph of 1922.[4] We now see it covered thickly with white snow. It is another desolate place, a blank spot.

Several scenes later, this private sublimity has its public and no less sublime outpouring: on Red Square, Stalin pronounces the Vow. He swears to fulfil Lenin's symbolic will. The multitude gathered in the square instantly recognizes the man speaking in the distance, just as they instinctively sense the sacred charge of the moment. Thousands of hands holding Party membership cards go up, and thousands of voices second Stalin's each time he pronounces solemnly, "We swear!" As if the sacramental public spectacle were not enough to convince us that Stalin has the mandate of the people as Lenin's true heir, the scene is capped off by a final, blatantly tautological gesture: the enormous crowd parts, giving way to Varvara, who approaches Stalin and hands him the letter from her husband. Intended for Lenin, it reaches, quite "naturally," his rightful successor. By the time it does, it is no longer the letter of a single person from a single locality: miraculously collected on this white sheet of paper are the voices of *all* Soviet people and places.

Participants in the public ritual, along with all the rest, have been our pilgrims: Varvara (who has made it an explicit point to swear on behalf of her entire family, as if knowing in advance the beneficial effects this will produce in the future); the Ukrainian, Baklan; the Georgian, Georgii; the Uzbek, Turgunbaev. As the authoritative voice of *Pravda* remarked soon after the film's release, this miniature model of Soviet society[5] is bound together by the binding power of the vow ("Kliatva" 3). By that same power they are elevated in status: within a few short years, which the film traverses almost instantaneously, we see them promoted to the ranks of *znatnye liudi,* the aristocracy of Stalinist socialism – those very beings I referred to earlier as "shiny, happy people." Of course, by these credentials, they also figure as the main characters in the film narrative.

There is no motivating transition between these two states of existence. Varvara and her children, as well as Baklan, Georgii, and Turgunbaev, each move from zero to hero without really accomplishing anything special. The transformation is really not their doing. Indeed, the doing comes later. First comes being, in this case, *being there.* Our heroes' "elevation" happens not through their knowledge or abilities, and even less through their accomplishments; it happens through the mere fact that they all were there on Red Square at the time of Stalin's vow.

That this is indeed the case is shown to us in a brief but remarkable exchange within the larger scene of the vow. The camera cuts into the crowd to find Turgunbaev, who is visibly disconcerted. While all the hands around him go up, his stays down. To the puzzled Baklan, he explains: "I don't know what it is. I feel strength, and then it's gone." He, an illiterate peasant without a Party card, feels unworthy of the great scene at which he is present. To this, his companion responds by drawing a striking verbal image:

"Take the vow! Let us all take it: you, and I, and everybody else. *You have nowhere to fall* [*Tebe i upast' nekuda*]."

Turgunbaev knows what makes him weak but does not know what makes him strong. This latter "something" is some mysterious, invigorating force that supports and uplifts him so that there is nowhere for him to fall; this is strangely reminiscent of the angelic hands that would not allow the Son to fall and dash His foot against a stone (Luke 4.11). Just as miraculously, the illiterate Turgunbaev will be uplifted to a place of distinction in Soviet society. But for this to happen, he must first raise his hand: He must do so not *out* of his convictions and knowledge, that is, not *out* of his consciousness. All his consciousness can tell him at this moment is that he is an insignificant, illiterate peasant with little or no awareness of even the basic tenets of Marxism-Leninism. But, as we ascertained already – first with the example of the institute employees, then with the example of ideologically misguided writers[6] – this fact matters very little in Stalinist culture. Consciousness is subsequent. It belongs to the dimension of the effect. First comes the gesture of partaking, or belonging. So Turgunbaev raises his hand and pronounces, together with the rest, "We swear." This gesture can be called "somnambulic" because it is not guided by prior knowledge and will. Quite the reverse: knowledge and will spring *from* the gesture. Only after he takes the vow, and as a direct result of doing so, will Turgunbaev become a conscious builder of socialism. All takes place within the paradoxical sequence of Pascal's prescription: "Kneel down, move your lips in prayer, and you will believe."

We continue to watch how belief is born out of somnambulic motions in the extended episode showing the construction of the Stalingrad tractor plant – itself part of the epic saga of Stalin's Five-Year Plans. Initially, the central figure here is Varvara's older son, Aleksandr. And, let it be said in advance, his centrality is in proportion to his un-consciousness. The grandiose project furnishes him with a long-awaited opportunity to transfer his engineering visions from the walls of his room, where they have been hanging as mere drawings on paper, to the world outside. But at first, like Turgunbaev, Aleksandr is a man of little faith. When he hears of the plans to build the enormous plant on the bank of the Volga, he gasps: "Where?! On these marshes?!" The film cuts promptly to a shot of Stalin standing on the very same bank, pointing to these very same marshes and confidently instructing the architects and engineers in his entourage that construction should indeed commence on this spot. Himself part of the entourage, Aleksandr listens carefully to the Leader's words but continues not to understand: "Still, why on *this* spot?!" The enigma the cerebral engineer finds so impenetrable is solved quickly and effortlessly in the simple words of a simple man. Varvara's brother, Ermilov, the film's figure of comic relief, spells out what every more or less attentive viewer has realized already: this empty spot, seemingly unfit for any construction project, is the same spot where Stalin defeated the Whites in 1918; moreover, it is a place marked with the historical presence of Ivan IV, Stepan Razin, and Emelian Pugachev; in short, it is a sacred place.

We see Aleksandr next when construction is under way. He does not yet seem fully possessed by faith, but by now this has ceased to matter. What is important is that he is there, he is standing in that spot. His motto now is: "We must work, not wonder!" (*Rabotat' nado, a ne udivliat'sia!*). The meaning of his words can be translated as: "We must work instead of analysing." The only one who still analyses is Anatolii. Rational analysis is the meta-position, which here means: the position of those who do not belong. Because they do not belong, they can never believe. So even as he half-heartedly participates in the construction work, Anatolii continues to mumble that the project is nothing but a crazy fantasy and that the Party leaders have lost touch with reality. When the plant is nearly completed, we will see him setting fire to one of the blocs; driven by his alien nature, he has found himself, quite naturally, in the ranks of the Trotskyist "wreckers."

If we agree that human labour consists of more than the menial operations performed – that it is not only physical but always also symbolic, permeated with meaning (whether consciously accessible or not to those who labour) – let us consider the labour through which the Stalingrad tractor plant is erected in the film. What does this work involve? Beyond the film plot, the question aims, of course, at the general plot in which the cultural act of Stalinism unfolds, giving rise to the erection called "socialism." Taking Aleksandr as our model (but remembering also the episode with Turgunbaev), we would describe this work as follows: to happen to be in the *right* spot and, while there, to *let go;* to labour in such a way that the effort produces material results just as it induces a self-forgetfulness of sorts, an abandon. In this effort, one abandons the possibility of grasping things in advance as well as the possibility that one's actions will be guided by such a preliminary grasp. Having let go, one can now be "moved," "acted," by the power that dormantly subtends the empty spot, which is also the "right" spot. Through this power, the seemingly fantastic project is fulfilled and the erection happens.

Through the same power, human life also "happens." If *The Vow* shows one thing clearly and absolutely consciously, it is this: that one cannot author one's own deeds and consequently one's being. They happen *to* the individual and may even surprise him at times. From the point of view of Stalinist ideology, there is nothing surprising about this; after all, socialism is supposed to bring out what is best in being human – that is, previously untapped, slumbering potentials. Thus, it is possible that *any* Soviet person could be caught unawares by the deeds that socialism elicits from the depths of his own humanity (just as the writers discussed in chapter 7 were caught unawares by a wholly new way of seeing things). Like Varvara, like Turgunbaev, and really, like all the other "heroes" in the film, Aleksandr begins as a nobody and becomes "somebody" through achievements that are not really his. Since this mechanism is already familiar to us, we can reiterate the earlier formula: in his stead, the heroic work of socialist construction is being done. The stark appeal of Pavlenko and Chiaureli's cinematic narrative comes from the fact that in it we see plainly what I previously elaborated only as an abstract, theoretical proposition: we see the "stead," the place where one is supposed to be standing, being demonstratively empty as well as separate from and antecedent to anyone who might actually come to stand there. In this particular episode of *The Vow*, it is a construction site. More broadly, it is the entire area of Stalingrad, the former Tsaritsyn. Most broadly yet, it is the place where socialism is being built: the land of the Soviets.

After the tractor plant is completed (and survives the diabolical schemes of the saboteurs), we leave Stalingrad for a time, with the utter certainty, by now instilled in us, that we will be returning to it. By now the film has established the pattern of "eternal return" to this spot. And sure enough, the Great Patriotic War begins, both in order to fulfil Stalin's prediction that the Soviet Union will one day have to be defended against the enemy and in order for us to witness one last time the power of the sacred place. We return to Stalingrad and see it once more as a desolate spot, this time because months of ferocious fighting have turned it into a ghost town. We find here, once again, Varvara (she is now in charge of an orphanage), Aleksandr, and his wife, Kseniia. Aleksandr is captured and executed by the Germans, but as everyone knows, the empty spot is once again victorious in the battle that effectively decides the fate of Hitler's Eastern campaign. Varvara takes one final walk before the ranks of jubilant Red Army soldiers shouting "Hurrah!" Through a cinematic cut, the walk takes her to the very heart of the Kremlin, where the Father of all Soviet people greets her as his symbolic mate.

The agency that brings Varvara to this symbolic apex is – with a nod in the direction of Lacan – the agency of the letter.[7] She comes onto the stage of the narrative because she carries a letter. But if we consider the situation more carefully, it is better to say that the *letter* carries *her*. It is a sheet of paper of whose contents she is initially unaware. More importantly, even when she becomes aware of those contents, their significance remains outside her grasp. How could she know that the letter will mysteriously absorb and express in a single voice the grievances of the whole Soviet Union of the NEP years? Varvara knows that she and the letter come from Tsaritsyn, but how could she possibly know that Tsaritsyn will turn out to be the *right* place and that the word hailing from there will turn out to be the fullest and most meaningful Word? How could she anticipate that this Word, swollen by the unanimous recognition of all Soviet people, will exceed its intended function of a report and take on the function of a popular mandate legitimizing the political succession in the Kremlin? Of all this, Varvara remains unaware. These unfoldings outrun her consciousness. They unfold *before* her, that is, ahead of her cognizance and will; and as they do, they direct her (subsequent) steps – they carry her.

Varvara's personal story is underpinned by another, greater story. The former is "hitched" to the latter; as the latter advances, it "moves" the former along. This mechanism accounts for the fact that Varvara's life "happens" – that is, it comes to her from somewhere else. At first, she happens to be the wife of Stepan, who happens to have fought alongside Stalin during the Civil War; as Stepan happens to die on the very site of Stalin's past exploits, Varvara happens to be chosen as a messenger (although her younger son would have been a more understandable choice); Lenin dies just when Varvara happens to be in Moscow; and so on. This logic is carried out with impeccable consistency in the film, not just in relation to Varvara but in relation to all the shiny, happy people. With reference to all of them and to the ideology of Stalinist culture as a whole, we can advance the following semantic equivalence: "to be" means "to happen to be."

As far as narrative art is concerned, this logic reminds us of times long past. Similarly structured plots are to be found in the tragedies and mythic tales of classical antiquity. There as well, the hero's life is often hitched to a larger, more essential story, which he either knows not at all or, as with Oedipus, fatefully misconstrues. Archaic but indelible familial memory has marked the landscape of the hero's journey and specified its precipitous course, visibly for us but unbeknownst to him. It is his "fate." In significantly modified form, this type of narrative persisted in the hagiographic literature of the Middle Ages, where fate was to be found in the predetermined path that led the righteous to their true Father. The modern period begins precisely where this circuitous route – from the preinscription of a mythic proto-story to its reinscription and reaffirmation through the fate of a particular "one" – is no longer capable of delineating the meaning of human experience. The first great narrative of the new era, the biography of a lunatic knight errant, presents us with a desperate desire for the signs of predestination and a pathetic effort to tease these signs out of the barren landscape of a decidedly post-mythic land. Precisely because of its failure, Don Quixote's quest shows the only road the hero can take from now on: because destiny is not *pre*destined (in either scriptures of faith or books of chivalry), it must be constructed out of the hero's own inner nature.

The possibility of providing a destiny for oneself has been, from the beginning of this new beginning, coextensive with the power of giving oneself representations. In Cervantes this power is equated with madness, since it offers only misleading apparitions, but since then that power has become normative. In *Hamlet,* madness springs not from the wanton self-giving of (illusory) representations but precisely from the impossibility of such self-giving. The ghost that appears at the beginning is an apparition that Hamlet has not given to himself from within himself; and as much as he would like to believe that this is all an illusion, he cannot: like the sacred Father of medieval Christianity, the royal Danish father has bestowed absolutely binding destiny upon his son. But this is now an unnatural, unexpected, and unwanted gift. Since it cannot be refused, its acceptance brings derangement.

The Vow returns us to that earlier time when the hero's steps were still "ordered by God," who "delighteth in his way" (Ps. 37.23). What makes God so happy? Certainly, it is the fact that the hero is a good man, that is, a good subject, who walks the way pointed out by his Master. We can easily relate to a divinity that rejoices for subjects who have chosen freely to follow the steps to the True. But in our context, which is Stalinist culture, there is pleasure to be had precisely insofar as subjects *do not* choose their steps but rather execute them in a somnambulic fashion. This modern-day authority enjoys the unconditional hegemony whereby those subjects are driven to do what they do and be what they are. It delights in their "creaturely" nature. For the more unconsciously their life narrative unfolds, the more emphatically it manifests and affirms the creation whose creatures they are, the order by which their steps have been preordered. Precisely in the spot where it catches the subject unawares, this order shows itself as most actual.

We have an accessible reference point for understanding such a libido: *Oedipus Rex.* The deities presiding over Oedipus's fate are satisfied to see the prophecy fulfilled, but the real crux of the play is the hero's hopeless effort to evade destiny – an effort whose every motion only strengthens

destiny's grip. With every conscious step towards escape, Oedipus unconsciously realizes what was meant to be. The same extended act through
which he shows himself to be a pathetic plaything of predestination exposes, at each stage and ultimately, the ancient story of familial sin. By the
same token, the act awakens the power through which this sin is being
punished, reconfirming it as the Power that be.

Keeping this famous archetype in mind, let us ask what is being aroused
in the act we watch unfold in the narrative space of *The Vow*. Enough has
been said so far to make the terms of the question less flippant than they
might appear. The sexual rhetoric is there to suggest that, even on the
grand scale of socio-cultural formations, we are dealing with the workings
of desire, even if this desire has congealed into an impersonal, alienated
form. But, as I am seeking to co-articulate this problematic with the theme
of creation, of building, giving shape, institutionalizing, terms like "arousal" and "erection" acquire a two-dimensional significance (which, hopefully, absolves me from the charge of frivolity). So: what is being aroused
in *The Vow*? The easy answer is: "Stalin."[8] And if we understand what
"Stalin" stands for, this is the correct answer.

In *The Vow*, unlike in the other Chiaureli films in the cinematic tetralogy
devoted to the Leader, Stalin appears in two distinct hypostases. On the
one hand, he is there "in the flesh," as an actual living person, although
by no means an ordinary person. He is just as Nikita Khrushchev would
later describe him in his secret speech to the Twentieth Congress of the
Communist Party: "a superman possessing supernatural characteristics,
akin to those of a god. Such a man ... knows everything, sees everything,
thinks for everyone, can do anything, is infallible in his behavior." This image is familiar. We find it, essentially, in every film or text of the period in
which the Leader makes an appearance.

But on the other hand – and this is where Pavlenko and Chiaureli's
mythography becomes truly radical – the Leader exists as a trace, that is, as
a proto-story that has been inscribed on the diegetic landscape, creating in
it patches of sacred space, of which Stalingrad is the largest and most significant. The whole point of there being a trace is that it should be retraced: ordinary characters are made to retread the ground once trodden
by Stalin. And as they do, they draw the sacred charge suffusing the seemingly empty spot and experience its miraculous effects.[9] Having become
"conductors" of this charge, our heroes begin to "shine." Put another way,
through the agency of the sacred trace, their lives "happen."

The Vow is a postwar Stalinist creation, which explains why in its ideological narrative it is not just the freshly built infrastructure of socialism

that acts individuals-cum-subjects. Rather, the entire history of Russia, at least since Ivan Grozny, has been turned into a mythic infrastructure that preconfigures the course of events as well as the fates of people. Stalin, of course, is aware of this history and consciously secures its reinscription in every new present. He knows what traces have been left by the (glorious) Russian past, and he confidently retraces them. As for the other, more ordinary characters, such knowledge proves to be superfluous. They tread upon the sacred ground, and while they might not see the trace that makes it sacred, they experience its effects all the same. They, the people, *are* those effects.

Given that "Stalin" is the name for two quite different things – a living person (even if a superman), and a trace circumscribing an empty spot – it behooves us to ask which deserves priority. Which of the two is the essential, authentic referent of "Stalin," the one we need to foreground in order to understand the phenomenon called "Stalinism"?

If we go by a straightforward logic, we must conclude: first comes the person who leaves the trace, then comes the trace left by him (Stalin comes along and defeats the Whites, and after that, the place of his exploits is marked as "sacred"). Following the same logic, only this time in the direction of opprobrium rather than adulation, subsequent Soviet historiography was to script the historical and cultural trauma of Stalinism as the trace (scar!) left by a particular human being named "Stalin." The term "cult of personality," first used in Khrushchev's secret speech of 1956, sloganizes this type of understanding, in which much of Cold War Western historiography has been complicit. Without disputing that the Leader's personality left a significant imprint on policies in virtually every sphere of Soviet life, including the artistic (one thinks first of the film industry, which produced Stalin's favourite art and was, to that extent, most consistently influenced by his tastes), I see this fact as belonging to a secondary, derivative dimension. We must turn Stalin's own words against him: It is *not* a matter of persons. Persons, of course, play a certain role. But we must first understand the power that the person in power has come to embody. If we approach this question from the perspective of culture, we must ask what sort of imagination was projected onto the real-life figure of the short, swarthy Georgian with a moustache.

We are familiar with the imagination in question. It is the ideological dream of the cannot-but, of the meant-to-be, of pure fulfilment. And there is probably no text from the Stalinist period that showcases this more vividly than *The Vow*. After all, it is the story of a vow, and a vow, as we know, is something that must be fulfilled. This, really, is the main movement of the narrative: from the word given to making it happen, from the course charted to its execution, from the delineation of an empty space to the erection that comes to stand there. For all these ful-fill-ments, "Stalin" is just as much the name of the heroic leader whom we watch in action on the grand stage of history, the personage through whose wisdom and will everything is accomplished, as it is the name of a mysterious agency guaranteeing that everything will be so *indeed.*

With its stark schematicism, Chiaureli's film demonstrates in plain view the reduction of the Leader's figure to this bare function. The human figure shows itself to be figurative of a strictly non-human automaton of reinscription. The mechanism produces one thing only: "More of the same." Stalin is the same as Ivan Grozny, Emelian Pugachev, and Sten'ka Razin. Stalin's greatness repeats the greatness of Lenin, for the worthy successor follows the same path. The Stalingrad of the Great Patriotic War is the same as the Stalingrad of the First Five-Year Plan, and the same as the Tsaritsyn of the Civil War and of Ivan Grozny's campaign against the Tatars several centuries earlier. Tatars, Whites, "wreckers," and Nazis are all enemies, all doomed to defeat, all the same. Kulaks all over the Soviet land are the same; likewise identical are the crimes they perpetrate. The hopes and dreams of people all over this same land are the same (which is why the letters they write echo one another). Everything is part of a cyclicity that spans time as well as space. The Same replicates itself over the space of the Soviet Union and thereby homogenizes it. The Same replicates itself over time and constitutes history as the never-ending materialization of predetermined outcomes. Everywhere – only the eternal return of the Same.

The seemingly empty spot that features so prominently in *The Vow* visualizes the moment of suspense before the same triumphantly returns to the same. Simultaneously, the blank space corresponds to the state of subjective (un-)consciousness: the ordinary subject does not see the preinscription, cannot fathom the pattern of eternal return and reinscription, and is unaware of its miraculous effects, including those that she is about to experience. All of this constitutes itself for the most part behind her back, forming a transcendental reserve, a "beyond" that springs suddenly upon the subject in a terminal moment of "happy recognition." This is precisely the "miracle" of Stalinism – how the emptiness dissipates to reveal the previously hidden inscription: "S" as in "Same," but also as in "Stalin." The ruling ideology triumphs with the arousal of the inscription from the state of dormancy, the dawning of the beyond, which lays bare the coupling of the same with the same. The miracle "miraculates" the subject: her life turns out to be driven by the unerring mechanism of reinscription.[10]

The scene of the vow provides a revealing illustration. The coupling has just taken place: Stalin stands in the place vacated by Lenin, Stalin is the same as Lenin – a fact confirmed by the admiration of the multitude as well as by Stepan's letter, which accomplishes a symbolic identification between original addressee and actual recipient. (In other words, the place is not actually vacated; the slate is wiped clean only to reveal the "miraculous" appearance of the same character.) The vow is obviously superfluous. There is no need for Stalin to promise that Lenin's will shall be followed and his dreams fulfilled. This has already been guaranteed by the manifest act of the coupling. The ambiguous state in which Turgunbaev finds himself can now be properly diagnosed: the weakness he feels arises from the mistaken perception that the vow is an actual promise that looks onto an open-ended future and requires personal credentials and exertions; the mysterious strength he feels comes from what is actually the case: the vow is fulfilled before being given. Baklan's words confirm this: there is "nowhere to fall" because nothing is left to chance, the future is anything but open, everything is decided in advance. The movement of the narrative has only one modulation; it is not a development but rather an oscillation, a pendulum swing: from subjective uncertainty to objective confirmation that the same does indeed return as the same.

The name of the Leader is the name of the automaton that produces this single oscillating motion. What we must recognize is that a very real desire is caught in the automaton's cogs. From the suspense of seeming emptiness to the fulfilment that fills that emptiness, the relay connects a historically determinate anxiety to its wishful ideological deflection. It is not difficult to see through the windswept fields and desolate places of Chiaureli and Pavlenko's film a vision of Soviet socialism as a tantalizingly blank slate, an open-ended project without guarantees, which sets out towards its highly uncertain future across the disheartening expanses of yesterday's semi-feudal, overwhelmingly rural empire. In *The Vow* this anxiety-laden vision is invoked – in images rather than statements – only to be immediately dispelled. The subject is subliminally teased by it before being reassured that there, in the blind (blank) spot of her consciousness, a constellation of objective historical forces has inscribed the success of the state project with the hard lines of ineluctable destiny.

It could be shown that all narratives of socialist realism, in one way or another, treat history as destiny. But the creation of Chiaureli and Pavlenko is exceptional in its insistence that history is an *unconscious* destiny for the ordinary Soviet subject. In the language of cinematic fiction, it addresses to the viewer a message very similar to Althusser's theoretical thesis: places come before acts; acts come before beliefs; the beliefs are believed in the acts; the acts are acted by the places. Each subsequent level is but a rein-scription of the previous, more fundamental dimension. Consciousness is the reinscription of practice; living practice is the reinscription of past practices that have congealed into an objective structure of "places." It is this objective structure that counts most; practices and beliefs merely me-diate its reproduction. The human individual, as subject, is but a support-ing player in the process of reproduction/reinscription. Her life is an effect of the relay; it is lived *for* her by the automaton that produces the repro-duction of the same. She indeed lives it as if it were life. But we, the viewers, can see the all-important fact that eludes her: the individual mans a stead whereby and wherein she is "lived."

I am offering Chiaureli's *The Vow* not as a sample of socialist-realist art but as a meta-commentary on it. The premise of my account throughout has been that socialist realism is an artistic practice embedded in a plot, an ideologically sanctioned performance that prescribes a certain type of symbolic behaviour on the part of the author. *The Vow* allows us to see this plot as it plays itself out in epic hyperbole on the screen. It is the story of people whose deeds are theirs and not really theirs. The authors of those deeds are not really authors, for in their actions they are acted all along by a tendency whose carriers they are. The tendency is the real author; it works by means of people; the people's deeds are the tokens of the ten-dency's objective presence and power; the tokens furnish proof that history obeys an iron logic, which is not abstract but runs through the veins of life, and, as such, equals destiny. Socialist realism is part of this plot. As an institution, it stages the rebirth of culture as the work of the Formative, the imprint of a common destiny. As a form of representation, it assumes that representations are "given" to individuals insofar as they are subjects of socialism. The purported realism of these representations lies not in their mimetic reproduction of an empirically accessible world but rather in their status as "objective dream" (analogous to the concept of objective belief) produced by the unconscious called History. Being a socialist-realist artist meant practising one's trade within this plot. It required showing oneself, through one's artistic production, as capable of having objective dreams (displaying "revolutionary romanticism"). It was not a matter of depicting (*darstellend*) socialism but of showing, by means of the depiction, that the real-life force of socialism had taken hold of the depicter, acted him in the practice of creation, and thought itself out in the finished work.

In practice, the business of socialist realism was much more prosaic, of course. Since no one could be certain that one's creative imagination was in line with the objective imaginary of history, it was always wise to find out in advance what the Party considered to be the dreams befitting the epoch. This involved emulating works that had already received official recognition. In those paragons, which were already on hand when socialist realism was proclaimed, and whose number increased over time, the epoch had already spoken in its authentic voice, its grand Style had already shown itself as an aesthetic phenomenon. Hence, if one wanted to show oneself as a good Soviet subject, a true son of the epoch, one had to create in light of the existing canon, to produce tokens of belonging by reproducing those already in circulation. Ideologically, the symbolic act of socialist realism was that of a pen or a brush moved along by the compelling force of destiny-laid-bare. Practically, in the great majority of cases, it was the act of reinscribing conventions that had been canonized as the genuine marks of the Formative.

Notes

Introduction

1 I take artistic modernism in a deliberately broad sense that encompasses not only the now-canonized figures and masterpieces of the early twentieth century (Proust and Kafka, Eliot and Pound, Faulkner and Joyce; in Russia, Khlebnikov and Bely, Zamiatin and Pilniak) but also those more radical impulses of experimentation traditionally grouped under the term "avant-garde." I am wary of drawing a sharp line of separation between "modernism" and "avant-gardism," for such a separation – quite common in scholarship – has served as the means for enshrining a new cultural canon and for keeping this canon clean of all radical politics. On this issue, see Eysteinsson (143–78). Russia of the 1910s and 1920s is certainly the national context in which such a separation is least likely to hold. Another understanding of modernism, both broader and more specialized, will become apparent in the course of this introduction. It relates, specifically, to the metaphor of the death of the author or subject. I identify modernism as the (historically extended) moment in which the decentring of the subject was still experienced as an imperative – as a call for a new kind of cultural practice in which art would be either radically redefined or abolished altogether.

2 It is difficult to disagree with the following characterization of modernism offered by Raymond Williams: "Although modernism can be clearly identified as a distinctive movement, in its deliberate distance from and challenge to more traditional forms of art and thought, it is also strongly characterized by its internal diversity of methods and emphases; a restless and often directly competitive sequence of innovations and experiments, always more immediately recognized by what they are breaking from than by what, in any simple way, they are breaking towards" (89).

3 For an early critical assessment of Groys's position, see Ivanov, Review.

4 Cf. Solov'ev's well-known pronouncement: "The most perfect art, in its ultimate task, must embody the absolute ideal not just in the imagination, but in
reality as well, it must spiritualize, trans-substantiate [*presushchestvat'*], our
actual life. And if someone says that this task goes beyond the limits of art,
then we should ask: who has established these limits?" ("Obshchii" 22). For
Ivanov's explicit endorsement of this statement, see "Vzgliad" 182. The theme
of life creation in the younger generation of Russian symbolists is treated at
length in Sarychev 46–139.

5 In an article by Blok's closest friend and poetic associate, Andrei Bely, we find
a similar imperative: "Art takes wing where *the call to creation is, at the same
time, a call to the creation of life*" (154; emphasis in the original).

6 Whenever a Russian source is cited, the translation is mine (PP). Where I
quote an existing English translation of a Russian original, the citation in
parentheses refers to the former. In such cases, the entry in Works Cited gives
the English translation first, followed by the source in Russian.

7 T.J. Clark has described the practice of UNOVIS in similar terms: "They believed in working together on all forms of visual imagery, putting their individual interests and styles on hold for the moment; and even this degree of
collectivity, which at times seems to have been real and productive, was conceived as a kind of way-station on the road to a more comprehensive dissolution of the self" (226).

8 For a meticulously documented account of these debates, see Khan-
Magomedov. See also pp. 94–9 in the present study.

9 For further discussion of Constructivism, see chapter 4 of this book.

10 According to Michel Foucault, the assault on the author is ultimately "a matter of depriving the subject (or its substitute) of its role as originator, and of
analyzing the subject as a variable and complex function of discourse" ("What
Is an Author?" 158).

11 In similar spirit are the observations in Burke (xxv–xxvi), where, among others,
we find this assertion: "Following Nietzsche, the most radical alternatives to
transcendental subjectivity [once again, Marx and Freud are the other two] have
sought to situate rather than detach the subject from its work and world" (xxv).

12 The slogan "slovo kak takovoe" figures as the title of an important Futurist
manifesto by Velimir Khlebnikov and Aleksei Kruchenykh, which appeared
in 1913.

13 The pursuit of an essential language that would reinstantiate the lost sacrality
of the word, even at the price of jettisoning commonly used human language,
is no less characteristic of Dada's radicalizations of poetry's medium. Thus
Hugo Ball boasted in his diary: "We have charged the word with forces and

energies that make it possible for us to rediscover the Evangelical concept of
the 'word' (logos) as a magical complex image" (68).

14 Ricoeur argues that not only in the demystifying hermeneutics of Marx,
Nietzsche, and Freud, but also in the hermeneutics of faith and revelation, the
dispossession of consciousness is carried out en route to its subsequent reap-
propriation in another "home of meaning," which "is not consciousness but
something other than consciousness" (55).

15 Ekaterina Bobrinskaia has cautioned against attempts to confine the significance of modernist artefacts to their internal dynamics: "The radical gestures
of the avant-garde have meaning only in the context of history. They operate
with massive contexts, and not with some meaning locked within the work itself" (117). To my mind, this statement applies fully also to the dynamics of
depersonalization.

16 "The avant-garde poet or artist tries in effect to imitate God by creating something valid solely on its own terms, in the way nature itself is valid solely on
its own terms, in the way a landscape – not its picture – is aesthetically valid;
something *given*, increate, independent of meanings, similars or originals"
(Greenberg, "Avant-Garde" 6). These words of modernism's most acclaimed
art critic appear to support Groys's demiurgic thesis. In the next paragraph,
however, Greenberg goes on to state that the analogy with divine creation is
in fact spurious.

17 "The 'obsolescence' or even irrelevance of art for the 'spirit of contemporane-
ity' is for the avant-garde more than just an occasion for nostalgic experiences.
Artists and literary authors insistently seek different methods for the reconstruction of what has been lost or the creation of a new mode for the existence of art. The need to justify art, the pursuit of new coordinates and new
meanings for its existence, is a component part of many experiments in art
after the First World War" (Bobrinskaia 9).

18 Jameson's theorization of modernism owes much to the insights of Perry
Anderson's "Modernity and Revolution," especially to his understanding of
"uneven development" in relation to culture. In Anderson's analysis, the cultural situation in early-twentieth-century Europe was determined, above all,
by the fact that capitalism had not yet succeeded in absorbing modes of economic production and ways of life belonging to earlier stages of development.
The resulting tensions generated revolutionary energy in both politics and
culture. Anderson's socio-historical vision could serve as an illuminating
background to the Formalists' theorizations of literature. It seems fitting that
a theory based on the perceptual tensions between old forms and new was
born in world in which striking juxtapositions of phenomena from different
epochs were ubiquitous.

19 "Let the picture imitate nothing and let it present nakedly its *raison d'etre!*" (Gleizes and Metzinger 6).

20 The problem of grounding the artistic act is the same one that Yve-Alain Bois addresses under the rubric of "motivation." For him, this is one of the cardinal dilemmas confronting the modernist author: "what is the mode of existence of the work of art once its expressive function has been discarded" (136). Drawing upon Bois's work, Gough has discussed the "discourse on motivation" in the context of Russian Constructivism. See Gough, *The Artist* 11–14, 27; "Faktura" 48–52. See also pp. 98–9, 133 in the present study.

21 For one example, see n24; for another, see Theo van Doesburg's pronouncement, quoted on p. 144.

22 "The more closely the norms of a discipline become defined, the less freedom they are apt to permit ... The essential norms or conventions of painting are also the limiting conditions with which a marked-up surface must comply in order to be experienced as a picture" (Greenberg, "Modernist" 8).

23 This general approach, which takes the medium's defining properties as the generative principles for the artistic work, is what Władysław Strzemiński has called the "law of organicity." In *Painting as a Model*, Bois summarizes Strzemiński's thesis: "[The] work of art must be engendered from its 'primary given,' according to its 'first principles,' which means that this law functions differently for different media. As far as painting is concerned, these 'first principles' belong to three different orders, all of which are indissolubly linked to the fact that 'a picture is, or rather ought to be, something designed for *looking at* only': flatness, deduction of forms from the shape of the frame, abolition of the figure/ground opposition" (136; emphasis in the original).

24 For the fullest treatment of medieval conceptions of authorship, see Minnis.

25 For the cultural policies of the NEP, see Kemp-Welch; Fitzpatrick, *The Cultural Front* 1–15, 91–114.

26 As Evgenii Dobrenko has demonstrated, the dethroning of the "creative personality" was the dominant theme in the cultural-theoretical discourse of those years (*Formovka* 16–133). With this I fully agree, as it is also the guiding assumption of the account I offer in Part I of this book. But I cannot follow Dobrenko in his evaluative approach, which has led him to conclude that all of those theories of impersonality were a symptom of creative impotence, a clever ploy on the part of the uncultured plebeians to whom the Revolution had opened the shrine of art. Dobrenko does not acknowledge that the Soviet post-revolutionary episode – for all its uniqueness – was still part of a broader transnational crisis of culture. Nor does he pay sufficient attention to the fact that gestures of impersonality had currency far beyond the territory of Soviet Russia, with its lumpenproletarian parvenus. As I have been arguing so far, such gestures were common across the landscape of European modernism.

Some of those who performed them – Flaubert, Mallarmé, Rilke, Eliot, Joyce – easily meet Dobrenko's lofty standards for artistic talent.

27 The phrase "the victory of socialism ... in one separately taken country," from a 1915 article by Lenin ("O lozunge" 354), later encapsulated Stalin's position in the Party debates of 1926–7 regarding the possibility of building socialism in the Soviet Union. Against Trotsky – whose stance was likewise identified with a slogan, "permanent revolution" – Stalin maintained that socialism (but not communism) could be achieved without assistance from victorious proletarian revolutions in other countries.

28 The following humorous observation made by Maksim Gor'kii captures the atmosphere of that period: "If A belongs to a group B, then all other letters of the alphabet are for him either inimical or nonexistent" ("O pol'ze" 323).

1. The Imperative of Form

1 The designation was not chosen by the members of Opoiaz and the Moscow Linguistic Circle. It was foisted upon them by largely unsympathetic commentators.

2 For prominent examples of the type of literary criticism the Formalists rejected, see Erlich 51–5, 71.

3 For these lines of influence, see Erlich 23–32, 59–60. For a detailed discussion of Heinrich Wöfflin's influence, see Dmitrieva.

4 "The deeper justification for the use of the linguistic model or metaphor must, I think, be sought elsewhere, outside the claims and counterclaims for scientific validity or technological progress" (Jameson, *The Prison-House* viii). Jameson goes on to claim, predictably, that the reign of the linguistic model and the scientificity to which it laid claim are rooted, ultimately, in the socioeconomic system of Western capitalism, whose functioning becomes ever more dematerialized: "There is therefore a profound consonance between linguistics as a method and the systematized and disembodied nightmare which is our culture today" (ix).

5 Jameson describes in just these terms the revolutionary significance of Saussure's linguistic theory. Saussure's dissatisfaction with diachrony, according to Jameson, is an intellectual unease with the kinds of objects whose dynamics are to be explained by causes external to them. By contrast, Saussure's turn to synchrony and "system" is a turn to a new matter of knowledge, a matter determined fully by factors and relationships internal to it. See Jameson, *Prison-House* 7–8. For the Formalists' own unease with explaining literary phenomena by reference to a different "order" (*riad*) of facts, see Eikhenbaum's polemic with Trotsky in Eikhenbaum, "Vokrug voprosa."

6 We have Shklovskii's clearly stated admission: "In its essence, the Formal
   method is simple: a return to craftsmanship" (qtd in Steiner, "Three
   Metaphors" 63). Artisanal production as an implicit model for Shklovskii's
   conception of art has been noted by Jameson, who has commented also on
   the Aristotelian descent of the notion of art as craft or skill (*Prison-House*
   81–3). The reduction of art to skill, technical competence, would be a central
   idea of productivism – an avant-garde current closely associated with the
   Formalist school. The main theoretical explication of this idea is to be found
   in Arvatov, *Iskusstvo i proizvodstvo*.

7 On Shklovskii's personal fondness for machines and machine metaphors, and
   on the general mechanistic tendency of the Formalist method, see Steiner,
   "Three Metaphors" 63–71. Steiner's account suffers from the facile subsump-
   tion of *techne* under "technology." His characterization of Shklovskii as an
   "arch-mechanist" (72) fails to take into account the powerful strain in
   Shklovskii's writings that points, nostalgically, away from the alienating and
   benumbing effects of modernity towards a pre-industrial mode of production
   and perception. "It is at the same time part of a general feeling in the modern
   world that life has become abstract, that reason and theoretical knowledge
   have come to separate us from a genuine existential contact with things and
   the world" (Jameson, *Prison-House* 55).

8 For the most thorough treatment of the term "defamiliarization" and its uses,
   see Stacy. For its connection with psychological conceptions current during
   the early twentieth century, see Svetlikova 72–98.

9 Shklovskii's pronouncements were not always consistent with such a dynamic
   definition of artistic creation. In *The Knight's Move* (*Khod konia*; from which
   the quoted passage is taken) we also read: "*Faktura* is the principal characteristic of this peculiar world of deliberately constructed objects, the totality of
   which we call art" (102). Here it seems that the aesthetic is not the evanescent,
   contextually conditioned and, hence, contextually bound blossoming reached
   in a particular moment in the renewal of form, but rather a more or less identifiable property (*faktura*) that clings to the object and ascertains its belonging
   to art (which is, thus, also a supposedly stable "world … of objects"). Erlich
   has pointed out the same ambiguity in Shklovskii's understanding of form:
   "The Russian Formalist leader seemed to fluctuate between two differing interpretations of the term: he could not make up his mind as to whether he
   meant by 'form' a quality inherent in an esthetic whole or an esthetic whole
   endowed with a certain quality" (187). The concept of *faktura* will be discussed on several occasions in this book. See pp. 74, 83–4, 97–100. For the
   meaning of the term and the history of its use in Russian modernism, see
   Gough, "Faktura." Following Gough's suggestion (33), I have opted not to

translate *faktura* as "texture," for this rendition proves inaccurate or misleading in some contexts.

10 This translates the German *Differenzqualitaat*, a term borrowed from Broder Christiansen's *Philosophie der Kunst*. The treatise appeared in Russian before the Revolution, and evidence of familiarity with it is there already in Shklovskii's early "Sviaz' priemov" (1916). Another major borrowing from Christiansen is the concept of the "dominant" (*Dominante*). See Davydov.

11 Barthes has proposed a provocative distinction between diachrony and history, the former encompassing the systematic generation of oppositions and differences, the latter functioning as an unsystematic principle of inertia and contingency that disturbs the smooth operation of the diachronic automaton ("Literature" 265).

12 In another place, Shklovskii compares the laws of artistic tradition with those of Brownian motion: "The artist, whether he be the inventor of the internal-combustion engine or a poet, plays the role of just such particles, which make manifest [*vyiavliaiut*] motions that are, in themselves, invisible to the naked eye" (*Khod* 70).

13 The term the Formalists used was "constructive principle." See the quotation from Tynianov, "Literatyrnyi fakt" 108, above.

14 The Formalists delighted in showing how the personality projected by literary works or oeuvres had little to do with the biographical persona of the author. This personality was merely the enabling condition for the effects the text set out to realize: the extraliterary self dissolved into the literary device. Outstanding examples of Formalist demystifications of the self are Eikhenbaum's studies of the young Tolstoy and Anna Akhmatova. In the latter, Eikhenbaum argues that the contradictory lyrical "I" of Akhmatova is a little more than a projection on the plane of human psychology of a specific stylistic figure, the oxymoron. What appeared to be (the poet's) dramatic personality is revealed to be the literary device of dramatism.

15 Here is how Jakobson describes the workings of this automaton in the history of painting: "It is necessary to learn the conventional language of painting in order to 'see' the picture ... This conventional, traditional aspect of painting to a great extent conditions the very act of our visual perception. As tradition accumulates, the painted image becomes an ideogram, a formula, to which the object portrayed is linked by contiguity. Recognition becomes instantaneous. We no longer see [the painting]. The ideogram needs to be deformed. The artist-innovator must impose a new form upon our perception, if we are to detect in a given thing those traits which went unnoticed the day before. He may present the object in an unusual perspective; he may violate the rules of composition canonized by his predecessors" ("On Realism" 39–40). The

imperative "must" (*dolzhen*), which Jakobson uses repeatedly, issues, of course, from the automaton-like logic underlying the history of art.

16 The insistence on separating poetic from practical language – a mainstay of early Formalism – appears already in Lev Iakubinskii's "O zvukakh stikhot-vornogo iazyka" of 1916 (37). This definition was criticized by Medvedev 96–7. The Formalists themselves soon recognized its limitations. In 1925, Boris Eikhenbaum reminisced: "But these general acknowledgements that there are differences between poetic and practical language and that the specific quality of art was shown in its use of the material were not adequate when we tried to deal with specific works. We had to find more specific formulations of the principle of perceptible form so that they could make possible the analysis of form itself – the analysis of form understood as content. We had to show that the perception of form results from special artistic [devices] which force the reader to experience the form" ("The Theory" 113).

17 This early position of Jakobson's remained virtually unchanged until 1960, when it received a much more systematic treatment in his seminal lecture "Linguistics and Poetics." There, the poetic function was defined as an "orien-tation" (*ustanovka*) toward the "message"; this time it was framed not simply in opposition to pragmatic communication but in a paradigmatic distinction from all possible types of verbal performance: "referential," "phatic," "meta-lingual," "emotive," "conative" ("Closing Statement" 53–8).

18 "The existence of a fact as *literary* depends on its differential quality (i.e., on its relation to either the literary or the extra-literary series), or in other words – on its function" (Tynianov, "O literaturnoi" 273; emphasis in the original).

19 "We apprehend every fact of poetic language in an inevitable juxtaposition with the following three moments: the current poetic tradition, the practical language of the present, and the poetic tendency preceding the emergence of the given fact" (Jakobson, "Noveishaia" 19–20).

20 "Of course, the deformation can be noticed only against the background of literary and social history. Therefore Tynianov states that it is unwise to speak of aesthetic qualities in general, as aesthetic qualities are the result of a con-crete act of perception within a particular historical context" (Fokkema and Ibsch 23).

21 "If we are dealing with poets of the past, these three moments must be recre-ated – a difficult work, which can only be partially successful" (Jakobson, "Noveishaia" 20).

22 See Zhirmunskii 20–2.

23 For a nuanced discussion of Shklovskii's, Tomashevskii's, and Tynianov's views on the dichotomy *fabula–siuzhet*, see Todorov, "Some Approaches" 12–19. Jameson suggests that Shklovskii's work in cinema, which routinely

required the assembling of filmed pieces en route to the finished narrative product, made him particularly sensitive to this dichotomy (*Prison-House* 61).

24 "[The] fable is not a phenomenon which is logically prior to the subject; rather it follows after it. The fable is a pure construction thought up by the reader ... When we read a novel, we see its events in an (eventually) inverted order, which is sometimes presented by a special character in the story, or in a distorting version, and so on. During the course of our reading, we begin to assemble our own personal impression of the real events portrayed by the text. This personal image of the story will only be definitely fixed when we finish reading the last page of the book ... Throughout our reading of the story we only grasp the *subject*; we are incapable of reconstructing a complete version of its fable" (Todorov, "Some Approaches" 18). "Subject" here fails to convey the meaning of the French *sujet* (in the original of Todorov's article) and the Russian Formalist *siuzhet*.

25 Here, Shklovskii quotes Tolstoy on the conception of Andrei Bolkonskii's character in *War and Peace*: "In the battle of Austerlitz, which will be described, but with which I began the novel, I needed a brilliant young man to be killed; in the further course of the novel, I needed only the old Bolkonskii with his daughter, but since it was awkward to describe a person who was in no way related to the rest of the novel, I decided to make the brilliant young man a son of the old Bolkonskii. Then I got interested in him, a role turned up for him in the further course of the novel, so I spared his life, severely wounding, instead of killing him" ("Sviaz'" 55). As we can see, what spares the life of Andrei and allows him to grow into a major literary character is, really, the formal need for cohesion in the character scheme of the novel.

26 "A new form engenders new content" (Shklovskii, *Khod konia* 38). Here Shklovskii is only rephrasing one of the slogans of the Russian Futurists (Kruchenykh, "New Ways" 77). See n41.

27 Instead of the earlier talk of art being that which allows us to experience the thing as *made*, Tynianov now spoke of literature as a "dynamic verbal construction," which is to say, a "linguistic contruction which is experienced as construction" ("Literaturnyi fakt" 261).

28 For a classic account, see Abrams 156–225.

29 "Thus, the plot in Gogol has only a superficial significance and is, therefore, quite static ... The true dynamic, and, hence, the composition of his works, consists in the construction of the *skaz*, in the play of language" (Eikhenbaum, "Kak sdelana" 50; see also 46).

30 For more on the Romantic echoes in Formalist criticism, see Todorov, "Three Conceptions" 135–8. On the Hegelian connection in Russian Formalism, see Paramonov.

31 For the representative status of dreams in psychoanalysis, see Freud's own statements in *The Interpretation* 483; *New Introductory Lectures* 8. For an illuminating discussion of dreams' privileged role in the psychoanalytic approach to culture, see Ricoeur 159–63. In Book II, Part II, of *Freud and Philosophy* (159-254), Ricoeur proceeds to show how Freud's analysis of cultural and religious phenomena consists in the "gradual extension of the model of dreams and the neuroses to all cultural representations" (258).

32 See Freud's discussion in *Jokes* 14–105, which shows these same principles at work in the generative poetics of witticism.

33 See pp. 42–3 in this book.

34 It was Paul de Man who captured most memorably this modern being of the textual, when he asserted that "literature exists at the same time in the modes of error and truth; it both betrays and obeys its own mode of being" (163–4). For him too, the "error," the "blindness," the "betrayal" – all of them referring to what I have called dissimulation – are not pathological or accidental moments, introduced from some detachable outside, but are constitutive of the text as such.

35 "Three masters, seemingly mutually exclusive, dominate the school of suspicion: Marx, Nietzsche, and Freud" (Ricoeur 32).

36 Tsvetan Todorov has commented on how the Formalists ended up losing the very object on which their science of the literary was to be based ("Three Conceptions" 142–4).

37 In the words of Shklovskii: "The violation of the canon is possible only while the canon exists, and sacrilege presupposes a religion that is still alive" (*Khod konia* 73).

38 For the idea of *fabula* as corollary of the reader's presence within the text, see Todorov, "Some Approaches" 18.

39 Consider, for instance, Viktor Zhirmunskii's characterization of the movement: "The fact is that Russian Formalism ... took shape not as a school of literary studies, but as a working theory of creative practice. Our Formalism was begun by poets" (qtd in Dobrenko, *Aesthetics* 68). Dobrenko's *Aesthetics of Alienation* is largely a translation of the Foreword to his *Formovka sovetskogo pisatelia.* I cite the former volume in those cases where a quotation from the text is given.

40 The following statement by Teodor de Wyzewa (1862–1914) conjoins – very much like Shklovskii's program later will – the rhapsody of habitualization with the imperative for an art of renewal: "We have been the slaves of the world, and the sight of this world, where we engaged our interests, has since ceased to give us pleasure. And the Life which we had created – created in order to give us the joy of creating – has lost its original character. It is

necessary therefore to recreate it; one must build, over and above this world of defiled, habitual appearances, the holy world of a better life: better, because we can make it intentionally, and know how to make it. This is the very business of Art" (17). Here, too, Romantic precedents are to be found. Shelley's description of the (artistic) imagination is particularly pertinent: "It creates anew the universe after it has been annihilated in our minds by the recurrence of impressions blunted by repetition" (qtd in Burke, *The Death and Return* xx).

41 Here is Kruchenykh, in 1913: "A new content *becomes manifest only* when new expressive devices are achieved, a new form. Once there is new form, a new content follows; form thus conditions content" ("New Ways" 77; emphasis in the original). And here is his Futurist associate, Mayakovsky, writing in the following year: "It is not the idea that gives birth to the word, but the word to the idea" (qtd in Garzonio and Zalambani 8).

42 See Kruchenykh, *Sdvigologiia*; Kruchenykh, *Faktura*. For a discussion of the continuities between Futurist and Formalist theorizing, see Cherniakov.

43 Kruchenykh, "New Ways" 73–5.

44 Kruchenykh, "New Ways" 72.

45 I borrow this expression from Cherniakov.

46 For this widespread perception, see Khodasevich 320; Lunacharskii, "Formalizm"; Trotsky, *Literature* 138–53. It is a rather telling fact that Trotsky's first salvo in the direction of Formalism, his 1923 article in *Pravda*, was titled "The Formalist School of *Poetry* and Marxism" (this became the fifth chapter in his *Literature and Revolution*). See also ch. 1 n39, ch. 2 n4, ch. 3 n2.

47 Jameson's statement to this effect is even stronger: "Thus an ultimate evaluation of Formalism as a concrete literary phenomenon will bring it much closer to genuine creative movements such as German Romanticism or Surrealism than to a purely critical doctrine like that of the American New Criticism" (48).

2. The Imperative of Content

1 See n4 in this chapter.

2 The chief statement of this antagonism was, of course, Trotsky's polemic in *Literature and the Revolution* (138–3). For other representative critiques of Formalism from Marxist positions in the 1920s, see Bukharin, "O formal'nom"; Lunacharskii, "Formalizm"; Medvedev 54–174. Lunacharskii's text appeared as an entry in the debate on Formalism published in a special section of the journal *Pechat' i revoliutsiia* (No. 5, 1924).

3 For the particular fate of the term *pereverzevshchina*, see Lenhert 320–1, 327–36.

4 This was true at least until 1936, when a diatribe in *Pravda* against Shostakovich's *Lady Macbeth of Mtsensk* set off a massive campaign against "formalism," thus giving the latter the pre-eminent place among the cardinal sins of artistic practice in the Soviet Union. But "formalism" was no longer associated exclusively, or even principally, with the critical-theoretical school of the 1920s. It had become synonymous with all of the perceived evils of modernist aesthetics.

5 "Sociological school" is the more ambiguous of the two designations, as it has also been used to refer to the group around Vladimir Friche, while also serving as a blanket reference for the various sociological trends in the literary criticism of the 1920s. For a detailed review of these trends, see Novozhilova. Pereverzev himself objected when the label "sociological" was applied to his Marxist approach to literature ("Essential Premises"; qtd in Poliakov 14).

6 This volume was projected as the first in a series of publications on literary methodology and criticism; it remained the only one.

7 During a discussion at the Communist Academy in 1930, whose outcome was the *de facto* elimination of the Sociological school, one of the speakers, N.I. Efimov, remarked: "Methodological unity was represented in their works with such exclusive consistency that the 'Pereverzevtsy,' or members of the Pereverzev school, like the Formalists, were always identifiable by their style and by the methodological orientation of their works" (qtd in Scott 7).

8 As Poliakov points out, opposition between the sociological and Formalist methodologies was the defining dynamic in the literary criticism of the 1920s (12–13). The polemic between the two schools did not prevent the Pereverzevians from admitting, on occasion, the methodological superiority of their opponents. Thus Ul'rikh Fokht wrote in 1927: "Marxist literary scholarship cannot yet meet the Formalists on their own grounds; it lacks a well worked out system of literary concepts; it does not yet have its own poetics" (qtd in Erlich 114).

9 In Anatolii Lunacharskii's colourful characterization: "Before October, Formalism was a vegetable in season. Today it is a stubborn relic of the *status quo*, the last refuge of the unreconstructed intelligentsia, looking furtively toward bourgeois Europe" (qtd in Erlich 107).

10 This aversion to causal explanations was stated by Eikhenbaum in no uncertain terms: "To seek out the prime causes of literary forms or literary evolution is sheer metaphysics" (qtd in Erlich 125).

11 Pereverzev finds support for this monistic view in Marx's critique of earlier materialist philosophies: "The main defect of materialism up to and including Feuerbach consisted in the fact that it regarded reality, the objective world perceived through the external senses, as only an object of contemplation,

not as concrete human activity, not as practical activity, not subjectively" ("Essential Premises" 58).

12 "[The] main contradiction [of materialist critical thought of the 1860s] consisted in the fact that having advanced the strictly materialist proposition that art reproduces reality and having denied the idealistic view of art as the fruit of free thought unencumbered by objective conditions, the mechanists immediately began talking about art as engendered by thought, and very often thought that diverged from reality. This contradiction was inescapable for those who, in speaking of the reproduction of reality, meant not subjective reality with its inherent consciousness but the objective world opposed to consciousness, for those who did not include the consciousness peculiar to reality in the reality reproduced by art. Under such circumstances, art was the result not of a single actual reality but of the interaction between two essences – reflected reality and reflecting consciousness, the objective world and subjective thought, i.e., a fact of both real and ideal order" (Pereverzev, "Theoretical Premises" 42–3).

13 See p. 43 in the present study.

14 In this context, it is instructive to recall the passage in Marx's "Introduction to a Critique of Political Economy" in which he criticizes the "Robinsonades" of eighteenth-century economists – their attempts to derive the principles of socio-economic development from fictional scenarios in which the human individual appears as a fully independent agent in confrontation with "nature." Marx proceeds to expose these scenarios as misrepresentations characteristic of a specific phase in the historical life of bourgeois society. The human individual in question, "the joint product of the dissolution of the feudal form of production and of the new forces of production which have developed since the sixteenth century" (267) is represented as most independent precisely when, in actuality, "the inter-relations of society ... have reached the highest state of development" (268). Yet this misrepresentation is due neither to accidental blindness, nor to some inborn defect of human reason; it is itself a product – and a necessary product, at that – of the very actuality it obscures, the actuality of social existence under capitalism, in which "the different forms of social union confront the individual as a mere means to his private ends, as an outward necessity" (267).

15 "The non-coincidence between reality and its depiction is inherent in the historical process itself. The convergences between reality and representation are always relative; they are limited in respect to both history and class" (Bespalov, "Problema" 25).

16 "We should judge about style neither from the author's pronouncements, nor from his belonging to this or that literary group, neither from manifestoes,

nor from the author's plans and intentions. Historical scholarship studies not the wills and desires of people, but the facts that emerge, at times, despite the will of people, *behind their back*. The formation and individuation of a given style occurs *not on people's will, but, sometimes, regardless of their will, albeit through them*" (Bespalov, "Problema" 32; emphasis added). Bespalov's thesis, while replaying the main theme of the present investigation, recalls this classical passage from Marx's *The Eighteenth Brumaire*: "Upon the different forms of property, upon the social conditions of existence, rises an entire superstructure of distinct and peculiarly formed sentiments, illusions, modes of thought and views of life. The entire class creates and forms them out of its material foundations and out of the corresponding social relations. The single individual, who derives them through tradition and upbringing, may imagine that they form the real motives and the starting point of his activity" (47).

17 Cf. Marx and Engels's *The German Ideology*: "First the productive forces appear as a world for themselves, quite independent of and divorced from the individuals, alongside the individuals: the reason for this is that the individuals, whose forces they are, exist split up and in opposition to one another, whilst, on the other hand, these forces are only real forces in the intercourse and associations of individuals. Thus, on the one hand, we have a totality of productive forces, which have, as it were, taken on a material form and are for the individuals no longer the forces of the individuals but of private property, and hence of the individuals only insofar as they are owners of private property themselves. Never, in any earlier period, have the productive forces taken on a form so indifferent to the intercourse of individuals *as* individuals, because their intercourse was formerly a restricted one. On the other hand, standing over against these productive forces, we have the majority of the individuals from whom these forces have been wrestled away, and who, robbed thus of all real life-content, have become abstract individuals, but who are, however, only by this fact put into position to enter into relation with one another *as individuals*" (91–2; emphasis in the original).

18 In most other cases, "tendency" would be an inadequate translation of the Russian *ustremlenie*, which is traditionally rendered as "striving" or "aspiration." For translating Bespalov's usage, however, the teleological connotations of "striving" and "aspiration" seem out of place. The notion has some affinity with what the Formalists termed *ustanovka* ("orientation," "set"). In both cases, it is a matter of of seeing the literary text as organized in accordance with a definite principle; the plurality of artistic signs composing the text is functionally unified, "directed," so to speak. For the Formalists, the normative instance of such unifying directedness is the focus on the verbal medium's own properties (Jakobson's *ustanovka na vyrazhenie*). By contrast, the

Pereverzevian *ustremlenie* is a definite orientation or configuration of consciousness that endows the literary whole with something akin to personality.

19 At this point, Bespalov's reading echoes Pereverzev's early study of Dostoevsky, in which the position of the petty bourgeoisie is described in the following terms: "Over the petty bourgeoisie a curse hangs, as over the biblical fig tree: it is sociologically fruitless, incapable of a historically constructive role. The tragedy of this class lies in the fact that its revolutionary impulse neutralizes its reactionary impulse, and its reactionary impulse neutralizes its revolutionary impulse; the stormiest tensions of revolutionary energy are resolved in reaction, and the most intense reaction must be resolved in revolution" (qtd Jackson 48).

20 "Being immanent in relation to the socio-historical conditions which have brought it into existence, the [socio-psychological] complex is also immanent in relation to the structure of the [text]. The latter is a result of this complex's realization" (Pospelov, "Stil'" 162).

21 Hans-Jürgen Lehnert emphasizes this immanentist or, as he calls it, "poetological," perspective, after which he quotes the following statement by Pereverzev: "The social nature of the literary fact can and must be uncovered with the means of purely literary analysis and minimal reliance on the data of sociology, because the social nature of the literary work is manifested in its very structure, in the peculiarities of the elements that compose it" (321).

22 For Eikhenbaum's insistence that the Formalists were, above everything else, specifiers, see "Vokrug voprosa" 3.

23 See, for example, "Problems" 161–3, where Pereverzev speaks of the text as a "complex organic structure" constituted by the interaction of "living images."

24 It should be said that Pereverzev himself has not been fully consistent in the separation of the (higher-order) *obraz* from the (particular) *kharakter*. On this point, see Poliakov 27–8.

25 See Fokht's reading of the character of Lermontov's Demon, Pospelov's analysis of Lavretskii's character in *A Nest of Gentlefolk* ("Stil'"), and Pereverzev's discussion of character types in the novels of Goncharov ("K voprosu").

26 Poliakov elaborates on this point: "The genesis and existence of the work are intimately bound. The intermediary link between these two sets of problems is the concept of the work's structure. It is precisely the structural organization of the work that creates the unity of the two levels on which literature functions as a social phenomenon: as a *pronouncement* about reality and as an *image* of that reality" (7; emphasis in the original).

27 "Style is a phenomenon relative to class. The psychology of this or that class is imprinted in the whole aggregate of elements in the literary work, which represents a unity. In each historical period, the psychology of a given class

possesses certain basic features that define the psychological character of that class. These basic features are, so to speak, the foundation, the kernel, around which the other elements of class psychology are concentrated; they serve as the organizing principles of the given psychology, giving it a definite form ...

"These organizing psychological elements are reflected in the formative principles of the artistic work, in general, and of literature, in particular; they are realized, *materialized, so to speak, in the laws of literary construction*.

"We must emphasize that the basic elements of [class] psychology are not, by themselves, [identical with] style; style is the product of class consciousness objectivated in the literary work; being objectivated, its basic elements serve as the principles of organization of [literary] images" (Khrapchenko 27; emphasis in the original).

28 Pospelov explains the relation between particular character-images *in* the text and the overall "image" *of* the text in the following terms: "Within the limits of the poetic work, an order of social group experiences manifests itself as a *concrete system of motifs*. When speaking about poetic structures, we will refer to this system as a *complex of psychological motifs* – a socio-psychological complex, by which we understand that very same subjective aspect of social relations between people, which has been poetically canonized" ("K metodike" 67; emphasis in the original).

"If we call [this] entire complex, in all of its aspects, an 'image,' it is because the distinctive being of the socio-psychological complex becomes particularly visible and intelligible for us exactly in the plane of poetic imagery, within the well-defined logical confines of the 'image.' The images of the 'dramatis personae,' of the agents in the work of fiction, are its main constituents." ("K metodike" 78; emphasis in the original).

29 Robert Louis Jackson has used the compound in its reversed form ("image-character") to render Pereverzev's use of *obraz*.

30 See also Pereverzev, "Theoretical Premises" 16 and Pospelov, "K metodike" 59.

31 In Northrop Frye's system, the anagogic is the last level of figural representation, the furthest possibility for a figural embodiment of meaning. See Frye 151–8.

32 Thus, from Bespalov's analysis of Gor'kii's early stories (see p. 62 in the present study), it becomes clear that the "character" reproduced in the text is not to be confused with either of the two central character-types; it emerges from their structural opposition, which articulates the vacillating social position of the urban *petit bourgeoisie*.

33 "The order of experiences of a given social group, fixed in a verbal structure, creates through its features the characteristics that permeate all aspects of this

verbal structure, thus forging a distinctive poetic style" (Pospelov, "K metodike" 66).

34 See pp. 44–5 in the present study.

35 The same ambiguity emerges also in the Formalist dialectic of "device," where, in relation to the governing constructive principle (*dominanta*), a given formal element or group of them can stand as privileged carriers of the said principle. Thus, for instance, in Sterne's *Tristram Shandy* the device of narrative digression is clearly in privileged relation to the operative dynamic of the whole. But this is so because, to remember, the dynamic in question consists simply in the fact that a given creative gesture (in the case of *Tristram,* the idiosyncratic meandering of fictional narration) is promoted at the expense of others (namely, those associated with the habitual unfolding of an autobiographical story). Although the latter are equally "form," they necessarily appear as less "formal," or not "formal" at all (which makes Tynianov's reminder – that the subjugated elements, i.e., the so-called material, are also formal – a necessary one).

36 Lehnert declares that "Pereverzev understood the sociological nature [*sotsiologichnost'*] of literature to be tantamount to the determined character [*determinirovannost'*] of the writer's work. In this sense, his point of departure was the unfreedom of the writer's work" (329).

37 Deviation from the proper course (of reasoning, action), distortion.

3. Knowledge Become Practice

1 "A commodity appears at first sight an extremely obvious, trivial thing. But its analysis brings out that it is a very strange thing, abounding in metaphysical subtleties and theological niceties. So far as it is a use-value, there is nothing mysterious about it, whether we consider it from the point of view that by its properties it satisfies human needs, or that it first takes on these properties as the product of human labour. It is absolutely clear that, by his activity, man changes the forms of the materials of nature in such a way as to make them useful to him. The form of wood, for instance, is altered if a table is made out of it. Nevertheless the table continues to be wood, an ordinary, sensuous thing. But as soon as it emerges as a commodity, it changes into a thing which transcends sensuousness. It not only stands with its feet on the ground, but, in relation to all other commodities, it stands on its head, and evolves out of its wooden brain grotesque ideas, far more wonderful than if it were to begin dancing of its own free will" (Marx, *Capital* 163–4).

2 Cf. Vladislav Khodasevich: "In art, theory almost always comes after practice. *As the spiritual child of futurism*, there arose the formal method of critical

scholarship, which is now if not dominant, then extremely fashionable and vocal, which makes it seem 'advanced'" (320; emphasis added).

3 This prototypical *zaum* piece appeared first in the booklet *Pomada,* handwritten by Kruchenykh and illustrated by Mikhail Larionov. There the verse is to be found sandwiched between an explanatory note by its author and a rayonist sketch by Larionov. On the significance of this juxtaposition, see Perloff, *Futurist Moment* 123.

4 For the political and ideological contest between Lenin and Bogdanov, see Ballestrem; Joravsky 24–44; Sochor, esp. 3–20.

5 See also Bogdanov, "Taina" 404–5.

6 For the ambition of supplementing Marx with Mach, see Bogdanov, *Empiriokrtitsizm* 10. For Bogdanov's objections to the empiriocriticism of Mach and Avenarius, see *Filosofiia* 152–79. The principal of these objections is that empiriocriticism is a reflective philosophy, that is, a form of systematic knowledge that has not abandoned the contemplative stance in favour of the active, transformative engagement with reality (*Filosofiia* 200–3). In the same text, Bogdanov also criticizes Marx and Engels's dialectical materialism (201–11, 219–21).

7 The relationship between philosophy and tektology is the exclusive subject of Bogdanov, "Ot filosofii."

8 As Bogdanov explained in an earlier treatise, the human world and the collective doings of mankind are only the highest level of the organizational continuum that is universal being (*Filosofiia* 255–6).

9 On Bogdanov's understanding of matter as resistance, see *Filosofiia* 48–9, 58–9, 83. The notion has a long historical pedigree, reaching back to the early modern philosophy of nature. Cf. Definition III of Newton's *Principia,* which speaks of *vis insita*, the force innate to matter, as the power of resisting change (*The Mathematical Principles* 2). At a shorter historical distance, Bogdanov's position can be traced – via Mach – to Herbert Spencer's conception of matter as the abstraction through which we represent to ourselves everything in our world that opposes our muscular exertions (Spencer 136–45).

10 Bogdanov's tektological elements are a slightly refashioned version of Mach's elements-sensations, which comprise the entirety of the universe, traversing the duality between psychical and physical, human interiority and the exteriority of nature. See Mach 12–18; 20–2. On the difference between Bogdanov's and Mach's understanding of experience and its analytical units, see Jensen 124–6.

11 See Bogdanov, *Tektologiia* 57.

12 See ch. 2 n11.

13 The reference is to Marx, "Theses" 243. Bogdanov's own narrative of philosophy's divorce from life and plea for their integration can be found in *Filosofiia*
3–17.

14 See the quotation from Arvatov above.

15 See also Bogdanov, "Taina" 407–8.

16 "The problem is that specialization … undermines the homogeneity of the
[class] collective, it engenders disunity, mutual misunderstanding, and thence
also contradictions between its differentiated elements; then [the class collec-
tive] is no longer one in its life and constructive work, and is incapable of producing a unified and whole structure for the entire society. Such was the case
with the bourgeoisie: it never became a true collective, it could not devise any
form of organization other than the anarchic. And to the extent to which the
proletariat is ruled by the specializing powers of bourgeois culture, it too
manifests disunity, which turns into direct contradictions" (Bogdanov,
Tektologiia 50).

17 This (productive) ambiguity has been noted in Jensen 113.

18 Purportedly, such was not the case for prehistoric man. In the earliest human
communities, Bogdanov tells us, the span and depth of accumulated experience was extremely limited. This made it possible for each individual's organizational know-how to be equal to that which the community, as a whole,
commanded. Another way of stating the same is to say that there was, at this
earliest stage, still no true "I" as separate from the primitive collective identity
("Sobiranie" 31–2).

19 See also Bogdanov, *Filosofiia* 60–9, where the failure to recognize the social
character of every human activity is viewed both as a principal feature of
bourgeois consciousness and, thus, as the source of all fetishism of bourgeois
philosophical thought.

20 See ch. 2 nn14, 16.

21 Bogdanov develops this idea at length in "Sobiranie."

22 See also Bogdanov, "Sotsialisticheskoe obshchestvo" 91–4; "Kollektivisticheskii stroi" 296–9.

23 "Machine production transforms the proletariat … into a class infused with
working consciousness, infused with positive attitude toward labor, a class
that realizes the meaning and value of labor … In the worker's thinking, the
idea of labor occupies a central position: it serves as a starting point for him.
In his inner world … there develops, firstly, the love of labor and, secondly,
the pride in labor, because he sees constantly … how labor overcomes nature,
overcomes the elemental forces. All this is done by the machine, which carries
the self-consciousness of labor" (Bogdanov, *Elementy* 38–9).

24 For Bogdanov, the prehistoric stage of primitive communal life showed no signs of *systematic* knowledge, and thus also no distinct notion of causality (*Filosofiia* 226–7).

25 On this view, a cause is something active in itself, although not necessarily anthropomorphic. The effect is something the cause itself "does" in its sovereign agency. See, for example, Bogdanov's discussion of Thales's *arche* in *Filosofiia* 76.

26 By contrast with the authoritarian model, the paradigm of abstract necessity treats "cause" not as an existent but as a general principle definable by a cognitive scheme, a law. Newton's gravity, for instance, is not thought as an entity to be found in the physical world; only physical bodies can be found existing in it; gravity is simply the law that generalizes their interactions. See Bogdanov's summary of Francis Bacon's method in *Filosofiia* 141.

27 There is an unmistakable affinity between Bogdanov's schema of human cognitive history and Vladimir Solov'ev's plotting of history as a progression of forms of social organization. In *The Philosophical Principles* 32–56, Solov'ev distinguishes three dialectically related phases of such organization. The earliest, as in Bogdanov, is the authoritarian, characterized by a primitive unity imposed from the outside. The second is a stage on which external compulsion falls away, but unity is lost as well, as the elements composing the social whole strive for independence. The third and final stage is one of synthesis and reconciliation between totalizing rule and pulverizing freedom: the "free theocracy," as a voluntarily undertaken and realized unity of mankind and the divine. In Solov'ev, too, the gradations of social life are found to correspond to different configurations of knowledge. His integral knowledge arrives on the scene – just as it does in Bogdanov – with the appearance of an integral form of communality.

28 Bogdanov referred to this as the principle of "sociomorphism"; see *Filosofiia* 241–3. See also pp. 86–7 in the present study.

29 See p. 70 in the present study.

30 "Ideas of universal significance are not thought up by individual consciousness, but are formed by social practice" (94). It is worth noting that Bogdanov's determinism is stringent only when it comes to the most basic structures of knowledge, the fundamental ideological premises of social consciousness.

31 On Althusser, see chapter 8 of this book.

32 See pp. 7–9.

33 "Such is the objective meaning of labor, which exists for the collective, but usually eludes the consciousness of the person, the narrow, fragmented thinking of the contemporary individual" (*Filosofiia* 48).

4. The Organization of Things

1 In 1922, young Andrei Platonov, a follower of Bodganov and member of the Voronezh Proletkult, wrote about this return of art to its essential dimension: "After the proletarian epoch, poetry will be not the organization of symbols, the ghosts of matter, but the organization of matter itself, the transformation of reality itself. Proletarian poetry is the transfiguration of matter, a struggle with reality, a fight with the universe for its alteration in accordance with the inner requirement of man" (31). That same year, Platonov abandoned his literary pursuits to devote himself to the direct "transformation of reality itself"; he took up work as an engineer on irrigation and electrification projects.

2 For a book-length study of Proletkult, see Mally. Other useful sources are Brown 6–20; Fitzpatrick, *The Commisssariat* 89–109; Sochor 125–60. On the formation of the proletarian self and its expression in poetry, see Steinberg. For the poetry of Proletkult, see also Dobrenko, *Formovka* 176–234; Levchenko.

3 A member of the "Objectivist" group at INKhUK, Nataliia Udal'tsova summarized the group's program for new art in this one sentence: "We regard art not as a representation of reality, but as its *organization*" (qtd in Khan-Magomedov 86; emphasis in the original).

4 See pp. 21–2, 29–30 in this book.

5 For the early-Soviet cult of the machine, see Stites 145–64.

6 As the director of the Central Institute of Labor, Gastev's most nagging preoccupation was that of reducing the gap between the "human, all too human" nature of physical labour and the inexorable functioning of the machine: "The contemporary machine, especially the machine complexes, have their laws of calibrations, executions, and rests, which are not in correspondence with the rhythmics of the human organism ... We must introduce some corrective coefficients in [the machine's] iron, disciplined oppression; but history insistently demands that we address not these small problems of individual safety, but the bold engineering of human psychology in accordance with such a decisive factor as machinism" (Gastev, *Nashi zadachi* 10).

7 The minute and seemingly trite mechanics of daily life were also of concern to Arvatov, who expressed himself in terms strikingly similar to Tretiakov's: "The ability to pick up a cigarette-case, to smoke a cigarette, to put on an overcoat, to wear a cap, to open a door, all these 'trivialities' acquire their qualification, their not unimportant 'culture'" (qtd in Kiaer 34).

8 "Rejection of the 'creative personality,' the *idée fixe* of all the revolutionary theories of creativity, found among the LEFists the most radical and logical supporters" (Dobrenko, *Aesthetics* 75).

9 To the latter, Tarabukin devoted in the same year a lecture emphatically titled "The Last Picture Has Been Painted."

10 Mikhail Matiushin imaged this moving-outward from the traditional surface of representation in the following allusion to the new art of material assemblage: "The artist was jumping out from the canvas by means of boxes, sticks, a rag, glass, metal, endeavoring to force his own and his neighbor's eye to understand depth" (qtd in Bobrinskaia 101). But the turning inside out (or hereto-there) of the traditional space of representation was perhaps most clearly demonstrated in theatre. In the projects of Vsevolod Meyerhold and Liubov' Popova (as in those of Berthold Brecht in Germany), the stage was to encroach on the space formerly reserved for the audience and become the site of political demonstration, or the training ground for the rhythmics of movement and the efficiency of labour (Meyerhold's school of "biomechanics"; see further in this chapter, pp. 100–2.

11 Gough coins for this the term "materiological determination" ("Faktura" 41–2). See further in this study, pp. 98–9.

12 The more immediate and relevant reference is to Aleksei Gan's programmatic pamphlet, *Constructivism*, where "tectonics" figures as one of the three definitive elements of the new practice, along with *faktura* and "construction" (40). For a discussion of this conceptual triad, see pp. 98–9 in this book.

13 In the rest of the paragraph, I gloss Arvatov's narrative in *Iskusstvo i klassy* 3–13.

14 See ch. 3 n1.

15 See above, p. 74.

16 Kiaer sees Tatlin's creation of everyday objects of use as a variation on the "materiological determination" exemplified by his corner reliefs (52). She distinguishes Tatlin's procedure (and ideology) from the functionalist direction followed by the constructivists of INKhUK. She believes, along with Gough, that the latter leads to an imposition of form dictated by extrinsic factors rather than by the material itself (50–2). As the current discussion should make clear, I do not subscribe to this view, as I find the distinction between "intrinsic" and "extrinsic" factors much too neat to do justice to the Constructivist program. As will be argued further in this chapter, one of the most intriguing features of this program is how it manages to present ostensibly extrinsic factors (e.g., communist ideology) as something pertaining to the material; see pp. 98–9.

17 Regarding the widely divergent interpretations of the concept of *konstruktsiia* among the early Constructivists, see Khan-Magomedov 45–6.

18 Thus Rodchenko spoke of contemporary expediency (*tselesoobraznost'*) as "construction laid bare [*obnazhennaia konstruktsiia*]" (qtd in Khan-Magomedov 39).

19 For Rodchenko, the leader of the initial group of Constructivists, construction was the very principle of utilitarian organization; it amounted to the expedient use of the properties of materials (Khan-Magomedov 44, 61). In other words, he saw it as a certain general approach to materiality. It should be said, however, that *konstruktsiia*, too, permits the dual meaning of act and fact. It can refer to *what* one does or *how* one does it (a method or approach); but it can also refer to the objectivated outcome of practice. In fact, the members of INKhUK invested the term with one or the other of these meanings without signalling – and often without being conscious of – the difference. This often made the distinction between *konstruktsiia* and *faktura* appear tenuous and uncertain. This was one reason why some Constructivists found the latter term redundant.

20 I do not believe that Gan intended to arrange the parts of his program as a progression, but I do think it is possible to interpret them as I have done here.

21 Gan's manifesto, *Constructivism*, opens with the bold-faced cheer "Long Live the Communist Expression of Material Constructions!" (5).

22 Gan stressed repeatedly Constructivism's task of uniting the ideological aspects of production with the formal-technological (54, 60, 61).

23 In Gan's text, the order of exposition is different: *faktura* is discussed after *tektonika* and before *konstruktsiia*.

24 Those members of INKhUK who would later call themselves "Constructivists" first came together in a tellingly named "Working Group for Objective Analysis," which distanced itself from the leadership of Vasilii Kandinskii. As the very first items on the agenda for its inaugural meeting (23 November 1920), the group proposed: "a) objective *analysis of artistic works* in order to uncover [their] elements (basic and peripheral) and the laws of their organization; 2) *analysis* of elements and the laws of their organization in individual works" (qtd in Khan-Magomedov 37; emphasis added). One would be hard-pressed to find any differences between this proposal and an agenda for an Opoiaz meeting.

25 In another place, Chuzhak states: "It would be a huge absurdity to understand the 'thing' only as an externally perceptible materiality – an error committed by the first productionists, who relied on vulgar-fetishistic, metaphysical materialism; the 'idea' should not be excluded from the concept of the thing, inasmuch as the idea is the necessary prerequisite of any real construction – a model for tomorrow" (Chuzhak, "K zadacham" 145–6).

26 On the development of biomechanics, as a theoretical platform and as a training program for actors, see Law and Gordon 33–59. Important original documents pertaining to biomechanics can be found in the same volume, 93–253.

27 On the Taylorist inspirations of Meyerhold's biomechanics, see Law and Gordon 34–6; Pozdnev. Arkadii Pozdnev, a student of Meyerhold, concludes

his article by proclaiming: "The Taylor of the theater is Vsevolod Meyerhold" (151).

28 Meyerhold admitted that his dualistic formula of acting was inspired by Constant Benoît Coquelin's conception of the actor as an aggregate of two distinct selves. See Braun, *Meyerhold* 202.

29 These laws extend to and encompass the entire space of theatrical performance: "The stage and the theater are to be an enormous machine with very complex construction, which works with mathematic precision according to the laws of mechanics" (Sokolov 21).

30 Compare this pronouncement with Gan's programmatic postulate: "The sociopolitical system conditioned by the new economic structure gives rise to new forms and means of expression. The emergent culture of labor and intellect will be expressed by intellectual-material production" (21).

31 *Komfut* is the acronym of the "Communist-Futurist collective" founded by Mayakovsky and Brik in Petrograd in late 1918. The short-lived association (dissolved in 1921) aimed at integrating Futurism with the organization and ideology of the Communist Party. See "Organizatsiia," "Partiia."

32 *Kino-glaz* ("kino eye" or "cinema eye") was to provide the title of Vertov's film project of 1924. From the compound *kino-oko* (cine-eye) was derived *kinoki* – the name adopted by a group of documentary filmmakers who gathered around Vertov in the early 1920s.

33 "The cinema eye lives and moves in time and space; it perceives and records impressions in a manner entirely different from that of the human eye. The position of our body during observation, the amount of features of this or that sensory event that we are able to apprehend, is not at all obligatory for the camera, which perceives more and better the more perfect it is.

"We cannot make our eyes better than they already are, but we can perfect the camera endlessly" (Vertov, "Kinoki" 138).

On the superiority of the cinema-eye over the human, "naked" eye, see also Vertov "Kino-Eye" 67 and "From Kino-Eye to Radio-Eye" 87. In "We: Variant of a Manifesto," Vertov echoes Tretiakov's dissatisfaction with man's imperfect motions: "The machine makes us ashamed of man's inability to control himself, but what are we to do if electricity's unerring ways are more exciting to us than the disorderly haste of active men and the corrupting inertia of passive ones" (7).

34 See Rodchenko's critique of traditional (artistic) photography in "Puti," esp. 36.

35 *Life Caught Unawares* (*Zhizn' vrasplokh*) is also the alternative title of Vertov's 1924 film *Cinema Eye* (*Kinoglaz*).

36 On the dialectic of "life facts" and "film facts" in Vertov, see Petric 38–9.

37 On the conceptual relation of Vertov's method to the theoretical Constructivism of Gan and the practical Constructivism of Tatlin, see Michelson xxviii–xxxv.
38 "Cine-Eye is not the end. Cine-Eye is a means. To show without masks" (qtd in Hicks 32).
39 On the top of the list in Vertov's various definitions of the kino-eye stands "kino-eye as cinema analysis" ("The Birth" 41).
40 See pp. 47–51 of this book.
41 See Vertov, "From Kino-Eye" 88–90.

5. The Organization of Minds

1 To be sure, Meyerhold's actor possesses emotions and moods, but these are in strict subordination to the physiological-kinetic aspect of human being – what Meyerhold calls the "physical prerequisite" (*fizicheskaia predposylka*; "Akter" 11).
2 So named after the journal *On Guard* (*Na postu*), which the group published between 1923 and 1925. From 1926 to 1931, the journal *On Literary Guard* (*Na literaturnom postu*) took its place. In the first half of the 1920s, *napostovstvo* (onguardism) became the name of a recognizable literary-critical platform and a very distinct type of cultural activism. After 1925, when the Party resolution on literature caused a split in the movement, *napostovstvo* was often associated with the left wing of VAPP (Rodov, Lelevich, Vardin, Bezymenskii).
3 This description is hardly more than an echo of RAPP proclamations like the following: "The power and meaning of RAPP now consists in this: that its literary production is thought through and programmed, that there is a five-year plan, [that] signposts are marking the point of departure and the point of arrival, [that] the strategic map is plain to see" (Berkovskii 123).
4 See Rodov's passionate proselytizing of this principle in "Organizatsionnye" and "O kruzhkovshchine."
5 Lenin, an old foe of Bogdanov's, personally directed the coup. See Lenin, "On Proletarian Culture"; "On the Proletkults."
6 In noting the continuity between Proletkult and the Onguardist movement, two essential divergences should be kept in mind. First, whereas Proletkult had sought complete independence from the Party and the structures of Soviet government (in the first place, from NARKOMPROS), the Onguardists wished nothing more than to function as a representative of the Party in the literary sphere. Second, the Proletkult program for proletarian culture presumed that this culture would be the work of the proletarians themselves. As

will be discussed further in this chapter, the Onguardists fought for a literature that would represent the (ideological) *point of view* of the newly victorious class.

7 See Lelevich, "O marksizme"; Vardin, "Revoliutsiia" 77–80.

8 These formulations remained unchanged throughout the decade. We find them in the resolution adopted by the First Congress of Proletarian Writers in 1928: "Being one of the means for the cognition of social life and of the whole world which surrounds man, art organizes the feelings and thoughts by means of images influencing the psyche of the reader, listener, etc., through 'emotional infection'" (qtd in Brown 62).

9 On the concatenation Proletkult–"Smithy"–"October," see Dobrenko, *Formovka* 41–8. Dobrenko argues that the most essential continuity between Proletkult and RAPP is to be sought in the "act of overcoming the personality of the creator" (35).

10 On this issue, see Brown 62–3.

11 Cf. the following passage from Marx and Engels's *Holy Family*, which serves as the epigraph to Lukács's chapter "Class Consciousness": "It is not a question of what this or that proletarian, or even the whole proletariat, at the moment *regards* as its aim. It is a question of *what the proletariat is*, and what, in accord with this *being*, it will historically be compelled to do" (53; emphasis in the original).

12 I offer here only a minimal gloss on the tangled organizational history of the movement. For a more comprehensive account, see Brown 12–20, 46–57; K. Clark, "RAPP."

13 The All-Union Organization of Proletarian Writers' Associations (*Vsesoiuznoe ob"edinenie assotsiatsii proletarskikh pisatelei*, VOAPP) coordinated the activities of the separate national organizations.

14 In subsequent Soviet history, RAPP became – through a sort of retroactive genealogy – the blanket reference for the entire movement of proletarian literature initiated by the Octobrists. For a detailed historical account of the "proletarian episode" in Soviet literature, see Brown.

15 On the conflict between the Onguardists and Voronskii, see Brown 21–45; Maguire 156–87; McLean.

16 "Grimasa NEPa" is the title of a 1927 short story by Mikhail Zoshchenko.

17 On the notion of "restoration of the superstructure," see Lelevich, "Otkazyvaemsia" 100–1. Without mentioning NEP, Lelevich writes about moments in history in which the superstructure of earlier epochs can make a return, provided that some of the socio-economic conditions associated with the said superstructure have been restored as well.

18 As Voronskii himself was a card-carrying Communist, the confrontation with
    RAPP could be viewed as a fractional battle within the Party (K. Clark,
    "RAPP" 213).

19 On the position of the Party on cultural and literary affairs during NEP, see
    Kemp-Welch.

20 For the distinguished history of *Krasnaia nov'*, see the classic study by Maguire.

21 For comprehensive accounts of Voronskii's ideas and positions in the cultural
    debates of the 1920s, see Belaia; Maguire 188–311.

22 For the Onguardist credo that writers *should* carry Party cards, see Vardin,
    "O politgramote" 94. Paraphrasing Nekrasov, the leading Onguardist poet,
    Bezymenskii, mandated: "A poet you need not be/but a communist you must
    be" (*Poetom mozhesh' ty ne byt'/no kommunistom byt' obiazan*; qtd in
    Libedinskii, "K voprosu" 59–60).

23 Voronskii's position was certainly more nuanced than that; it was also less re-
    mote from the position of his opponents. He insisted that all cognition pro-
    ceeds from a class-determined point of view. But when a class gains strength,
    when it is the "progressive" class of its day, objective cognition becomes both
    necessary and possible for it ("Iskusstvo" 378). It is the objective historical be-
    ing of a social group that opens to it the possibility for objective knowledge
    of reality.

24 When RAPP's main theoretician, Libedinskii, put to paper his views on the
    writer's relationship to reality, they turned out to be embarrassingly similar to
    those of Voronskii. In the "The Artistic Platform of RAPP," Libedinskii as-
    cribes to the writer the ability to raise himself, by an act of will, above the pre-
    vailing interpretation of reality (Libedinskii, "Khudozhestvennaia" 16).

25 See pp. 96–7.

26 Confusing the *actual* consciousness of the proletariat with the class's *imputed*
    system of cognition became, during the 1920s, the distinguishing mark (and
    stigma) of political "opportunism."

27 As has been noted, this emphasis on ideological position, at the expense of
    class origin, suited quite well the social profile of RAPP. Although all of its
    leaders were Party members, none of them were from a working-class back-
    ground (K. Clark, "RAPP" 212; Brown 62–63).

28 See above, p. 103.

29 On the different "interpretations" of the social commission during the 1920s,
    see Dobrenko, *Formovka* 97–116.

30 See above, p. 60.

31 Since the organization of proletarian literature, Averbakh reasoned, rested on
    ideological rather than formal principles, the problem of artistic method was

overridden by considerations of the author's ideological position: "The writer's artistic method cannot be torn away from ideology, from his worldview as a whole. Moreover, the writer's artistic method is fully subordinate to ... his ideological stance" (Averbakh, "Tvorcheskie" 9).

32 See, for example, Zonin 14–15.

33 The term "sociolect" (*sotsiolekt*) was coined by Mikhail Bakhtin, in whose theory of culture and novelistic discourse it designates a modulation of the common language, marked stylistically and ideologically as issuing from a particular social position. In the present context, Reich's sociographics claims to be an exclusive discourse in which the heterogeneity of the various conflicting sociolects has been resolved. This type of discourse, which belongs to the proletariat by objective entitlement, cannot be identified with any *particular* position within society, but only with the objective existence of the social as a whole (the universal).

34 For example, in Vertov: "Cinema's unstrung nerves need a rigorous system of *precise* movement. The meter, tempo, and type of movement, as well as its *precise* location with respect to the axes of a shot's coordinates and perhaps to the axes of universal coordinates (the three dimensions + the fourth – time), should be studied and taken into account by each creator in the field of cinema. Radical necessity, *precision*, and speed are three components of movement worth filming and screening. The geometrical extract of movement through an exciting succession of images is what is required of montage" ("We" 8; emphasis added).

35 See Dobrenko, *Formovka* 54.

36 On the history and significance of these notions, which were to become mainstays of the doctrine of socialist realism, see Balina, esp. 368–75; James 8–14.

37 On the concept of *narodnost'*, see Günther; James 1–11.

38 For the passage from cultural revolution to Stalinist *kul'turnost'* (a difficult-to-translate term that implies the veneer of civilization more than the spiritual depth of culture), see Boym 120–1; Durham 22–3; Fitzpatrick, *The Cultural Front* 218; Volkov.

39 Just a few months before his execution, still hoping to prove himself to Stalin, Bukharin wrote in prison: "[Socialism] gathers people together and creates a human type that is truly an integrated individual [*tselostnyi chelovek*], one who has a multitude of functions and a fullness of life and a richness of life that is developing historically more and more" (*Socialism* 41). Bukharin was not describing a hypothetical situation, but something he asserted to be the contemporary reality in the Soviet Union: "for almost twenty years socialism has been living a real existence in the form of the USSR" (3).

6. The Anonymous Centre of Style

1 "The avant-garde exists in a situation of constant reflection upon the nature of art, in constant questioning 'what is art?', and also in a situation of constant doubt, a maniacal search for arguments to justify art's existence. A sense of art's dubiousness and irrelevance is one of the principal ingredients of avant-garde culture" (Bobrinskaia 20).

2 Ludwig Kirchner made it clear that answering these questions was a prerequisite for membership in *Der Blaue Reiter*: "Everyone who with directness and authenticity conveys that which drives him to creation, belongs to us" (qtd in Perloff, "Violence" 69).

3 Thus Christopher Butler has identified modernism with "the disruption of the very idea that the arts should have a socially agreed reflective content" (20).

4 See also Berdiaev 32.

5 Eysteinsson has made a very similar point: "It is true that many modernists have extolled the autonomy of art. But nothing obliges us to take such views as adequately representative of their own work or of modernism in general" (12).

6 This, I believe, is what the following lines by Giorgio de Chirico seek to communicate: "A work of art must narrate something that does not appear within its outline. The objects and figures represented in it must likewise poetically tell you of something that is far away from them and also of what their shapes materially hide from us" (439).

7 See pp. 9–14 in this book.

8 This fact is also clearly spelled out by the intertitles that open the film.

9 "Thirty foreheads damaged – scrap the people."

10 Олошадить жителей Австралии.

Омолодить на 30 лет канадцев.

Принять рапорт в три минуты от полмиллиарда спортсменов.

Сделать сводку рапортов телемашинами в 10 минут.

Включить солнце на полчаса.

Написать на ночном небе 20 километров слов.

Разложить сознание на 30 параллелей.   (Gastev, "Pachka orderov" 219).

11 Панихида на кладбище планет.

Рев в катакомбах миров.

Миллионы, в люки будущего.

Миллиарды, крепче орудия.

Каторга ума.

Кандалы сердца.   (Gastev, "Pachka orderov" 217–18)

12 "Speech travels between the separate parts. But in the perfect One there is perfect silence and bliss" (Lawrence 423).

13 "We do not [wish to] preempt the forms of the word's technicization, but it is clear that this will be more than a mere amplification of sound; [the word] will gradually separate itself from its living carrier – man" (Gastev, "Kontury" 333).

14 For a useful summary of these polemics, see DeKoven 675–9. Some of the main Marxist texts in the debate can be found in *Aesthetics*.

15 Such comparisons were highly typical in the intellectual culture of the nineteenth century. Writing in 1831, John Stuart Mill observed: "The 'spirit of the age' is in some measure a novel expression. I do not believe that it is to be met with in any work exceeding fifty years in antiquity. The idea of comparing one's own age with former ages, or with our notion of those which are yet to come had occurred to philosophers; but it never before was itself the dominant idea of any age" (51).

16 For the influential treatment of style as individual signature, see Goodman.

17 This is what an art review of 1906 characterized aptly as the "sauce of history" (qtd in Gray 71).

18 Simmel continued: "Earlier times, which only had one style which was taken for granted were situated quite differently in these difficult questions of life. Where only one style is conceivable, every individual expression grows organically from it; it has no need to search first for its roots; the general and the personal go together without conflict in a work. The unity and lack of problems we envy in Greek antiquity and some periods of the Middle Ages are based on such an unproblematic general foundation of life, that is to say, on the style, which arranged its relationship to the individual production much more simply and freer of contradictions, than is possible for us, who have a variety of styles at our disposal in all areas, so that individual work, behavior and taste have a loose optional relation to the broad foundation, the general law, which they do require after all. That is the reason why the products of earlier times often seem to have so much more style than those of our own age. For we say an object is devoid of style if it appears to have sprung from a momentary, isolated, temporary sentiment, without being based on a more general feeling, a non-contingent form" (70).

19 See p. 15 in this book.

20 "All the intellectual attainments of mankind, all the wealth of achievements, knowledge, and values accumulated by centuries have become oppressive to me of late as an annoying burden or too heavy, too confining garment ... I am thinking what happiness it would be to plunge into Lethe, so as to wash

forever from the soul the memory of all religious and philosophical systems, of all knowledge, all arts, poetry" (Gershenzon and Ivanov 11).

21 Eight years later, in "The Building of a New Culture and the Question of Style," Lunacharskii offered a more cautious prognosis. He still hypothesized about a future epoch endowed with a singular style, but its preamble, the period of proletarian dictatorship, he saw as a protracted span of stylistic diversity.

22 "Horizon is the metaphor for what approaches without ever becoming a possessed object" (Ricoeur 526).

23 Consider, for instance, Freud's classic distinction between the "aim" and "object" of sexual instincts (*Three Essays* 1–2), whose crucial import is that the aim is constitutive and guides the selection of objects. For this reason, the objects of desire are variable, interchangeable, contingent, and no single one of them can be said, in *sensu stricto*, to be the "right one." Consider also Hegel's classic discussion of desire in the *Phenomenology* (109–11), where every object and objectivation proves transient, since desire is nothing other than the path of consciousness's return to itself.

24 See n25 of this chapter and n14 of the next chapter.

25 An editorial in *Krasnaia nov'* celebrating the First Congress of the Union of Soviet Writers captured also this chief characteristic of the grand new style: "The style of our art, the style of socialist realism, demands *organicity* in creative work, because this is the style of the most truthful art ever known …

"Precisely insofar as we provide artists with the possibility for organic creativity, we now find ourselves on the eve of an unseen blossoming of art, on the eve of a socialist Renaissance" ("Privet" 1; emphasis in the original).

26 Compare with Wilhelm Worringer's enormously influential understanding of style as a will-to-form that stems from a "world-feeling" (*Weltgefühl*) characteristic of a given historical epoch (17). See also n18 of this chapter for Simmel's notion of style as grounded in "a more general feeling" (*ein allgemeineres Empfinden*).

27 Paul Cézanne described the creative process in these terms when he wrote: "The landscape reflects itself, humanizes itself, thinks itself in me. I objectify it, project it, fix it onto my canvas. Perhaps what I am saying doesn't make sense, but it seems to me that I am the subjective consciousness of that landscape, and my canvas is the objective consciousness" (qtd in *Arte Moderna*, 68). An even better example, of course, would be the art of the Surrealists, which deliberately abandoned itself to the power of the unconscious.

28 Spengler had been given a prominent place also in the lecture "Fundamental Problems of Contemporary Culture," which Bukharin delivered in Paris on

3 April 1936, several months before his arrest (243, 257–8). The lecture addresses most of the topics that Bukharin's prison manuscript will treat at greater length.

29 Bukharin mentions Simmel, Max Scheler, and Karl Lamprecht.

30 There is an analogous passage in Bukharin, "Fundamental Problems" 237–8.

31 "The growth of socialism in the USSR has already worked out new forms (laws, customs and a world outlook)" (Bukharin, *The Prison Manuscripts* 199).

32 In the speech concluding the Sixteenth Congress of the CPSU (July 1930), Stalin announced: "It is clear that we have already entered the period of socialism, for the socialist sector now holds all the levers of the entire people's economy, although the construction of a socialist society and the elimination of class distinctions are still far ahead" ("Zakliuchitel'noe" 6).

33 See the quotation from Simmel in n18 of this chapter.

34 On the question of Stalinist literary criticism as an arbiter of vitality, see Iampolski.

35 For a detailed discussion of these categories and their genesis, see James 2–14, 84–102. For a more recent treatment, see Balina and Günther.

7. The Unbearable Light of Being

1 The distinction between *Darstellung* and *Vertretung* is a pivotal theoretical point in Gayatri Spivak's appropriation of Marxism for post-colonial criticism (276–9).

2 The Seventeenth Party Congress, which has remained in history as the "Congress of Victors," was held in late January–early February 1934, in Moscow. It celebrated the achievements of the First Five-Year Plan and, on the basis of them, charted a course towards a classless society over the next five years. The congress also celebrated the unity of the Party now that the "rightist deviation" (led by Bukharin, Rykov, and Tomskii) had been neutralized.

3 Gor'kii's rhetoric may well be a conscious echo of Stalin's. Panferov has reported the following statement made by the Leader during one of his meetings with writers: "Let the writer learn from life [*uchitsia u zhizni*]. If he reflects the truth of life in a highly artistic form, he cannot fail to arrive at Marxism [*nepremenno pridet k marksizmu*]" ("Rech'").

4 Cf. also in Gor'kii: "it goes without saying that socialist realism can only be created on [the basis] of the facts of socialist experience" ("O sotsialisticheskom" 614).

5 In his speech at the First Congress of the Union of Soviet Writers, Nikolo Mitsishvili formulated a similar thesis: "In the years prior to the Second Five-Year Plan, the transformation of people's consciousness, the liquidation of the leftovers of capitalism in the consciousness of authors, was determined *not so much by ideological factors, as by the very progress of socialist construction*" (*Pervyi* 155; emphasis added).

6 See pp. 118–19 in this book.

7 The following statement, from a review of Ehrenburg's *Ne perevodia dykhaniia* (*Not Catching One's Breath;* 1935), highlights these shortcomings while also providing a revealing explanation for them: "The internal principles [*zakonomernosti*] of our development and their iron logic have not yet fully *etched themselves* [*otchekanilis'*] in Ehrenburg's consciousness, so as to *cast themselves* [*otlit'sia*] into the sharply-defined plot lines of his books. Hence – the amorphous structure of *Ne perevodia dykhaniia*, its formless, musical-lyrical construction" (Gal'perina 233; emphasis added). Note how the author is displaced as the subject of the sentence and his consciousness as the agency of representation. They appear, instead, as locatives. In the place they circumscribe, another agency does its work. This other agency is "reality" itself, which, through the internal dynamic of its "principles," proves capable of "etching" and "casting" itself in the receptive medium and thus giving birth to representations. Since this power of reality is constant and axiomatic, the shortcomings of actual artistic representations (Ehrenburg's books, with their discordant plot structure) can only be explained through the inadequacies of the human medium. The critique's implicit message is that the place of inscription – Ehrenburg's consciousness – is still a "dense" one, if the hard tip of history's iron logic has been unable to inscribe therein the neat lines of a coherent story.

8 Since Russian lacks markers for the definite form of nouns, their translation into English always involves interpreting the semantic context. In the present case, the choice is between "in search of truth" and "in search of *the* truth." I believe the latter is more appropriate when the context is Stalinist discourse. In it, "truth" usually figures as something already known, quite definite, and definitive.

9 See a similar characterization in another critical response to *Den' vtoroi*, which likewise undertakes to demonstrate the extent of Ehrenburg's transformation: Selivanovskii 227.

10 In a discussion of John Dos Passos's work, a Soviet critic explained how someone living under capitalism can be made to see: "Even a relatively revolutionary position on the part of the artist in the conditions of contemporary

capitalism *opens his eyes* for a truthful seeing and truthful depiction of reality and saves art from destruction in the hopeless and hideous confusion of empirical detail" (Kirpotin 40; emphasis added).

11 In the words of Régine Robin: "The general laws that govern nature apply to the realm of History, taking into account the specificity of human societies. History is no longer anything but a natural phenomenon; it produces only singularizing effects growing out of the laws of nature-History, illustrations of a general evolution, phenomena actualizing an essence ... History thus becomes a version of nature in the service of the political; it is preinterpreted, events are already foreseen; or, if an event takes place that does not coincide with the path already traced, this is because the struggle includes resistance from forces hostile to socialism, which may take various forms (rightists, Trotskyites, kulaks, saboteurs, spies, neo-Mensheviks, and so on)" (xxvii).

12 "It is a peculiarity of socialist society that it consciously plans its future; the reality of its tomorrow becomes indubitable, it can be verified, controlled. Stalin's five-year plans give the opportunity to each Soviet citizen to breathe the air of a future being actually created, being 'made' by history" (Tager 211). The same critic went on to speak of socialist realism as the "art of a guaranteed future" (211).

13 See Stalin, "K voprosam" 141–2; "Otvet" 232.

14 One is reminded of Rilke's disenchanted invocation of what it means to live and die as a modern: "One comes along, one finds a life all prepared, one only has to put it on. One wants to leave or is forced to; no strain: *Voilà votre mort, monsieur'*. One dies as one happens to; one dies the death that belongs to the diease one has (for all diseases are known, one also knows that their various fatal conclusions belong to the diseases and not to the person, and the ill person has, so to speak, nothing to do)" (*Notebooks* 5–6).

15 Here is how the journal *Literaturnyi kritik* described the acquisition of ideological knowledge by Soviet writers: "When the writer, the artist, leaves the narrow walls of his studio and plunges head-first into the thick of life [*golovoi okunutsia v gushchu zhizni*], when he sees in practice and feels with his own hands the great transformations taking place in our country, the enormous shifts in the consciousness of people ... then he will master in the best way possible the dialectics of life and will educate himself as a true communist, a Marxist-Leninist" ("Marksizm-Leninizm" 10). We recognize here the gist of Gor'kii's story, in which dialectical materialism figures not as a prerequisite for knowing the world, but as a point of arrival.

16 For testimonies on the blinding effects of socialism, see pp. 206–7 in this book.

17 Just how widespread this rhetoric was can be seen from a letter published in
    Literaturnyi kritik, in which a reader avows Soviet reality's power of "argu-
    mentation" (Lenobl' 108).

18 Rozental' was deputy editor of the journal for the first five years of its exis-
    tence. He replaced Pavel Iudin as editor-in-chief in 1938 and remained at this
    post until 1940, when the journal was closed. At the end of the 1940s,
    Rozental' became a target of the "anti-cosmopolitan campaign."

19 The tragic fate of *Bezhin Meadow* (1935–7), which the authorities ordered de-
    stroyed before final editing, and the ensuing vociferous campaign against its
    director, proved that the "sins" of Eisenstein's modernist past were never quite
    forgotten.

20 John Locke once defined reflection as the "inner perception" by which the
    mind is aware of its own thoughts. Before him, Descartes had famously
    grounded the being of the ego in the self-evidence of this same inner percep-
    tion. Kant's version of it was the unity of apperception.

8. Ideology as Authentication

1 The first appearance of the term "socialist realism" was in *Literaturnaia gazeta* on 23 May 1932, quoting a speech by Ivan Gronskii (qtd in "Obespechim
   vse usloviia" 1). Subsequent accounts, however, routinely attributed the term
   to Stalin, along with the definition of writers as "engineers of human souls."
   This is already the case in the 1935 volume of *Bol'shaia sovetskaia entsiklopediia* (see "Iskusstvo"). See also p. 204 in this book.

2 In a revealing pronouncement made in 1933, the art critic Abram Efros noted
   the seemingly paradoxical situation that the new Soviet style was both present
   and absent: "We know its name; it is on everyone's lips; everything speaks of
   'socialist realism.' *And yet there is nothing to which [this name] can be applied.*
   Not a single artist, not a single work, is yet equal to its parameters. Our art
   falls behind our reality" (560; emphasis added). The new artistic style is absent to the extent that no artist or work adequately conveys it. Yet it is present
   insofar as it is presupposed by the socialist infrastructure, which, as Efros tells
   us, has run ahead of the superstructure. In the same vein is the following
   statement in the inaugural issue of *Literaturnyi kritik* (June 1933): "*Soviet literature has not yet become what it could and should become*" (qtd in "Nashi zadachi" 4; emphasis in the original). Implicit in these typical pronouncements
   is the Stalinist ideologeme of theory's lag behind practice, which can be interpreted, more broadly, to mean the lag of superstructural phenomena in relation to those of the base; see p. 165 of this book.

3 See K. Clark, *Soviet* 27.

4 See above, pp. 164–5.

5 The thesis was advanced in Stalin's speech to the Central Committee plenum of July 1928 and elaborated in numerous subsequent pronouncements. See Stalin, "Ob industrializatsii i khlebnoi probleme" 170–1; Stalin, "O pravom uklone" 34–9; Stalin, "Politicheskii otchet" 302; Stalin, "Itogi" 211–12.

6 For examples of such accounts, see Kosarev 39; Kaganovich 18–21; Shubrikov 32–3.

7 In a footnote, Althusser points out that this explanation was prevalent even in Communist circles, where various "deviations" were blamed on the actions of such "cliques" of bad men ("Ideology" 165). It may be added that for a long time this was also the prevalent explanation for the epochal historical deviation called Stalinism. The ideological lies that covered up the tragedies and crimes of this period were deduced straightforwardly from the actions of Stalin and his clique. In recent years this type of historical demonology has mostly descended to the shelves of semi-scholarly literature, yet its currency in popular consciousness – both in Russia and in the West – remains high.

8 The way this insight is phrased in the text differs ("in letter, not in spirit") from my formulation. In Althusser's words, the question of ideology cannot be a question of "cause" ("Ideology" 165).

9 "[Ce] n'est pas leurs conditions d'existence réelles, leur monde réel, que les 'hommes' 'se représentent' dans l'idéologie, mais c'est avant tout leur rapport à ces conditions d'existence qui leur y est représenté" (emphasis added).

10 "[The] Law, that has been lying in wait for each infant born since before his birth, and seizes him before his first cry, assigning to him his place and role, and hence his fixed destination" (Althusser, "Freud" 211).

11 Althusser expresses this with the statement that "individuals are 'abstract' with respect to the subjects they always already are" ("Ideology" 176); and in another place: "concrete subjects exist insofar as they are supported by a concrete individual" ("Ideology" 174).

12 The case for an epistemological break between the thought of the early and late Marx is developed at length in Althusser, "On the Young Marx." For an unsparing critical attack on this thesis, see Kolakowski. The idea of the "break" as the principal object of Althusser's theoretical oeuvre is treated in Balibar.

13 Althusser has characterized *The German Ideology* (along with the *Theses on Feuerbach*) as a "work of the Break" (Althusser and Balibar, *Reading Capital* 31, 39).

14 See Marx, *Capital* 163–77. This inspiration is not acknowledged in the ISA essay itself, but see Althusser and Balibar, *Reading Capital* 66, 191; Althusser, "Reply" 51–2.

15 "Thus fetishism is not simply an illusory appearance. It is the *mode of existence* of capitalist production. The mystified character of the system results not from some accidental feature of it, or from the skill of the capitalists in fooling workers, but from its very heart, from the nature of the commodity, that is, from the very form that the products of labour must take under the capitalist mode of production" (Callinicos 49; emphasis in the original).

16 This is what Slavoj Žižek has termed the "objectivity of belief." Commenting on the same text in Marx, Žižek states: "*The point of Marx's analysis is that things (commodities) themselves believe in the place of subjects:* it is as if all their beliefs, superstitions and metaphysical mystifications, supposedly surmounted by the rational, utilitarian personality, are embodied in the 'social relations between things'. They no longer believe, *but the things themselves believe for them*" (317; emphasis in the original). There are serious difficulties in turning Marx's account of fetishism into a comprehensive view of ideology, apart from Marx's own unwillingness to do so. It is rather obvious that the vast array of practices Althusser deems ideological – the actions of mourners at a funeral, those of fans at a soccer match, and so on – do not stand in the same relationship of straightforward determination by basic economic mechanisms. But if this is the case, the thesis that these practices constitute a *necessary* imaginary relation becomes unsupportable. Conversely, one could grant to Althusser that individuals necessarily engage in activities through which *some* form of social identity is exercised. But if ideology is nothing more than this general assumption of *some* social roles, then it becomes logically impossible to demonstrate that it always serves to reproduce existing relations of production.

17 For how Althusser understands Lacan's role in transmitting and enriching Freud's legacy, see Althusser, "Freud." For a critical commentary on Althusser's intellectual debt to Lacan, see Macey.

18 This twofold dynamic is the subject of Althusser's meditations in the first part of the essay, where he endeavours to distinguish between the reproduction of the *forces* of production and the reproduction of the *relations* of production.

19 In another text, borrowing an expression from Lacan, Althusser describes the generation of ideology as a "theatrical machine" ("Freud" 216). On Althusser's mechanistic metaphors, see Thompson 132–42, 46.

20 See above, pp. 176–8.

21 Thus Lévi-Strauss famously declares that his interest is "not how men think in myths, but how myths operate in men's minds without their being aware of the fact" (12).

22 The popularity of Althusser's work, after the publication of *For Marx* (1965) and *Reading Capital* (1968), ensured that his theorizations were criticized

early and often, especially in Marxist circles. See Kolakowski, Lewis, Rancière, Thompson.

23 It should be said, in all fairness, that Althusser devotes considerable effort to eschewing the trap of economic determinism. The related notions of overdetermination (borrowed from Freud) and structural causality are aimed precisely against the treatment of the infrastructure as an essence of which superstructural realities are phenomenal expressions (see Althusser, "Contradiction"). Still, I believe that "Ideology and Ideological State Apparatuses" surrenders a large part of these earlier conceptual gains. It would seem that the concept of overdetermination is most useful when applied to particular historical situations, when it can be shown that a given social formation is constituted by "instances" of various levels and degrees of effectivity. But in the ISA text, Althusser is dealing with ideology in general in its relation to society in general. From this perspective, ideology is the product of an abstractly conceived structure of economic relations. If Althusser is thinking in terms of Marx's notion of fetishism – as I believe he is – the same conclusion suggests itself: ideology is the necessary form of appearance of a fundamental economic mechanism.

24 As Terry Eagleton has pointed out, things are not quite in order with Althusser's transplantation of psychoanalytic categories. He seems to confuse the constitution of the ego with that of the unconscious (Eagleton 144–5). In the ISA essay, he speaks often of ideology as an imaginary relation, with obvious reference to Lacan's Imaginary, but many passages make it clear that Althusser's ideology is also Lacan's Symbolic Order. For instance, the child's entrance into a life already prestructured in terms of expectations, obligations, and family and social roles (Althusser, "Ideology" 176) is, most certainly, an entrance into the Symbolic, not the Imaginary. Althusser offers no argument for how these two aspects of ideology can be made compatible or shown to interact. If – as one would have to assume – the imaginary relation is what makes the necessary symbolic assignments bearable, livable, then ideology becomes unbelievably omnipotent. It is both that which creates roles and that which ensures their manning (through the primary function of interpellation).

25 This possibility is prepared by Althusser himself, who holds that ideology remains a component of the social whole even in communism. See the glossary definition of the term at the end of Althusser and Balibar, *Reading Capital* (314).

26 On this point, see Rancière 131.

27 It is necessary to read Thompson's vitriolic attack on Althusser with an understanding of its immediate historical and intellectual context. On the British Left after the mid-1960s, an old guard of intellectuals, including

Thompson, saw itself displaced by a new generation intent on infusing Marxism with fresh theoretical vigour. For the latter group, Althusser's writings held a promise of pushing through the impasses of postwar Western Marxism. When Thompson speaks of "Althusserianism," he certainly means Althusser's French pupils (Étienne Balibar, in particular), but also British followers like Barry Hindess, Paul Hirst, and – less directly – Perry Anderson, the editor of *New Left Review*. For Anderson's response to Thompson, see Anderson, *Arguments*. A judicious arbitration of the sparring match between Thompson's *The Poverty* and Anderson's *Arguments* can be found in Jacoby. For in-depth treatments of the structuralist turn in Western Marxism, see Benton and Resch. For an advocacy of Althusser's *anti*-Stalinist thinking and politics, see Lock.

28　*"So ideology is as such an organic part of every social totality*. It is as if human societies could not survive without these *specific formations*, these systems of representations (of various levels) which are ideologies. Human societies secrete ideology as the very element and atmosphere indispensable to their historical respiration and life" (Althusser, "Marxism" 232; emphasis in the original).

29　See "Priem."

30　The "workday" (*trudoden'*) was legislated in 1930 as a unitary measure for quantifying and remunerating labour on the newly created collective farms. The basic meaning of *trudodni* is this: units of socially necessary work that, after being performed by the farmer and registered in his "work book" (*trudovaia knizhka*), can be exchanged for money or a share of the *kolkhoz*'s own products.

31　The Russian *baza* is both "basis" and the (Marxist) "base." The latter is awkward in English, yet in this and many other instances, Stalin intends precisely the meaning drawn from Marxist political economy. His point is that the characters of these remarkable women could only have grown from a socialist infrastructure.

32　The speech did appear in *Pravda* the following day, 11 November 1935.

33　Cf.: "The biological men are only the *supports* or bearers of the guises [*Charaktermasken*] assigned to them by the structure of relations in the social formation" (Althusser and Balibar, *Reading Capital* 320; emphasis in the original).

34　The next day the *Pravda* editorial reported these words of Mariia Demchenko, one of the celebrities of the shock-work movement: "We can be confident in our merry life [*radostnoe zhit'e*]. The old [times] won't come back, when my father worked for the landlords and my mother was in tears almost every day because there was nothing to eat. Now my mother says, 'It is as if I live in paradise.' 'No, mom,' I answer to her, 'This is not yet paradise. Paradise is still ahead of us, and we will attain it. We will study, we will work, and we will have it all" ("Priem" 1).

35 In the early 1930s, it was common to read stories of transformation in which inanimate entities like the *kolkhoz* were the subjects of action, while animate entities like the Soviet farmers were its object. A local Party activist, comrade Zharkov, wrote in a letter to the journal *Bor'ba klassov* ("Class Struggle"): "This is how the kolkhoz mass was educated in the struggle for socialism. The kolkhoz firmly *imparted upon it* new thoughts, habits, notions" ("Bor'ba" 69; emphasis added).

36 Here is another report from the provinces, which describes the transformation of a certain Ershtadt under the beneficial influence of "socialist competition" (*sotssorevnovanie*): "His psychology was not ours, not proletarian. He took no part in social work, was not interested in the kolkhoz production, and only thought of how to get home more quickly after work. Now he carries social responsibilities and fulfills them conscientiously ... The [socialist] competition fundamentally changed his worldview" ("Odna" 2).

37 See p. 165 in this book.

38 See above, p. 160.

9. The Blind, the Seeing, and the Shiny

1 On the topic of objective enemies, see Arendt 423–5.

2 "[The objective enemy] is never an individual whose dangerous thoughts must be provoked or whose past justifies suspicion, but a 'carrier of tendencies' like the carrier of a disease" (Arendt 424).

3 "I think that in our country, under the conditions of proletarian dictatorship, there is not and there cannot be a single, more or less important, political or economic fact that did not reflect the existence of class struggle in town and country" (Stalin, "Ob industrializatsii i khlebnoi probleme" 169). "It stands to reason: it is impossible, given the existence of the petite-bourgeois element [*stikhiia*] and the pressure of this element on our party, to not have Trotskyist tendencies. It is one thing to arrest the Trotskyist cadres or expel them from the party. It is another thing to eliminate the ideology of Trotskyism. This is more difficult" (Stalin, "Ob industrializatsii strany" 278). Obviously, by "ideology" here Stalin means not simply a certain doctrine associated with Trotsky and his supporters, but the general mechanism by which "opportunist" ideas are bred by the conditions of class struggle in the Soviet Union. To eradicate Trotskyist ideology is difficult because it requires the elimination of those objective conditions.

4 "The strength of the right opportunism lies in the force of the petite-bourgeois element, in the force exerted upon the party by capitalist elements in
general, and by the kulak class in particular. And precisely because the right
deviation reflects the resistance of the main elements of the dying classes, the
right deviation constitutes the main danger to the party in our times" (Stalin,
"Politicheskii otchet" 361).

5 Cf. later in the same speech: "There are people in the ranks of our party who
are attempting to adapt – *perhaps without even noticing it* – the work of socialist construction to the needs of the 'Soviet bourgeoisie'" (Stalin, "O pravoi
opasnosti" 226; emphasis added).

6 Here is the impression the accused Piatakov left on one of the notable foreign
guests in attendance, the German writer Lion Feuchtwanger: "I shall never
forget how [he] stood in front of the microphone, a middle-aged man of average build, rather bald, with a reddish, old-fashioned, sparse, pointed beard,
and how he lectured. Calmly and at the same time sedulously he explained
how he had managed to sabotage the industries under him. He expounded,
pointed his finger, gave the impression of a school teacher, a historian giving a
lecture on the life and deeds of a man who had been dead for many years,
named Piatakov, anxious to make everything clear even to the smallest details
so that his listeners should understand fully" (125).

7 Cf. earlier in the same speech by Vyshinskii: "Like a cinematic reel played in
reverse, this trial has reminded us of and shown us all the stages of the historical path of the Trotskyists and Trotskyism, which needed more than 30 years
to prepare, at last, its transformation into an advanced detachment of
Fascism, one of the departments of Fascist police" (*Protsess* 168–9).

8 Given how such confessions were obtained, it is hardly suprising that they
often echoed Vyshinskii's rhetoric. The following passage is taken from
Kamenev's last plea: "I ask myself, *is it an accident* that alongside of myself,
Zinoviev, Evdokimov, Bakayev and Mrachkovsky are sitting emissaries of
foreign secret-police departments, people with false passports, with dubious
biographies and undoubted connections with the Gestapo. *No! it is not an accident.* We are sitting here side by side with the agents of foreign secret-police
departments because our weapons were the same, because our arms became
intertwined before our fate became intertwined here in this dock" ("Last
Pleas of Kamenev"; emphasis added).

9 Compare Vyshinskii's harangue with Stalin's words from the beginning of
1929: "The Trotskyists' struggle against the VKP(b) had its own *logic*, and
this *logic* led the Trotskyists into the anti-Soviet camp. Trotsky began by ad-
vising his followers in January, 1928, to attack the leadership of VKP(b),
without opposing themselves to the USSR. However, *given the logic of the*

struggle, Trotsky reached the point where the blows he aimed at the leadership of VKP(b), against the leading force of the proletarian dictatorship, were *inevitably* directed at the very dictatorship of the proletariat, against the USSR, against our entire Soviet society" ("Dokatilis'" 314–15; emphasis added).

10 See ch. 8 n33.

11 "We represent a most brutal gang of criminals who are *nothing more or less* than a detachment of international fascism" ("Last Pleas of Mrachkovsky"; emphasis added).

12 For Vyshinksii's explanation of this logic of degradation, see *Protsess* 21.

13 This was the trial of the so-called Anti-Soviet Right Trotskyist Bloc. Among the accused were Bukharin, Aleksei Rykov, and the former chief of OGPU/NKVD, Genrikh Iagoda.

14 An editorial in *Krasnaia nov'* summarized the manifest significance of the assembly days after it was over: "The congress of Soviet writers showed with concrete clarity that our country is truly becoming the center of world culture, that the best among the creators of truly cultural values are drawn to the Soviet Union ...

"Moscow became the centre uniting the thoughts and feelings of the best people of all humanity, the greatest artists of the era, the bravest, the most honest, the most devoted to the very essence of art" ("S"ezd" 4).

In a recent book (*Moscow*), Katerina Clark has investigated the campaign for a Soviet Renaissance in the 1930s, which projected Moscow as the centre of a global socialist culture. While it usefully draws attention to the cosmopolitan aspects of Stalinism, the study tends to downplay the staged character of the campaign.

15 In the words of a distinguished foreign guest, André Malraux: "All delegations, which brought to us, along with their gifts, the human warmth and extraordinary friendship amidst which your literature grows, what did these delegations say? – 'Express us, show us'" (*Pervyi* 286). Similarly, in the speech of Aleksandr Afinogenov: "New people came onto this podium, and they said: 'Describe us, write about us'" (*Pervyi* 429).

16 Otto Schmidt (1891–1956) was the leader of the 1934 Arctic expedition of the icebreaker *Cheliuskin*. After it was crushed by icepacks and sunk, 104 crew members survived on the ice for two long months. During these desperate times, Schmidt behaved as a true political and moral leader of the group: he organized poetry readings, lectured on philosophy and world politics, and even published a wall newspaper (!). In April 1934, the crew was rescued by Soviet airplanes, which landed directly on the ice. The seven pilots participating in this unprecedented rescue mission were among the first to be awarded the newly instituted title "Hero of the Soviet Union." Schmidt received the same honour in 1937.

17 The coal miner Nikita Izotov (1902–52) was a pioneer of the shock-work movement in the USSR. A 1932 article in *Pravda* devoted to him inaugurated the Izotovite movement for training young workers and improving productivity.

18 Bill' Belotserkovskii: "These days, every corner of the Soviet Union is saturated with unusual life – a kind of life that may provide material for a truly universal [literary] theme. Unfortunately, *we do not see life*, we do not study it sufficiently, and know it very little" (*Pervyi* 428; emphasis added).

Anna Karavaeva: "Our enormous country has been seized, from end to end, by the grandiose processes of building and transforming absolutely all aspects of life. Great discoveries of Soviet science and technology are taking place all around us. There is a serious flaw in our life as writers: we stand quite far from the intellectual life of our country, we still live boring, limited, and insufficiently social lives" (*Pervyi* 203).

Boris Romashov: "To study, read, people, the new people, is enormously difficult ... I am not only not familiar with the new [Soviet] man – I often *do not know, cannot do, cannot hear...*" (*Pervyi* 426; emphasis in the original).

19 From 1932 to 1938, Iudin was the director of the Institute of Red Professors, while serving as the deputy to the head of the Agitprop and Press sections of the Party's Central Committee from 1934 to 1937; he was also editor-in-chief of the journal *Literary Critic* (*Literaturnyi kritik;* 1933–7).

20 I have treated the issue of truth in Stalinist culture in another text; see Petrov.

21 I am in no way questioning the patent fact that Marxism-Leninism was an institutionalized body of knowledge urged upon all Soviet citizens. I wish only to emphasize that this knowledge led a double life in the Soviet period: on the one hand, it was a supposedly scientific doctrine to be studied, understood, and followed with conviction; on the other, it was a teaching-become-life, that is, the very stuff of everyday experience. The latter aspect is the one that interests me here. On the issue of life's priority over "book" knowledge as a foundational trait of socialist realism, see Ermolaev 154–7, 164–7.

22 See also ch. 7 n3.

23 It is worth remembering here that "sincerity," understood precisely in these traditional terms, was to become the slogan word for Thaw culture's attempt to veer off the course set by Stalinist socialist realism.

24 On the notion of sensibility in the context of eighteenth-century Sentimentalism, see Todd 1–9.

25 An almost identical phraseology is to be found in Bukharin's report to the congress: "We, USSR, are *the apex of the whole world*, the backbone of future humanity. We need to understand, think through, feel through [*prochuvstvovat'*], this" (*Pervyi* 498; emphasis in the original).

26 See Stalin, "O pravom" 10–18.

27 As one Stalinist critic expressed it years later, "it is a great happiness to feel the surrounding world as one's own world, to see in one's native country the embodiment of one's own ideal, to have the right to depict actual reality as a realized dream" (Bialik 195).

28 See p. 81 in this book.

29 Consider the following statement by the eminent artist Isaak Brodskii, which collates the theme of belonging with the imperative for sincerity discussed earlier: "Now all subjects [*temy*] are close, dear to us, these are the subjects of socialist construction, the subjects of the proletariat's revolutionary struggles, subjects close to the heart of every artist, every citizen.

"If such subjects are commissioned to the artist, [he] will work upon them with love, *as long as this artist is an honest Soviet citizen; and an artist should be, in the first instance, an honest, decent, earnest, citizen of his Motherland.* There is no need to chase after some freely chosen subjects and consider the commissioned subject as something terrible. I find it wrong to allow students to choose [their] subjects" (*Pervyi* 755; emphasis added).

30 See ch. 6 n25.

31 The "heaven," in this case, refers to the celestial heights in which the objectivity of the Marxist-Leninist "scientific" analysis is reinscribed as the effective force of destiny that rules Soviet society.

32 Gusev's improvised poem was read by Gor'kii during his closing speech.

33 This impression was captured in Vladimir Ermilov's frequently quoted equation, "The beautiful is our life" (*Prekrasone – eto nasha zhizn'*).

10. Life Happens

1 *The Great Dawn* is set on the eve of the October Revolution, during the last days of Russia's participation in the First World War. Next in the chronological sequence is *The Unforgettable 1919*, which follows Stalin through the years of the Civil War, focusing particularly on his leadership during the defence of Petrograd. Broadest in its historical scope, *The Vow* covers the years from 1924 to 1945. *The Fall of Berlin* mythologizes the Leader's role in the Great Patriotic War of 1941 to 1945.

2 Chiaureli's screenwriting partner for *The Great Dawn* was Georgii Tsagareli, while on *The Unforgettable 1919* he collaborated with Vsevolod Vyshinskii (on whose original play the script was based) and Aleksandr Filimonov.

3 Apart from the symbolic association with pilgrimage, the episode is modelled, quite deliberately, I believe, on the traditional image of the Russian peasant appearing before the Tsar Himself as a last resort in the pursuit of social justice.

4 This widely reproduced photograph is among the very scant evidence suggesting any kind of close personal relationship between Lenin and Stalin. Needless to say, it was heavily exploited for purposes of propaganda throughout the Stalinist period.

5 Chiaureli and Pavlenko will redeploy the formula in *The Fall of Berlin*, where we meet a multinational family of Red Army soldiers fronted by a modern-day Russian *bogatyr'*, Ivan.

6 See p. 183.

7 I am alluding both to the classic essay "The Agency of the Letter in the Unconscious or Reason since Freud" (delivered first as a lecture in the Sorbonne on 9 May 1957) and to Lacan's famous reading of Edgar Alan Poe's "Purloined Letter" in his seminar of 1954–5, hosted by the Société Française de Psychanalyse (see *Seminar* 191–205). In both texts Lacan emphasizes the independent and determinative workings of signification, the preponderance of its "material" aspect (the "letter," the signifier) over its "ideal" counterpart (the intended meaning, the signified).

8 Dušan Makavejev's film *W.R.: Mysteries of the Organism* (1971), which interpolates several scenes from *The Vow*, makes an explicit connection between phallic sexual arousal and the idolization of Stalin.

9 An identical logic is at work in the ritualistic traditions of many Indigenous cultures. Particular places within the tribal territory are associated with the archetypal journey of the ancestor (cultural hero). This trajectory is retraced and the places are revisited during holiday celebrations, when specific rituals evoke the memory of mythic times, just as they evoke, for quite practical purposes, the energy of the ancestral *loci*. See, for example, the discussion in Durkheim 330–40.

10 "Miraculation" is a term deployed by Gilles Deleuze and Felix Guattari in *Anti-Oedipus* to designate a mechanism of mystification characteristic of socio-economic life under capitalism (10). While wealth is – as always – created by human agents and their labour, in the inverted world of bourgeois economic relations it is as if wealth (in the form of capital) is the engine that drives production and "activates" the labour of humans (a fact captured in such common pronouncements as "investment *creates* jobs"). "Miraculation" refers to this effect of inversion whereby capital serves as the (quasi-)cause of the subject's actions and in a deeper sense *produces* the subject. As I have been trying to show, Stalinist socialism possessed its own version of the ideology of miraculation.

Works Cited

Abrams, M.H. *The Mirror and the Lamp: Romantic Theory and the Critical Tradition.* London: Oxford UP, 1953.

Adorno, Theodor. *Aesthetic Theory.* Trans. Robert Hullot-Kentor. Minnesota: U of Minnesota P, 1998.

Aesthetics and Politics: The Key Texts of the Classic Debate within German Marxism. London: New Left Books, 1977.

"AKhRR: Declaration of the Association of Artists of Revolutionary Russia." *Russian Art of the Avant-Garde: Theory and Criticism, 1902–1934.* Ed. John Bowlt. New York: Viking. 266–7.

Althusser, Louis. "Contradiction and Overdetermination." *For Marx.* Trans. Ben Brewster. New York: Vintage, 1969. 87–128.

– *For Marx.* Trans. Ben Brewster. New York: Vintage, 1969.

– "Freud and Lacan." *"Lenin and Philosophy" and Other Essays.* Trans. Ben Brewster. New York: Monthly Review Press, 1971. 195–219.

– "Ideology and Ideological State Apparatuses (Notes towards an Investigation)." *Lenin and Philosophy and Other Essays.* Trans. Ben Brewster. New York: Monthly Review Press, 1971. 127–86.

– "Marxism and Humanism." *For Marx.* Trans. Ben Brewster. New York: Vintage, 1969. 219–48.

– "On the Young Marx." *For Marx.* Trans. Ben Brewster. New York: Vintage, 1969. 49–86.

– "Reply to John Lewis." *Essays in Self-Criticism.* Trans. Grahame Lock. London: New Left Books, 1976. 34–77.

Althusser, Louis, and Étienne Balibar. *Reading Capital.* Trans. Ben Brewster. London: New Left Books, 1970.

Al'fonsov, V.N. Introduction. *Poeziia russkogo futurizma.* Sankt-Peterburg: Akademicheskii proekt, 2001. 5–66.

Anderson, Perry. *Arguments within British Marxism.* London: New Left Books, 1980.
– "Modernity and Revolution." *New Left Review* 144 (1984): 317–38.
Arendt, Hannah. *The Origins of Totalitarianism.* San Diego: Harcourt, 1985.
Arte Moderna: 1870–1944, Dall'impressionismo al surrealismo. Vol. 1. Ed. Hanz Wener Hozwarth. Milan: Taschen, 2011.
Arvatov, Boris. "Aleksei Gastev. *Pachka orderov.*" *LEF* 1 (1923): 243–5.
– *Iskusstvo i klassy.* Moscow: Gosizdat, 1923.
– *Iskusstvo i proizvodstvo. Sbornik stat'ei.* Moscow: Proletkult, 1926.
– "Rechetvorchestvo (Po povodu zaumnoi poezii)." *LEF* 2 (1923): 79–91.
Averbakh, Leopol'd. "Nekotorye momenty kul'turnoi revoliutsii." *Na literaturnom postu* 7 (1927): 4–7.
– "O sovremennykh pisatel'skikh nastroeniiakh." *Na literaturnom postu* 3 (1927): 5–13.
– "Po etu storonu literaturnykh transhei." *Na postu* 1 (1923): 79–94.
– "Tvorcheskie puti proletarskoi literatury." *Na literaturnom postu* 10 (1927): 5–16.
Balibar, Étienne. "Althusser's Object." *Social Text* (Summer 1994): 157–88.
Balina, Marina. "Ideinost', klassovost', partiinost'." *Sotsrealisticheskii kanon.* Saint Petersburg: Akademicheskii proekt, 2000. 362–76.
Baljeu, Joost. *Theo van Doesburg.* London: Studio Vista, 1974.
Ball, Hugo. *Flight out of Time: A Dada Diary.* Trans. Ann Raimes. Berkeley: U of California P, 1996.
Ballestrem, Karl G. "Lenin and Bogdanov." *Studies in Soviet Thought* 9 (1969): 283–310.
Barthes, Roland. "The Death of the Author." *Modern Literary Theory: A Reader.* Ed. Philip Rice and Patricia Waugh. 3rd ed. London: Arnold, 1996. 118–22.
– "Literature and Signification: Answers to a Questionaire in *Tel Quel.*" *Critical Essays.* Trans. Richard Howard. Evanston: Northwestern UP, 1972. 261–79.
– *The Pleasure of the Text.* Trans. Richard Miller. New York: Hill and Wang, 1975.
Belaia, Galina. *Don Kikhoty 20-kh godov: "Pereval" i sud'ba ego idei.* Moscow: Izvestiia AN SSSR, 1989.
Bely, Andrei. "Teatr i sovremennaia drama." *Simvolizm kak miroponimanie.* Moscow: Respublika, 1994. 153–66.
Benjamin, Walter. "The Task of the Translator." *Illuminations.* Trans. Harry Zohn. London: Fontana, 1973. 69–82.
Benton, Ted. *The Rise and Fall of Structural Marxism: Althusser and His Influence.* London: Palgrave Macmillan, 1984.
Berdiaev, Nikolai. *Krizis iskusstva.* Moscow: Izdanie Lemana i Sakharova, 1918.

Berkovskii, Naum. "Bor'ba za prozu." *Kritika 1917–1932 godov.* Moscow: Astrel',
2003. 123–52.

Bernshtein, Sergei. "Esteticheskie predposylki teorii deklamatsii." *Poetika* 3
(1927): 25–44.

Bespalov, Ivan. "Problema literaturnoi nauki (Metodologicheskie osnovaniia
nauki o literature)." *Literaturovedenie.* Ed. V.F. Pereverzev. Moscow: GAKhN,
1928. 19–38.

– "Stil' rannikh rasskazov Gor'kogo. (Opyt analiza)." *Literaturovedenie.* Ed. V.F.
Pereverzev. Moscow: GAKhN, 1928. 273–347.

Bialik, Boris A. "Gor'kii i sotsialisticheskii realizm." *Problemy sotsialisticheskogo
realizma.* Moscow: Sov. pisatel', 1948. 115–96.

Bobrinskaia, Ekaterina. *Russkii avangard. Granitsy iskusstva.* Moscow: NLO,
2006.

Bogdanov, Aleksandr. *Elementy proletarskoi kul'tury v razvitii rabochego klassa.*
Moscow: Gos. iz-vo, 1920.

– *Empiriomonizm: Stat'i po filosofii.* Vol. 1. Moscow: Izd. S. Dorovatskogo i A.
Charushnikova, 1905.

– *Filosofiia zhivogo opyta. Populiarnye ocherki. Materializm, empiriokrititsizm,
dialekticheskii materializm, empiriomonizm, nauka budushchego.* Saint
Petersburg: Izd. M.I. Semenova, 1913.

– "Kollektivisticheskii stroi." *Voprosy sotsializma. Raboty raznykh let.* Moscow:
Politizdat, 1990. 296–305.

– "Ot filosofii k organizatsionnoi nauke." *Neizvestnyi Bogdanov.* Vol. 1. Moscow:
ITs "AIRO-XX," 1995. 110–19.

– "Sobiranie cheloveka." *Voprosy sotsializma. Raboty raznykh let.* Moscow:
Politizdat, 1990. 28–46.

– "Sotsialisticheskoe obshchestvo." *Voprosy sotsializma. Raboty raznykh let.*
Moscow: Politizdat, 1990. 90–8.

– "Taina nauki." *Voprosy sotsializma: Raboty raznykh let.* Moscow: Politizdat,
1990. 391–410.

– *Tektologiia: Vseobshchaia organizatsionnaia nauka.* Vol. 1. Moscow: Ekonomika,
1989.

Bois, Yve-Alain. *Painting as a Model.* Cambridge: MIT P, 1993.

"Bor'ba za sotsializm v derevne." *Bor'ba klassov* 1 (1932): 68–9.

Bowlt, John. "Introduction." *Russian Art of the Avant-Garde: Theory and
Criticism, 1902–1934.* Ed. John Bowlt. New York: Viking. xix–xl.

Boym, Svetlana. "Paradoxes of Unified Culture: From Stalin's Fairy Tale to
Molotov's Lacquer Box." *Socialist Realism without Shores (Post-Contemporary
Interventions).* Ed. Thomas Lahusen and Evgenii Dobrenko. Durham: Duke
UP, 1997. 120–34.

Braun, Edward. *Meyerhold on Theatre*. London: Methuen, 1988.

Brik, Osip. "Fiksatsiia fakta." *Novyi LEF* 11–12 (1927): 44–50.

– "Ot kartiny k foto." *Novyi LEF* 3 (1927): 29–33.

– "T. n. 'formal'nyi metod'." *LEF* 1 (1923): 213–15.

Brodskii, I. I. "Ovladet' masterstvom kompozitsii." *Russkaia sovetskaia khudozhestvennaia kritika, 1917–1941*. Ed. L.F. Denisova and N.I. Bespalova. Moscow: Izobrazitel'noe iskusstvo, 1982. 753–9.

Brown, Edward J. *The Proletarian Episode in Russian Literature, 1928–1932*. New York: Columbia UP, 1953.

"Budem sozdavat' bol'shuiu literaturu strany sotsializma." *Literaturnaia gazeta*, 17 May (1932): 1.

Bukharin, Nikolai. "Fundamental Problems of Contemporary Culture." In *The Prison Manuscripts. Socialism and Its Culture*. Trans. George Shriver. New York: Seagull, 2006. 227–58.

– "O formal'nom metode v iskusstve." *Krasnaia nov'* 3 (1925): 248–57.

– *The Prison Manuscripts: Socialism and Its Culture*. Trans. George Shriver. New York: Seagull, 2006. Trans. of *Tiuremnye rukopisi N.A. Bukharina. 1. Sotsializm i ego kul'tura*. Moscow: Airo-21, 1996.

Bürger, Peter. *Theory of the Avant-Garde*. Trans. Michael Shaw. Minnesota: U of Minnesota P, 1984.

Burke, Seán. *The Death and Return of the Author: Criticism and Subjectivity in Barthes, Foucault, and Derrida*. 3rd ed. Edinburgh: Edinburgh UP, 2008.

Butler, Christopher. *Early Modernism: Literature, Music, and Painting in Europe, 1900–1916*. London: Oxford UP, 1998.

Callinicos, Alex. *Althusser's Marxism*. London: Pluto, 1976.

Cassedy, Steven. *Flight from Eden: The Origins of Modern Literary Criticism and Theory*. Berkeley: U of California P, 1990.

Cherniakov, A.N. "Dva fragmenta 'poeticheskoi filologii' russkogo avangardizma." *Vestnik Baltiiskogo federal'nogo universiteta im. I. Kanta* 8 (2012): 87–93.

Chiaureli, Mikhail, and Petr Pavlenko, screenwriters. *The Fall of Berlin* [*Padenie Berlina*]. Mosfilm, 1949.

– *The Vow* [*Kliatva*]. Mosfilm, 1947.

Chiaureli, Mikhail, dir. *The Great Dawn* [*Velikoe Zarevo*]. Tbilisi Film Studio, 1937.

– *The Unforgettable 1919* [*Nezabyvaemyi 1919*]. Mosfilm, 1951.

Christiansen, Broder. *Philosophie der Kunst*. Hanau: Clauss und Feddersen, 1909.

Chuzhak, Nikolai. "K zadacham dnia (Stat'ia diskusionnaia)." *LEF* 2 (1923): 145–52.

– "Pod znakom zhiznestroeniia (Opyt osoznaniia iskusstva dnia)." *LEF* 1 (1923): 12–39.

Clark, Katerina. *Moscow, the Fourth Rome: Stalinism, Cosmopolitanism, and the Evolution of Soviet Culture, 1931–1941.* Cambridge, MA: Harvard UP, 2011.

– "RAPP i institutsializatsiia sovetskogo kul'turnogo polia v 1920-kh—nachale 1930-kh godov." *Sotsrealisticheskii kanon.* Ed. Hans Günther and Evgenii Dobrenko. Saint Petersburg: Akademicheskii proekt, 2000.

– *The Soviet Novel: History as Ritual.* Bloomington: Indiana UP, 2000.

Clark, T.J. *Farewell to an Idea: Episodes from a History of Modernism.* New Haven: Yale UP, 1999.

Collins Cobuild English Dictionary. London: HarperCollins, 1995.

Dadamian, Genadii G. *Atlantida sovetskogo iskusstva, 1917–1991. Chast' I, 1917–1932.* Moscow: Gitis, 2010.

Davydov, Sergei. "From the 'Dominant' to 'Semantic Gesture': A Link between Russian Formalism and Czech Structuralism." *Russian Formalism: A Retrospective Glance. (A Festschrift in Honor of Victor Erlich).* Ed. Robert Louis Jackson and Stephen Rudy. New Haven: Yale UP, 1985. 96–113.

De Chirico, Giorgio. "Metaphysical Art." *Artists on Art: From the XIV to the XX Century.* Ed. Robert Goldwater and Marco Treves. London: Pantheon, 1972. 439–41.

de Man, Paul. *Blindness and Insight: Essays in the Rhetoric of Contemporary Criticism.* Minnesota: U of Minnesota P, 1983.

DeKoven, Marianne. "The Politics of Modernist Form." *New Literary History* 3 (1992): 675–90.

Deleuze, Gilles, and Felix Guattari. *Anti-Oedipus: Capitalism and Schizophrenia.* Trans. Robert Hurley, Mark Seem, and Helen R. Lane. Minneapolis: U of Minnesota P, 1983.

Descartes, René. *Discourse on Method* and *Meditations on First Philosophy.* Indianapolis: Hackett, 1993.

Dmitrieva, Ekaterina. "Genrikh Vel'flin v Rossii: Otkrytie Italii, barokko ili formal'nogo metoda v gumanitarnikh naukakh?" *Evropeiskii kontekst russkogo formalizma (K problem esteticheskikh peresechenii. Frantsiia, Germaniia, Italiia, Rossiia).* Ed. Ekaterina Dmitrieva, Valeriia Zemskova, and Michel Espagne. Moscow: IMLI RAN, 2009. 98–131.

Dobrenko, Evgenii. *Aesthetics of Alienation: Reassessment of Early Soviet Cultural Theories.* Trans. Jesse M. Savage. Evanston: Northwestern UP, 2005.

– *Formovka sovetskogo pisatelia. Sotsial'nye i esteticheskie istoki sovetskoi literaturnoi kul'tury.* Saint Petersburg: Akademicheskii proekt, 1999.

Doesburg, Theo van, El Lissitsky, and Hans Richter. "Declaration of the International Fraction of Constructivists of the First International Congress of Progressive Artists." *Art in Theory, 1900–2000: An Anthology of Changing Ideas.* Ed. Charles Harrison and Paul Wood. New York: Blackwell, 2003. 314.

Durham, Vera. *In Stalin's Time: Middle-Class Values in Soviet Fiction.* Cambridge: Cambridge UP, 1976.

Durkheim, Emile. *The Elementary Forms of Religious Life.* Trans. Karen E. Fields. New York: The Free Press, 1995.

Eagleton, Terry. *Ideology: An Introduction.* London: Verso, 1991.

Efros, Abram M. "Vchera, segodnia, zavtra." *Russkaia sovetskaia khudozhestvennaia kritika, 1917–1941.* Ed. L.F. Denisova and N.I. Bespalova. Moscow: Izobrazitel'noe iskusstvo, 1982. 531–60.

Eikhenbaum, Boris. *Anna Akhmatova: Opyt analiza.* Petrograd: Petropechat', 1923.

– "Kak sdelana 'Shinel'" Gogolia." *O proze. O poezii. Sbornik stat'ei.* Leningrad: Khud. lit., 1986. 45–63.

– *Literatura (Teoriia, kritika, polemika).* Leningrad: Priboi, 1927.

– *Moi vremennik: Slovesnost'. Nauka. Kritika. Smes'.* Leningrad: Izd. pisatelei v Leningrade, 1929.

– *Skvoz' literaturu. Sbornik stat'ei.* Leningrad: Academia, 1924.

– "The Theory of the Formal Method." *Readings in Russian Poetics: Formalist and Structuralist Views.* Ed. Ladislav Matejka and Krystyna Pomorksa. Cambridge: MIT Press, 1971. 3–37. Trans. of "Teoriia formal'nogo metoda." *Literatura. Teoriia, kritika, polemika.* Chicago: Russian Language Specialties, 1969. 116–48.

– "Vokrug voprosa o formalistakh." *Pechat' i revoliutsiia* 5 (1924): 1–12.

Eisenstein, Sergei. "Razborchivaia nevesta." *Literaturnaia gazeta.* 29 June 1933: 2.

Eliot, T.S. "Tradition and Individual Talent." *Prospecta* 19 (1982): 36–42.

Emerson, Caryl. "Literary Theory in the 1920s: Four Options and a Practicum." *A History of Russian Literary Theory and Criticism: The Soviet Age and Beyond.* Ed. Evgenii Dobrenko and Galin Tikhanov. Pittsburgh: U of Pittsburgh P, 2011.

Ermolaev, Herman. *Soviet Literary Theories, 1917–1934: The Genesis of Socialist Realism.* Berkeley: U of California P, 1963.

Erlich, Victor. *Russian Formalism: History and Doctrine.* The Hague: Mouton, 1969.

Eysteinsson, Astradur. *The Concept of Modernism.* Ithaca: Cornell UP, 1992.

Feuchtwanger, Lion. *Moscow, 1937: My Visit Described for My Friends.* Trans. Irene Josephy. New York: Viking, 1937.

Fitzpatrick, Sheila. *The Commissariat of the Enlightenment: Soviet Organization of Education and the Arts under Lunacharsky, 1917–1921.* Cambridge: Cambridge UP, 2002.

– *The Cultural Front: Power and Culture in Revolutionary Russia.* Ithaca: Cornell UP, 1992.

Fokkema, Douwe, and Elrud Ibsch, eds. *Theories of Literature in the Twentieth Century: Structuralism, Marxism, Aesthetics of Perception, Semiotics.* New York: St Martin's, 1995.

Fokht, Ul'rikh. "'Demon' Lermontova, kak iavlenie stilia." *Literaturovedenie.* Ed. V.F. Pereverzev. Moscow: GAKhN, 1928. 107–46.

Foucault, Michel. *The Order of Things: An Archeology of the Human Sciences.* New York: Vintage, 1970.

– "What Is an Author?" *Textual Strategies: Perspectives in Post-Structuralist Criticism.* Ed. Josué V. Harari. Ithaca: Cornell UP, 1979. 141–60.

Freud, Sigmund. *The Interpretation of Dreams.* Trans. A.A. Brill. New York: Macmillan, 1913.

– *Jokes and Their Relation to the Unconscious.* Trans. James Strachey. New York: W.W. Norton, 1990.

– *New Introductory Lectures on Psychoanalysis.* Trans. James Strachey. New York: W.W. Norton, 1989.

– *Three Esssays on the Theory of Sexuality.* Trans. James Strachey. New York: Basic Books, 2000.

Frye, Northrop. *The Anatomy of Criticism: Four Essays.* Princeton: Princeton UP, 1957.

Gabo, Naum, and Antoine Pevsner. "The Realistic Manifesto." *The Tradition of Constructivism.* Ed. Stephen Bann. New York: Viking, 1974. 7–11. Trans. of *Realisticheskii manifest.* Moscow: n.p, 1920.

Gal'perina, E. "'Ne perevodia dykhaniia' Erenburga." *Novyi mir* 8 (1935): 232–8.

Gan, Aleksei. *Konstruktivizm.* Tver': Tver'sko izd-vo, 1922.

Garzonio, Stefano, and Maria Zalambani. "Literary Criticism during the Revolution and Civil War, 1917–1921." *A History of Russian Literary Theory and Criticism: The Soviet Age and Beyond.* Ed. Evgenii Dobrenko and Galin Tikhanov. Pittsburgh: U of Pittsburgh P, 2011. 1–16.

Gastev, Aleksandr. "Kontury proletarskoi kul'tury." *Literaturnye manifesty. Ot simvolizma do "O'ktiabria."* Ed. N. Sidorov and N. Brodskii. Moscow: Agraf, 2001. 328–33.

– *Nashi zadachi.* Moscow: Tsentral'nyi Institut Truda, 1921.

– "Pachka orderov." *Poeziia rabochego udara.* Moscow: Khud. lit., 1971. 215–20.

– *Vosstanie kul'tury.* Khar'kov: Molodoi rabochii, 1923.

Gershenzon, Mikhail, and Viacheslav Ivanov. *Perepiska iz dvukh uglov.* Peterburg: Alkonost, 1921.

Gladkov, Fedor. *Cement.* Trans..S. Arthur and C. Ashleigh. New York: International Publishers, 1929. Trans. of *Tsement.* Moscow: Zemlia i fabrika, 1927.

Gleizes, Albert, and Jean Metzinger. "Cubism." *Modern Artists on Art.* Ed. R.L. Herbert. New York: Dover, 2000. 2–18.

Goodman, Nelson. "The Status of Style." *Critical Inquiry* 1 (1975): 799–811.

Gor'kii, Maksim. "Moshchnaia energiià klassa." *Literaturnaia gazeta.* 20 January 1934: 1.

– "O pol'ze gramotnosti." *Sobranie sochinenii v 30 tomakh.* Vol. 24. Moscow: Sov. pisatel', 1953. 319–26.

– "O sostsialisticheskom realizme." *Sobranie sochinenii v 30 tomakh.* Vol. 27. Moscow: Sov. pisatel', 1953. 5–13.

Gough, Maria. *The Artist as Producer: Russian Constructivism in Revolution.* Berkeley: U of California P, 2005.

– "Faktura: The Making of the Russian Avant-Garde." *Res* 36 (1999): 32–59.

Gray, Camilla. *The Russian Experiment in Art, 1863–1922.* London: Thames and Hudson, 1986.

Greenberg, Clement. "Avant-Garde and Kitsch." *Art and Culture: Critical Essays.* Boston: Beacon P, 1961. 3–21.

– "Modernist Painting." *Modern Art and Modernism: A Critical Anthology.* Ed. Francis Frascina and Charles Harrison. San Francisco: Harper and Row, 1982. 5–10.

Greimas, A.J. "Actants, Actors, and Figures." *On Meaning: Selected Writings in Semiotic Theory.* Trans. Paul J. Perron and Frank H. Collins. Minneapolis: U of Minnesota P, 1987. 106–20.

– *Structural Semantics: An Attempt at a Method.* Trans. Daniele McDowell. Lincoln: U of Nebraska P, 1983.

Groys, Boris. *The Total Art of Stalinism: Avant-Garde, Aesthetic Dictatorship, and Beyond.* Trans. Charles Rougle. Princeton: Princeton UP, 1992.

Guro, Elena. "Govoril ispugannyi chelovek ..." *Sochineniia.* Berkeley: Berkeley Slavic Specialties, 1996. 104–5.

Günther, Hans. "Totalitarnaia narodnost' i ee istoki." *Sotsrealisticheskii kanon.* Saint Petersburg: Akademicheskii proekt, 2000. 377–89.

Hegel, Georg Wilhelm. *Phenomenology of Spirit.* Trans. A.V. Miller. Oxford: Oxford UP, 1977.

Hicks, Jeremy. *Dziga Vertov: Defining Documentary Film.* London: I.B. Tauris, 2007.

Howe, Irving. *Thomas Hardy.* New York: Macmillan, 1967.

Iakubinskii, Lev. "O zvukakh stikhotvornogo iazyka." *Sborniki po teorii poeticheskogo iazyka* 1 (1916): 37–49.

Iampolski, Mikhail. "Censorship as the Triumph of Life." *Socialist Realism without Shores.* Ed. Thomas Lahusen and Evgenii Dobrenko. Durham: Duke UP, 1997. 165–77.

"Iskusstvo." *Bol'shaia sovetskaia entsiklopediia.* Vol. 29. 1926–47. Print.

Ivaniushina, Irina Iu. *Russkii futurizm. Ideologiia, poetika, pragmatika.* Saratov: Izd. Saratovskogo universiteta, 2003.

Ivanov, Viacheslav. "Poet i chern'." *Sobranie sochinenii.* Vol. 1. Brussels: Foyer Oriental Chrètien, 1971. 709–14.

– "Vzgliad Skriabina na iskusstvo." *Sobranie sochinenii.* Vol. 3. Brussels: Foyer Oriental Chrètien, 1971. 171–89.

Ivanov, Viacheslav. Rev. of *The Total Art of Stalinism: Avant-Garde, Aesthetic Dictatorship, and Beyond,* by Boris Groys. *Slavic Review* 3 (1993): 600–1.

"Iz materialov grupy 'Oktiabr'." *Na postu* 1 (1923): 199–200.

Jackson, Robert L. "The Sociological Method of V.F. Pereverzev: A Rage for Structure and Determinism." *Literature and Society in Imperial Russia, 1800–1914.* Ed. William Mills Todd III. Stanford: Stanford UP, 1978. 29–60.

Jacoby, Russell. Rev. of *Arguments within British Marxism,* by Perry Anderson. *Theory and Society* 2 (1982): 251–7.

Jakobson, Roman. "Closing Statement: Linguistics and Poetics." *Style in Language.* Ed. Thomas Sebeok. New York: Wiley, 1960. 350–77.

– *Noveishaia russkaia poeziia. Nabrosok pervyi: Velimir Khlebnikov.* Prague: Politika, 1921.

– *O cheshskom stikhe, preimushchestvenno v sopostavlenii s russkim.* Berlin: OPOIaZ, 1923.

– "On Realism in Art." *Readings in Russian Poetics: Formalist and Structuralist Views.* Ed. Ladislav Matejka and Krystyna Pomorksa. Cambridge: MIT P, 1971. 38–46. Trans. of "O khudozhestvennom realizme." *Readings in Russian Poetics: Michigan Slavic Materials* 2 (1962): 30–6.

– "Randbemerkungen zur Prosa des Dichters Pasternak." *Slavische Rundschau* 7 (1935): 357–73.

James, C. Vaughan. *Soviet Socialist Realism: Origins and Theory.* New York: St Martin's, 1973.

Jameson, Fredric. *The Political Unconscious: Narrative as a Socially Symbolic Act.* Ithaca: Cornell UP, 1981.

– *Postmodernism, or the Cultural Logic of Late Capitalism.* Durham: Duke UP, 1990.

– *The Prison-House of Language: A Critical Account of Structuralism and Russian Formalism.* Princeton: Princeton UP, 1972.

– *A Singular Modernity: Essay on the Ontology of the Present.* London: Verso, 2002.

Jensen, Kenneth M. *Beyond Marx and Mach: Aleksandr Bogdanov's Philosophy of Living Experience.* Dordrecht: D. Reidel, 1978.

Joravsky, David. *Soviet Marxism and Natural Science.* London: Routledge and Kegan Paul, 1961.

Kaganovich, Lazar M. "Tseli i zadachi politicheskikh otdelov MTS i sovkhozov." *Bol'shevik* 1–2 (1933): 12–37.

Kant, Immanuel. *Critique of Pure Reason.* Trans. Paul Guyer and Allen W. Wood. New York: Cambridge UP, 1998.

Kantor, Kh. "O literaturnoi kritike." *Bol'shevik* 23 (1933): 85–96.

Kemp-Welch, A. "'New Economic Policy in Culture' and Its Enemies." *Journal of Contemporary History* 3 (1978): 449–65.

Khan Magomedov, Selim O. *INKHUK i rannyi konstruktivizm.* Moscow: Arkhitektura, 1994.

Khodasevich, Vladislav. "O formalizme i formalistakh." *Kritika ruskogo zarubezh'ia.* Vol. 2. Ed. O.A. Korostelev and N.G. Mel'nikov. Moscow: Olimp, 2002. 319–25.

Khrapchenko, M. "K probleme stilia." *Na literaturnom postu* 19 (1927): 22–9.

Khrushchev, Nikita S. "The Cult of the Individual." *The Guardian.* http://www. theguardian.com/theguardian/2007/apr/26/greatspeeches1. Web 25 June 2011. Trans. of *Doklad na zakrytom zasedanii XX s"ezda KPSS: O kul'te lichnosti i ego posledstviiakh.* Moscow: Gospolitizdat, 1959.

Kiaer, Christina. *Imagine No Possessions: The Socialist Objects of Russian Constructivism.* Cambridge: MIT P, 2005.

Kirpotin, Valerii. "O sotsialisticheskom realizme. Zakat burzhuaznogo iskusstva (Lozh' o iskusstve)." *Literaturnyi kritik* 1 (1933): 32–48.

"Kliatva." *Pravda.* 1 July 1946: 3.

Kolakowski, Leszek. "Althusser's Marx." *The Socialist Register, 1971.* London: Merlin, 1971. 11–28.

Korabel'nikov, G. "Konets chekhovskoi temy." *Literaturnyi kritik* 1 (1933): 80–99.

Kosarev, A. "O zadachakh komsomola." *Bol'shevik* 23–24 (1932): 35–54.

Kruchenykh, Aleksei. *Faktura slova. Deklaratsiia. (Kniga 120-a.)* Moscow: n.p, 1923.

– "New Ways of the Word." *Words in Revolution: Russian Futurist Manifestoes, 1912–1928.* Ed. Anna Lawton and Herbert Eagle. Ithaca: Cornell UP, 2004. 69–77. Trans. of "Novye puti slova." *Manifesty i programmy russkikh futuristov – Die Manifeste und Programmischriften der Russischen Futuristen.* Munich: Fink, 1967. 64–73.

– *Sdvigologiia russkogo stikha. Trakhtat obizhalnyi (Trakhtat obizhalnyi i pouchalnyi). Kniga 121-a.* Moscow: n.p, 1923.

Kruchenykh, Aleksei, and Velimir Khlebnikov. *Slovo kak takovoe.* Peterburg: Tipo-lit, 1913.

Kuleshov, Lev. "Ekran segodnia." *Novyi LEF* 4 (1927): 31–4.

Lacan, Jacques. "The Agency of the Letter in the Unconscious or Reason Since Freud." *Écrits: A Selection.* Trans. Alan Sheridan. New York: W.W. Norton, 1977. 146–78.

– *The Seminar of Jacques Lacan. Book II. The Ego in Freud's Theory and in the Technique of Psychoanalysis, 1954–1955.* Trans. Sylvana Tomaselli. New York: W.W. Norton, 1991.

"Last Pleas of Kamenev, Zinoviev, Smirnov, Olberg, Berman-Yurin, Holtzman, N. Lurye, and M. Lurye." *Report of Court Proceedings: The Case of the Trotskyite–Zinovievite Terrorist Centre.* The Art Bin. Web. 17 April 2008. Trans. of *Sudebnyi otchet po delu trotskistko-zinov'evskogo terroristicheskogo tsentra.* Moscow: Narodnyi kommissariat iustitsii, 1936.

"Last Pleas of Mrachkovsky, Evdokimov, Dreitzer, Reingold, Bakayev, and Pickel." *Report of Court Proceedings: The Case of the Trotskyite–Zinovievite Terrorist Centre.* The Art Bin. Web. 17 April 2008. Trans. of *Sudebnyi otchet po delu trotskistko-zinov'evskogo terroristicheskogo tsentra.* Moscow: Narodnyi kommissariat iustitsii, 1936.

Law, Alma, and Mel Gordon. *Meyerhold, Eisenstein, and Biomechanics: Actor Training in Revolutionary Russia.* Jefferson: McFarland, 2012.

Lawrence, D.H. *Women in Love.* New York: Thomas Seltzer, 1922.

Lefebvre, Henri. *Everyday Life in the Modern World.* Trans. Sacha Rabinovitch. London: Continuum, 1984.

Lelevich, Grigorii. "O marksizme, bogdanovshchine, proletarskoi literature i tov. Rumii." *Na postu* 1 (1925): 171–88.

– "Otkazyvaemsia li my ot nasledstva?" *Na postu* 2/3 (1923): 43–60.

Lenhert, Hans- Jürgen [Khans Lenert]. "Sud'ba sotsiologicheskogo napravleniia v sovetskoi nauke o literature i stanovlenie sotsrealisticheskogo kanona. Pereverzevshchina / vul'garnyi sotsiologizm." *Sotsrealisticheskii kanon.* Ed. Hans Günther and Evgenii Dobrenko. Saint Petersburg: Akademicheskii proekt, 2000. 320–38.

Lenin, Vladimir I. *Materialism and Empiriocriticism: Critical Comments on a Reactionary Philosophy.* Moscow: Progress, 1952.

– "O lozunge soedinennykh shtatov Evropy." *Polnoe sobranie sochinenii.* Vol. 26. Moscow: Izd. polit. lit., 1965–75. 351–5.

– "On Proletarian Culture." *Soviet Socialist Realism: Origins and Theory.* New York: St Martin's, 1973. 112–13. Trans. by C. Vaughan James of "O proletar-skoi kul'ture." *Polnoe sobranie sochinenii.* Vol. 41. Moscow, Izd. polit. lit-ry, 1970. 336–7.

– "On the Proletkults (Letter from the Central Committee R.C.P.)." *Soviet Socialist Realism: Origins and Theory.* New York: St Martin's, 1973. 113–15. Trans. by C. Vaughan James of "O proletkul'takh: Pis'mo TsK RKP." *Lenin o literature i iskusstve.* Moscow: Izd. polit. lit-ry, 1967. 408–10.

Lenobl', G. "Nenavist' rozhdennaia liuboviu." *Literaturnyi kritik* 3 (1934): 97–112.

Levchenko, Mariia. *Industrial'naia svirel'. Poeziia Proletkul'ta 1917–1921*. Saint Petersburg: SPGUTD, 2007.

Lévi-Strauss, Claude. *The Raw and the Cooked: Mythologiques*. Vol. 1. Chicago: U of Chicago P, 1983.

Lewis, Jon. "The Althusser Case (Part I)." *Marxism Today* 1 (1972): 23–8. "The Althusser Case (Part II)." *Marxism Today* 2 (1972): 43–8.

Libedinskii, Iurii. "K voprosu o lichnosti avtora." *Na postu* 1 (1924): 37–70.

– "Khudozhestvennaia platforma RAPP." *Na literaturnom postu* 19 (1928): 9–19.

– "Problemy tematiki." *Na literaturnom postu* 13 (1927): 15–21.

– "Temy, kotorye zhdut svoikh avtorov." *Na postu* 2–3 (1923): 118–26.

Lisitskii, El. *El Lissitzky: Life/Letters/Text*. Ed. Sophie Lissitzky-Küppers. Greenwich: Graphic Society, 1968.

Lock, Grahame. Introduction. *Essays in Self-Criticism*, by Louis Althusser. London: New Left Books, 1976. 1–32.

Locke, John. *An Essay Concerning Human Understanding*. New York: Dover, 1959.

Lukács, Georg. *History and Class Consciousness: Studies in Marxist Dialectics*. Trans. Rodney Livingstone. Cambridge: MIT P, 1968.

Lunacharskii, Anatolii S. "Formalizm v nauke ob iskusstve." *Pechat' i revoliutsiia* 5 (1924): 19–23.

– "Revolution and Art." *Russian Art of the Avant-Garde: Theory and Criticism, 1902–1934*. Ed. John Bowlt. New York: Viking. 190–96. Trans. of "Iskusstvo i revoliutsiia." *Sobranie sochinenii v 8-i tomakh*. Vol. 7. Moscow: Khud. lit., 1967. 134–6.

– "Stroitel'stvo novoi kul'tury i voprosy stilia" ["The Building of a New Culture and the Question of Style"]. *Sobranie sochinenii v 8-i tomakh*. Vol. 8. Moscow: Khud. lit., 1967. 62–6.

Macey, David. "Thinking with Borrowed Concepts: Althusser and Lacan." *Althusser: A Critical Reader*. Ed. Gregory Elliott. Oxford: Blackwell, 1994. 142–58.

Mach, Ernst. *The Analysis of Sensations and the Relation of the Physical to the Psychical*. Trans. C.M. Williams. Chicago: Open Court, 1914.

Maguire, Robert A. *Red Virgin Soil: Soviet Literature in the 1920s*. Evanston: Northwestern UP, 1968.

Makavejev, Dušan, dir. *W.R.: The Mysteries of the Organism*. Neoplanta Film, Telepool, 1971.

Mally, Lynn. *Culture of the Future: The Proletkult Movement in Revolutionary Russia*. Berkeley: U of California P, 1990.

Marc, Franz. "Aphorisms, 1911–1912." *Manifesto: A Century of Isms*. Ed. Mary Ann Caws. Lincoln: U of Nebraska P, 2000. 275–6.

– "Two Pictures." *Art in Theory, 1900–2000: An Anthology of Changing Ideas*. Ed. Charles Harrison and Paul Wood. New York: Blackwell, 2003. 94–5.

Marcuse, Herbert. *One-Dimensional Man: Studies in the Ideology of Advanced Industrial Society.* London: Routledge, 2002.

"Marksizm-Leninizm i khudozhestvennaia literatura." *Literaturnyi kritik* 3 (1933): 3–11.

Marx, Karl. *Capital: A Critique of Political Economy.* Vol. 1. Trans. Ben Fowkes. New York: Vintage, 1977.

– *The Eighteenth Brumaire of Louis Bonaparte.* New York: International Publishers, 1963.

– "Introduction to the Critique of Political Economy." *Contribution to the Critique of Political Economy.* Trans. N.I. Stone. Chicago: Charles H. Kerr, 1918. 265–312.

– "Theses on Feurbach." *Basic Writings in Politics and Economy.* Ed. Lewis S. Feuer. Garden City: Anchor, 1959. 243–5.

Marx, Karl, and Friedrich Engels. *The German Ideology: Part One, with Selections from Parts Two and Three, together with Marx's "Introduction to the Critique of Political Economy."* New York: International Publishers, 2004.

– *The Holy Family, or Critique of Critical Critique.* Moscow: Foreign Languages, 1956.

"Materialy pervoi moskovskoi konferentsii proletarskikh pisatelei." *Na postu* 1 (1923): 193–200.

Mayakovsky, Vladimir. "Broadening of the Verbal Basis." *Russian Futurism through Its Manifestoes, 1912–1928.* Ed. Anna Lawton. Ithaca: Cornell UP, 1988. Trans. of "Rasshirenie slovesnoi bazy." *Novy LEF* 10 (1927): 14–17.

– *Misteriia Buf. Geroicheskoe, epicheskoe i satiricheskoe izobrazhenie epokhi. Polnoe sobranie sochinenii.* Vol. 2. Moscow: Gos. izd. khud. lit., 1956. 167–355.

Mazaev, A.I. *Kontseptsia "proizvodstvennogo iskusstva" 20-kh godov. Istoriko-kriticheskii ocherk.* Moscow: Nauka, 1975.

McLean, Hugh, Jr. "Voronskii and Vapp." *American Slavic and East European Review* 3 (1949): 185–200.

McLuhan, Marshall, and Quentin Fiore. *The Medium Is the Message: An Inventory of Effects.* New York: Bantam, 1967.

Medvedev, Pavel N. [Mikhail Bakhtin]. *The Formal Method in Literary Scholarship: A Critical Introduction to Sociological Poetics.* Trans. Albert J. Wehrle. Baltimore: Johns Hopkins UP, 1978. Trans. of *Formal'nyi metod v literaturovedenii: Kriticheskoe vvedenie v sotsiologicheskuiu poetiku.* Leningrad: Priboi, 1928.

Meier-Graefe, Julius. "The Mediums of Art, Past and Present." *Art in Theory, 1900–2000: An Anthology of Changing Ideas.* Ed. Charles Harrison and Paul Wood. New York: Blackwell, 2003. 51–7.

Meyerhold, Vsevolod. "Akter budushchego i biomekhanika. (Doklad 12 iunia 1922g.)" *Ermitazh* 6 (1922): 10–11.

Michelson, Annette. Introduction. *Kino-Eye: The Writings of Dziga Vertov.* Trans. Kevin O'Brien. Berkeley: U of California P, 1984.

Mill, John Stuart. "The Spirit of the Age." *The Spirit of the Age: Victorian Essays.* Ed. Gertrude Gimmelfarb. New Haven: Yale UP, 2007. 51–79.

Minnis, Alastair. *Medieval Theory of Authorship: Scholastic Literary Attitudes in the Later Middle Ages.* London: Scolar P, 1984.

"Nashi zadachi." *Literaturnyi kritik* 1 (1933): 3–10.

Newton, Isaac. *The Mathematical Principles of Natural Philosophy.* Vol. 1. London: Motte, 1729.

Nietzsche, Friedrich. *Thus Spake Zarathustra. The Complete Works of Friedrich Nietzsche.* Vol. 11. Trans. Thomas Common. New York: Macmillan, 1911.

Novozhilova, L.I. *Sotsiologiia iskusstva.* Leningrad: Izd. Leningr. un-ta, 1968.

"Obespechim vse usloviia tvorcheskoi raboty literaturnykh kruzhkov. (Na sobranii aktiva litkruzhkov Moskvy.)" *Literaturnaia gazeta.* 23 May 1932: 1.

"Odna iz dvadtsati vos'mi tysiach." *Pravda.* 29 April 1932: 2.

"Oktiabr'." *Na postu* 1 (1923): 205–6.

"On the Reformation of Literary-Artistic Organizations. (Decision of the Central Committee, V.K.P.(b), 23 April 1932." James, C. Vaughan. *Soviet Socialist Realism: Origins and Theory.* New York: St Martin's, 1973. 124. Trans. of "Postanovenie Politbiuro 'O perestroike literaturno-khudozhestvennykh organizatsii' 23 aprelia, 1932 g." *Vlast' i khudozhestvennaia intelligentsia. Dokumenty TsK RKP(b) – VKP(b), VChK – OGPU – NKVD o kul'turnoi politike. 1917–1953.* Ed. A.N. Iakovlev. Moscow: Demokratiia, 1999. 172–3.

"Organizatsiia 'Komfutov' (Petrograd 1919)." *Ot estetiki k ideologii. Khudozhest-vennye deklaratsii i literaturno-politicheskie dokumenty 1900-1920-kh gg.: Khrestomatiia.* Ed. E.G. Serebriakova. Voronezh: IPTs VGU, 2007. 35–7.

Panferov, Fedor. *Bruski.* Moscow: Khud. literatura, 1947.

– "Rech' na XVII s"ezde VKP(b)." *Khronos.* Web. 12 July 2012.

Paramonov, Boris. "Formalizm: Metod ili mirovozzrenie?" *NLO* 14 (1995): 32–52.

"Partiia i komfut." *Ot estetiki k ideologii. Khudozhestvennye deklaratsii i literatur-no-politicheskie dokumenty 1900-1920-kh gg.: Khrestomatiia.* Ed. E.G. Serebriakova. Voronezh: IPTs VGU, 2007. 37.

Pereverzev, Valerian F. "Essential Premises of Marxist Literary Scholarship." *Soviet Studies in Literature* (Spring–Summer 1986): 54–63. Trans. of "Neobkhodimye predposylki marksistskogo literaturovedeniia." *Literaturovedenie.* Moscow: GAKhN, 1928. 9–18.

– "The Formalists' Sociological Method." *Soviet Studies in Literature* (Spring–Summer 1986): 127–49. Trans. of "Sotsiologicheskii metod formalistov." *Literatura i marksizm* 1 (1929): 3–26.

– "K voprosu o monisticheskom ponimanii tvorchestva Goncharova." *Literaturovedenie.* Moscow: GAKhN, 1928. 201–30.

– "Problems of Marxist Literary Scholarship." *Soviet Studies in Literature* (Spring–Summer 1986): 150–76. Trans. of "Problemy marksistskogo literaturovedeniia." *Literatura i marksizm* 2 (1929): 3–32.

– "Theoretical Premises of Pisarev's Criticism." *Soviet Studies in Literature* (Spring–Summer 1986): 36–53. Trans. of "Teoreticheskie predposylki pisarevskoi kritiki." *Vesinik komunisticheskoi akademii* 31 (1929): 35–46.

– *Tvorchestvo Dostoevskogo. Kriticheskii ocherk.* Moscow: Gos. izdatel'stvo, 1922.

Perloff, Marjorie. *The Futurist Moment: Avant-Garde, Avant Guerre, and the Language of Rupture.* Chicago: U of Chicago P, 2003.

– "'Violence and Precision': The Manifesto as an Art Form." *Chicago Review* 2 (1984): 65–101.

Pertsov, Viktor. "'Igra' i demonstratsiia." *Novyi LEF* 11–12 (1927): 33–44.

Pervyi vsesoiuznyi s"ezd sovetskikh pisatelei. Moscow: Sov. pisatel', 1990.

Petric, Vlada. "Dziga Vertov as a Theorist." *Cinema Journal* 1 (1978): 29–44.

Petrov, Petre. "The Industry of Truing: Socialist Realism, Reality, Realization." *Slavic Review* 4 (2011): 873–92.

Pilniak, Boris. *The Naked Year.* Trans. Alec Brown. New York: AMS, 1971. Trans. of *Golyi god. Sochineniia v trekh tomakh.* Vol. 1. Moscow: Lada M, 1994. 5–160.

Platonov, Andrei. "Proletarskaia poeziia." *Kuznitsa* 9 (1922): 28–32.

Poggioli, Renato. *The Theory of the Avant-Garde.* Trans. Gerald Fitzgerald. Cambridge: Harvard UP, 1971.

Poliakov, M. "V.F. Pereverzev i problem poetiki." *Gogol'. Dostoevsky. Issledovaniia.* Ed. V.F. Pereverzev. Moscow: Sov. pisatel', 1982.

Pospelov, Genadii. "K metodike istoriko-literaturnogo issledovaniia." *Literaturovedenie.* Ed. V.F. Pereverzev. Moscow: GAKhN, 1928. 39–104.

– "Stil' 'Dvorianskogo gnezda' v kauzal'nom issledovanii." *Literaturovedenie.* Ed. V.F. Pereverzev. Moscow: GAKhN, 1928. 147–200.

Pozdnev, Arkadii. "Taylorism on the Stage." *Meyerhold, Eisenstein, and Biomechanics: Actor Training in Revolutionary Russia.* By Alma Law and Mel Gordon. Jefferson: McFarland, 2012. 148–51.

"Priem kolkhoznits-udarnits sveklovichnykh polei rukovoditeliami partii i pravitel'stva." *Pravda* 11 November (1935): 1.

"Privet s"ezdu sovetskikh pisatelei (Tol'ko strana sotsializma obespechivaet podlinnyi rastsvet iskusstva)." *Krasnaia nov'* 7 (1934): 3–4.

Propp, Vladimir. *Morphology of the Fairy Tale.* Trans. Louis A. Wagner. Austin: U of Texas P, 1968. Trans. of *Morfologiia skazki.* Leningrad: Academia, 1928.

Protsess antisovetskogo trotskistkogo tsentra. (23–30 ianvaria, 1937 goda). Moscow: Iuridicheskoe izdatel'stvo, 1937.

Rancière, Jacques. *Althusser's Lesson.* Trans. Emiliano Battista. New York: Continuum, 2011.

Reich, B. "K diskusii o tvorcheskikh putiakh: O romantizme, realizme i natural-izme." *Na literaturnom postu* 14 (1927): 15–21.

Resch, Robert Paul. *Althusser and the Renewal of Marxist Social Theory.* Berkeley: U of California P, 1992.

Richter, Hans. *Dada: Art and Anti-Art.* Trans. David Britt. New York: Thames and Hudson, 1964.

Ricoeur, Paul. *Freud and Philosophy: An Essay on Interpretation.* Trans. Denis Savage. New Haven: Yale UP, 1970.

Rilke, Rainer Maria. *The Notebooks of Maltis Laurids Brigge.* Trans. Burton Pike. New York: Penguin, 2009.

– *The Selected Poetry of Rainer Maria Rilke.* Trans. Stephen Mitchell. New York: Vintage, 1989.

Robin, Régine. *Socialist Realism: An Impossible Aesthetic.* Trans. Catherine Porter. Stanford: Stanford UP, 1992.

Rodchenko, Aleksandr. "Puti sovremennoi fotografii." *Novyi LEF* 9 (1928): 31–9.

Rodov, Semen. "O kruzhkovshchine, platformakh, i otryve ot mass." *Zvezda* 4 (1924): 310–21.

– "Organizatsionnye voprosy proletarskoi kul'tury." *Na postu* 1 (1925): 83–103.

Rozhkov, P. "Sotsialisticheskii realizm i 'zdorovaia empiriia'." *Novyi mir* 6 (1934): 168–201.

Rudnitskii, K.L. *Rezhiser Meierkhol'd.* Moscow: Nauka, 1969.

Sarychev, V.A. *Estetika russkogo modernizma: Problema zhiznetvorchestva.* Voronezh: Izd. Voronezhsk. un-ta, 1991.

Sayre, Henri M. *The Object of Performance: The American Avant-Garde since 1970.* Chicago: U of Chicago P, 1989.

Sartre, Jean-Paul. "What Is Literature?" *What Is Literature? and Other Essays.* Cambridge: Harvard UP, 1988. 21–246.

Schlegel, Friedrich. "On Goethe's *Meister.*" *German Aesthetic and Literary Criticism.* Ed. Kathleen M. Wheeler. Cambridge: Cambridge UP, 1984. 59–73.

Shubrikov, V. "Srednevolzhskaia partorganizatsiia v bor'be za bol'shevistskie kolkhozy." *Bol'shevik* 12 (1933): 32–44.

Scott, Helen Gifford. "Introduction: V.F. Pereverzev, 1882–1968." *Soviet Studies in Literature* (Spring–Summer 1986): 6–35.

Selivanovskii, A. "Rozhdenie novogo khudozhnika." *Krasnaia nov'* 6 (1934): 217–27.

"S"ezd bor'by za velikoe iskusstvo sotsializma." *Krasnaia nov'* 9 (1934): 3–5.

Shaginian, Marieta. "Besedy s nachinaiushchim avtorom." *Novyi mir* 3 (1934): 201–10.

Shklovskii, Viktor. "Art as Technique." *Russian Formalist Criticism: Four Essays.* Ed. Lee T. Lemon and Marion J. Reis. Lincoln: U of Nebraska P, 1965. 3–24.

Trans. of "Iskusstvo kak priem." *O teorii prozy*. Moscow: Federatsiia, 1929. 7–23.

– *Khod konia: sbornik stat'ei*. Moscow: Glikon, 1923.

– *Rozanov (iz knigi "Siuzhet kak iavlenie stilia")*. Petrograd: OPOIaZ, 1921.

– "Sterne's *Tristram Shandy*: Stylistic Commentary." *Russian Formalist Criticism: Four Essays*. Ed. Lee T. Lemon and Marion J. Reis. Lincoln: U of Nebraska P, 1965. 25–57. Trans. of *"Tristram Shandy" Sterna i teoriia romana*. Petrograd: Opoiaz, 1921.

– "Sviaz' priemov siuzhetoslozheniia s obshchimi priemami stilia." *O teorii prozy*. Moscow: Federatsiia, 1929. 24–67.

Simmel, Georg. "The Problem of Style." *Theory, Culture, and Society* 8 (1991): 63–71.

Sochor, Zenovia A. *Revolution and Culture: The Bogdanov–Lenin Controversy*. Ithaca: Cornell UP, 1988.

Sokolov, I. "Teilorizm v teatre." *Vestnik isskustv* 5 (1922): 11–12.

Solov'iev, Vladimir. "Obshchii smysl iskusstva." *Literaturnye manifesty. Ot simvolizma do 'Oktiabria'*. Ed. N. Sidorov and N. Brodskii. Moscow: Agraf, 2001. 11–22.

– *The Philosophical Principles of Integral Knowledge*. Trans. Valeria Z. Nollan. Grand Rapids: Wm B. Eerdmans, 2008. Trans. of *Filosofkie nachala tsel'nogo znaniia. Sochineniia v dvukh tomakh*. Vol. 2. Moscow: Mysl', 1988. 139–288.

"Sotsialisticheskii gumanizm i sovetskaia literatura." *Literaturnyi kritik* 7 (1935): 4–20.

Spencer, Herbert. *First Principles*. London: Watts & Co., 1937.

Spengler, Oswald. *The Decline of the West: Perspectives of World History*. 2 vols. London: George Allen, 1928.

Spivak, Gayatri Chakravorty. "Can the Subaltern Speak?" *Marxism and the Interpretation of Culture*. Ed. Cary Nelson and Lawrence Grossberg. Urbana: U of Illinois P, 1987. 271–313.

Stacy, R.H. *Defamiliarization in Language and Literature*. Syracuse: Syracuse UP, 1977.

Stalin, Iosif V. "Dokatilis'." *Sochineniia*. Vol. 11. Moscow: Politlit, 1949. 313–17.

– "Itogi pervoi piatiletki: Doklad na ob"edinennom plenume TsK i TsKK VKP(b) 7 ianvaria 1933g." *Sochineniia*. Vol. 13. Moscow: Politlit, 1951. 161–215.

– "K voprosam agrarnoi politiki v SSSR: Rech' na konferentsii agrarnikov-marksistov 17 dekabria 1929g." *Sochineniia*. Vol. 12. Moscow: Politlit, 1949. 141–72.

– "Ob industrializatsii i khlebnoi probleme. Rech' na plenume TsK VKP(b) 9 iulia 1928." *Sochineniia*. Vol. 11. Moscow: Politlit, 1949. 157–87.

- "Ob industrializatsii strany i pravom uklone v VKP(b): Rech' na plenume TsK VKP(b) 19 noiabria 1928." *Sochineniia.* Vol. 11. Moscow: Politlit, 1949. 245–90.
- "O pravoi opasnosti v VKP(b): Rech' na plenume MK i MKK VKP(b). 19 oktiabria 1928g." *Sochineniia.* Vol. 11. Moscow: Politlit, 1949. 222–38.
- "O pravom uklone v VKP(b). Rech' na plenume TsK i TsKK VKP(b) v aprele 1929g (stenogramma)." *Sochineniia.* Vol. 12. Moscow: Politlit, 1949. 1–107.
- "Otvet t. M. Rafailu." *Sochineniia.* Vol. 12. Moscow: Politlit, 1949. 231–2.
- "Politicheskii otchet tsentral'nogo komiteta XVI s"ezdu VKP(b) 27 iunia 1930g." *Sochineniia.* Vol. 12. Moscow: Politlit, 1949. 235–373.
- "Rech' na prieme kolkhoznits-udarnits sveklovichnykh polei 10 noiabria 1935 goda." *Sochineniia.* Vol. 14. Moscow: Pisatel', 1997. 76–7.
- "Rech' na prieme rukovodiashchikh rabotnikov i stakhanovtsev metallurgicheskoi i ugol'noi promyshlennosti 29 oktiabria 1937 goda." *Sochineniia.* Vol. 14. Moscow: Pisatel', 1997. 236–7.
- "Zakliuchitel'noe slovo na XVI s"ezde VKP(b)." *Sochineniia.* T. 13. Moscow: Politizdat. 1951. 1–16.
Steinberg, Mark D. *Proletarian Imagination: Self, Modernity, and the Sacred in Russia, 1910–1925.* Ithaca: Cornell UP, 2002.
Steiner, Peter. "Three Metaphors of Russian Formalism." *Poetics Today* 2.1b (1980–1): 59–116.
Stites, Richard. *Revolutionary Dreams: Utopian Vision and Experimental Life in the Russian Revolution.* New York: Oxford UP, 1991.
Svetlikova, Ilona Iu. *Istoki russkogo formalizma: Traditsiia psikhologizma i formal'naia shkola.* Moscow: NLO, 2005.
"S"ezd bor'by za velikoe iskusstvo sotsializma." *Krasnaia nov'* 9 (1934): 3–5.
Tager, E. "Gor'kii i problemy sovetskoi literatury." *Problemy sotsialisticheskogo realizma.* Moscow: Sov. pisatel', 1948. 197–240.
Tarabukin, Nikolai. *Ot mol'berta k mashine.* Moscow: Rabotnik prosveshcheniia, 1923.
Thompson, E.P. *The Poverty of Theory, or an Orrery of Errors.* London: Merlin, 1995.
Todd, Janet. *Sensibility: An Introduction.* New York: Methuen, 1986.
Todorov, Tsvetan. "Some Approaches to Russian Formalism." *Russian Formalism.* Ed. Stephen Bann and John E. Bowt. Edinburgh: Scottish Academic P, 1973. 6–19.
- "Three Conceptions of Poetic Language." *Russian Formalism: A Retrospective Glance. (A Festschrift in Honor of Victor Erlich).* Ed. Robert Louis Jackson and Stephen Rudy. New Haven: Yale UP, 1985. 130–47.
Tret'iakov, Sergei. "Otkuda i kuda? (Perspektivy futurizma)." *LEF* 1 (1923): 192–203.

Trotsky, Leon. *Literature and Revolution.* Trans. Rose Strunsky. Chicago: Haymarket, 2005. Trans. of *Literatura i revoliutsiia.* Moskva: Glavlitprosvet, 1923.

- "Vneokt'iabr'skaia literatura." *Pravda* 17 September 1922: 2.

Tynianov, Iurii. "Literaturnyi fakt." *Poetika. Istoriia literatury. Kino.* Moscow: Nauka, 1977. 255–70.

- "O literaturnoi evoliutsii." *Poetika. Istoriia literatury. Kino.* Moscow: Nauka, 1977. 270–81.

- "Oda kak oratorskii zhanr." *Poetika. Istoriia literatury. Kino.* Moscow: Nauka, 1977. 227–52.

"V poiskakh pravdy." *Literaturnaia gazeta.* 17 March 1933: 4.

Vardin, Illarion. "O politgramote i zadachakh literatury." *Na postu* 1 (1923): 91–100.

- "Voronshchinu neobkhodimo likvidirovat': O politike i literature." *Na postu* 1 (1924): 10–36.

- "Revoliutsiia i literatura (Dve glavy iz knigi)." *Na postu* 1 (1925): 69–82.

Varst [Varvara Stepanova]. "Kostium segondniashnego dnia – prozodezhda." *LEF* 2 (1923): 65–6.

Vertov, Dziga. "The Birth of Kino-Eye." *Kino-Eye: The Writings of Dziga Vertov.* Trans. Kevin O'Brien. Berkeley: U of California P, 1984. 41–2. Trans. of "Rozhdenie 'kinoglaza'." *Stat'i. Dnevniki. Zamisly.* Moscow: Iskusstvo, 1966. 73–5.

- "The Essence of Kino-Eye." *Kino-Eye: The Writings of Dziga Vertov.* Trans. Kevin O'Brien. Berkeley: U of California P, 1984. 49–50. Trans. of "Osnovnoe 'kinoglaza'." *Stat'i. Dnevniki. Zamisly.* Moscow: Iskusstvo, 1966. 81–2.

- "From Kino-Eye to Radio-Eye." *Kino-Eye: The Writings of Dziga Vertov.* Trans. Kevin O'Brien. Berkeley: U of California P, 1984. 85–92. Trans. of "Ot 'kinoglaza' k 'radioglazu'." *Stat'i. Dnevniki. Zamisly.* Moscow: Iskusstvo, 1966. 109–16.

- "Kinoki. Perevorot." *LEF* 3 (1923): 135–43.

- "Kino-Eye." *Kino-Eye: The Writings of Dziga Vertov.* Trans. Kevin O'Brien. Berkeley: U of California P, 1984. 85–92. 60–79. Trans. of "Kinoglaz." *Stat'i. Dnevniki. Zamisly.* Moscow: Iskusstvo, 1966. 72–3.

- "To the Kinoks of the South." *Kino-Eye: The Writings of Dziga Vertov.* Trans. Kevin O'Brien. Berkeley: U of California P, 1984. 50–1. Trans. of "Kinokam iuga." *Stat'i. Dnevniki. Zamisly.* Moscow: Iskusstvo, 1966. 82–4.

- "We: Variant of a Manifesto." *Kino-Eye: The Writings of Dziga Vertov.* Trans. Kevin O'Brien. Berkeley: U of California P, 1984. 5–9. Trans. of "My. Variant manifesta." *Stat'i. Dnevniki. Zamisly.* Moscow: Iskusstvo, 1966. 45–9.

Volkov, Vadim. "The Concept of *Kul'turnost'*: Notes on the Stalinist Civilizing Process." *Stalinism: New Directions.* Ed. Sheila Fitzpatrick. London: Routledge, 2000. 210–30.

Voronskii, Aleksandr. "Iskusstvo kak poznanie zhizni i sovremennost'." *Iskusstvo videt' mir: Portrety. Stat'i.* Moscow: Sov. pisatel', 1987.

Vyshinskii, Andrei Ia. "Delo antisovetskogo trotskistkogo tsentra." *Sudebnye rechi.* Moscow: GIIuL, 1953. 425–84.

Watten, Barret. "Modernism at the Crossroads: Types of Negativity." *Modernism.* Ed. Astradur Eysteinsson and Vivian Liska. Vol. 1. Amsterdam: John Benjamins, 2007. 219–32.

Williams, Raymond. "The Metropolis and the Emergence of Modernism." *Modernism/Postmodernism.* Ed. Peter Brooker. London: Longman, 1992. 82–94.

Worringer, Wilhelm. *Abstraktion und Einfühlung.* Munich: Piper, 1921.

Wyzewa, Teodor de. "Wagnerian Painting." *Art in Theory, 1900–1990: An Anthology of Changing Ideas.* Ed. Charles Harrison and Paul Wood. New York: Blackwell, 1992. 17–20.

"Zakrytoe pis'mo TsK VKP(b): O terroristicheskoi deiatel'nosti trotskistsko-zinov'evskogo kontrrevoliutsionnogo bloka." *Sochineniia,* by I.V. Stalin. Vol. 16. Moscow: Pisatel', 1997. 286–313.

Zhirmunskii, Viktor. *Voprosy teorii literatury: Stat'i, 1916–1926.* Gravenhage: Mouton, 1962.

Zonin, A. "Kakaia nam nuzhna shkola?" *Na literaturnom postu* 11–12 (1927): 8–15.

Žižek, Slavoj. "How Did Marx Invent the Symptom?" *Mapping Ideology.* Ed. Slavoj Žižek. London: Verso, 1994. 296–331.

Index